Building a New Educational State

Building a New Educational State

FOUNDATIONS, SCHOOLS, AND
THE AMERICAN SOUTH

Joan Malczewski

Joan Malczewski (signature)

The University of Chicago Press   CHICAGO & LONDON

The University of Chicago Press, Chicago 60637
The University of Chicago Press, Ltd., London
© 2016 by The University of Chicago
All rights reserved. Published 2016.
Printed in the United States of America

25 24 23 22 21 20 19 18 17 16   1 2 3 4 5

ISBN-13: 978-0-226-39462-6 (cloth)
ISBN-13: 978-0-226-39476-3 (e-book)
DOI: 10.7208/chicago/9780226394763.001.0001

Library of Congress Cataloging-in-Publication Data

Names: Malczewski, Joan, author.
Title: Building a new educational state : foundations, schools, and the
    American South / Joan Malczewski.
Description: Chicago ; London : The University of Chicago Press,
    2016. | Includes bibliographical references and index.
Identifiers: LCCN 2016001730 | ISBN 9780226394626 (cloth : alk.
    paper) | ISBN 9780226394763 (e-book)
Subjects: LCSH: Education—Southern States—Finance. |
    Endowments—Southern States.
Classification: LCC LA230.5.S6 M35 2016 | DDC 371.2/060975—dc23
    LC record available at http://lccn.loc.gov/2016001730

CONTENTS

ACKNOWLEDGMENTS

I am indebted to the many people who made this work possible. I am fortunate to have had great teachers and mentors throughout my life, including Dorothy Fordyce, Bud Woods, and Patricia Woods, who inspired me to learn, helped me to find opportunities, and provided an important example of the significant role that teachers and schooling can play in the lives of rural students. My career path has not been conventional, and a number of people encouraged and supported my academic pursuits, including Mary Brabeck, Robby Cohen, Tom James, Ron Robin, Steve Thornton, Diana Turk, and Jonathan Zimmerman.

The arguments for this book have been developed over a number of years. Many colleagues both encouraged the work and helped me to refine my arguments with extremely valuable comments at conferences and in response to written work. Those individuals include Brian Balogh, Elisabeth Clemens, Adam Fairclough, James Leloudis, Tracy Steffes, and Christine Woyshner. The writing group at New York University has provided me with detailed and constructive comments on my work, as well as invaluable career support from colleagues, including Gretchen Aguiar, Lisa Andersen, Zoe Burkholder, Victoria Cain, Ansley Erickson, Cody Ewert, Nick Juravich, Rachel Lissy, Natalia Mehlman Petrzela, and Jon Zimmerman. I appreciate the invaluable comments that I received on the introduction from Christopher Loss, Jim Fraser, and Tracy Steffes, and useful information from Larry Kramer and David Yaffe that helped me to shape my arguments. In addition, I am especially grateful to Jonathan Zimmerman and Ellen Condliffe Lagemann for providing feedback on significant sections of the manuscript, and to Robby Cohen and Richard

Arum for graciously agreeing to read and comment on the entire manuscript, which included reviewing some sections more than once.

I was fortunate to receive a grant from the Spencer Foundation that supported numerous trips to the archives, as well as research assistance. Thanks to the archivists at the Atlanta University Center, Robert Woodruff Library, the State Archives of North Carolina, Special Collections at the University of North Carolina at Chapel Hill, Special Collections at Fisk University, and Special Collections at the University of Chicago, and in particular to Tom Rosenbaum at the Rockefeller Archive Center. Jordan Mylet, Hannah Hendler, Jennifer Villarosa, Amy Karwoski, Daniel Hyman-Cohen, and Jade Bettine are incredibly talented students who were instrumental to me completing the work. I am particularly indebted to Jade, who remained with the project to the end. Thank you also to the Steinhardt School at New York University, which provided an IDEA Grant and encouraged me to pursue my interest in this topic. Special thanks are also due to Timothy Mennel at the University of Chicago Press, who shepherded the manuscript through publication, and to Carol McGillivray for her detailed copyedits. I am also grateful to the anonymous reviewers whose extremely helpful and detailed feedback strengthened the book in numerous ways.

Anyone who has written a book knows how consuming a project it can be. Fortunately, I have an incredible family that supports everything that I do. My parents taught me to work hard and to make good choices, even difficult ones. My brothers and sisters remind me to have a sense of humor. Sydney, Eero, Luke, Zora, and Elias may bring some added work to my life but, with Sam, also bring endless joy and balance. Finally, thanks to Richard, who has been a constant source of encouragement and support.

Introduction

William C. Chance established the Parmele Industrial Institute in Martin County, North Carolina, in 1910.[1] A local newspaper reported that the school was located in a region where the percentage of black illiteracy was high and the "greatest hope for the colored race is in their being trained to the habits of industry, thrift, and economy."[2] Chance, an experienced educator who had studied law at Howard University and took classes at the Hampton Institute, the North Carolina College for Negroes at Durham, and LaSalle University in Chicago, appealed to students at the institute's first commencement exercises to "aspire to lofty ideals, and at all times cultivate such habits as go to make real men and women."[3] However, it was difficult in 1910 in the Jim Crow South to sustain an independent black school with such aspirations. Chance advertised regularly in local papers to attract students and financial contributions. While state reports on the institution indicated that he was doing good work, with guidance from a board of directors that included prominent white southerners, many southern whites were opposed to black schooling in the South.[4] In 1914, Chance's house was dynamited, substantially damaging the structure though he escaped without injury.[5] It was in that year that he decided to accept annual foundation and county contributions to the institute in exchange for turning the school over to the county, which the state would then develop to provide teacher training to rural blacks in the region surrounding Martin County. While Chance would remain principal of the school, he would report to the county superintendent.

The decision to turn the institute over to the state was more complicated than it might seem because black educators and white southerners did not necessarily agree on how best to educate rural blacks. Chance hoped to provide educational opportunity to the region's black students and believed in academic and industrial training. However, the foundations and the state hoped to bring independent black schools into a public system and to dictate the type of education made available. The Parmele Industrial Institute was renamed the Martin County Training School, a precursor to regular public high schools for rural blacks in the South. Chance made a difficult choice to grant formal control of the institution to the public system, but hoped he could have enough control to expand educational opportunity for blacks in the region.

Chance understood what he was up against. A few months before his decision to give up Parmele as an independent institution, he had joined prominent black educators from across the state at the First North Carolina Conference for Negro Education. He was named secretary of the conference, reflecting the respect that black and white educators had for his work. The conference was organized by Nathan Newbold, the white state agent for Negro education in North Carolina's Division of Instruction, to promote black teacher training in industrial education and greater standardization of public schooling.[6] Conference presentations by white educators focused on the need for an education system that differentiated between black and white students. Newbold had been instrumental in working to transfer the Parmele Industrial Institute over to Martin County.

Newbold's salary was paid by the General Education Board (GEB), a white northern philanthropic fund that promoted southern education reform. Other foundations, including the Rosenwald Fund and the Negro Rural School Fund, also appointed agents throughout the South to promote education reform at the state and local level and sent representatives to the conference. Newbold's report of the proceedings was one of hundreds submitted to northern philanthropists by education field workers located *within* state and local political systems with salary provided, at least in part, through funding from northern philanthropists. The result was an array of public-private collaborations that helped to develop an education infrastructure for rural blacks, and created institutional arrangements that strengthened state and local governance capacity in some regions of the South. The stories of those efforts are the focus of this book, which explores rural black school reform, the nature of foundation power, and the relationship of both to political development in the early twentieth century.

Scholarship in the history of education has considered the important influence of northern foundations on southern reform. Much of that work has presented a more instrumentalist view of foundation work, rather than one that acknowledges its relationship to broader national goals of state building. That scholarship demonstrates that foundations sought to impose their own education vision on southern communities, one that would promote their own power and serve their business interests by stabilizing both the labor force and the economy.[7] It has also provided evidence that philanthropists gave significantly less funding to programs for southern blacks than whites and promoted an inferior industrial-education curriculum in local segregated schools.[8] In fact, on the eve of World War II, decades after foundations began their work in the South, a report on southern black schools in Mississippi made clear that the profound inequities in that state had not been addressed. There was a "dire need for furniture and teaching materials—comfortable seating facilities, stoves, blackboards, erasers, crayons, supplementary reading materials, maps, flash cards, and charts . . . in hundreds of rural schools there are just four blank, unpainted walls, a few old rickety benches, an old stove propped up on brickbats, and two or three boards nailed together and painted black for a blackboard."[9] This was not the case in most white communities, where the state had been building a more modern public system of education since the early part of the century.

Such anecdotal facts paint a compelling picture of the extent to which foundation programs failed to address adequately the gross inequality between black and white schooling in the South. However, northern foundations expanded schooling and were important to southern education and political development, contributions that are apparent when viewed through the lens of progressivism and state building in the early twentieth century. Foundation leaders collaborated with black and white reformers from both the North and the South, and sought to modernize the South by creating an education infrastructure at the state and local level. In the process, a reform dynamic developed that precluded merely a top-down process, simultaneously influencing not just education reform but also the interest groups and institutions that promoted it. Schooling was an essential component of state formation in the South, especially in rural black communities. It provided a central organizing venue for creating stronger ties among local, state, and federal governance, and an important conduit for disseminating education ideals not just to children in classrooms but also beyond school walls and into the homes of community members. Blacks promoted rural education with or without foundation funding. However, collaborative action created a dynamic process for reform and opportunities to move black participation outside the boundaries of rural communities into formally established institutional sites that might sustain reform over the longer term and create new opportunities to expand political participation. Schooling provided institutional venues for philanthropists and rural blacks to promote a variety of goals that were sometimes contradictory and sometimes complementary.

This book considers the dynamic process of black education reform in two southern states, North Carolina and Mississippi. Extensive archival research that explores the initiatives of foundations and reformers at the top, the impact of that work at the state and local level, and the voices of southerners, including those in rural black communities, demonstrates the importance of schooling to political development in the South and challenges us to reevaluate the relationships among political actors involved in education reform. Leaders of the modern foundations were self-conscious state builders and policy entrepreneurs who aimed to promote national ideals through a public system of education, efforts they believed to be critical in the South, and black education reform was an important component of this national agenda. Through extensive efforts to create a more centralized and standard system of public education that would bring isolated and rural black schools into the public system, schooling served as an important site for expanding state and local governance capacity. Schooling provided opportunities to reorganize local communities and affect black agency in the process. Foundations could not unilaterally impose their education vision on the South, particularly in local black communities, and the collaboration that developed between foundation agents and local citizens could expand schooling and open political opportunity structures in rural areas. Unfortunately, this potential was realized in only a limited number of southern regions. While foundations were effective at developing the institutional configurations necessary to education reform, they were less effective at implementing programs consistently in local areas due to each state's distinctive political and institutional context.

PUBLIC EDUCATION AND THE SOUTH

Northern efforts to reform southern education began with Reconstruction, when philanthropists and denominational organizations descended upon the South in an effort to promote educational opportunities for free blacks.[10] Education programs, coordinated by the Freedmen's Bureau and staffed by black and white teachers from both the North and the South, sought to equip the freed men and women for citizenship and promote self-reliance, self-discipline, and spiritual and moral regeneration.[11] Private organizations provided support for teachers and initiatives that included small rural schools, denominational academies, higher-education institutions, and teacher-training programs.[12] These efforts represented the first comprehensive effort to create a public system of schooling in the South.

The South had been relatively unaffected by the nineteenth-century common school movement in the North. Most antebellum southern whites attended denominational or subscription schools or were part of the plantation elite and educated by private tutors. Wealthy plantation landowners who relied on tutors also dominated southern politics and had little interest in educating poorer whites.[13] Some antebellum southern states, typically the more progressive states that were closer to the Mason-Dixon line, considered public-school legislation by the middle of the nineteenth century, but North-South sectionalism in the decade preceding the war made southerners deeply suspicious of northern institutions, and many linked abolitionist sentiment with northern free-school advocacy.[14] The development of public schooling after the war was a monumental task given the economic devastation and the lack of an existing education infrastructure. Many southerners were reluctant to pay taxes or establish state-level supervisory mechanisms for common school systems, especially if based on northern institutions and funding.

White supremacy posed the most important impediment to the expansion of public education both before and after the war. Nat Turner's 1831 slave rebellion led to severe restrictions on education for slaves and free blacks, ensuring that most blacks in the antebellum South would be illiterate.[15] It was illegal for enslaved African Americans to learn how to read and write, and severe penalties were legislated not just for the slaves who attempted it but also for the freed blacks who tried to teach them. However, laws that prevented black literacy simultaneously reinforced southern white perceptions that the black race was inferior, and created in southern blacks the perception that education was the antithesis to slavery. The very feeling of inferiority forced upon southern blacks by slavery gave them an intense desire to be educated, a hunger met by northerners after the war who hoped to make provisions for it.[16] In a context in which many southern whites failed to see the benefits of expanded educational opportunity for either race, "It was only the other part of the laboring class, the black folk, who connected knowledge with power; who believed that education was the stepping-stone to wealth and respect, and that wealth, without education, was crippled."[17] Efforts to expand educational opportunity in the black community came from blacks themselves, who established their own schools with or without outside support.

While there were education gains after the war, by the end of the nineteenth century northern interest waned, and the planter class regained power.

The expanded education infrastructure created during Reconstruction, when most southern states had established racially segregated schools, was effectively dismantled. The end of Radical Reconstruction, the emergence of Jim Crow segregation, a stronger Democratic Party, and the plantation sharecropping economy made it virtually impossible to create a public school system, especially one that included blacks in any meaningful way. In addition, those earlier reforms had not reflected any agreement about the relationship of schooling to southern progress. Some reformers had promoted education as the foundation of a new egalitarian order that supported free labor, while others believed that education was best used to address racial limitations in segregated schools, rather than as a vehicle to modernize and reconstitute the South.[18] Yet, education remained an important vehicle by which reformers from both the North and the South hoped to shape southern society.

The idea that education could shape American society was certainly not new. Education had also been critical to state formation in the early days of the Republic when legislators and reformers across the nation regarded the common school as the sine qua non of republicanism, and the "safest branch of the government."[19] Schooling was important to addressing the social tensions and risks of industrialization, when reformers believed that it could safeguard democracy and provide for the individual and collective welfare of children.[20] By the end of the nineteenth century, when American farmers expressed their dissatisfaction with rural life through such populist movements as the Grange, education was considered important to addressing agrarian concerns. The Country Life Commission, organized by President Theodore Roosevelt in 1908, recommended public education in rural areas, along with better roads and rural free delivery of the mail to address the relative isolation of these communities.[21]

While the commission's work was national in scope, the South presented a difficult context, given a majority black population in many rural areas and white southern attitudes about both public schooling and race. Most southerners, if they even supported black education, believed that white education was the first priority. Many southern states promoted legislation at the beginning of the twentieth century that would serve rural whites, including consolidated school districts that would benefit from economies of scale and a wider tax base to support better facilities and teachers. However, strict parameters for education reform limited progress, and southern blacks were mostly unaffected by comprehensive efforts to make rural life more palatable in a modern age, except in the case of federally mandated rural free mail delivery.[22]

Problems of taxation and local governance also impeded reform. States across the nation in the early twentieth century were considering tax legislation that would place a greater burden on corporations and railroads, address rising income inequality through inheritance taxes, and equalize property values in order to increase tax revenues and have citizens share equally in payment.[23] Southerners shared these concerns, but their conversations about tax reform reflected important regional differences. Southern states also relied on property tax revenues, but most states relied on regressive taxes, particularly the poll tax, to fund education. Statewide property taxes that were collected locally augmented the school revenues raised through the poll tax. However, poll-tax revenues decreased after Jim Crow disfranchisement, making it difficult to find sufficient funding for education. Many southerners were deeply suspicious of tax increases after the Civil War and Reconstruction, when they were taxed heavily to cover the costs of war and its related debts. As a result, post-Reconstruction southern constitutions typically disallowed local tax levies or placed strict constitutional limits on the combined total of state and local levies.[24] In addition, unequal assessments across counties within states ensured that local communities would fight for scarce resources, which always went to benefit white schools first.[25] White supremacy complicated conversations about tax reform across the region and limited what was available to black communities.

It was difficult to separate conversations about tax reform from the problems of governance. Local governance in the South, where most people lived in areas that were relatively rural, was based on a county system that relied on patronage politics and single-party rule, and was generally managed by part-time officials with limited expertise. The region had relatively less administrative capacity than the North, limited funding to invest in county governance structures, and little incentive to alter them. The Brookings Institution issued a series of reports beginning in 1928 that explored the administrative capacity of a number of states across the nation and indicated that many in the South failed adequately to distribute duties and responsibilities between the state and its political subdivisions, including county governments, or to direct and control the provision of public services. The administrative oversight of county finances, taxation, health and human services, schooling, and roads was often underdeveloped.[26]

Local governance issues created particular problems for school reform. The rural nature of the South meant that many regions lacked town centers and did not perceive that schools were a central defining feature of their communities. The smaller, rural communities that had developed their own schools were generally isolated from formal governance structures. The lack of state standards for a public system of schools, combined with limited managerial or education expertise at the local level meant that there was minimal oversight, little data available, and wide variation in school terms, teacher training and remuneration, curriculum and pedagogy.[27] Further, southerners during Jim Crow were against policies that would lead to a loss of local control and threaten the racial state.

The US commissioner of education reported in 1910 that the "the percentage of illiteracy was greatest in the South, negro population largest, and urban population smallest, [with] the percentage of the school population enrolled, the ratio of average daily attendance, average length of school term, average salaries of teachers, and per capita expenditures for schools smaller than any other region."[28] The average year for enacting compulsory schooling was 1912 in the South as compared to 1870 in the North, and there were typically not measures in the South guaranteeing enforcement, especially for rural black students, with school terms shaped by agricultural cycles well into the 1930s.[29] The total budget for public schooling was significantly smaller in the South where schools met on average one hundred days fewer than northern schools with barely more than one-third of school-age children enrolled.[30] The South was significantly behind in developing a public system of schools that extended to rural areas and included members of both races.

Southern blacks faced a formidable challenge. While they continued to fight for expanded educational opportunity in spite of Jim Crow, the politics of white supremacy was especially significant at the local level and limited what they could do. The Supreme Court's 1896 decision in *Plessy v. Ferguson* legalized "separate but equal," and its 1899 decision in *Cumming v. Richmond County Board of Education* legalized segregation in the schools. However, segregated schools in the South were anything but equal. Expenditures for southern black students averaged only half of that for southern whites, with shorter school terms, fewer schoolhouses, and far lower pay scales for black teachers.[31] A merely quantitative description of the disparities that existed between black and white schools does not adequately capture the social and political context of the Jim Crow South. Most southern whites could simply see no benefit in providing blacks with greater educational opportunity, regardless of whether expanded public schooling required higher taxes and a loss of local control. Black citizens across the South understood that, yet continued to fight for greater equality in education, often at great risk to themselves and their schools.

The Jim Crow environment shaped black behavior and raised the constant specter of white reprisals that could further limit resources and result in personal harm. Between 1889 and 1929, 2,785 blacks were lynched in the South, and inhabitants of the most sparsely populated regions were at a much higher risk than someone living nearer to urban areas.[32] Civil rights activist Minnie Ripley recalled attending the Piney Woods boarding school for blacks in Mississippi in 1918. "To establish that school he [founder Laurence Jones] had to go through some hardships with the landowners . . . because he bought that land, and a black man had problems buying land back then. . . . Sharecroppers was [sic] coming there to school, even grown people were coming there to school, and they attempted to hang him once about that." She recalled that students and teachers hoped to expose the plight of southern blacks to outsiders. "We would publish a pamphlet, and we had to hide those pamphlets, and I wouldn't let any of those pamphlets be thrown around on the campus, and these pamphlets would be sent up North."[33] Teacher reports from Mississippi in 1919 illustrate the severity and intractability of the problem. A teacher in Coahama County said that there were eighty-five black schools, but half were in churches and half were in lodges because most had been "injured by storms and should be condemned." A teacher in Noxubee County noted that most of the sixty-three schools were in churches and shacks.[34] Black communities typically organized their own schools in makeshift spaces, with inadequate equipment, school terms tied to the agricultural cycle, and too few classrooms and teachers to meet the needs of rural communities.

Significant variation existed among states and among communities within the same states or regions in the South, providing evidence of the extent to which local politics determined and limited educational change.[35] Bura Hilbun, the white state agent for Negro education in Mississippi, who was also funded by the GEB, visited Carroll County in 1917 and "found schools in a very unsatisfactory condition." He thought that the "county Superintendent would do more for the negroes were it not for the fear of his losing his hold on the people in a political way."[36] Local politics made improving the black schools almost impossible in many regions. The appointment of Bura Hilbun in Mississippi suggests that northern foundations could exercise significant control over education reform in the South. Yet, most of Mississippi's white politicians and constituents, echoing the beliefs of many across the South, adamantly opposed establishing a public, tax-supported universal system of education. Education reform, however, was not just a southern issue but also a national one that inspired foundation involvement.

SOUTHERN EDUCATION AND THE EMERGENCE
OF THE TWENTIETH-CENTURY FOUNDATIONS

The modern foundation emerged in the early twentieth century, guided by professional expertise and research to inform goals, and made direct efforts to influence public opinion.[37] While foundations had existed since the earliest days of the state, scholars have called the first half of the twentieth century the "classic period of American foundations," in which a small group of philanthropic organizations played an outsized role in American life. Many focused on education and some continued a legacy of philanthropic giving in the South that began with emancipation. The newer foundations played critical roles in the dramatic transformation of several key areas in American life, underwriting policy work that was nonsectarian, secular, and science based. In the process, they helped to create institutions and agencies devoted to the study of particular sets of public problems, often in tandem with state universities and government agencies.[38] The GEB, Negro Rural School Fund (Jeanes Fund), and the Rosenwald Fund shared these important characteristics and contributed significant sums of money in the early twentieth century to build a publicly funded system of universal schooling in the South. Other philanthropists, including Anson Phelps-Stokes and Andrew Carnegie in the North and the Duke family in the South, also funded southern reform efforts. However, the trustees of the GEB, Jeanes Fund, and Rosenwald Fund worked closely together, and members often served simultaneously on more than one of the boards, creating an interlocking directorate that was a powerful force in education reform.

George Foster Peabody had established the Peabody Fund in 1867 as the first large, secular foundation operating in the South, and John Slater followed in 1881 with the Slater Fund. These foundations served as a model for the newer foundations. The GEB, funded by John D. Rockefeller in 1902, contributed to a range of initiatives and helped to coordinate and oversee the work of all of the funds that were active in the South. The Jeanes Fund was established with a bequest by wealthy Quaker Anna T. Jeanes in 1907, and provided supervising teachers to rural communities. The Rosenwald Fund, established by Sears, Roebuck magnate Julius Rosenwald with initial gifts in 1912 and a formal endowment in 1917, is best known for its contributions for schoolhouse construction but also funded such education initiatives as the extension of school terms and school libraries.[39]

The Conference for Education in the South, an annual meeting that began

in 1898 in Capon Springs, West Virginia, shaped the agenda of these foundations. These meetings brought together leaders in farming, business, church,
and education from both the North and the South and became an important
venue for far-reaching collaboration between reformers, university scholars,
northern businessmen, and southerners who represented state interests.[40]
The conference established the Southern Education Board (SEB) in 1901,
with sufficient funding for annual operating expenses to oversee the evolving
work, but no endowment. The SEB provided executive oversight but did not
fund specific education initiatives. That was left to the foundations. Edgar
Garner Murphy, a clergyman from Arkansas who served as a vice president of
the annual conference, encouraged philanthropic participation and believed
their gifts were in service to the nation. "When the people, through their government, educate themselves, they educate themselves for government. . . .
Every true gift of a genuine philanthropy represents the thought of what is due
not only to the child but to our country."[41] The GEB was a direct outgrowth
of conference efforts.[42]

The main goal of the conference was to develop a universal system of
education in the South, supported by public taxation and administered as
a public business.[43] However, it was difficult to separate education goals for
the South from loftier national ideals. As one prominent member of the conference pointed out, the common belief was that the great social duty of the
age was the salvation of society, which began with the salvation of the child,
and was intended to promote democratic values that would be dominant and
universal. "Thus, in a very special way, our political institutions unfold an
inspired mission that deeply concerns the moral progress of the world. Thus
the state should become the universal missionary of a political gospel both at
home and abroad."[44] Conference participants also believed universal education should include both races.

> The issues presented by the negro in American life are national . . . because
> of the principles, because of the industrial and political assumptions, which
> they involve. The national welfare is the larger context of every local prob-
> lem; and while the negro question finds its locality in the South, it must find
> its ultimate adjustment—if it ever receives adjustment—in the conscience,
> the wisdom, the knowledge, the patience, the courage of the nation.[45]

Reformers did not promote education equality, but "universal education"
for conference participants meant the education of both black and white stu-

dents, which they believed necessary for a stronger state. "We declare such education to be the foremost task of our statesmanship, and the most worthy object of philanthropy."[46]

While reformers were inspired by national goals, they also understood that the work had to take place locally. The foundations designed programs and bureaucratic structures that could enhance state and local governance capacity. Programs included the state agents for Negro education, Jeanes teachers, county training schools, and teacher-training programs. They also promoted tax reform, school consolidation, term extensions, minimum teacher salaries and standards for certification, and a philanthropic mode of funding that both coexisted with state and local budgets and operated discretely.[47] These initiatives helped to coordinate public schooling and overcome problems of administrative capacity, rationalize state education policy by creating minimum standards, and promote appropriate forms of oversight that connected local schools to state-level governance structures.[48] Foundation reformers hoped to create bureaucratic autonomy for public education based on education expertise rather than partisan and local rule.

Foundation reformers understood that an effective public system required an infrastructure supported by local citizens, and their programs encouraged such participation. They realized that philanthropic donations could never be adequate to building the education system that they envisioned; they understood that private donations and local taxation both transferred the burden of public schooling to the public and provided an avenue for citizens to demonstrate attitudes of self-help. Tax reform was an important means of promoting the connection between citizens and an emerging public system of schooling. The Jeanes teachers were central to foundation-based local reform because of their roles as community organizers, fundraisers, and supervisors of rural black schools. With the assistance of these local teachers, foundations promoted networks that extended across local and state boundaries and fostered dynamic relationships between white and black reformers.

Foundation programs used schooling to promote collaboration at every level of government, which could strengthen governance in the process. Education field workers who were located within state and local political systems with at least partial funding from northern philanthropists helped to strengthen administrative oversight of both schools and local communities. Both state agents and Jeanes teachers had positions in the formal governance structure, but reported to their foundation benefactors and to white state and local politicians, including the county superintendent. Foundations believed that the county Jeanes teachers would be important for local initiatives, implementing foundation programs and promoting stronger administrative structures and oversight. They also believed that the teachers could help to end the isolation of rural schools because they were required in their positions to participate in the broader reform dynamic. Public-private collaboration was instrumental to developing an education infrastructure for rural blacks in some southern regions and to producing institutional arrangements that enhanced state and local governance capacity.

A Reconsideration of Reformers' Goals

The profound racism of the South influenced the agenda for education reform. Southern blacks worked to enhance their own educational opportunities, often in ways that diverged from white conceptions of black schooling. However, rural blacks were politically marginalized and lacked resources— and as a result northern foundations had particular influence by virtue of their largesse and efficiency.[49] Yet a conversation that starts and ends with racism can diagnose the limits of what was possible in the South, but neglects other important dimensions of foundation work and black agency. Education reform influenced the southern social and political structure in ways that went well beyond schooling. We can better understand its impact by considering it in the context of progressivism and state building in the early twentieth century.

Many of the foundation objectives make sense in the context of progressivism. The particular goals of foundation reformers, including taxation, bureaucratic supervision, and standardization were in line with broader efforts during the time period to make government efficient. Municipalities across the nation reformed local governance structures to rely more on professional expertise and modern managerial theories. Reformers hoped to overcome a system of local and partisan representation that expanded representative government and grassroots impulses but that reformers considered inefficient and irrational.[50] Business leaders, including such philanthropists as Andrew Carnegie and John D. Rockefeller, objected to local and particularistic interests that dominated public institutions, and in New York in 1906 they provided the funding for the New York Bureau of Municipal Reform, which aimed to provide nonpartisan expertise on governance matters.[51] In the South, similarly, northern philanthropists perceived egregious examples of local, partisan, and inefficient rule, and they believed that efficiently designed governance systems would provide greater opportunity to develop and implement policy decisions that reflected the best scientific knowledge available. This required state and county governments that were led by experts with modern managerial ability, tax policies that allowed for sufficient revenues to support both governance and public education, and administrative systems that could develop and implement the policies of a modern industrialized state.

Foundation reformers wanted governance structures run by experts, so that they might advance their own ideas about policy development. They acted similarly in their efforts to expand public health initiatives in the South. For example, the Rockefeller Sanitary Commission, formed in 1909, found most state public health agencies inadequate to meet the demands of a rigorous campaign to battle the hookworm, a parasite estimated to have infected as much as 40 percent of the southern population in the early twentieth century.[52] The commission recognized that the best way to promote an efficient and scientific campaign to eradicate the parasite was through a network of established state agencies—yet these had been mostly ineffectual in the South. The commission also recognized that the most glaring deficiency in the South's public health system was the lack of county organization.[53] A first priority was to strengthen existing governance structures by appointing scientifically minded state and local agents who reported to the commission. A decade of education reform in the South provided a blueprint for this work.

Efforts to expand state authority over the general well-being of children in this time gave the state a defining role in both education and the lives of American families.[54] Foundations believed that the creation of a public system of education, with formal oversight by efficient state and local governance structures, would help them promote ideals in the most public of spheres. In this way, education reform and state building were inextricably linked.[55] Yet, education reform was a complicated terrain.

The development of rural black schools required compromises among groups that often held contrasting racial conceptions. Some southern whites, including Mississippi governor James Vardaman, incited violence against blacks and asserted that any money spent on their education was a waste, while other virulent white supremacists, including North Carolina governor Charles Aycock, believed that universal and unequal education for blacks and whites was a key to the state's political and economic development. Foundation officials and other participants in the Conference for Education in the South were similarly divided between those who believed that blacks were capable and deserving of only an inferior education and those who believed that education might positively affect perceived racial differences over time. More broadly, all of these groups differed in their conceptions of how racial difference affected the strength of the American nation-state and translated into state and local education policy.

The dynamic nature of education change, especially in local communities where rural black citizens participated in reform, adds an important bottom-up dimension to these efforts. Indeed, assuming that philanthropists exercised hegemonic control over education obscures the important role of locals, especially rural black teachers. The decentralized nature of the public system of schooling that foundation reformers developed in the South during the first half of the twentieth century allowed for a broad range of ideas and practices from both southern whites and black reformers.

Broad collaboration occurred because there were important areas of consensus. Many white reformers agreed on the need to address a southern problem that both related to and transcended views about race and equality. The failures of Reconstruction had led to a reduction in labor-force productivity, a focus on separatist political power, and a general retardation of southern political and economic development.[56] Southern separatism and backwardness challenged the nationalist ideals that inspired northern reformers and philanthropists, who believed that American national strength depended upon regional unity.[57] Further, a dependent black labor force in a region that provided the world's cotton supply threatened the nation's economic supremacy and cultural authority.[58] Colonialism around the world in the early twentieth century influenced perceptions of southern backwardness and generated a discourse about the South, resulting in an enduring paradox of southern reform that was simultaneously "compounded colonialism" and a "nation building project."[59]

An early report on southern education is illustrative, claiming it was "more than a Southern problem; it is a national problem. . . . We cannot afford to let a great section of the country, containing one-sixth of our entire population, remain longer in this condition. . . . The education of the people of the South is today the supreme national question."[60] Public schooling could transform rural blacks into citizens who might govern themselves in preferred ways, promote national unity by disseminating shared ideals, aid in efforts to rehabilitate the South by providing an institutional means to reach rural communities, and make government more efficient in the process.[61]

Concerns about southern rehabilitation and political development also reflected another important area of consensus. Many reformers recognized the problem of extreme white supremacy and found the views of people like Governor Vardaman to be not just embarrassing, but also economically problematic. Even Governor Aycock conceded that economic welfare depended upon an educated workforce that would simultaneously prevent black migration to other states and prevent race warfare, which would be inimical to investment. Many foundation collaborators had extreme racial views, but recognized the need to limit the reach of white supremacy. This agreement provided a space for political action, even though the people who occupied that space often had extreme views about race and differed in their conceptions of the purposes of schooling.

Southerners of both races who collaborated with foundation reformers made difficult compromises that they believed served their interests. This was true for white-supremacist politicians who considered foundation initiatives politically expedient. It was especially true, however, for southern blacks, who had to make difficult choices about how best to promote black progress. Beginning with Reconstruction, black southerners worked to change the southern caste system, often with the help of outside intervention. Some black educators believed that industrial education had its advantages and that it might lead to more schooling in rural black communities, while others adamantly opposed this curriculum on the grounds that it limited black opportunity and might lead to a system overseen by white reformers committed to the racial state.[62] Rural black teachers stood to gain significant support if they promoted foundation policies, even when those policies contradicted their political ideals. They saw the decision to work closely with foundations and their agents as a Faustian bargain that might simultaneously expand educational opportunity and limit local control and individual aspirations.

Foundation programs provided opportunities for marginalized citizens to participate in extrapolitical alliances as democratic citizens despite white supremacy. They influenced how rural black communities understood their relations not only with the government but also with their fellow citizens.[63] Local control was also a powerful source of education development and innovation in rural black communities, just as it was in white ones.[64] This does not mean that local communities defined reform initiatives or that rural blacks had significant power in the reform dynamic. However, foundation programs affected rural black agency, in some regions more than in others, and education organizations affected political opportunity structures over the longer term. Because southern whites often abrogated responsibility for rural black schools, local black teachers had relatively greater autonomy than white oversight of schools would seem to provide, and their positions created avenues to join the professional middle class. They worked to meet simultaneously the

needs of both the rural black communities that they served and their foundation benefactors.

In the long and perilous road to civil rights, southern blacks often had to
make such difficult choices. Black reformers recognized that foundations offered a ray of hope for expanded education in the short term, and for new
possibilities over the longer term. Historian Nelson Lichtenstein argues that
southern black support for labor unions presented similar complexities. While
national labor unions failed to promote black labor interests adequately, the
unions provided opportunities to challenge entrenched local elites.[65] Blacks
could not vote in the South, but were allowed to vote in union elections. Historian Robert Norrell argues that Booker T. Washington's work with northern
foundations and southern white politicians and educators reflected a sophis-
ticated strategy whereby he hoped to link black progress with the fortunes of
the South. Washington wanted blacks to acquire land, wealth, skills, health,
and education; his gradualism reflected difficult compromises.[66] Rural black
citizens who sought to expand educational opportunities faced similar dilem-
mas. Foundations failed to challenge the gross inequality of white supremacy,
yet offered an opportunity to challenge the political structure of the South
through schooling.

Foundation initiatives in the early twentieth century present another example of northern efforts to address the problems of the southern racial state.
These include the abolitionist movement, Radical Reconstruction, civil rights
organizers, and the Freedom Riders, Freedom Schools, and voting rights
militants of the 1960s. Most southerners considered Yankee reformers to be
dangerous meddlers and demonized them as fanatics, carpetbaggers, mis-
cegenationists, and Communists. Yet wealthy philanthropists were far more
conservative in their approach to the problem South. They remained defer-
ential to southern mores and, for the most part, escaped the extreme derision
of southern whites. Many liberal and radical historians have been far more
critical of their work because, by comparison with other interventions, they
lacked a sense of egalitarianism and social justice. They were concerned with
black education, but not necessarily as a way to promote greater equality, and
they failed to end the inequities of public education. However, the philanthropists correctly perceived that the problems of the South required education
and effective government, and they came to understand that outside intervention would be the only means to overturn the racial caste system there. They
facilitated the expansion of administrative capacity in both governance and in
the area of education, and provided resources to support black agency. Their

contributions do not provide an inspiring story of breaking down the door of Jim Crow, but they did lead to incremental change. By our present standards, these contributions might seem small, but many blacks in the South collaborated with foundation reformers to promote an expanded education system and considered their programs important in the long path to civil rights.

Brown v. Board of Education in 1954 called for an end to the "separate but equal" idea defined in *Plessy v. Ferguson* in 1896. However, between *Plessy* and *Brown*, foundation programs provided an organizational structure to expand black schooling at a time when almost nobody outside the black community had the will or resources to do so. It is hard to imagine what the South would have looked like at the midpoint of the twentieth century without the efforts of the foundations that are explored here. The Rosenwald Fund facilitated the construction of 5,357 buildings in 883 southern counties across the South; the GEB and Slater Funds developed county training schools that promoted teacher training and a movement toward black high schools; the Jeanes Fund provided supervising teachers who organized both rural schools and their communities; and foundation programs in general promoted reform of local governance.[67] These programs expanded education for rural blacks relative to what might have been. Historian Howard Rabinowitz describes how southern blacks sought greater education equality in a number of urban school systems in the late nineteenth century, and how southern whites refused to accommodate them. However, these same whites were willing to respond to requests that more black teachers be provided for black students, placating many of the protestors who came to recognize that "half a loaf" was better than none.[68] While "success" during this time period in the South can usually be understood only as limited progress in a very unequal system, it remains important to understand what that progress looked like, where it was greatest, and how it affected both state and local communities.

Southern Education Reform and Political Development

Foundations and education were both important to state-building efforts in the early twentieth century, though much scholarship has focused on the national level.[69] This book focuses on the distinctiveness of education as a state-building effort at both the state and local level, through a comparison of education reform in North Carolina and Mississippi between 1900 and 1940. These two states represent regions that responded differently to foundation efforts in black education reform, often in complicated ways.[70] Foundation reformers distinguished between the "Upper South" and the "Deep South" in their reports, and these two states represent extremes within those regions. Yet, the story of reform in each state adds important nuance to southern education history and political development. The juxtaposition of the relatively progressive education actions of North Carolina against the extreme unwillingness to act in Mississippi demonstrates that education-policy development was dependent upon administrative structures that affected both governance and rural black agency. State differences illustrate the dimensions and limitations of foundation power and efficacy.

The differences between North Carolina and Mississippi make clear that it is simplistic to generalize about foundation efforts across the South.[71] Racial attitudes in each state translated differently into education policy.[72] North Carolina was more interested in economic and political development and believed it could be achieved by educating all citizens. That vision led to an administrative structure conducive to deep collaboration with foundations and relatively greater evidence of foundation efficacy and progress, education reform, and political development at the state and local level. Mississippi did not develop a vision for universal education tied to economic and political development, and it had a weak administrative structure. Most politicians there had little interest in foundation collaboration, leading to a relative lack of education reform and political development.

Some important insights from scholarship in American political development inform this analysis and help to recast the more traditional narratives in the history of education. The earlier scholarship addresses the problem of a "weak" federal state in the early twentieth century.[73] Indeed, educational opportunity for the South's rural blacks at the beginning of the century was so limited that it should have been a national matter, but the federal government neglected to take on this important matter directly because of general white indifference and contemporary conceptions of federalism that limited the government's ability to act. However, classic state theory does not adequately capture a more diffuse form of state power, one that develops more on the periphery than at the center. Interest groups and institutions were critical to the development of the American state.[74] The problem was not a "weak" state, but perhaps a "hidden" one, meaning that the federal government could mobilize both public and private resources for national policymaking, rather than using unilateral state power, and policies often developed outside the boundaries of formal governance systems through associated action.[75] Education reform had the potential to incite fears of concentrated government power, but the delegation of authority to nongovernmental organizations provided an alternative means of public intervention.[76] These relationships were important to early twentieth-century policy development in both the North and the South.

Recent scholarship that suggests that American foundations might have engineered reform to promote their own power and corporate interests does not sufficiently explore the mechanisms by which corporate interests could direct and control social policy.[77] It is not clear to what extent business elites had that ability, especially in the Jim Crow South.[78] The modern foundations integrated professionals from a range of institutions and created complex ideological configurations to promote reform. They also played a major role in preparing the way for the modern state by developing links between disparate groups of reformers.[79] Their members were among the "new liberals" of the Progressive Era, who embraced a range of national nongovernmental associations, including voluntary, religious, and even corporate organizations.[80]

The federal government did not explicitly promote the education objectives of the private foundations, but it supported the work. Through efforts like the Country Life Commission and vocational and agricultural education programs, the federal government promoted a set of national ideals that helped to shape rural education and encouraged the relationships that developed among northern foundations, business interests, universities, and political actors from the North and the South across every level of governance. Such associated action was central to education reform.[81] Associated action was important to expanding educational opportunity in rural black communities. The relationship of foundation work to both federal and state governance provides important lessons for understanding foundation efficacy in the present. While early twentieth-century collaboration helped to redefine the relationship between education and the individual states, reformers in the early twenty-first century are restructuring the relationship between education and the national state, with the possibility of greater federal intervention and foundation influence.

Southern blacks were so marginalized in the early twentieth century that it would seem almost impossible for them to make meaningful contributions to the interest groups and institutions that promoted political development.[82] However, foundation efficacy required collaboration at every level of government, with both public and private actors, and with local black citizens. Foundations were but one of a set of institutional actors, and a powerful one at that, but still not sufficiently powerful relative to the formal institutions that existed at the federal, state, and local level. Collaboration often included disparate participants and resulted in organizational structures that were widely dispersed, ensuring that it would be impossible for one group to control southern reform. The policies associated with education reform in the South did not emerge because northern foundations imposed them, and their implementation resulted in interactions between various interest groups and organizations. Blacks had a marginalized role in that broader dynamic but were essential at the local level, and foundation reform programs could not have happened without them. Educational policy specifically and political development generally were driven not just by experts and policymakers at the top but also locally by reformers, including rural black citizens.

Foundation officials believed that their programs should operate within the political system as much as possible, a difficult strategy given that concerns over local control and states' rights created strict parameters around policy development. They established and implemented administrative systems that operated within, parallel to, and discretely from formal governance systems. These systems were essential to establishing new policy, enacting reform, and managing social policy.[83] Foundations sought to institutionalize their policies by layering tracks onto existing institutions and developing arrangements that varied by state in order to create environments that were more conducive to education reform.[84] Their programs recognized and limited where possible the strength of local white majorities, and created public agencies to deliver a public system of education that state and local politicians could not easily influence. Foundations tailored initiatives to local conditions; their programs were open to decentralization and policy experimentation, strategies that were instructive as race-based social policy developed with greater breadth in the New Deal.[85]

Institutions structure politics and have the potential to influence subsequent policy and political development.[86] Thus, schooling was an essential component of state formation in the South, especially in rural black communities. Local schooling provided a central organizing venue that could create stronger ties among local, state, and federal governance, and provided an important conduit for disseminating education ideals not just to children in classrooms but also beyond school walls and into the homes of community members.

Programs that successfully promoted broad collaboration had the potential both to strengthen and change the shape of state and local governance, sometimes in ways that could have a considerable impact in local communities and provide new sources of power for rural black citizens. Political change increases when there is greater friction among multiple political orders, such as government institutions, the organizational environment, and the ideological and cultural repertoires that organize discussion.[87] While the segregated school system was intended to undergird white supremacy, its implementation through decentralized and local initiatives led to forms of policy feedback that incited such friction.[88] This does not mean that education development was the sole precursor to political change in the South, but it was certainly an important component.

It is difficult to convey adequately the array of institutional arrangements that developed in the South. Forms of state and local governance that developed through foundation efforts varied by region, as did the range of actors involved in them, and might have been initiated either from the top of the governance structure or locally. Foundations relied upon a range of collaborative efforts, each designed to fill a policymaking void in state and local governance. Referred to here as "interstitial collaboration," this idea recognizes that foundations cooperated with a range of political actors in an effort to fill gaps in state policy and practice regarding education development for rural black citizens.[89] It is based on a concept in legal scholarship, "interstitial lawmaking," by which the courts fill gaps in laws enacted by Congress, often with diverse results. This form of lawmaking acknowledges that silence in law is no reason for limiting its reach.[90]

The foundations operating in the South recognized that many states promoted new legislation in the early twentieth century to benefit white schools. However, most of the states left gaps in policy and practice with regard to black schools. The foundations developed a range of methods, also with diverse results, to fill those gaps. Interstitial collaboration provided for extra political associations that promoted collective action. It created opportunities for the participation of marginalized black citizens, even if severely circumscribed, incorporating them into the state through the developing public-school system. This occurred formally, through organizational structures that developed within and outside of existing governance systems, and informally, through the political and professional networks that existed as part of these structures. Industrial schools reinforced and magnified the white power structure at the same time that schooling, as an institution, provided interesting and unintended opportunities for rural blacks to exercise agency beyond what white supremacists ever envisioned.

Organization and Methodology

The nature of state and local government in the South in the early twentieth century makes it difficult to generalize about education reform, either by region or time period. Political decisions were often influenced by sectional interests, which were defined in terms of race and the agricultural economy, and defended in terms of states' rights. Change did not occur at the same rate throughout the South, even though states operated in the same broad historical context and felt events such as *Plessy v. Ferguson*, World War I, the Great Migration, the decline of the cotton economy, and the Great Depression. All of these events affected foundation work, yet education gains in the early part of the century in one rural community were often not matched in another rural community within the same period, despite their temporal and physical proximity.[91] One way to understand the differences between North Carolina and Mississippi is to consider not just the acts of individual reformers, whether located in foundations or in local communities, but also the institutional sites in which reform took place. While this book analyzes four decades of education activism, the key period is 1900 to 1920, when foundations initially implemented programs. Archival information from local communities is richer in earlier years in North Carolina, where the appointment of the first state agent for Negro education in 1913 had an immediate and significant effect on education reform, and in much later years in Mississippi, where foundation efficacy was much harder to achieve.

The chapters that follow discuss efforts to reform rural black education in the South from the perspective of foundation reformers, state and local politicians, and rural black citizens, especially the teachers who promoted education in their own communities. Their stories converge in the formal networks and administrative systems that were promoted through foundation initiatives, even as black teachers and parents implemented them at a local level. Ultimately, this is a comprehensive history of southern education reform in that it captures the important roles of interest groups and institutions and transcends the work of individual teachers and reformers.

The first two chapters discuss rural black education reform from two different perspectives. The first is that of the twentieth-century foundations. Chapter 1 argues that foundation leaders believed education reform, which promoted universal and unequal education, was instrumental to the broader goal of state building at every level of government. The second perspective, discussed in chapter 2, is that of rural blacks, particularly the Jeanes teachers. This chapter argues that the Jeanes teachers were also state builders, who collaborated with foundations and their agents to strengthen the organization and administration of local communities. Schooling helped to expand political opportunities, organizational strength, shared cognitions in the community in some areas of the South, and opportunities for black reformers to promote community goals.[92] Taken together, these two chapters provide a top-down and bottom-up analysis of foundation programs implemented in collaboration with rural blacks. They illustrate the significance of decentralization to education-policy innovation and implementation, and the formal role of black teachers in organizing their communities and working to meet the communities' education needs in the early twentieth century.

The remainder of the book is devoted to a more detailed study of North Carolina and Mississippi. Chapter 3 explores the institutional and contextual differences between the two states and establishes that foundations required an array of institutional arrangements across the South that were responsive to regional differences and granted differential power to the state, foundations, interest groups, and rural black citizens.[93] Chapter 4 describes education reform in North Carolina, where the public system of education evolved with greater state centralization and local decisions about public education became part of the public sphere. Foundation programs expanded translocal networks for rural black teachers and provided connections between rural black communities and political actors outside the community, giving some black educators a more formal and participatory role.[94] In Mississippi, schools remained isolated and disconnected, and rural blacks covertly promoted educational opportunity. It proved difficult in these circumstances to sustain progress because education reform was initiated privately rather than publicly, and programs did not result in any comprehensive changes to the public system of schooling. Rural blacks came to understand that public education in Mississippi would never progress without grassroots organizing within the state and help from actors outside of it.

The United States is made up of citizens who exist in a society of institutions. The leaders of the early twentieth-century foundations believed in the connection between education and a stronger American state, but recognized that it would not be possible to promote national ideals about education one school at a time. Foundation leaders and their agents sought to modernize the South, and education reform was important to that cause. Their programs, however, did not sufficiently alter the public system of schooling for rural blacks across the South, nor did extensive collaboration prevent southern blacks in any region from being politically marginalized. Historian Louis Harlan concluded that by 1915 the Southern Education Board failed to expand southern black education and to "challenge or deflect the anti-Negro movement which it paralleled," and the GEB had ceased to focus on black education.[95] This book takes a longer view. Foundations were instrumental in establishing an education infrastructure that contributed to state and local governance capacity, and provided a means to organize rural black communities and expand black agency through schooling.

William Chance, who attended the First North Carolina Conference for Negro Education in 1913, spent the first half of the twentieth century promoting black education in collaboration with white reformers, and allowed the state to subsume his beloved Parmele Institute into the public system. He had a different conception of black schooling than white North Carolina educators or northern benefactors. In 1948, after being ejected from a railroad car, arrested, and jailed, Chance successfully sued the Atlantic Coast Line Railroad, outlawing segregation on railroad cars in interstate travel.[96] He put himself at risk to promote political equality, and his decades of collaboration with northern foundations demonstrated that he understood public schooling to be central to that fight. Organizational change is always a dynamic process, with both intended and unintended consequences, and nowhere is this more evident than in the development of rural black education in the South.

CHAPTER ONE

"The Thrill of This State-Building Work"

When the Confederate Congress met in 1862, Jabez Lafayette Monroe Curry seemed an obvious choice to represent Alabama.[1] He was a member of the Democratic Party and a southern aristocrat, educated on a large plantation with private tutors and then at the University of Georgia and Harvard Law School. He served in the Alabama Congress from 1847 to 1856 and was a representative to the US Congress from 1857 to 1862. He was also a Baptist minister with a gift for public speaking. In an 1859 address to the House of Representatives on the eve of the Civil War, Curry seemed the perfect spokesman for his southern colleagues. "In all possible modes of government there will be a conflict between sections and interests and classes . . . every separate community must be able to protect itself [and] . . . this power of self-protection, according to my judgment and my theory of politics, resides in each State."[2] Although Curry was adamant enough about his views to serve in the Confederate Army, he spent the four decades following the Civil War promoting public, universal education in the South that was "organized, controlled, and liberally supported by the State" but national in scope and developed outside the boundaries of Alabama.[3] He not only advocated universal education but also encouraged the federal government to give aid to southern schools.[4] As a general agent to the Peabody Fund beginning in 1881, and a trustee of the Slater Fund, he was instrumental to the development of the Conference for Education in the South, the Southern Education Board (SEB), and the General Education Board (GEB). Curry's participation in these endeavors illustrates that southern education reform, as promoted by northern foundations, was a collaborative process, developed in partnership with southern reformers, and implemented in partnership with southern states. His interest in promoting universal education for both races seems inconsistent with his earlier views, alluding to the possibility that he believed education reform might achieve something beyond simple learning.[5]

Curry's role was particularly important to southern education reform. He influenced an agenda that would be more acceptable to southerners, helped northerners to manage the southern sociopolitical culture, fostered cooperation between the North and the South, and brought the legitimacy that foundations needed in their campaign for universal education. The influence of an ex-Confederate like Curry and, indeed, the willingness of foundations to rely so heavily on him, provides evidence that foundations neglected to use the power of their largesse to overturn the South's unjust, racial state. They focused instead on their belief that public schooling was essential to southern development. The philanthropists brought a paternalistic perspective to southern education reform. They hoped to save not just the South but also the nation. Indeed, when the president of the Fifth Conference for Education in the South made his address to the assembly, he was clear about the import of the work: "As one of our number so often remarks, we must come to these people that they may have life and have it more abundantly. Truly this work is Christ-like."[6] Their messianic aspirations included supreme faith in the expertise and organizational skills that they brought to the task.

Southern education reform was indeed a scientific business. William Baldwin, head of the Long Island Railroad and first chair of the GEB, called for the application of business methods to reform and the elimination of references to past differences between the North and South.[7] Indeed, an effective business model required a new era of post–Civil War collaboration between northern and southern reformers. The Conference for Education in the South, which began in 1898 at Capon Springs, West Virginia, brought together an assembly of southern citizens who were leaders in farming, business, church, and school, but quickly became an important venue for far-reaching collaboration between reformers, university scholars, northern businessmen, and southerners who represented state interests.[8] Edwin Alderman, a prominent reformer who served as president of three southern universities and a member of the SEB, spoke to the importance of cooperation in his presentation to reformers at the 1902 conference. "I believe that this assembly is the largest event in the direction of national American unity which occurred in this generation."[9]

Alderman's comments reflected both an interest in the kind of associated action that defined policy making at the federal level at this time and also reformers' hopes that education reform might promote a stronger state and overcome problems of southern development and separateness. Failed Reconstruction policies created a separatist attitude in a South that remained wary of northern influence, including that of the federal government, and resentful that southern life might be reconstituted in service of northern political and economic goals. However, southern education reform was a popular cause among disparate groups of white donors and reformers long before the first annual conference. Their ideas converged in a shared belief that education was central to building a more powerful American state, aspirations that required the rehabilitation and uplift of the South, and national unity. Curry spoke to members of the annual conference in 1899 about the commitment to those national ideals. "Our country is the glory of earth, the hope of the oppressed of all lands, the realization of the dignity of man as man, the fulfillment of the dreams of all who have built their hopes on human capabilities and human liberty, and nothing can surpass the duty to omit no exertion of transmitting unimpaired all these blessings and hopes to those who are to come after us."[10] He promoted support for every education agency from kindergarten through the university in pursuit of these ideals, serving all citizens both black and white. However, he was explicit about the need to educate whites first. "The white people are to be the leaders, to take the initiative, to have the directive control in all matters pertaining to civilization and the highest interests of our beloved land. History demonstrates that the Caucasian will rule. He ought to rule. . . . This white supremacy does not mean hostility to the negro, but friendship for him."[11] Education reformers sought to expand public schooling without imposing ideals that challenged these beliefs in rural regions of the South. Yet, education reform did challenge southerners to think differently about the purposes of schooling and its relationship to the state.

In general, foundation reformers wanted government that was effective, efficient, and would provide an appropriate venue for disseminating policy. However, while efforts to increase participation in schooling might seem at first glance to be motivated by democratic concerns that promoted civic participation, this was not the case. Foundations required local participation for program efficacy but ultimately believed that foundation ideas based in scientific knowledge and expertise would be superior to local ideas. Indeed a conference resolution called on members to promote "free education of such efficiency as shall make the coming generation of citizens of the Southern States the best trained men and women that an enlightened democracy can produce. To this end it urges the increase of taxes for school use, the lengthening of school terms, the better payment of teachers as fast as prudent regard for the economic conditions of every community will permit."[12] These initiatives required the administrative capacity that might be achieved through state education standards and accountability, as well as mechanisms that connected small rural communities to the state. An effective public system of education required governance structures that had the capacity to provide sufficient oversight, integrate a range of state and local agencies, and promote the organization and participation of local communities. Foundation programs often resulted in parallel governance systems used to establish new policy, enact reform, and ensure bureaucratic management over social policy in the South. Their programs encompassed an array of initiatives aimed at state formation. The development of bureaucracy and standardization, to the extent that states were willing to undertake it, would likely lead over time to greater centralization at the level of individual states. For states that did not develop such bureaucracy, foundation programs that promoted community organizing and imposed standards through alternative systems of governance might promote administrative hierarchies and capacity. As later examples illustrate, foundations often awarded funds on the condition that local schools standardized practice, including Rosenwald gifts for school construction that required minimum teacher salaries and school terms.

School reformers across the nation in the early twentieth century worked to transform the public school as a governing institution.[13] This was also true in the South, where foundations conceived of a public system of education that would promote national ideals through decentralized and local systems of public education. But southern school reform proved far more complicated. The region lacked administrative capacity, was defined by white supremacy and perceived as holding the nation back from greatness. In most southern communities, nearly all power resided at the county level in governance units much smaller than their northern counterparts and led primarily by elected and part-time officials. Southern whites perceived this type of governance structure conducive to promoting their narrow interests; they mistrusted centralization that might extract resources for expanded governance capacity and diminish local control. Foundation officials were concerned about such forms of governance and hoped to design programs that promoted a public system of education and enhanced governance capacity at the level of both individual states and localities. Success depended upon men like Curry, who could facilitate connections between northern and southern reformers, southern political systems, and participants at the state and local level across the South.

Ultimately, foundation programs had the potential to strengthen both governance capacity and black agency. However, local programs limited the educational attainment of rural black citizens whose aspirations were impacted by the foundations' infatuation with industrial education. One way to keep white southern politicians involved was to provide some guarantee that rural black education would not upset the racial state. However, this does not mean that northern reformers and philanthropists promoted industrial education in a merely instrumentalist fashion, or had an alternative, more liberal conception of black education that was compromised through collaboration. As one reformer said, "Negro education is recognized as a part of the public education system in every state, both South and North. The education of every child in our country is an admitted national duty."[14] This reflects simultaneously a commitment to black education and an indication that some reformers grudgingly promoted it only because both the law and perhaps conscience required it. At least in the short term, northern philanthropists and reformers were comfortable with an unequal system of universal education. Ultimately, foundation programs extended black educational opportunity into rural communities, yet restricted the quality of education that would be available to rural black citizens. Yet, their programs also strengthened local governance capacity through schooling and affected black agency over the longer term.

THE CONFERENCE ON SOUTHERN EDUCATION AND COOPERATION FOR SOUTHERN REFORM

Dr. Hollis Frissell, principal of the Hampton Institute, helped to organize the first Conference for Education in the South in 1898 and delivered the opening address, advocating an industrial-education curriculum that would become a central feature of education reform in rural black communities.[15] However, Reverend A. B. Hunter, who was elected secretary and treasurer of the conference, delivered a paper that was even more instructive. "If our work lies outside the jurisdiction of the national government; we ought to constitute a republic or confederacy among ourselves."[16] Frissell, like many participants, agreed with Hunter. "It became clear in 1898, at this first Capon Springs Conference, that to accomplish the greatest good in the Southern education field the North and South must enter into closer relations . . . since the Federal Government had given the South practically no assistance, the North should help in a fraternal sprit, not to meddle or interfere, but to 'stand by' as fellow-citizens of a common country."[17] At its inception, the conference was an important site to promote cooperation, especially in the absence of explicit and strong government participation at the national or state level, and that cooperation determined the agenda that would develop.

This is not meant to minimize the importance of Frissell's opening address. Industrial education, a curriculum intended to train rural blacks for agricultural and domestic labor in the South, became a defining feature of foundation support, and its limitations were clear. It promoted the idea that hard labor was a principle of civilized life. Samuel Chapman Armstrong established the Hampton Institute in 1867 to promote education for the freed blacks. Booker T. Washington, a graduate of the Hampton Institute, was chosen to be the founding principal of the Tuskegee Institute. Both institutions promoted a strict industrial-training curriculum that sought to cultivate black citizens who would dignify labor and contribute to the South's prosperity.

The work in these two institutions heavily influenced the philanthropists and their associates. Robert Curtis Ogden, head of the New York branch of Philadelphia's Wanamaker Stores, was appointed vice president of the second Conference for Education in the South, and then president of the SEB and the GEB. Ogden had helped to establish the Hampton Institute in 1867 and served as a trustee for both Hampton and Tuskegee. He organized railroad tours of southern communities in conjunction with the annual conferences to generate greater participation from potential northern donors. The events highlighted for many the rural nature of the South and its lack of both community centers and an administrative infrastructure to deliver public education. George Foster Peabody and William Baldwin also served as trustees at both institutions. They found it easy to make the case that economic prosperity depended upon an educated black labor force, and industrial education could achieve it.

An address by William Baldwin at the first conference clarified that southern education reform was not designed to challenge the Jim Crow order. "Social recognition of the negro by the white is a simple impossibility, and is entirely dismissed from the minds of the white, and by the intelligent Negroes. . . . Properly directed he is the best possible laborer to meet the climatic conditions of the South."[18] Baldwin's statement reflected both racial attitudes and national trends that made it easier for philanthropists and reformers to become enamored of industrial education. The needs of a modern yet racialized industrial "democracy" influenced education reformers in the late nineteenth century, who became more interested in the practical applications of knowledge and developed manual-training programs in the emerging high schools. Educators advocated its benefits, recognizing the industrial need for trained workers. In combination with literacy, science, and math, reformers believed manual training could aid in the selection of occupations, "cultivate the mechanical and scientific imagination . . . and, increase the bread-winning and home-making power of the average boy."[19] Francis Parker, an early propo-

nent of progressive education, developed ideas about manual training when
he served as superintendent of schools in Quincy, Massachusetts, beginning
in 1875. "Out of real work, the child develops a motive that directs his life
work. Doing work thoroughly has a great moral influence."[20] The country
life movement at the end of the century extended these ideas to rural life by
promoting agricultural-training programs that led to vocational-education
legislation beginning with the Smith-Lever Act in 1914.

Southern white reformers promoted industrial education for rural blacks
and invoked progressive reformers, including John Dewey, with claims that
"the educational ideal must conform to the social ideal."[21] Industrial education, however, was a different model of manual training altogether. Charles
Dabney, president of the University of Tennessee and active in the annual
conferences, was explicit about the connection between industrial education
and southern reform. "It is simply carrying out the great modern principle
of education, namely, that each race, and each individual in fact, must be
educated in accordance with its or his own capabilities and needs. No man
hopes more sincerely than I do that the time may speedily come when this
kindly, generous, but still infant race may have many representatives prepared
for the highest university training."[22] Many conference attendees could only
conceive of universal education in grossly unequal terms, promoted with language that made clear the extent to which white reformers perceived blacks
as second-class citizens. Further, for most southerners, it was the least threatening curriculum model, with little potential for overturning the South's
racial state. Indeed, the annual conference excluded black educators in its
earlier years, including Booker T. Washington, who believed that industrial
education would ensure the economic success of southern blacks and was an
effective fundraiser for the cause, responsible for the initial gifts from Anna T.
Jeanes and Julius Rosenwald.[23] Washington's success at generating these initial donations for Tuskegee demonstrated his fundraising abilities but also
illustrated the extent to which industrial education appealed to many reformers as the best possible basis for a public system of education that included
rural blacks.

While the Hampton and Tuskegee Institutes figured prominently, and
some black educators saw merit in the curriculum, there were black schools
throughout the South beginning with Reconstruction that differed in philosophy. Black educators established Sabbath schools, moonlight schools, and
private academies in their communities, and the Freedmen's Bureau cooperated with organizations to expand educational opportunities to freed blacks.
By the end of 1865, there were 740 black schools in operation in the South and

90,589 students enrolled, numbers that continued to increase in subsequent decades.[24] Many southern blacks saw a classical curriculum as the path to political equality, and many of these schools promoted a liberal education and continued to receive private support after Reconstruction and the Freedmen's Bureau's involvement ended. Frissell's correspondence following the first and second meetings highlighted his plans to promote simultaneously the broader goals of the conference and the particular goals of the Hampton Institute, where he served as president. He wrote that many southern schools were doing work that might be "valuable, but it is certainly questionable" and lamented that many institutions were receiving money from the North for a more classical curriculum that was "not at all helpful to the negroes."[25]

Frissell sought an alliance of industrial schools and private funders. He planned a meeting with New York banker and philanthropist George Foster Peabody so they "might direct the giving in the north, into proper channels. It is too bad that our northern friends should be continually pestered by appeals from schools that are not doing good work and are really of no advantage to the negro."[26] His efforts reflected anxiety about Hampton, which he explicitly addressed in correspondence with banker and philanthropist Morris Jesup. "I am sure I rejoice in all Mr. Washington's success, and yet of course it is quite natural for Hampton to feel the effects of it somewhat. I think you know that instead of being at all jealous, I am glad, and yet when I write to one and another of our friends and am told by them that their contributions must now go to Tuskegee, it makes me feel that Hampton has got to put forth an earnest effort if its work is not to lag behind."[27] He wrote a similar appeal to other northern financiers, suggesting that cooperation between men of the north and the south would ensure that northern funding was "appropriately awarded." He also sought Washington's help, asking him to meet with Jesup and Long Island Railroad executive Baldwin, to foster cooperation between Hampton, Tuskegee, and northern financiers.[28]

Other southern educators who sought northern benefactors recognized Frissell's influence. For example, the president of the Georgia State Normal School was eager to cooperate with the group that Frissell put together and was explicit in his correspondence about the potential benefits. "While in New York, I had the most pleasant of conversations with Mr. Ogden, Mr. Peabody, Dr. Parkhurst, Mr. Page, Mr. Plympton, Dr. Russell, Dr. Butler and others, and in December I hope the way may be opened for direct assault upon our moneyed friends. I did not dare to trench upon your preserves. I should want to do nothing without your advice in this direction; you seem to have on your string about all the generous people in the city, however."[29] Frissell's efforts ensured that when the second conference convened, members would resolve to develop industrial education "upon lines now well established by noteworthy models," and would recognize "a basis for hearty and united cooperation on the part of all funds in southern education."[30] Participants needed little encouragement to support such a resolution. Frissell acknowledged in his correspondence that there was a real need to transfer the cost of the burden of public education to taxpayers, but felt that a campaign for publicly supported schooling would fail without an industrial-education curriculum. Frissell's and Washington's appeals influenced financiers and scholars, but also reflected general beliefs about how best to structure a public system of education.

Almost every discussion of universal education in the South focused on separate models for each race, noting the merits of industrial education to the southern economy and to individual needs. "We must make money before we can even have schools, and the very first thing is to train our people to produce. The book education we give them leads too many away from the industries in which they must make their living. . . . We shall then be reduced to an industrial dependency even worse than our present political and commercial dependency."[31] These discussions included dubious assertions of industrial education's merits to individual aspiration. "All the industries of the South are still open to negro employment. The door of his opportunity is not yet closed; but, unless he speedily enter, armed with skill, industry and character, it will close, and close forever. . . . The new generation must be taught to work, to submit to authority, to respect their superiors."[32] Edgar Garner Murphy was even more direct about the form that industrial education would take, making clear that it would "supply, under the conditions of freedom, those elements of skill, those conditions of industrial peace, which our fathers supplied under the conditions of slavery."[33]

While most reformers active in southern education agreed that the Hampton and Tuskegee Institutes provided an appropriate program for educating southern blacks, there was significant disagreement about what would be needed over the longer term, a reflection of the ways in which the range of racist attitudes translated into education policy. While Murphy promoted the curriculum, he also recognized that reformers disagreed about its ultimate use. Everyone understood that industrial education would ensure white supremacy, and some believed it to be essential to southern prosperity. Some reformers also believed it to be a short-term need as blacks progressed to greater equality with whites. Murphy explicitly acknowledged this disagreement. "All are agreed that this [industrial education] is the next step. The next step to what?"[34] Many of the conference participants and foundation reformers believed that education would create greater equality over time. "It may take another generation or two generations before the work is complete; but now we know the way, and conscientious effort will make speedy progress."[35] Industrial education was one of a set of objectives that reformers anticipated would lead to a universal system of education, publicly supported at the state and local level. The curriculum reflected an unjust and unequal system of education. However, it was also one that promoted the collaboration necessary to achieve broader goals and, at least for the short term, resonated with the beliefs of most reformers.

The first conference generated a great deal of enthusiasm and resulted in the appointment of a Committee on Permanent Organization that would arrange annual meetings.[36] Curry was one of the more influential reformers, having worked with the Peabody and Slater Funds for more than twenty years and declined an offer to lead the US Bureau of Education. Beginning with emancipation, Curry developed a more progressive view than the vast majority of southerners about the need for black education, influenced by his religious views and a paternalistic concern that education was the only way to manage and promote black progress. He maintained his belief in states' rights, but urged southerners to join him in promoting education and industry.[37] He joined the Committee on Permanent Organization and was named president of the second annual conference. He had extensive contacts with universities and philanthropists, especially those affiliated with the boards he served; his southern background and devotion to national unity through public education made him a trusted ally to white northerners and southerners alike. His participation ensured that collaboration would be far-reaching and extensive.

While Curry might have been the most prominent southern education reformer, there were certainly more like him. Walter Hines Page was born in North Carolina but settled in New York and Boston, where he became editor of the *Atlantic Monthly* and established a popular magazine, *The World's Work*, which was a forum for discussion of southern social problems. He was also a member of the SEB and the GEB. Men like Curry and Page represented a "New South" sensibility that sought economic prosperity through "new conditions, new adjustments and . . . new ideas and aspirations," for which education would be a central component.[38] In a 1902 article in the *Atlantic Monthly*, Page contended that the force for reckoning with the "arrested development" of the South was the "new impulse in public education" and argued that education involved more than the teaching of youth; it would be the building of a new social order. He called on reformers to recognize that,

"Any man who has the privilege to contribute even so small a thing as applause to this great movement feels the thrill of this State-building work."[39] Page believed that efforts to train the "hand and mind together," including for black students at the Hampton Institute, served as an important model because the southern problem was not about race or political difference but simply the training of the untrained masses.[40] White education was the primary focus of the work, but most conference participants supported universal education that included rural blacks.

The New South sensibility converged with the ideas of northern reformers, who also believed that education was essential to a strong national state. The foundations and members of the annual conference were explicit about the need for national unity. Edgar Garner Murphy spoke to these goals in 1904:

> More than once I have expressed the conviction that, in a certain local and palpable sense, the peculiar problems of the South are sectional in their form. And yet such a view is in no way inconsistent with the contention that the time has now come when every problem of every section of our country is to be conceived in the terms of the Nation's life. . . . If national action could be really inspired by the wholesome and constructive spirit of a truly national policy, could be pursued really in the interest of the whole people, rather than in the interest of sectional bitterness or partisan advantage, it would bring significant and lasting benefits.[41]

Curry expressed similar sentiments, though both brought to the task a southern perspective.

In his work with the Peabody Fund, Curry promoted universal education and focused on the relationship between education and the state. He worked to establish state systems of schooling that would make adequate and permanent provision for universal education, where state authorities would have more power and general influence than individuals, denominational groups, or private corporations. As he explained:

> [Public systems] represent the whole people, are held to a strict accountability, protect 'from the charge of sectarianism and from the liability of being overreached by interested parties.' State systems, besides, have a continuous life and are founded on the just principle that property is taxable for the maintenance of general education. The Fund now acts exclusively with State systems, and continues support to the negroes more efficiently through such agencies.[42]

Curry's views reflected foundation concerns about governance. He advocated states' rights and used democratic language about representing the "whole people." However, his conception was based in national conversations about unity, expertise in policy development, and the relationship of universal education to state aspirations. Indeed, while conference attendees included northerners, southerners, educators, businessmen, and members of the clergy, all of whom likely had varied beliefs about curriculum and pedagogy, this diverse group was able to reach consensus about the general importance of education to the health of the American state.

Members of the fourth annual conference established the SEB in 1901 to serve as an executive group that would oversee the work. The SEB board included Robert Ogden as president, Edgar Garner Murphy as executive secretary, and George Foster Peabody, Holliss Frissell, J. L. M. Curry, Charles Dabney, William Baldwin, and Walter Hines Page.[43] The group, of whom a majority were white southerners, had power and limited funding from conference participants to direct the development of an education program for the South. The resolution that established the organization was instructive:

> The overshadowing and supreme public need of our time, as we pass the threshold of a new century, is the education of the children of all the people. . . . With the expansion of our population and the growth of industry and economic resources, we recognize in a fitting and universal education and training of the home, for the farm and the workshop, and for the exercise of the duties of citizenship, the only salvation of our American standards of family and social life and the only hope for the perpetuity of our institutions, founded by our forefathers on the four cornerstones of intelligence, virtue, economic efficiency and capacity for political self-control.[44]

The SEB was supposed to promote education development and school improvement in the southern states but not actually develop and implement the particular programs that would lead to such reform.

Robert Ogden explained the distinction in 1903 in an article published in the *Annals of the American Academy of Political and Social Science*, one indication that members recognized the far-reaching and political dimension of their efforts:

> The Southern Education Board carries on a crusade for education. Its organization is comprehensive and actively covers the larger part of the

country from the Potomac to the Rio Grande, from the Ohio to the Gulf. Its large expenses are privately defrayed. The General Education Board administers such funds as may come to it for the assistance of education. In this connection they cannot be considered separately—their work is a unit; they are the halves of a complete sphere; they are interdependent, subjectively and objectively.[45]

Foundations that came later would take on the actual reform, but the SEB could make the job easier. Its primary roles would be to conduct the campaign for universal education, supply literature to newspapers and periodicals, participate in educational meetings and general correspondence, and develop data to inform the agenda.[46] The organizational plan included a Bureau of Information and Investigation, located in Knoxville, Tennessee, under the leadership of Charles Dabney. During the first year, the bureau created a weekly publication, "Southern Education," sent to newspapers throughout the South. District directors included Charles McIver, Edwin Alderman, and Hollis Frissell, all of whom would serve on a campaign committee led by Curry. Finally, Booker T. Washington and George Dickerman were appointed as field agents.[47]

Foundation programs were simultaneously national in scope but local in implementation. However, efforts to change the structure of state and local governance in the South required persuasion. Southerners were reluctant to increase state and local governance capacity if it meant greater centralized control or higher taxes. One job of the SEB was to translate foundation ideals into a set of state and local objectives and disseminate them for publication in southern newspapers. The organization wrote articles that not only promoted education in terms of local and agrarian needs but also made clear that successful schools required local buy-in. "The agency that organizes country life must be a permanent agency; it must be a country agency, an instrument in the country peoples own hands for their own uplift; the school is the only permanent institution that can do the work at all." Articles conveyed that the purposes of community organization included increased production, income, and life, all of which would be developed through "common power, resulting from partnership or combined efforts."[48] The foundation and SEB reformers hoped to change the discourse about southern education.

After the 1902 conference, John D. Rockefeller provided the initial endowment to establish the GEB, a direct outgrowth of the SEB, with sufficient funding to make substantial investments in southern education reform. As Ogden pointed out in his 1902 conference address, "seven gentlemen are members of both Boards. Perfect cooperation is thus secured. In addition, the Boards of the Peabody and Slater Funds are represented in both the newly-formed Boards, and the outcome of the whole matter is a community of interest that secures harmony and economy and prevents duplication."[49] Rockefeller's endowment of the GEB was followed by gifts over the next two decades by Anna T. Jeanes for the Negro Rural School Fund (Jeanes Fund), and Julius Rosenwald for the Rosenwald Fund. While the SEB was directly related to the establishment of the GEB, no equivalent connection existed with either Rosenwald or Jeanes. Both of those endowments resulted, in part, from conversations with Booker T. Washington about the education needs of rural blacks, and his beliefs influenced northern philanthropists. The SEB did not call specifically for supervising teachers or schoolhouse construction in rural areas, though those two objectives fit nicely with a program that extolled universal education. Yet, the organization ensured a coordination of efforts that was responsive to conference ideals between disparate philanthropists and reformers. Once the Rosenwald Fund and the Jeanes Fund were established, the membership of their boards had considerable overlap with the GEB, SEB, and conference membership. In fact, when the SEB determined that its bureau of information lacked sufficient time for all of its responsibilities, given special projects and publication efforts, the investigation of southern schools was delegated to the GEB. Over time, the GEB increasingly took responsibility for managing the education programs of all of the foundations that promoted education in the South.

The three donors gave considerable sums of money to southern education reform, though each brought a different perspective to the work based upon their backgrounds. Rockefeller, a strict Baptist and relatively conservative, had been encouraged to fund the GEB by Wallace Buttrick, a Baptist minister who became the first secretary of the board in 1902. Jeanes was a reclusive Quaker from Philadelphia, who had belonged to the more radical Hicksite meetinghouse where Lucretia Mott had practiced, and was encouraged by Booker T. Washington to support rural black teachers.[50] She died in 1907, and her bequest was managed by a board that shared members with the GEB. Rosenwald's philanthropy had often focused on Jewish causes, and his giving was generally influenced by his relationship to his rabbi, but Booker T. Washington also encouraged his initial gifts for southern education, which resulted in the formal endowment of the Rosenwald Fund.[51] These three donors had different worldviews, which spanned the religious and political spectrum, though their interests converged in the possibility that they might positively influence the future of the South and, by extension, the American state.[52] While these foundations were part of a larger group that included the Peabody Fund, the Slater Fund, the Phelps-Stokes Fund, and numerous smaller foundations, the overlap between the GEB, the Jeanes Fund, and the Rosenwald Fund provides an opportunity to explore the relative power of foundation work in the South.

In formal declarations of the fourth conference, education was declared to be "the only salvation for our American standards of family and social life, and the only hope for the perpetuity of our institutions."[53] That idea became more pervasive in subsequent conferences, as evidenced by an address in 1904:

> That education is the key of Southern as of Northern security, that education does not mean the shirking of political service or the increase of racial antagonism, that education begins at the bottom and not at the top, that the South and the North have a common stake in the education of the whole people, that illiteracy is inconsistent with democracy, that the part of the North is not to patronize or criticize but to reinforce the initiative for the South, and that the strength and sacrifice of the Southern States for education present the most honorable and gallant achievement of modern American statesmanship—all this is conclusively determined, and this is the common faith in which we meet.[54]

As this statement illustrates, reformers recognized the need for educating citizens and connected it to a stronger democracy. They also acknowledged that actual reform would need to focus locally.

It is not clear that reformers all agreed on the elements of a "strong state," particularly at the local level. Southerners held tightly their commitment to states' rights but did not generally support increased state or local power, especially when it required higher taxes and threatened local tradition. At the same time, such education reformers as Curry and Page understood that universal education required a reconsideration of the administrative systems in place to deliver it. The Blair Education Bill, proposed in Congress between 1883 and 1890 to provide federal aid for education, provides a useful lens for understanding southern attitudes about education and the state. Southerners estimated the annual cost of adequate public schooling in the South to be $40 million, and many whites believed that the federal government should provide a substantial portion of the cost because it was an undue burden for southerners to have to give up slavery and then be solely responsible for the cost of educating the freed blacks.[55] The first bill proposed that $105 million be distributed to states based on illiteracy rates, which promised a significant boon to the southern economy. Each version of the bill required that states spend the money equally at the state level required and provide matching funds from its own or local resources, which would lead to a sharp increase in education expenditures in the South.[56]

While the Republican Party included federal aid for education in its 1880 platform, the Democratic Party did so with the caveat that it opposed centralization in government.[57] Many southern democrats supported the idea of federal funding, but were concerned about federal control. The second version of the bill provided for a smaller total appropriation but gave almost complete control over funds to state officials. In the end, four different versions of the bill ultimately failed to pass congressional approval. Southerners who opposed the bill feared that spending a treasury surplus would lead to tariff increases and thought federal support was unconstitutional. Others believed that it would alleviate an education emergency at the expense of southern self-reliance, postponing efforts to address important local issues like taxation. Moreover the bill might lead to a nationalized and integrated school system that would recreate Reconstruction patterns of northern influence. While many dominant democratic leaders in the lower south supported the bill because it spread the burden of educating a majority black population in some regions, many were also ambivalent about the centralized power that might come with it. Many Democrats and agrarian states-rights southerners, as well as Republican leaders, opposed it.[58]

The debate provides an interesting lens for understanding why southern whites were willing to support foundation initiatives, especially given their genesis in the North. From a southerner's perspective, private funding might be more likely to sustain a southern way of life. Federal or state involvement had the potential to result in legislation that supported national ideals, which might not favor white supremacy in the future. One conference participant, in speaking about general differences between communities in the South, said, "Some things are possible to private beneficence which are not so to legislation. Sometimes legislation cannot discriminate where discrimination is essential. It has to lay down general principles and treat all alike, even if it does more harm than good. . . . One community requires what another does not and the treatment that would help one might hurt another."[59] There was some recognition that a state-run system of schooling, even if developed by southern politicians, might pose a bigger threat to the racial state over the longer term. Indeed, scholarship on race-based social policy confirms this possibility.[60] Outside interference was necessary to promote greater equality in the South, but it may have seemed to many southerners that public-private collaboration might be easier to control. Gifts could be refused.

Northern reformers saw education reform as a moral imperative, and believed it the best remedy for the weak and inefficient southern economic and political system, which ultimately limited the possibility for more centralized and efficient approaches to national governance. Baldwin asked southerners to consider education reform as a business proposition that would lead to greater prosperity, but also said that it was a call for "universal intelligence," because "the magic power of popular education, [will] evoke forces that make for progress—progress that gives intelligence to the State, and commands respect for the town."[61] William Torrey Harris, the prominent philosopher and educator who was US commissioner of education in 1902, also commented on the work of the conference: "Everyone who loves his country and can take the far-reaching view must feel that this conference is doing more for the United States as a whole than any other one agency, because it is seeking to develop the directive powers of the individual and to furnish him with the ability to change his vocation, and when these ends shall have been accomplished we will have diversified our labor and enormously increased the nation's producing power."[62] These testimonies to the relationship between education and state became the defining objective of the annual conference.

Many prominent businessmen supported national efforts to reform government in the early twentieth century. The conceptions about the most appropriate form of government among progressive reformers took many forms, with some focused on ballot measures that provided for greater democratic opportunity, including referendum and recall at the local level, and the constitutional amendment for direct elections of senators at the federal one. Most business interests, however, were less interested in strengthening local and direct democracy. Business reformers, including prominent philanthropists like Rockefeller, advocated municipal reform because it mitigated the possibility for partisan and particularistic concerns that were detrimental to enlightened and scientific governance.[63] Efficient government provided a venue more conducive to the expertise available through private interests.

While each foundation had a distinctive agenda that helped to build and sustain a particular part of the education infrastructure, all worked in tandem as one part of the southern reform dynamic that included southerner actors at every level of government. The Jeanes Fund provided black teachers who would supervise education in rural black communities; the Rosenwald Fund assisted with the construction of school buildings; and the GEB con-

tributed to a range of initiatives that included state agents for Negro education and money to augment the work of the other funds. The GEB helped
to coordinate and oversee the work of all of these funds, especially after the
SEB stopped providing oversight in 1914. Their boards consisted of an interlocking directorate that reflected the depth of associative action that grew
out of the conference. This might support a view that foundations exercised
complete control over southern education reform in the early twentieth century and used it to promote and sustain an unjust and racialized system.[64]
However, even if they sought such unlimited power, the process of creating
an education infrastructure in the South required a more dynamic process.
It is important to look at the programs that developed through cooperation
and consensus, and consider how those programs were implemented and
sustained locally. Foundation reformers recognized the enormity of the task
and developed a comprehensive strategy to achieve their goals, but they did
not do it alone.

The overlap between membership in the conference and on foundation boards supported a form of collaboration that was not anomalous at
the beginning of the twentieth century. Institutions like regulatory agencies
and political-party structures played an important role in establishing new
policy and provided the organizations necessary for managing social policy.
This model defined foundation efforts. The federal government lacked the
ability, will, and interest in the cause of rural black education to employ the
experts necessary to inform and implement change in the South. The Republican administrations of McKinley, Roosevelt, and Taft were increasingly
unsympathetic to African Americans, and progressivism took an even more
white-supremacist turn when southerner Woodrow Wilson ascended to the
presidency.[65] The philanthropists filled the void in federal, state, and local
policymaking, cooperating extensively with a range of political actors to develop organizations that would lead to a stronger infrastructure for delivering
public schooling.[66] In 1915, the board issued a comprehensive report of more
than a decade of work that spoke to these goals:

> It was recognized that the feasibility of cooperation between private and
> governmental agencies and the large opportunity open to individual initia-
> tive in dealing with social and educational problems are among the dis-
> tinct advantages of a democratic social order. . . . The devotion of private
> fortunes to public ends on these terms is highly desirable; and leaders in
> social and educational endeavor can and do render intelligent and patriotic
> service by participation in these characteristically American enterprises.[67]

Their work provided the basis for public-private partnerships with state and local governments, but varied by state. The foundations also quickly realized that cooperation had to include both elite and local actors, within government and outside of it. These forms of interstitial collaboration were intended to substitute for the lack of federal or state leadership in education-policy development.

The federal government's education bureaucracy did not stand in the way of this work either and gently promoted it in unobtrusive ways.[68] When Curry reported in 1895 on education progress in the South, he acknowledged that the Peabody Fund and the US Bureau of Education had been "most helpful allies in making suggestions in relation to legislation in school matters, and giving, in intelligible, practical form, the experiences of other states, home and foreign, in devising and perfecting educational systems."[69] Two years later, US commissioner of education Harris promoted the annual conferences.[70] When Philander Claxton, who was born in North Carolina and served as chairman of the Executive Committee of the Conference for Southern Education in its early years, became US commissioner of education in 1911, he remained connected to the work of the conference in his new role and maintained relationships with its members.

While the commitment to states' rights and local control impeded reform, a changing political climate forced the southern political parties to facilitate some progress toward universal education after 1900, making incremental change possible. The rise of populism and agrarian discontent in the 1890s, and the addition of several new western states, destabilized the parties and led to realignments. Ultimately, both major parties had to pander for greater power at the national level, especially by appealing to the agrarian vote, which had implications subsequently for both federal and state politics.[71] While populism was essentially defeated and the southern Democrats regained power by the end of the 1890s, it resulted in a factionalized and entrepreneurial system throughout the Progressive Era.[72] At the federal level, the Republican Party was less likely to promote sweeping change in the South, and the Democratic Party recognized that regional discontent could have broader implications for realizing their own cohesive political platform. The federal government also promoted a national set of ideals for rural education and encouraged the relationships that developed between northern foundations and southern political systems.

President Theodore Roosevelt formed the Country Life Commission in 1908, recognizing that the "social and economic institutions of the open country are not keeping pace with the development of the nation as a whole."[73] The commission was one outgrowth of the country life movement, an associative movement of urban reformers that included government officials, academics, and business leaders who sought to address what they perceived as the backwardness of the nation's rural populations. The movement sought regulation and expanded educational opportunity in rural areas as remedies that would help to modernize rural populations. In his letter appointing the commission, Roosevelt included mention of southern agricultural problems and included Walter Hines Page as a member.[74] Page was an active member of the annual Conference for Education in the South and instrumental in establishing both the GEB and the SEB; his presence ensured a connection between commission work and conference-related organizations.[75] The commission focused on rural life as a national concern. The group conducted extensive surveys of rural inhabitants and held hearings in thirty locations, including Raleigh, North Carolina, and Athens, Georgia. However, the final report did not focus on the needs of particular regions and ignored racial problems in the South, except to point out that problems of intemperance complicated the race problem there. W. E. B. Du Bois had written to members in 1908, urging them to include black farmers in their study and confront directly the issue of race.[76] Instead, the report pointed out that "the ultimate need of the open country is the development of community effort and of social resources" and called for effective cooperation among farmers on a level with business interests, rural schooling, and better communication through good roads and rural free delivery.[77] At the same time, Page's participation influenced southern reform.

The commission's final report recommended a nationalized extension service that was formalized with the Smith-Lever Act in 1914. It also encouraged greater university and government attention to rural life, including ongoing data collection and a campaign for rural progress.[78] The commission resulted in the development of agricultural extension services through the US Department of Agriculture beginning in 1906 in Mississippi and extending throughout the South by 1908. One of the recommendations called specifically for enhanced local governance and reflects the foundations' agenda in the South. The report specifically noted that rural progress depended upon local government that "must be developed to its highest point of efficiency, and all agencies that are capable of furthering a better country life must be federated . . . it is specially necessary to develop the cooperative spirit."[79] The final report also focused on the important role of schooling as the center of the community. "Inasmuch as the school is supported by public funds, and is therefore an institution connected with the government of the community, it should form a natural organic center."[80]

Foundation reformers similarly believed in the constructive value of education, which may have foreshadowed patterns for state intervention in poor communities in subsequent decades.[81] Historian Ellen Condliffe Lagemann pointed out in her research on the Carnegie Corporation that foundation work was "rooted in a long tradition of philanthropic efforts to establish the values, shape the beliefs and define the behaviors that would join people to one another, but it represented an effort to bring greater deliberateness and a more national orientation to the definition and fulfillment of common needs and interests."[82] Beyond that elevated role for schooling, the commission report recognized that a "voluntary union of associative effort, from the localities to the counties, States, and the nation," would be necessary and that both "state and national government, as suggested, might exert a powerful influence toward the complete organization of rural affairs."[83] The language of the report reflects not just the conversation among participants of the Conference for Education in the South during the previous decade but also the actual work of the foundations, echoing the national discourse about rural life and Page's influence in both domains.

Many recommendations of country life reformers, as well as the final report of the Country Life Commission, were welcomed by populist groups that had initiated national interest in rural America and influenced subsequent progressive legislation in areas that included trade policies, the income tax, banking regulations, better roads, and education. The populist coalition increasingly marginalized African Americans, an attitude that was reflected in the final report of the commission.[84] Ultimately, the report failed to address specifically the needs of rural black communities, though it informed a general interest in the need to use education to reorganize rural life. Rural groups resented the paternalism of urban reformers who sought to reorganize their communities without sufficient understanding of their needs. Rural southerners were not willing merely to let northerners dictate local reform.[85] Most white southerners wanted local governance systems that promoted particular community needs and had no real desire for local life to be reconstructed based on northern models. Foundation initiatives focused on local areas but recognized that reform programs were not necessarily welcome there.

Foundations provided funding for agricultural clubs in rural black communities through salary support for the Jeanes teachers and, in the early years, with Smith-Hughes funding from the federal government. The federal role provides more evidence of the relationship between foundation initiatives and national concerns. Initially, the GEB provided full funding for agricultural-extension work through the USDA budget. The federal government did not support these foundation efforts because of any egalitarian set of ideals about black education, but instead because of a general concern about the problems associated with rural life, especially in the South.[86] However, the program was an early example of public-private collaboration that might lead to not only greater cooperation but also contributions from weakly integrated rural black populations, a particularly important goal in the context of new nationalism.[87] However, when members of Congress discovered the arrangement between the GEB and the USDA in 1914, it led to a vigorous debate about the appropriateness of public-private collaboration at the national level.[88] Indeed, many perceived that such delegated authority might threaten American ideals of self-governance, reflecting disagreement between foundation reformers and citizens about the nature of the state.

The foundations collaborated with the federal government in other ways. For example, with the funding and expertise of foundations, the US Department of Education issued an extensive 1917 report on southern black schools and recommended that these schools develop in line with national movements, reflected in reports like the 1916 Commission on the Reorganization of Secondary Education and the 1918 Cardinal Principles of Secondary Education. W. E. B. Du Bois wrote a scathing critique of the Department of Education report, and responded to its substance. He made clear that many reformers had a different conceptualization of education needs in the South and pointed out that the report "stresses the adaptation of education to the needs of the community, evidently meaning the 'white' community." He castigated the author of the report, white reformers, and philanthropists for promoting a system of education that would "deliberately shut the door of opportunity in the face of bright Negro students."[89] Indeed, both black and white southerners were suspicious of northern philanthropy because of the potential for white outside interests to dominate southern policy.

Foundations would need to promote a national vision while recognizing that individual southern states often had varied conceptions about education, were reluctant to acquiesce to outside interference, and differed sharply in their administrative capacity to support reform. There were impediments to developing greater oversight of rural schools, white or black. "Step outside the city limits in nearly every county in the entire South and you will find a different state of affairs. The county is composed of neighborhoods, each with a school. . . . The grounds are unkept, often barren. . . . The school has practically no supervision. The county superintendent often receives as salary from five hundred to seven hundred and fifty dollars, hence he is a farmer, or a preacher, or a lawyer, who gets the office merely to supplement his income."[90] There was a strong commitment to local autonomy and an aversion to government intervention of any type. Patronage politicians were likely to resist government efforts at reform in principle, out of a fear that any strengthening of federal or even state government would threaten the more traditional bases of power in the political-party system of the late nineteenth century. As a result, foundations created a complicated array of institutionalized programs that took various forms and differed by state. Flexible implementation of programs helped to manage the tension that existed between national conceptions of education and southerners' ardent commitment to states' rights and local control in the racial state. The creation of institutions that could evolve in a dynamic fashion on a regional basis within this political context was most likely to ensure sustained reform. This is a process by which education policy specifically, and political development generally, developed from the bottom up, even as it promoted national unity through extensive collaboration at the top.[91]

While all reformers shared the view that education was a central component of a stronger national state, they differed in some of their particular beliefs. Across the nation, schooling was fundamentally altering the relationship between individual states and local communities, and the courts affirmed that schools were state not local institutions.[92] Indeed, outside of the South, states took on increasing responsibility for both school funding and equalization initiatives after World War I and into the Depression.[93] In line with national trends, foundation reformers tended to be in favor of programs that would lead to greater centralization at the state level, accompanied by standards consistently enforced at the county level with regard to school terms, compulsory education, teacher certification, and the curriculum. They recognized that it would be easier to implement standards in consolidated school systems that reported to the state and were adequately supported through a system of local taxes. Yet, this was difficult in a South where commitment to local control, white supremacy, and poverty limited progress in many regions.

Foundations recognized the parameters in which they worked, and one strategy was to make greater coordination a first order of business. In 1911, the GEB recommended "cooperation with state and local authorities to develop rural public schools," and this strategy was a basis for their efforts to implement policy in the South.[94] The foundations wanted their field agents to "get the cooperation of county superintendents" and expected that a "well trained negro teacher" would bring about a "spirit of cooperation" in rural areas.[95] County training schools would ultimately be "maintained by public funds and . . . built and equipped by the cooperation of the two races."[96] Cooperation was necessary for education reform, which required state and local participation, and it was essential to southern state development. Ultimately, this would ensure the state participation that was necessary to developing a public system of education supported by state and local taxes.

Cooperation was a two-way street and required willing partners. Foundations had no interest in providing private support over the longer term to any state education system, which they believed was an essential public institution.

> The agency to which the South must look for the education of the masses of its people of the Negro race as of the white is the state system of schools supported by public taxation and administered as a public business. This is the agency upon which all modern states depend for training the masses in the arts of civilization. It is the only educational agency yet devised that is at all equal to a task of such enormous proportions.[97]

There was a purposeful rejection of sweeping change. A reform program implemented in this manner would insure that ultimately, over the longer term, the states and local communities— not the northern philanthropists—would be responsible for education.

While the conference ensured consensus between northern and southern reformers, cooperation with state and local political systems required that foundations work within local communities and not impose a system from the outside. In the first year of the work, Frissell complained to Curry that a field-worker in Virginia seemed to have "antagonized many of the people. I know that your thought was that he should act in harmony with the Superintendent of Public Schools and the officials generally, but there are those it is not wise to oppose, but rather to bring them over to our side."[98] They were institution builders, who used money and ideas to help establish sustainable organizations in the South that not only led to a stronger education infrastructure, which would be institutionalized in state and local government, but also contributed to a stronger national state through a unity of effort.[99]

The biweekly publication of the SEB, *Southern Education Notes*, was filled with education news, statistics, statements, and brief articles on education policy. It served the sole purpose of disseminating the education campaign to the newspapers of the South, especially in rural districts, and provided commentary for the "convenience of the press."[100] The board also advertised directly to communities and fostered cooperation between local organizations and state agencies. "If you are thinking of organizing a club, or a league for community development, write to us and we shall be glad to send blanks for getting the data you need concerning the homes, the schools and the churches. We can furnish model forms for Constitution and By-Laws of the different kinds of clubs which you may need and enlist the Experts in the Federal Department, and possibly other agencies to help you in your undertaking."[101] This illustrates the extent to which the SEB promoted cooperation and community building and provides evidence of foundation efforts to influence public opinion in the South. Foundations recognized that their success depended on organization, information, and local support.

The SEB issued a report in 1912 that outlined ten ways in which it could facilitate reform in North Carolina. The report called for a general plan of action, developed and adapted to the state's needs, which included conferences with state superintendents, college presidents, farm demonstration agents, officials of state boards of health, extension workers of the colleges of agriculture and state universities, and other state and county leaders. The report recommended that the SEB provide information about programs that had proven effective, as well as plans, ideas, and suggestions from leaders throughout the nation. For example, the SEB planned to facilitate communication between the National Bureau of Education, the Department of Agriculture, other departments in Washington, and the state supervisors. The report recommended that the SEB keep tabulations of state laws for use by reformers and provide information on southern reform to authors, editors, and magazine and newspaper reporters. At the same time, the recommendations made clear that the state would need to develop and implement its own particular agenda at the local level.[102] This general plan for North Carolina reflected an effort to promote national conceptions of education reform, a willingness to adapt it to each region, and a commitment to collaborative relationships that permeated the state and local political and education system.

Efforts to promote greater coordination reflected broader concerns about the lack of political development in southern state and local communities. It was easy for the GEB to take over the work of the SEB, given the overlap of members, and to extend that work, given the power of their largesse to concentrate efforts through a vast array of programs. However, as the GEB pointed out in 1914, several states had "serious obstacles" to implementing reforms, which included state education organizations that were "more or less defective," inefficient methods for raising money, and constitutions that prohibited local taxation for school purposes. The board felt that perhaps nowhere in the South had an "entirely proper relationship between state, county, and district officials been worked out."[103] They recognized that it would be easier to accomplish their goals in some states more than others, and it would be necessary to design programs accordingly.

Page and Buttrick were clear that the organization of rural areas had to be a priority and recommended that the US Department of Agriculture create a "Rural Organization Service" to promote "greater efficiency in such governmental functions as making roads and conducting schools and administering justice and in the social upbuilding of the people. . . . It will show the states and state institutions that they must do their proper tasks and pay for them."[104] The authors felt that this would lead to greater efficiency, in part because such an organization could connect disparate agencies and be in a position to develop comprehensive information about rural life. While this particular recommendation was not adopted, it reflected the tenor of foundation work. By 1912, newspaper reports of the annual Conference for Education in the South included references not just to the meeting agenda but also to an expansive set of subconferences and roundtable conferences that were organized in conjunction with the main meeting. This included the Association of State Superintendents of the Southern States, state elementary-school inspectors, state boards of health, southern school-improvement workers, state departments of agriculture, presidents and professors of agricultural colleges, district agents and cooperators of the farm-demonstration work of the southern states, progressive farmers, and even members of the US Department of Agriculture.[105]

The US commissioner of education recognized these efforts in his 1916 report: "The funds and associations interested in the education of Negroes in the United States . . . have developed a correlation of activities that adds much to the value of their work [and] this correlation of effort probably originates in the conviction, common to all of them, that the educational progress of the Negroes in the United States requires the increasing cooperation of public authorities in the Southern States."[106] The commissioner explicitly addressed the GEB's success in working with private funds, church boards, and individual institutions, work that was supported by field agents who brought education expertise to setting policy goals in rural areas, and often focused on providing integrated services and expanding bureaucracy.[107] The foundations developed a cadre of field workers throughout the South, who provided monthly reports of visits to rural communities, including itinerant data and written summaries of findings. This included general field agents, those appointed within particular state and local governments, and even secondary professors in southern universities who would conduct research and promote the cause.

In 1909, the professor appointed through GEB funding at the University of Mississippi issued his annual report, which underscored the theme of cooperation:

> I am persuaded, when I look around at the detached, sporatic [sic] and spasmodic efforts in educational and industrial directions that this state needs integration as much as it needs differentiation in its efforts to educate the people. . . . Integration is the word . . . to note the waste of uncoordinated energy and the groping in the dark of good men from the South and from the North, moves me to say that the Educational Conference for the South *might* become the agency through which this work of Co-ordination could be done. *But the co-operation of the masses of the people would have to be obtained.* [emphasis in original][108]

Foundation reformers believed rural schools were important to communities for the same reason: "The Principal of the School is the natural agent to bring the farm demonstrator, the extension worker, and the health official and the preacher into a harmonious co-working for the development of the center into a vital community institution."[109] Everyone involved in the southern program, including foundations and their agents, as well as southern reformers, spoke of the need for greater cooperation and a coordination of efforts, not just among reformers but also between the North and the South, and among foundations, states, and local communities.

The GEB reinforced and supplemented the work of the other foundations, often by providing oversight. However, this was a situation that other funds welcomed and makes it difficult to describe the work of the funds in discrete ways. The North Carolina Department of Public Instruction produced a report on GEB funding: "The constant aim of the Board has been to stimulate progress and to increase efficiency, and in all of the gifts to institutions it has sought to assist the officials and not to act as a patron."[110] There was a great deal of intellectual overlap between funds, but that was strengthened through funding allocations; the GEB provided supplemental money for Jeanes teachers and for Rosenwald building efforts. The Jeanes Fund and the Rosenwald Fund had more specific missions, while the GEB was somewhat broader. All three sought to promote universal education in ways that would, over time, transfer responsibility for the funding and oversight of a universal school system to the state. These three foundations worked in tandem to promote a set of objectives in the early twentieth century that did not lead to a system of universal and equal education that challenged the racial state. However, this work did serve to strengthen the administration of state and local governance through schooling in some regions of the South.

The Foundation Program in Rural Areas

Most southern states had weak state and local administrative systems, and relatively little bureaucracy for accomplishing any kind of centralized school system. Many white southerners were happy to keep it that way. The foundations recognized that a state system of public schooling in the South required organizational capacity and stronger administrative structures. There were already many rural black schools before the foundations began their work, typically established with the initiative of the black community. Some of these were one-room, makeshift schools in whatever space might be available, while others were more formally organized with endowments and ongoing support from a range of benefactors that included both philanthropic and denominational organizations. Foundations sought to establish new schools and to design a comprehensive set of programs that connected existing schools to a state system. The foundations hoped for a more bureaucratic and centralized school system, supported by tax dollars and sufficient administrative systems. This newly designed school system would address the isolation and poverty of rural communities and promote stronger governance systems across the South.

The foundations designed programs that would promote a stronger education infrastructure. For example, the state agents for Negro education and the local Jeanes teachers strengthened the general administration of state and local schooling by providing greater oversight and promoting standardization. These agents organized systems to collect data, which was necessary for designing, implementing, and replicating programs. The philanthropic mode of giving provided funding that both coexisted with state and local budgets and operated discretely. Foundation gifts could promote private fundraising and local taxes. Efforts to influence tax legislation were essential not only to the expansion of schooling but also to restructuring governance. At the local level, programs for teacher training, schoolhouse construction, and the development of county training schools might improve not only pedagogy and practice but also rural black access to education.

The foundations created programs in spite of state and local politics, and often designed them to operate in parallel fashion to established governance. This made reform relatively less coercive than direct governmental intervention and potentially helped it to become part of the state and local political

system. At the same time, there was a clear relationship between foundation initiatives and local state building objectives. By 1931, the trustees of the
Rosenwald Fund recognized progress in the South but also realized that it
would be beneficial to continue to focus efforts explicitly on county-level governance. Their report recommended that the fund "cooperate in experiments
in a unified county organization which would include schools, health, library
service, and general welfare, for white and colored in both rural and urban
sections of the county. Such experiments, although they may be difficult to
carry out, may throw a great deal of light on what can be accomplished under
the best organization for all the people of the county."[111] However, the path
to stronger county organizations, inclusive of rural black schools, proceeded
slowly in many areas of the South.

The appointment of a state agent for Negro schools in those states that
could accommodate such a position was an important method for achieving
foundation objectives. The GEB conceived of these positions as being central
to the southern program because the agent would be located in state departments of education but have "'entre' to all the counties, communities, and
schools of the state; he could transact the state's business with county superintendents, county school boards, local trustees and teachers . . . and then
get the two races to cooperate in its improvement." The GEB believed that
the state agent could promote consolidation and influence the plan and construction of schools, get both races to contribute through private donations
to supplement the public school building fund, and secure an increase in the
appropriation of public funds. In short, "he can stimulate and direct state,
county and local effort in developing an effective system of public schools for
the training of the negro children of the state."[112]

Each agent was formally appointed by the state but paid by the GEB with
the hope that over time each state would legislate funds for this purpose. However, in providing the salary, the GEB could control who was selected and
monitor the work. The initial investment and then ongoing support in most
states provided the foundation with a basis for participating in selection and
oversight. For example, when Nathan Newbold was selected as state agent for
Negro education in North Carolina, the state superintendent for education
wrote to the GEB about the appointment and explained, "the selection of the
man would be subject to your approval, and that I had no authority to offer
him the position at this time; but . . . I should like for him to consider the matter and let me know how he would feel about it in case the position should
be tendered him, and that I would take the matter up with you."[113] These appointments led to the development of rural black education departments that

functioned within the state departments of education, but could also operate in discrete ways. The foundations were clear that it was up to the state to decide exactly how to define the state agent's work. The GEB sent a standard letter to states interested in having an agent about the most effective way that "generally speaking, the rural school agents can be employed. I say 'generally speaking' advisedly, for we all realized the necessity of local adjustments and, in any event, this note, like all our communications oral and written, is, as you know, intended as a suggestion, and not as an instruction. Every superintendent is to be himself the judge as to what it is wise and feasible to attempt in his own state."[114] At the same time, those states that aligned the work with these general suggestions could positively influence foundation efficacy.

The system for appointing state agents was especially significant given the politics of civil administration in the decentralized American government at the turn of the century, where governmental functions at all levels were staffed through the appointment of the governing political party.[115] The agent would be a "state official, an officer of the state department of education, and would have in all his work the powers and responsibilities of such position . . . [which would] combine the advantages of official authority with freedom from arbitrary political interference."[116] Hence, it was a noteworthy innovation to create an appointment to work in tandem with, rather than as an appointee of, a more partisan government. The GEB sought to make every position a part of the state civil administration. It was clear the foundations believed that their programs would have greater success if administered through a state-level agency that would not be influenced by other interests, with the potential to overcome the strength of local politics.[117] The agents and the organizations that they directed at the state level added a layer onto existing state institutions.[118] In states where these agents were most successful in garnering state and local resources to institutionalize reform, the agent became responsible for a budget and staff.

By 1914, the GEB was funding state agents who were selectively appointed in Alabama, Arkansas, Georgia, Kentucky, North Carolina, and Virginia.[119] The secretary of the GEB reported in 1914 on progress in making these appointments: "Under the present State administration in South Carolina it does not seem practicable to appoint a man in that state now. The same condition is found in Louisiana and to less extent in Mississippi. I should deem it unwise to appoint men at this time in any one of the three states named. I have had a request from Florida but, to speak plainly to you and in confidence, I do not fully trust the State Superintendent in this particular matter."[120] While most of the southern states had state agents by 1920, many did not legislate funding to support the position. North Carolina provided funding to do so by 1924, while other states, such as Mississippi and Georgia, still had not provided state funds to support the office in the mid-1930s.[121] The GEB produced reports that predicted whether state support for Negro education was "strong, medium, or weak." The reports also detailed the reason behind each classification and a plan for overcoming it, where possible, often providing similar data by county.[122] With the assistance of a state agent, it was possible to coordinate efforts around achieving particular goals at a more local level. The state agents typically had a significant role in establishing parallel systems in local communities. However, it was important for foundation efficacy that the programs were managed at the state level of government, even if local participation was required for successful implementation.[123]

Foundations recommended that states build efficient central administrative organizations, including the establishment of special divisions and "qualified persons to carry on increasingly specialized work."[124] The longer-term goal was a strengthening of administration without regard to race, even if the specific education policies for the segregated system were unequal. The objective was an organization that would improve public education by stimulating the state to develop its central organizations and, eventually, to assume the total expense of administration.[125] Funders anticipated that state-level administrative improvements would lead to the creation of a comprehensive school system at the local one.

Rural organization was easier with consolidated schools than disconnected one-room schoolhouses. The annual conference of the Rosenwald school-building agents in 1923 devoted an afternoon discussion to rural school consolidation, and appointed a "Committee on Resolutions" to consider the problems of bad roads, widely scattered schools, inadequate transportation, and the peculiar systems of supervising schools.[126] School consolidation required not just that entire communities be reorganized but also that the states develop programs to facilitate consolidation. A number of state agents reported positively on progress but also acknowledged that the fund should recognize that "every state and section has its own peculiar problem."[127] The fund agreed to provide one and one-half times the regular funding allocation for the first real consolidation in a county.[128] Consolidation was popular with foundation reformers from the beginning and was gaining favor in rural black areas by 1925, with "wretched one-room schools being abandoned for the centrally located larger school. There is a steady increase in the provision of transporting the children by bus. . . . The County Training School idea is growing so rapidly that it is being followed closely by greatly increased enthusiasm for high schools for Negroes."[129] Progress varied and foundations hoped that the agents could make it more uniform and comprehensive across states.

The state agent could promote initiatives that institutionalized the public school system, including schoolhouse construction, an increase to the local tax base, the extension of school terms, and teacher training. However, reform required a cadre of workers at the local level who could promote particular initiatives and generate community support for reform. The appointment of a state agent, in combination with Jeanes teachers in counties throughout the state, provided a means for the GEB to address the full range of problems that existed across local communities in the South, and between the South and other regions of the country. These teachers promoted their own agenda, transforming the program of the philanthropists from the bottom up, providing the most important evidence of the organizational dynamic in southern reform. The work was truly local in nature and reflected grassroots efforts that were central to the development of a state system of schooling. This was a strength of state building through education reform, in that it allowed for greater experimentation and innovation at the local level, as well as opportunities to disseminate education policy effectively into rural areas.[130] At the same time, it also meant that universal education was promoted simultaneously by the state and by local interests. Policy implementation at a more parochial level meant that local majorities and private interests could more easily use foundation programs to their own ends.

The GEB appointed Jackson Davis to serve as the first state agent for Negro education in Virginia, where he hired the first Jeanes teacher in Henrico County in 1909. Davis considered industrial education to be a defining feature of rural black education and hoped the Jeanes teachers could promote it. However, he also perceived that a capable teacher could do more than just foster industrial education in the schools by using that ideal to promote greater cooperation at the local level. He thought that whites would be willing to drop their objection to public schooling for rural blacks if philanthropists could "adjust the training of the negro to his needs," based upon the Hampton model of industrial education, rather than a more liberal arts curriculum that might make them "dissatisfied with their environments." The supervising teacher would be effective at "showing the teachers how to connect the school with the child's everyday life through simple forms of industrial work, and by planning a course of study and work that will fit them for a useful and happy life in their own community."[131] Davis's description of the first teacher in Henrico County illustrated the central role that industrial education played in early foundation efforts, especially at the local level.

The Jeanes Fund organized its teacher program similar to that of the state agents. The county superintendent selected and hired the teachers, who reported to that office on a daily basis. The foundation stipulated that a part of their salary would be paid through the county tax funds in order to receive funding from the Jeanes Fund[132] However, the teachers were also on the payroll of the foundations, and both the state agent and the foundation approved each appointment before a county could receive funding. The foundations collected reports from the teachers and organized regular meetings within states and across the South, where teachers could meet to share their work. The first circular letter from the Jeanes Fund to these teachers throughout the South explained that work would focus on both schools and communities and would vary by place; the letter then suggested that teachers keep in regular contact with school officials, be willing to help fellow teachers, assist in organizing the people of the community into associations for self-help, cooperate with the minister or ministers of the community, and introduce industrial work.[133] The GEB appointed a teacher only in those counties where a significant portion of the population was black or where more than ten black teachers were employed. As late as 1933, 804 of the 1,415 southern counties were eligible. By 1919, 213 counties (26 percent) employed Jeanes teachers; the number rose to 354 (44 percent) by 1930, and to 390 (48 percent) by 1935.[134]

To succeed in these positions, the teachers had to answer to multiple constituencies and ensure the support of local whites. The teachers and the organizations they created had the imprimatur of the white communities, who typically provided at least some of their funding; in return those communities expected to see community improvement and a commitment to industrial education. Foundations recognized that their supervising role was essential to the whole range of reforms because Jeanes teachers were at the center of their communities and could coordinate and sustain community participation. The Jeanes teachers served as an essential liaison between foundation efforts and local communities. The director of the Jeanes Fund was clear about the benefits of these teachers to school governance. "This work would be made much more useful if brought under the direction of a state supervisor of rural schools and made an integral part of the state system."[135] They had the potential to influence positively the relationship of the state agent to local communities and were central to many of the foundation programs.

The trustees of the Jeanes Fund were clear that any definite work and assistance undertaken should be carried out with the approval and cooperation of the regular public-school officials. "There are already abundant indications of opportunity for developing our work under the sanction of the school authorities, and we believe that in this way we shall best promote the cause of equitable appropriations as well as the activity of local efforts."[136] When the state agents met in 1929, they were explicit about how supervision had evolved in rural counties and felt that the Jeanes program had created greater opportunity for general county oversight. They recommended that the original Jeanes program, which had provided separate supervision of black schools, be replaced with a "program of general supervision of all schools within a local (county) jurisdiction."[137]

In line with the "scientific giving" that characterized progressivism in general and the northern philanthropists in particular, extensive data were collected on every detail of implementation, including successes and failures by state and locality, by state agent, by individual Jeanes teachers, in teacher-training programs, and in school-building construction. The GEB used these data to inform regional action and to consider longer-term reforms that might be implemented across broader areas of the South. The foundations relied on this process beginning with the earliest days of the conference, when they assigned Curry the task to "ascertain such facts with respect to southern education, both public and private, as will make clear what methods and agencies are to be encouraged, and what to be avoided or reformed." [138] He became the supervising director of field work, and Charles Dabney, president of the University of Tennessee, the chief of a bureau of investigation and information.

The SEB engaged in the earliest effort to collect comprehensive data about rural black schools, and foundations were subsequently responsible for most of the information that was generated in subsequent decades. When the US government issued its two-volume report on black schools in 1917, the report was supported with funding from Anson Phelps-Stokes, and a majority of the information came from the state agencies that were managed by state agents for Negro education who were on the payroll of the northern foundations and relied on field workers and Jeanes teachers to generate local data.[139] Scientific giving required that state and local governments produce an accurate accounting of revenues and expenses.

The commissioner of education reported that while financial accounts and student records were essential to the sound management of every school, the large majority of southern schools were defective in both types of record keeping. The commissioner called on states to standardize and centralize reporting requirements because the complexity of funding practices required expertise in record keeping for philanthropic donations, contributions from state and local governments, private donations, and asset management.[140] During the early decades of the century, however, most southern states lacked the capacity to address these problems through state agents. The Jeanes teachers strengthened this reporting in their respective communities, often surpassing county and state governments, and their reporting helped to highlight the needs of black schools and school funding inequities. States such as North Carolina made early progress in developing budget systems, while states in the Deep South such as Alabama required no annual state review of county budgets until 1935, the same year that Mississippi finally developed a formal system for preparing school budgets.[141]

Correspondence between foundations and reformers typically focused on the need for better data to inform decision making. The state supervisors of rural schools met in 1911 and concluded that the improvement of the rural schools depended upon data from all over the world with regard to legislation and taxation, the curriculum, community activities, consolidation, supervision, and experimental schools. They developed a survey that would generate data for each of the southern states regarding rural schoolhouses, teachers, attendance, instruction, conditions, community attitudes, and consolidation.[142] The GEB held meetings regularly for state agents, with a detailed agenda that required discussion on every aspect of state and local education reform. For example, in 1921 the extensive agenda included teacher training, county training schools, and Rosenwald schools, and specifically asked a range of questions about each that included the collection of data and sharing of information about best practices.[143] The foundations also scheduled regular meetings of the Jeanes teachers within and across states, and worked to facilitate reporting between groups of field workers. In states with greater administrative capacity or a more effective state agent, similar meetings were held for state field workers and typically included the Jeanes teachers.

Good data helped foundations to develop strategies. A report to the GEB in 1927 assessing the impact of education reform efforts in the previous decade illustrates the relationship between data and policy:

> We are dealing in the several states with situations by no means uniform, and the state agents' opportunities for service are far from being equal. . . . Is it a wiser policy, for example, to continue for much longer to support state agents in some of the border states where the general level of Negro education approaches the level of white education, or to discontinue in a few years the state work in these states and concentrate upon the more

backward states? Would it be desirable in the border states to grant aid for the state agents for specific tasks, such as the building up of weak counties, improving state schools or the state facilities for training teachers?[144]

Data collection and flexible implementation allowed foundations to test objectives in discrete regions and gain an understanding of how and where successful reforms might be implemented.[145]

Foundations were eager to replicate programs that they deemed successful but were concerned with sustaining programs over the long term and integrating them with the public school system. This required that state and local political systems, and rural black communities, demonstrate a willingness to participate and share the financial burden. The differences in per capita expenditures between the North and South were extreme, $5.53 and $2.49 respectively in 1910, and the funds in the South were disproportionately provided for white students and urban areas.[146] There were also disparities across states and between communities within states.

It was difficult at best for states and local communities to find sufficient funding to maintain two separate school districts, but that problem was made worse by the hostility toward creating a school system that was both separate and equal. A 1903 report from Charles Dabney, who was directing the bureau of investigation and information of the SEB, was clear about the difficulty of providing public schooling in the rural South. "The average county in the rural districts of the South has eighteen children of school age to the square mile, eleven white and seven colored, thus practically making two counties, both having a very sparse school population. Where the number of negro children is very small, the cost of their proper schooling will be proportionately large; and the same is true of the white children."[147] However, such descriptions imply that unequal schooling was merely a problem of poor resources and administration when, in fact, most white southerners were committed to such inequalities, and many reports were clear about that aspect of the problem. "The cause for this very disadvantageous situation has been attributed to various reasons, but the principle one is that the available funds for school purposes are too limited to maintain the dual system of schools up to the standard the whites desire for themselves and neither the legal injunctions nor the common justice involved is sufficient to protect the interests of the politically powerless group of Negroes."[148]

States in every region addressed problems of taxation at the turn of the century, and the general trend beginning with the common school movement in the North was toward state systems of public schooling in which general oversight of schools, including tax support, moved from small, local districts to the county with stronger state oversight. When Arizona was admitted to the union in 1912, it established legislation to provide "for county control of county funds through county boards of education and nonpolitical county superintendents."[149] South Dakota, in line with national trends, revised its education codes to provide for a county-unit system, with county boards of education having specified powers and duties, including levying a uniform county school tax."[150] Idaho enacted a board of county commissioners in each county to levy a school tax for general purposes sufficient to meet a $15 per capita minimum for school-age children.[151] In northern states, legislation focused more on state aid laws that aimed to equalize funding across counties.[152] These trends accelerated after World War I. When the US Department of the Interior produced its Biennial Survey on Education for 1928–1930, education financing laws received "considerably more attention than did other education problems" and in the direction of placing more responsibility for funding and equalization with the individual states.[153]

The rising demand for better white schools in the South required that local tax revenues increase sufficiently. Many southern states funded education through regressive individual taxes that the state collected at the polls, and on sales, gifts, shows, exhibitions, and liquor, though the poll tax provided for a substantial portion of school funding and was typically augmented with property-tax revenues. Disfranchisement at the beginning of the twentieth century decreased the amount of revenues raised through poll taxes, and many southern whites believed that it would be unfair to redistribute poll taxes paid by whites to local black schools. Jim Crow disfranchisement decreased the total amount of revenue raised through poll taxes, transferred the burden of education expenses to white citizens, and precluded blacks from voting in local elections regarding tax levies.

Many southern states did not provide for sufficient local property-tax levies and often legislated caps on the amount of money that could be raised. Most local white citizens opposed increased local taxes because of both poverty and the fear that it would require them to spend additional funds on black schools.[154] In those counties where the population was primarily black, the redistribution of local property-tax revenues could be very lucrative for whites. While states in the North and West were able to implement tax reforms that transferred some of the burden of taxation to corporations, including the railroads, the South had a relatively smaller industrial base. Additional *ad valorem* taxation would place an undue burden on farmers, the southern white politicians' primary constituents.

Foundations hoped to influence tax legislation in the South that would promote a public system of schooling that more closely mirrored national trends and bring southern states, over time, more in line with those in the North and West. Southern taxation policies exacerbated the problems of inadequate resources. Local counties were responsible for collecting state and local property taxes and poll taxes. The state allocated the school funds to counties based on a fixed amount per student regardless of race. However, especially following disfranchisement, the poll tax was paid almost exclusively by whites and property taxes were used to augment the poll tax revenues in most states. Many southerners believed white tax revenues should go to whites and black revenues to blacks, and districts typically funneled the majority of these funds to white schools. One report on southern education in Mississippi was explicit that "one-third of your [Mississippi] counties spend less on Negro education than they receive from the state for Negro education."[155] These inequalities persisted throughout the first half of the century. Foundations did not provide sufficient funding to equalize support across schools or to fix the public school system. Instead, the foundations developed a method of giving that had as its primary goal the creation of a school system supported by the state and included the double taxation of rural black communities.

The regressive taxes on goods were often more palatable to white southerners because they were less visible. Foundations, however, favored more visible forms of taxation, particularly ad valorem taxes, because they believed local citizens would see the correlation between their local tax payments and improved educational opportunity, and would take on greater responsibility for public schooling. However, it was a double-edged sword. Campaigns to increase local taxes also created a demand from citizens for real improvement in the schools and the possibility of a backlash against reform if citizens saw too little improvement in white schools or too much improvement in black ones. Many local citizens perceived local taxes as a costly expense that translated into both a loss of local control and a redistribution of local funds to black schools.[156] Edgar Garner Murphy expressed his concerns about the weaknesses in southern campaigns for tax reform: "Unless there is a wiser co-ordination and unification of our educational policies, there is bound to be ere long a revulsion in sentiment. Men are already getting uneasy as to how their money is being spent. Unless the people gain an increasing confidence in the general policy under which their funds are collected and utilized, they will quit voting their funds with such generosity and a reaction will be inevitable."[157] Murphy pointed out that county superintendents had their salaries increased by 30 percent in an effort to promote greater county oversight and professionalism, but it typically did not result in a corresponding increase in efficiency.

Foundation leaders believed their funding might lead to a dependence on private gifts for a public good that belonged to the state. They also thought that the public's willingness to support education reform through private donations and a system of taxation indicated that citizens were interested in "self-help" and would be more committed to education. As one foundation agent explained, "For however poor a community may be, the people must go to some expense in order to prize their schools. People will not prize anything that costs nothing."[158] However, comprehensive reform required a new tax system that might be a longer-term endeavor. One of the most important goals was simply to lift the cap on state and local property-tax levies. This would provide a means for state and county governments to increase taxes to support the schools. The foundations were also interested in equalization policies that would raise substantial revenues in areas by increasing property assessments and get the state involved more directly in school funding by providing equalization funds.

Enrollment increases at the beginning of the twentieth century affected and were affected by funding policies. Initial funding was necessary to increase the number of schools and encourage consolidation. Those efforts, in turn, influenced transportation, compulsory-school enforcement, and the availability of secondary schools, all of which led to an increase in enrollments. As enrollments increased, state and local revenues would be necessary for the developing infrastructure. Because legislative changes to the tax structure, including local tax levies and equalization measures, would be a longer-term effort, foundations also developed short-term policies that could have immediate impact.

Foundation influence in the South had more to do with its method of giving than it did with the amount of money expended. Funding was strategically expended for initiatives that would not just help create infrastructure but also, more importantly, stimulate government spending. The provision of small philanthropic donations rather than full funding, with a requirement for matching funds, would force the creation of a tax-based revenue stream and public responsibility for the schools. The GEB, the Jeanes Fund, and the Rosenwald Fund all operated in this manner, with one report stating, "Very small sums properly administered may be made to stimulate local effort, to release large sums from the public treasury, and to direct all expenditures toward significant results."[159] The secretary of the GEB was explicit about this in extensive correspondence with Julius Rosenwald. In an early letter, he encouraged the use of private funds "to secure larger public support. Our experience shows that public action in these matters does not go backward."[160] He pointed out in subsequent correspondence "that a dollar accomplishes more if it can be used to stimulate the raising of funds by taxation than in any other way."[161] The Rosenwald Fund supplemented other foundation programs when it felt that project participation would lead to greater public support. Fund reports were explicit about this method of operating. When Rosenwald gave money in 1919 to the Jeanes Fund to help with the extension of school terms and to the Slater Fund to promote the creation of additional county training schools, records indicated, "These offers are made to secure larger public support."[162] The ideal was to ensure that the public assumed responsibility for the cost of schooling, and philanthropists believed that the use of public funds would make progress inevitable. In this manner, schooling would eventually be embedded in state and local political systems.

The state agents for Negro education played an important role in developing funding sources by promoting increases to the state and local tax base. The Georgia state agent reported in 1916, "During the year three counties have been added to the list of those which levy a general tax specifically for educational purposes—a step which signifies a real desire on the part of the people for better things."[163] The state agents in North Carolina and in Mississippi engaged in vigorous campaigns to promote legislative changes to the tax system. The agents supervised programs designed to garner private donations, particularly those run by local Jeanes teachers. However, many counties did not exhibit "real desire," and an important strategy was to promote it by encouraging private donations and measurable evidence of self-help. The Jeanes teachers were instrumental to this effort. The foundations expected matching funds, which were often obtained through private contributions that reflected a form of "double taxation" of the black community that was grossly unfair and is discussed in greater detail in the next chapter. However, the hope was that these matching funds would be developed and administered within county budgets, with some oversight by state agents and, by extension, the foundations. Rosenwald has been credited with building rural schools and gave significant amounts of money toward this cause, though he actually contributed a fraction of the total cost of each school, thereby ensuring that the school construction and operations became institutionalized in the county. For example, while the Rosenwald Fund provided a greater amount of appropriations in North Carolina than either the GEB or the Jeanes Fund, the money it provided brought correspondingly the greatest amount of contributions from local tax dollars and private donations, a goal that was in line with that of the other two funds.[164]This allowed for "parallel budgets" within state and local political systems that might ultimately be sustained through taxes.

Efforts to lengthen the school term are illustrative. One cause of disparity in per capita expenditures between the North and the South and between southern white and black communities was the different length of school term. In 1915, Mississippi required that schools be maintained in each district for at least four months per year but stopped short of enacting compulsory-schooling laws to ensure that students would attend.[165] In Louisiana, compulsory-attendance laws in 1915 required that all children eight to fourteen years old attend school at least four months per year, while the Louisiana towns of Caddo, East Carroll, and Franklin had terms for blacks that ranged from three to six months, and in Vermillion it was seven.[166] While the South legislated compulsory-school laws beginning with Reconstruction, there was an absence of governmental desire or institutions to implement legislation; enforcement was often nonexistent, and actual attendance varied considerably.[167] These differences were between states and the counties within them.

The GEB promoted efforts to lengthen school terms by agreeing to pay for an additional month of salary for teachers in schools where the teachers earned a minimum salary, and where matching funds were provided by the school district. This method ensured that salaries might be brought to a more consistent minimum, and the additional costs would be formally provided for in the local budget. The Mississippi state agent wrote to one superintendent in 1929 about the school term and said that funding might be available if the salary for teaching was already at a minimum of fifty dollars per month, the county provided half of the funding through public or private donations, and the school authorities agreed to continue the extended term beyond the two years of Rosenwald Funding. The agent was clear that the award for term extension would diminish in the second year to one-fourth of the salaries for term extension.[168] The Rosenwald Fund was eager to assist counties that were interested in extending the school term, but the application was explicit about these policies: "In accepting aid of one-half the salaries the first year, one-third the second year, and one-fourth the third year from the Julius Rosenwald fund, the school authorities agree to carry on the extended term without further aid."[169] Rosenwald's contracts for schoolhouse construction explicitly addressed the relationship between funding and the creation of a more comprehensive school system. The contract made clear that the fund would cooperate in order to both build and equip schools. However, the sites of all buildings had to be the property of public school authorities, the community had to provide an amount equal to or greater than the award from public funds and private donations, which could include land and labor, and the school terms had to be at least five months.[170]

The shorter school year was in part the result of the complicated issue of teacher hiring and training. Many of the teachers were well trained, often by private schools devoted to black education given the absence of public education opportunities.[171] Foundations and reformers also overstated the trained teacher shortage by defining "trained" not in the traditional terms of academic credentials and teaching experience but rather as showing the willingness and ability to promote industrial training. As a result, foundations provided less funding to private academies devoted to academic training, and many of those academies ended up being subsumed by the public system. Additionally, many counties were reluctant to hire trained teachers at all because of fears about the effect that education might have on the social structure of the South.[172] The US Department of Education 1917 report on black schools acknowledged the complexity with regard to evaluating teaching when it reported, "inadequate compensation is ample explanation of the poor teaching found in most of the rural public schools for colored people. It is little wonder that 70 percent of the teachers in the 'black belt' states have less than six grades of elementary education."[173] However, the report also noted that the exception was those teachers from private schools, who "teach their students to put service to their communities above consideration of self. The splendidly unselfish and effective work of so many of these young people is at once the glory and occasion of the institutions from which they come."[174]

In the context of a school system where the ratio of teachers to students was significantly smaller in black schools than in white, a successful campaign for universal education would dramatically increase the number of children enrolled, for longer periods of time, making these ratios even smaller. For example, in 1924, only 2.68 percent of black students were enrolled in high schools.[175] It was not just that there were fewer blacks interested in attending, or that there were an insufficient number of high schools available, it was also difficult to find a significant number of teachers trained for high school due to the lack of public high schools for blacks and the scarcity of private academies. It would be difficult to overstate the significance of this problem to the promotion of educational change. A sufficient supply of teachers was crucial to expanding educational opportunities.

This issue persisted throughout the early part of the century and significantly constrained what could be accomplished. In Madison County, Mississippi, in 1919, the Jeanes supervisor reported that there were seventy-one schools in the county, but "many of the schools closed; no teachers."[176] In

South Carolina, as late as 1928, only one state institution engaged in teacher training for blacks, yielding only seventy-five students a year from a two-year course, with another 225 provided through private state schools, to meet a total need of 4,339 teachers annually.[177] In Louisiana, the state superintendent reported that the "state is not trying to train all the Negro teachers needed" and noted that "for some years to come the high schools and training schools will be called upon to help supply the demand for rural teachers." The Alabama state agent reported that fewer than two hundred teachers a year were trained in two state institutions and four private colleges, and about 3,800 teachers were employed by the state, with nine four-year accredited high schools and fifteen private high schools not accredited.[178]

The foundations believed that the creation of a trained and certified teaching force that was in line with the industrial-training agenda was important. However, by the 1930s some states called for greater academic training, especially for certification purposes. In 1927, the North Carolina state superintendent of education wrote to the GEB for funding for high schools as a central component of teacher training:

> Elementary schools for negroes cannot be improved and built up until we get better high schools turning out high school graduates who are capable of going to the normal schools and coming back better prepared for teaching. In other words, so long as the teaching profession stays on the level of the elementary school, we will never be able to make the elementary school what it ought to be. The best work that can be done right now to build up the whole situation for the negroes, as I see it, is to strengthen the high schools.[179]

The GEB recognized the difficulty in accomplishing this goal and sought to achieve it in more subtle ways, recognizing that it might be more effective to stimulate instead an interest in elementary schools. Many local whites did not believe in education for southern blacks beyond a rudimentary level, so promoting elementary schools instead of high schools was a strategy that would be less threatening and would lead over time to greater change. Instead, the GEB resolved in its early years that "the public high school for negroes will be an inevitable outgrowth from any sincere effort to improve permanently the elementary rural school for negroes."[180]

In spite of a reluctance to promote high schools, the GEB strategically sought locations for county training schools that would be model schools to the rest of the county, would help to expand the teaching force, and could potentially lead to a more comprehensive public system for rural blacks. The schools would start out as comprehensive schools that went as high as grade seven and would extend through the twelfth grade where possible. In 1914, a letter was sent to all of the county superintendents in North Carolina by the state agent requesting sites for such schools, which would "belong to the county and be under the supervision of the county superintendent, thus forming a part of the regular public school system. Such a school should have a fairly satisfactory annual income from permanent sources, a good building reasonably well equipped, a curriculum of nine or ten grades at least, and be located where it can meet a real need. A public school of three or more teachers might be developed into a training school of this type."[181] While these schools were formally under the supervision of the county superintendent, as "separate" institutions, the supervision of the school and ultimate responsibility for its work fell to the state agents and Jeanes teachers, whose salary was paid by the northern philanthropists. The state budget did not always provide for these schools. However, county boards often recognized that northern largesse promoting the "right" kind of education might simultaneously lessen the local financial burden and placate the black community on issues of education. The Slater Fund provided funding for these schools and expected that each would be the beginning of a rural high school, lead to additional tax money of at least $750 in each county, increase the local supply of country teachers, and provide a means to convert some private schools into public ones.[182] However, in order to receive funding for a county training school, the county had to commit to providing sufficient funding for minimum school terms and teacher salaries.

County training schools are an example of how one particular program could have a much broader effect on the strength of the administrative state. In order to develop a county training school, counties had to agree to meet minimum requirements that expanded public schools. Beyond the explicit agreements for school terms and salaries, the schools would eventually need states to formulate and implement a state curriculum and certification requirements for rural black schools. Over time, as subsequent chapters illustrate, it became increasingly difficult for some southern states to develop, implement, and fund two separate curricula as determined by race. Ultimately, county training schools were an effective program for promoting greater centralization.

Many would argue that greater bureaucracy might take away from the power that blacks were able to yield over their neighborhood schools. However, a principle cost of devolving power to small local units in the American state has been the tendency to place policy making in the hands of oppressive local majorities, typically to the detriment of the black community.[183] When Bula Anderson sought a professional license to teach in Alabama, based upon her education in the Mississippi normal schools, the Alabama superintendent was informed that no such license could be granted because there were no black institutions in Mississippi accredited by the Southern Association of Colleges and Secondary Schools.[184] The Mississippi state superintendent advised the Alabama county superintendent to grant an exemption, as Mississippi typically did, so that Anderson would be able to continue teaching. However, in that same year, when the Mississippi state agent sent applications for the accreditation of the county's high schools, he instructed superintendents to use the same forms for black and white schools and pointed out that "a good many of our negro schools are going to be left off the list in the years to come if we do not change the requirements laid down for approving them. I feel now that we would get in a pick of trouble if we should use different standards for the negroes from the ones used for the whites."[185] Higher enrollments and more certified black teachers might help to equalize both standards and pay scales over the longer term by formally recognizing the work of rural teachers within the bureaucracy of the public sphere.[186]

The GEB tried to leverage the creation of a county training school in Mississippi because if "a carefully selected county were treated in this way in any given state, in course of time the demonstration would favorably affect other counties throughout the State."[187] The Mississippi plan reflected the general foundation strategy to create programs that could be supported by state and local taxes, integrated into the education infrastructure, and replicated. "The members and officers of the Board early realized that a permanent system of education must grow up from within and could not be imposed from without."[188] The foundations understood that it would be more strategic to encourage local communities to develop systems that might be replicated, rather than impose one from the outside. The county training schools might raise the standard for schooling and assume responsibility for the training of teachers in the community.

The GEB tried to persuade private black institutions to accept funding and convert to county training schools, but these institutions were reluctant to lose their identity, often denominational, and be required to transform the curriculum to accommodate the various constituencies, particularly when it involved industrial education. Many scholars have viewed the willingness of the GEB to allow numerous institutions of varying quality to close as evidence of a commitment to industrial education as a first priority. Many high-quality private institutions for southern blacks were converted to public schools that focused on industrial education, or closed down altogether in the name of educational progress. However, from a more narrowly defined goal of institution building, the conversion of private academies into county training schools also helped to institutionalize a greater number of schools extending into higher grades and substantially increased the public system. Of course, one take on the county training school is that it merely illustrated "separate but equal," as defined by *Plessy v. Ferguson*, and was grossly unequal at that. However, in the context of institution building, these schools operated initially as separate systems, with responsibilities to northern foundations, and provided a relatively greater opportunity to shape and expand local education.

The county training schools could train teachers, but foundations also addressed this problem through other means. Some state agents were successful in promoting state certification requirements for all teachers, including blacks. In a letter written in 1921, North Carolina state agent Nathan Newbold pointed out that the new state certification requirements included a provision that principals must graduate from a four-year normal school. However, there were no four-year schools for blacks in the state at that time, a problem that he worked to resolve through the creation of county training schools and alternative certification requirements for black teachers.[189] During 1923–24, 53.19 percent of rural black teachers in North Carolina held standard certificates, meaning that the teachers had attended a standard high school, enrolled in additional classes, or passed the standard high school equivalency test, and the remaining 46.81 percent had nonstandard certificates, which were provisional or granted on an annual basis, to acknowledge experience and more limited education.[190] The Georgia state superintendent reported in 1919 that there were seventeen Rosenwald schools in one county and that while most of the teachers in them held a first-grade certificate, all of them attended Spelman College every month for an institute funded by the GEB.[191] The standardization and professionalization of education practice in the South, through such initiatives, also provided another means to institutionalize change by providing a subtle form of coercion that promoted best practices and legitimated state leadership.[192] As later chapters discuss, teacher training and certification standards may have enhanced state centralization but often to the detriment of local teachers, who lost not just considerable power over their own schools but also possibly their jobs. Yet, many also recognized a potential for improving their schools through greater centralization over the longer term.

In 1928, the trustees of the Rosenwald Fund met to consider new possibilities for funding, but before turning to specific recommendations they were reminded of what they had learned from their experience in the first decade of work. Cooperation with government departments was "probably the soundest method of work for a Foundation in any field [because] large support for long periods of time can be counted upon most readily from tax funds. Insofar as governments can be brought to better procedures and higher standards, enduring results may be expected."[193] The report recommended that the fund make small contributions to private organizations for the purpose of conducting experiments, demonstrating successes, and setting standards, and recognized that the support of research, usually under university auspices, and the support of special studies were beneficial both to foundation work and to the larger society.[194] Foundations had learned a great deal about how to develop the organizations necessary to promote sustained reform.

CONCLUSION

Political authority in the South was controlled almost completed by whites hostile to universal education.[195] However, northern philanthropists recognized that they had considerable power through the funding and the social networks that they brought to southern education reform. They used that power to enhance the organizational capacity in both state and local governance structures. The foundations' focus on industrial education and the needs of rural citizens, and the responsibility they assumed in creating both the programs and the accompanying assessment data, created a discrete milieu of complex education issues that solidified their role as "expert policymakers" with regard to education for rural blacks, and gave them considerable policymaking leverage among competing interest groups in the South.[196] This did not give them greater authority, but did provide additional power than what already redounded to them through their largesse. Extensive collaboration ensured consensus around policy and the networks required for implementation. A more detailed look at foundation work in North Carolina and Mississippi will make clear, however, that cooperation developed in various ways. Each southern state had a unique political and economic context, leading foundations to create forms of collaboration that varied by region in order to fill the policy-making void in rural black education.

Foundation efficacy required participation from both state and local political systems and rural black communities. Foundations recognized the important relationship between a state system of public education, with strong elements of local control, and state political development. The Southern Education Board developed a public-relations campaign in the South, using the media to advertise the reorganization of rural communities through schooling. The willingness of the philanthropists and the experts they employed to acquiesce to the demands of white southerners has played prominently in the literature, especially the fact that racism made accommodation a simple task. However, within an organizational context, there are also alternative ways of thinking about foundation efforts. With regard to progressive reforms in general, the dynamic nature of organizational change required that experts often compromise ideals or act upon competing ideals in order to create an effective organizational structure. That is the nature of organizational change.

The foundations have been criticized for exercising unlimited control over education reform in the South and imposing an unjust system of education. However, education reform could not be unilaterally imposed on the South if it was to be sustained over the longer term. Most reformers understood that. The foundations hoped to promote a public system of schooling in the South, one that would strengthen the relationship between individual states and local communities and bring the South more in line with states in the North and the West. They believed in national ideals that would be disseminated through stronger state and local governance systems, and schooling was the force for change. Organizations that were established through northern largesse were intended to provide centralized control and maintain white supremacy, but over the longer term provided southern blacks with some opportunity to bypass the local political structure and participate in education reform. This created a reform dynamic that differed by region and had a significant impact not just on education reform but also on political opportunity structures in rural black communities.

CHAPTER TWO

"Organize in Every Community"

Reverend J. R. Faison attended Shaw University in Raleigh, North Carolina, the oldest historically black college in the South, and his academic credentials led to his appointment in 1909 as principal of the Zion Academic and Industrial Institute in Anson County, North Carolina, where he hoped to offer a high-quality academic education to the black community. Zion was exemplary of many of the private academies that were established throughout the South in the decades following Reconstruction, typically through the initiative of the black community. Many of the schools were improvised, meeting in makeshift spaces when a teacher could be found to hold classes, while others were more formally established and sustained through private contributions and endowments. Zion was fortunate to have funding from a local Baptist organization and a talented new principal with academic, administrative, and fundraising skills. Yet, the institution struggled with relatively fewer resources than were available to schools lucky enough to have the support of wealthier national organizations or foundations. Like many southern black educators, Faison was astute enough to recognize not only that considerable funding could be had from northern businessmen who were interested in southern education but also that their objectives might differ from his own goals for Zion and for the blacks of Anson County. It would be important to learn how to serve both.

Three years into his appointment as principal of Zion, Faison accepted a secondary appointment as the Anson County Jeanes supervisor, beginning November 1, 1912.[1] One goal of the Jeanes Fund was to encourage trained teachers to return to the rural communities from which they came in order to strengthen the teaching force throughout the South. Faison had been compelled to move from Raleigh to Anson County for the Zion appointment, but it was curious that he was given the Jeanes position while directing a private academy. Foundations often characterized denominational schools like Zion as, "marked by detachment, isolation, frequently carried to the point of open hostility toward contact with white people, and a more or less skeptical attitude toward public schools controlled by white officials."[2] However, the foundations also understood that an educator with Faison's community stature could be effective at promoting reform at the local level, while Faison likely perceived that such an appointment might provide him with greater opportunity to exercise education leadership across the county, expand black schooling, further his goals for Zion, and promote his own professional development. Faison's story is illustrative of the relationship between rural black teachers and northern foundations during Jim Crow, and provides a clearer understanding of what it meant for these teachers to collaborate with foundations.

Foundations could not force southern communities to implement their programs. Success depended upon a local cadre of workers, and Jeanes teachers like Faison were essential to these efforts. Schools were an important institutional component of state-building efforts, connecting rural black communities to the broader political structure. The Jeanes teachers, who were at least partially on the payroll of northern foundations, were instrumental to expanding schooling in rural areas and to promoting greater standardization and the community networks essential to long-term education reform, even when those teachers recognized the tension between their professional goals and those of the communities and the foundations that they served. When local reformers, including rural black teachers, cooperated with foundations, it was easier for them to expand education at the local level. Schools could be a platform for both foundations and teachers to promote their goals.

Faison mediated between a black community often more interested in a classical education than an industrial one and foundations that provided resources for a public school system devoted to the latter. Faison's work is typical of Jeanes teachers throughout the South, who were appointed to promote industrial education but had considerable autonomy at the local level to supervise the development of rural black schools. These teachers had to present an industrial-training model to their northern benefactors and to their state and local supervisors, but community work was far more nuanced. The teachers did not necessarily share reformers' concerns about the economy or the state but focused instead on expanding political and economic opportunity to rural blacks in their communities, in a context where blacks were completely marginalized. These goals united black educators, even if they differed in their beliefs about how to achieve goals in both the short and long term.

Efforts simultaneously to acknowledge the realities of rural black life and promote progress were as complicated for rural black teachers as they were for leaders like Booker T. Washington, and many of these teachers had a less cosmopolitan understanding of racial politics and black progress in the context of national discourse. They likely considered a range of conflicting viewpoints that would have been available through teacher associations and black publications, including whether industrial education was a key to economic progress or an attempt to use the democratic institution of public schooling to disempower black citizens. Many of these teachers believed in the merits of a classical education but accepted a position that required them publicly to support something else. Ultimately, many had to consider, given disagreement about short-term strategies, whether cooperation with white reformers was necessary to enhanced educational opportunity or made them acquiescent in establishing institutions that supported the racial state. Even for those who were against the industrial-education program that foundations were willing to fund, cooperation might bring them to the policy-making table in ways that would influence longer-term goals and provide security for their professional aspirations. Ultimately, southern black teachers who worked with foundations made a decision that it was useful to work within a system of disfranchisement and seek new paths for political engagement. The scope of their responsibilities provided those opportunities.

Faison's 1913 report to the state agent for Negro schools in North Carolina was both honest and strategic. He reported that in forty-three rural black schools in Anson County, with a total average attendance of 1,431 pupils, most "patrons, pupils and teachers alike knew nothing of the industrial work in the rural schools, nor did they seem to see their possibilities along this line." He made clear to white reformers in the opening lines of his report that he worked in a community whose views differed from foundation benefactors and that he would be mediating between the two competing conceptions of schooling. However, he then spoke about his accomplishments that were in line with foundation goals. He organized two school-betterment associations and a number of school clubs, which had raised funds to supplement a teacher salary, relocate a schoolhouse to the center of the district where "good water and a large playground" were available, and enlarge one of the schoolhouses.[3] He had also established a teachers' association and hoped to establish a county library for teachers.

In spite of community reluctance to consider industrial education, Faison reported that his most important work was the industrial-training programs that were introduced, where "girls were taught sewing, and the boys to make axe and hoe handles, picture frames, rustic tables, and the use of the pocket knife. Both boys and girls were instructed how to select seed corn and given lessons in clenliness [sic]."[4] Faison's report provides a powerful illustration of the role that black educators played in many southern towns. Faison clearly understood that many Anson County parents believed that industrial education would provide fewer benefits than an academic curriculum. Yet, he was also on the payroll of northern foundations that were willing to bankroll black education efforts that promoted an industrial-education program. He recognized that community support for industrial-education initiatives might lead to additional foundation funding.

Faison operated in a difficult political context, and it was important for him constantly to be strategic. In an effort to convince the community of the benefits of industrial training, he organized a fair at the end of the four-month school term where two-thirds of the black schools were represented and fifty-eight dollars was raised. At the same time, while the fair focused primarily on industrial education and fundraising for rural black schools, it also closed with a literary program and educational meeting, providing an important occasion to use foundation initiatives to extend educational opportunity. He concluded his report with a special commendation for the county superintendent, stating it has "largely been through his effort and untiring support that the industrial work in the colored schools in the county has met with success."[5] It is not clear that the superintendent was a real supporter of black schools in Anson County, but it made sense to acknowledge him positively in foundation reports as one way of fostering good race relations. Faison's political acumen had the potential to redound expanded educational opportunity for the community, better race relations, and an important community leadership role for Faison with greater job security. As one 1930s study of teacher education pointed out, "If there be an emancipator, it will not be a Lincoln, nor a New England missionary, but it will be Negro teachers themselves."[6] Black educators believed that education was essential to political opportunity, though collaboration with foundation programs and agents added significant complexity to their work.

The US Department of Education report in 1917 on southern black schools described Zion as a "crude one-teacher school," with thirty-two students in five elementary grades who "could be better cared for in the public schools, which is about a half mile distant."[7] It is not clear whether the school was truly subpar or merely failed to meet the expectations of white reformers, who had an alternative vision for public education. Philanthropists and denominational organizations supported many private academies in the South after Reconstruction. This first wave of philanthropy included gifts that supported particular schools, typically in response to the personal appeals of southern educators. The Peabody and Slater Funds, with a mission to expand education for freed blacks, also supported schools throughout the South. However, the annual Conference for Education in the South, and the organizations like the SEB and GEB that emerged from it in the early twentieth century, worked to direct these gifts to institutions and programs deemed more "worthy" of foundation support. These efforts had a significant impact in the South, forcing many high-quality private academies to close or merge with the public school system. The Department of Education 1917 report on black schools, paid for by the Phelps-Stokes Fund, recommended that Zion be merged with the public school system, reflecting foundation efforts to create a public and universal system of schooling supported by local tax dollars. Perhaps, however, Faison thought that such a merger would be beneficial to both Zion and his professional aspirations. The school was ultimately absorbed by the public system, and Faison remained in the position of county Jeanes teacher. He served as an administrator for many years in Anson County where a middle school that is named for him exists one hundred years later.

Faison's story is illustrative of the difficulties that southern blacks faced in promoting their own educational opportunities during Jim Crow. On the one hand, Zion was lost to the public school system and, in the process, the black community in general and Faison in particular no longer had complete control over the local school. Further, in accepting the Jeanes appointment, Faison committed himself to selling industrial education, at least publicly, and reporting in his position to the county superintendent, the state agent for Negro education, and the foundations that sought to impose a particular version of education in Anson County. At the same time, however, the transfer of Zion into the public school system led to the first publicly funded high school for rural blacks in Anson County, and Faison, in his new administrative role, was likely given limited oversight by the county and a virtual guarantee of his own professional development, though restricted by the boundaries of Jim Crow.

The Jeanes teachers answered to the foundations and often supported their objectives. They also served the community in which they worked. It would be impossible to generalize across all of these teachers regarding their goals for rural black education. There was a lack of unanimity in the black community regarding how best to educate southern blacks, just as there was in the white one.[8] In addition, much of what we know about southern blacks who worked on school reform is in letters written to foundations and their agents, or from accounts of black citizens seen through the lens of white reformers. Yet, these voices add an important dimension to understanding foundation work in the South. Indeed, even in the case of Faison, who promoted industrial education in his reports, it is unclear whether he considered collaboration to be purely instrumental, actually supported philanthropic goals, or became convinced of the long-term benefits of supporting at least some of them. These teachers likely cared deeply about their communities, but also sought opportunities for professional success.

Southern black teachers operated in a particularly difficult context and it is not possible to make broad generalizations about their motivations. Indeed, their actions were shaped by the local context as much as foundation programs were. It is likely, however, that many of these teachers perceived their work with northern foundations to represent a kind of Faustian bargain in which their collaboration both expanded schooling and provided a professional platform to promote community goals, but would likely lead to a loss of local control and an unknown future for rural black education. Teachers who were on the payroll of the northern foundations participated in a dynamic that included multiple constituencies, difficult politics, and a perception that action might have significant consequences, resulting in either increased funding and a new school or the loss of resources that already existed. The fractal nature of the reform dynamic in the South, created in the context of Jim Crow, made black teachers acutely aware of the benefits of collaboration and the need for quiet resistance. An important irony is that the teachers correctly perceived schools to be important institutional structures that would provide avenues for black agency, yet risked losing control over local institutional structures to education experts and politicians who existed outside of their community.[9]

Anne Chestnutt Waddell grew up in Fayetteville, North Carolina, with her brother, Charles Chesnutt, the noted African American author.[10] She was educated at the Howard School, a private academy that her father had helped to establish following Reconstruction, which became the North Carolina State Colored Normal School in 1877, from which Anne eventually graduated. She also attended the Hampton Institute and became a rural schoolteacher in Cumberland County, North Carolina, and then the county Jeanes teacher, where she served for twenty-two years. She facilitated the construction of seven Rosenwald schools and also had a school named for her in Fayetteville. For many educated blacks in the South, teaching was the rare professional aspiration available, and the foundations understood this and likely exploited it. An early report from North Carolina to the GEB was clear on this point. "In some sections the negro teachers are exceptionally capable. Directors of teachers' institutes have told me that they have sometimes found the negro teachers superior to the whites. The fact that school teaching is about the only sphere in which the negro can advance, in large part, accounts for this phenomenon. This encourages the belief that a sufficient supply of good negro teachers can easily be developed."[11] The story of Faison and Waddell is similar to that of many black teachers throughout the South. The profession attracted many southern blacks who were highly educated and capable, and their work was instrumental to educational development in rural black communities. Their stories make clear that educated and trained teachers existed throughout the South, in spite of numerous reports about the poor quality of southern black teachers. These teachers worked tirelessly on behalf of rural black communities, at the same time that they sought professional success through teaching careers, often in the context of working with northern benefactors who sought to define their work.

Teachers had relatively greater opportunity than many southern black reformers to promote the needs of rural black communities. As long as southern whites perceived black participation in foundation efforts as advancing the accepted goal of promoting industrial education, a curriculum they believed would ensure the continuation of the racial state, black teachers and reformers had considerably greater latitude to manage rural schools and organize the community around them.[12] Indeed, the ability of rural blacks across the South to promote expanded educational opportunity and shape education policies in the context of Jim Crow was severely circumscribed. Disfranchisement meant that normal avenues to political power were not open, options were restricted, and action was likely to invite repression. Hence, southern black educators and reformers sought a range of strategies to challenge the political system. Schooling provided one relatively safe haven. Many southern blacks were able to participate in collaborative relationships that had developed between the state and private interests through the institution of schooling, particularly through the program of Jeanes teachers.

Of course, thousands of teachers operated outside of these organizational structures. W. E. B. Du Bois documented the central role that southern blacks played in promoting their own education beginning with Reconstruction.[13] Teachers and community leaders were essential to education development, and members of the black community were a force for reform long before the twentieth-century foundations embarked on their southern program.[14]

Indeed, black teachers had developed their own teaching organizations that operated at the local, state, and national level. Rural black educators like Faison, however, worked within foundation programs to promote education and community. Organizational change is a dynamic enterprise, and while blacks had little power relative to whites, their participation in the development and administration of public schooling inserted them into that dynamic. Their collaborative role provided them with a voice and opportunities to shape education in their communities, not just in the short term by serving as the primary administrator of rural black schools but potentially in the longer term by helping to design and implement local foundation programs that might lead to redefined state systems of universal education.

The opportunity to influence and sustain education reform at both the local and the state level was greater when participation took place within the formal programs that foundations established. Many southern whites were reluctant to strengthen state and county oversight of schools because they recognized that it might be detrimental to the racial state. Black teachers sought to retain local control, but many recognized that education equality required outside influence. Many supported federal intervention in public schooling, indicating some understanding that national legislation was necessary to end the extreme racial inequality.[15] The Jeanes teachers in particular contributed to the full range of foundation initiatives, including rural school administration, data collection, school funding, teacher training, schoolhouse construction, and curriculum development. Bureaucracy in these domains helped to connect small, rural schoolhouses to a universal system of public schooling, where it was possible to begin to address the profound inequalities that existed between the two races.[16] Of course, as formal schooling evolved, the system was governed by an increase in formal rules, standardization, and levels of authority, which was obviously to the detriment of community control, especially in a context where there were differences of opinion among foundation initiatives and local black citizens about the nature of schooling.[17] However, localism promoted and sustained discrimination and inequality.[18] The transfer of resources from private to public schools in the South was not going to lead to a redistribution of power or resources in the short term because the public sphere was dominated by a local racial state. For rural blacks, the development of a centralized public school system that diminished local control and with it efforts by communities to improve their own schools could be detrimental to progress. However, over the longer term, centralization could have its benefits.

The example of the Zion Academy is illustrative. When the school was folded into the public school system and its principal went on the foundation payroll, a private academy devoted to classical training with oversight provided solely by black educators was lost. However, Faison and Anson County's black citizens had an alternative vision that was longer term. They anticipated that such a move would strengthen black schooling in the short term, and potentially help them to achieve greater education equality over time. The Zion Academy became a training school that could expand the teaching force and connect formally to the county, the state, and to northern foundations. The Jeanes teachers also helped to strengthen the administration of local communities and, in doing so, helped to connect local school organizations to the public sphere. Information about Faison's appointment is available because of his long, handwritten messages to the state agent for Negro education in North Carolina. At least during Jim Crow, bureaucracy could strengthen the administration of state and local political systems; it tended not to result in a locally centralized school system for rural black communities in most states because of the relative inattention paid to rural black schools by weak county administrative structures. Ironically, the developing bureaucracy provided greater latitude to local interest groups, especially under the leadership of the Jeanes teachers, to participate in education decision making both within their communities and beyond.

In the early years of the Conference for Education in the South, it was unclear which of the foundation objectives would be most successful, or how success would be defined in subsequent decades. For example, foundation programs might lead to an education system that ensured white domination in the South, but that system might also lead to greater equality over the longer term. An expanded school system had the potential to enhance governance capacity at the state and local level, which might ensure greater oversight by state actors who were opposed to black progress, but those enhancements might also mean organizational structures that created greater equality and political opportunity for rural blacks. Foundations worried that successful programs might lead to a political backlash in the South that precluded an expanded system of universal education at all. As subsequent chapters will illustrate, each of these possible outcomes occurred in different regions of the South.

Given organizational dynamics and the need for the participation of state and local actors, foundations recognized that they would need the participation of rural blacks. Most black schools were isolated from state and county governance, making it difficult to promote initiatives in a top-down manner. In addition, expanded education required additional revenues, and all foundation gifts required matching funds, which sometimes came from county governance and often were raised by private donations in the black community. However, counties were willing to provide such additional funds only in a context where they perceived black schools to be providing a useful function. Black teachers could help highlight the benefit of schooling, much as Faison did in his activities and reports. Because local whites typically paid little attention to rural black schools and would not likely actively work to improve them, it would be impossible for foundations effectively to implement programs at the local level without the help of rural blacks. However, they could not anticipate what effect that would have on foundation initiatives or black engagement specifically, or on education more generally. Black educators were similarly unsure of what cooperation might lead to over the longer term, but most shared a belief that it would lead to more schools.

Teachers like Faison and Waddell were instrumental to promoting education reform at the local level, especially when they were perceived as community leaders. And, of course these positions offered opportunities for real leadership. Regardless of the views of individual teachers, efforts at school reform connected them to the local and state political structure and to foundation field agents, or sometimes directly to foundation membership at the national level. While the teachers had to mediate between foundation initiatives and community goals that often were not in harmony, almost all shared a belief in cooperation, community building, and greater standardization at the local level. Standardization redounded greater power to individual teachers in the short run and had the potential to move isolated rural schools into the public sphere, where greater local control might be lost but greater equalization might be gained over the longer term. Ultimately, local teachers were also state builders. They saw the benefits that might result from programs that connected their communities to the governance structures that existed beyond. Unlike foundations, they cared little about creating a stronger national state because their needs were more local. Yet, in a context where they were completely marginalized from politics and policy, schools could expand political opportunity through both education and the platform it provided to garner additional funding and promote community needs.[19] Rural blacks promoted schooling, cooperated with foundations to achieve their goals, and often strengthened the community and local governance structures in the process.

THE JEANES TEACHERS: AN OVERVIEW

The foundations had high expectations for the county Jeanes teacher. The Jeanes Fund sought to appoint qualified and well-trained teachers to supervise the rural schools in each county. At least on the face of it, a primary goal was to reshape community expectations for a developing public school system. Foundations granted supervisory responsibilities to the Jeanes teachers, hoping that they could overcome local attitudes about schooling that foundations considered unacceptable. For example, one of the state agents expressed concern that the average rural teacher was "ambitious to use many books, and to teach the so-called 'higher branches.'"[20] However, at the outset, the depth and breadth of these positions ensured that the teachers could have a significant impact beyond the development of a "suitable" curriculum. These teachers served as the de facto superintendents of rural black schools and were instrumental to creating an education infrastructure in the early twentieth century. Their work also became central to a range of community initiatives. In the first letter from the Jeanes Fund to teachers appointed throughout the South, the teachers were told that the most effective appointees would keep in regular contact with school officials, be willing to help fellow teachers, assist in organizing the people of the community into associations for self-help, cooperate with the minister or ministers of the community, and introduce industrial work.[21] From the foundation perspective, those teachers who were successful at gaining the support of all of these groups could exercise significant leadership and create consensus for foundation-supported reforms.

There were three types of Jeanes teachers. The first was the "original home and school improvement type," regarded as more a community worker than a professional teacher, and likely to stress sanitation, hygiene, improving the schoolhouse, and beautifying the school grounds.[22] While early Jeanes agents, beginning in 1909, were all of this type, the positions evolved to include two other types of agents. The second, expected to have a "strong personality" and "qualities of leadership," recommended teachers for hiring, conducted teacher meetings and institutes, promoted and directed schoolhouse construction, and performed other administrative duties. The third included those who also supervised classroom work, tested pupils, conducted teachers' reading courses, and worked to improve instruction.[23] Over time, the majority was of the second or third type and exercised significant control over the rural schools where they were appointed.

Faison's appointment as the Jeanes teacher in Anson County in 1912 was atypical because he was male. Women often had greater success in organizing schools because they were perceived as nonthreatening by local whites, especially when they were organizing schools that promoted an industrial rather than academic education. Women might also be more effective at promoting an industrial curriculum because they were perceived to have closer relationships to families and homes, and the ability to develop and extend agricultural club work into the community. As such, foundations explicitly sought women to serve in these positions, and many of the state agents agreed. "I concur heartily in the opinion that women, as a rule, are capable of doing more effective work than men. My experience in Lauderdale County and my observation during the past few weeks thoroughly convinces me of this fact, and I am wondering if it would be advisable to go any further than recommend the employment of women in preference to men for this work."[24] This adds an interesting gender component to the important role that teachers played in organizing rural communities during Jim Crow. The initial job description that the foundations developed for these positions seem designed with women in mind. However, beyond the actual tasks at hand, local politics ensured that women would have a relatively greater role in developing a universal system of public education across rural communities in the South.

The job descriptions promoted a deep connection between work in schools and the life of the community, which brought the teachers in contact with a majority of families. They were expected to "encourage and promote better homes through campaigns and other activities," which included club work with children and adults, and assistance with community problems.[25] The expectation that they would work with schools, homes, and churches helped the community to "learn to regard the Jeanes Teacher as their friend and bring their problems to her."[26] While every teacher needed formal education training and experience, the intangible characteristics seemed to have far greater potential for navigating community politics to improve schools. "A Jeanes teacher should be a person who is well adjusted, and can get along with people. She must have a forceful personality and must be well trained. In addition to formal training, successful teaching experience, preferably in a rural school, should be a very important requirement. Good health is essential. In most cases the Jeanes Teacher occupies the place of leadership in the county and must work with people of both races."[27] Indeed, the job descriptions and early correspondence ensured that these teachers would be central to the organization of rural communities.

The range of foundation programs provided formal avenues for teachers to work with both whites and blacks, and promoted their role as community leaders. This ensured that each teacher might be a powerful ally in implementing foundation programs in rural black communities, while simultaneously shaping those programs to meet the needs of the families they served. The teachers also recognized this potential. Helen Whiting, who was appointed to a state-level position to supervise Georgia Jeanes teachers, recognized the opportunity. "Really, there is no Revolutionary Program, lest you become fearful. One can be FRANK, KIND, SPECIFIC, TACTFUL, POSITIVE, CAUTIOUS and ENCOURAGING at the same time . . . And, after all, any such program, of necessity, becomes one of Evolution, which is more desirable. The educator who warned the supervisor to MAKE HASTE SLOWLY, well knew that there is no other way, in spite of our zeal."[28] These teachers understood the parameters in which they worked but knew that the positions provided an opening for longer-term gains.

A teacher's ability to navigate smoothly between both races might be relatively easier where county administrators and even some of the state agents had little interest in managing or overseeing rural black schools, and tended to provide a more cursory oversight. The teachers were expected to report to the county superintendent regularly, especially given that the Jeanes Foundation expected local matching funds.[29] Over time, the share of county funding on average significantly increased, illustrating the extent to which these supervisors became institutionalized as part of the county school system. For example, in 1913–14, only 15.5 percent of the total salaries were provided through state and local revenue sources, but this amount increased to 57.7 percent of the total by 1924–25.[30] However, while counties assumed a larger share, the relationship between the teacher and most county supervisors did not necessarily change because of it. It would seem that the superintendents might feel that such additional tax-based remuneration warranted greater oversight of the supervisor's work and a stronger reporting line, but this was not typically the case. The state agent in Mississippi discussed the twenty-three Jeanes teachers appointed in that state in 1925, acknowledging that they are given "only a minimum amount of time which, of course, is a regret to us."[31] However, the teachers still had to answer to multiple constituencies and ensure the support of both local blacks and whites. The teachers also supervised a large black teaching force in the county that was not always amenable to the oversight. Helen Whiting, in her role as Georgia's state supervisor, explained that some Jeanes teachers had to convince local blacks to cooperate: "There was a subtle movement against her program seemingly, which was due to lack of enlightenment. . . . The people expected Mrs. Gregory to emphasize industrial work. It seems to be taking her some time to convince them that her program is for improvement of instruction."[32]Ann Short Chirhart aptly referred to them as "double agents," who simultaneously worked to achieve both foundation and community goals. But navigating the community was not always so simple. While local blacks wanted expanded educational opportunity, many were also uncomfortable with outside interference and additional oversight in their local schools.[33]

Local governments hired these teachers for a variety of reasons. Unfortunately, it was not always because local whites hoped to promote a better education system for rural blacks. One state agent reported on efforts to hire a teacher: "Supt. Blair was so much interested in reports of work done in other counties, he stated that he was going to get a barrel or more of lime for each of his negro schools, get the government recipe for making whitewash, then get his principals to urge the negro residents to whitewash their houses and premises, the schools, furnishing to each a bucketful or more of whitewash to do the work. Both these superintendents are anxious to have a supervisor."[34] In another example, the teacher in Martin County, North Carolina, organized "County Clean-up Day," in which residents cleaned 920 yards and 770 homes, while the "supervisor polished a stove that had been used in the same kitchen for sixteen years and had never had a coat of polish before."[35] The foundations and their agents were happy to accommodate such requests, and likely considered them beneficial, because every opportunity to appoint a Jeanes teacher provided for another potential ally in local communities. Once local whites perceived these teachers to be beneficial, the positions might be more effective in promoting expanded education.

Efforts to convince counties to appoint a Jeanes teacher were often degrading to local black residents. When the superintendent in Pasquotank County in North Carolina was reluctant to hire a supervising teacher, the state appealed by arguing that the appointment would help to "gain the co-operation of the educational authorities of the county in giving the colored people the *kind* of education and training that the southern people have for years believed they should have. . . . If a negro family in your city or county have measles, whooping cough, consumption, or smallpox, it is next to impossible to prevent it spreading to their white neighbors. Teach these people to be clean, to keep their homes and themselves clean, and the danger of contagious diseases spreading from them will be practically eliminated [emphasis in original]."[36] The superintendent was asked not to misinterpret the correspondence as insistence that the county cooperate with the Jeanes Fund but instead to understand that "I am only anxious to set the matter before your Board in what I believe to be the proper light and then leave them entirely free to act."[37] At the same time, however, such dubious arguments for appointing a Jeanes teacher might be advantageous to their work. Low expectations meant that local school-board members would not perceive school programs to be threatening. Black reformers in local communities were often able to organize with the imprimatur of whites, when reform was based in the context of industrial education.[38]

The relative autonomy meant that both the state and local school boards vested significant authority in these teachers over time. It was a quick transition from the "original home and school improvement type" to that of supervisor. The state agents recognized as early as 1921 that the teachers' roles had changed drastically across the South, with greater focus on Rosenwald schools, teacher selection and training, school-term extension, and adult illiteracy in order to promote education more generally.[39] For many teachers, it was easy to obscure the expansion of their duties by using the vernacular of industrial education and community improvement, an appropriate framework for the dictates of their position and one that would ensure support from local whites. However, while this work brought the teachers in direct contact with members across the community to promote industrial work, it also created a space for developing community awareness about education needs more broadly defined. In 1921, the state agent in Virginia reported that his fifty-four county Jeanes teachers had raised $100,000 for school improvements.[40] The Jeanes teachers in Alabama reported that they had supervised 995 schools in the state, 218 mothers clubs enrolling 1,744 members, and 1,509 parent-teacher associations. These groups raised $5,309 in private funding to support the addition of school buildings, the extension of the school term, and an increase to teacher salaries.[41] As one state agent pointed out, "The first efforts of the colored people after they have been organized into School Improvement Leagues has been to get equipment and a decent schoolhouse. After this has been done, the next step is to lengthen the term."[42] The agents recognized the extent to which the teachers' work had surpassed the original job description, but teachers understood that they could have a significant long-term impact by working within the organizations that the foundations had established.

Foundations also hoped that these teachers could promote standardization, which required administrative oversight. For the Jeanes teachers, who were responsible for overseeing all of the rural black schools in a particular county, greater bureaucracy could have its benefits. It added formal layers of authority that typically existed more in theory than in practice prior to World War II. However, the rules that promoted minimum standards for teachers and for the curriculum gave supervising teachers greater leverage for directing the work of local schools and created opportunities to equalize schools over the longer term in some regions. And, Jeanes teachers could possibly play even larger roles in oversight and organization when they worked in community schools that had been integrated into the local system and consolidated into larger schools. They participated in every aspect of the southern reform program in local communities.

THE JEANES TEACHERS AND LOCAL REFORM

The North Carolina state agent must have been pleased when he read the first report that Faison submitted in 1913. Prior to the appointment, the agent likely wondered whether it would be a good idea to hire a male whose position reflected a commitment to a more academic education for black students in Anson County. The agent must have felt relieved and gratified that, at least from the outside, Faison took his job responsibilities seriously and placed industrial education at the center of his work. At the same time, Faison's report made clear that Anson County might have been benefitting in more meaningful ways. Faison foreshadowed the extensive administrative oversight that he would have over the county's rural black schools, his impact on teacher training, teacher salaries, and schoolhouse construction, as well as his ability to work with local whites. Evidence from across the South illustrates that most teachers used their positions similarly, to strengthen administration and promote a range of education reforms that included schoolhouse construction, teacher and curriculum development, and extended school terms. Regardless of how teachers felt about the long-term benefits of industrial education, they talked explicitly about it in most of their reports. Their feelings about the role of such a narrowly defined curriculum did not matter as much as how they might use it to achieve other goals.

However, black educators did not always agree on how to design rural black education. While black southerners had connected education to progress, seeing it as the antithesis to slavery, there was disagreement about how to define progress and the best form of education to achieve it. Booker T. Washington spoke eloquently on the merits of an industrial education and was extremely successful at getting funding for southern education institutions. He played a role in promoting the development of the larger, mission driven endowments like the Rosenwald Fund and the Jeanes Fund, and their significant investment in the South. Many black intellectuals argued against Washington's stance, particularly after he seemed to acquiesce to white supremacy with the Atlanta Compromise speech in 1895. The public debate between Washington and W. E. B. Du Bois is well known, but many other blacks in both the North and South were also uncomfortable with Washington's views, as well as his close collaboration with northern reformers. However, Washington's advocacy of industrial training also illustrated the realities of the Jim Crow South, where blacks were increasingly marginalized and educational opportunity was severely circumscribed.[43] In a region defined by white supremacy, foundation programs provided an opening for expanded schooling and political participation, even if defined in terms that are deeply problematic.

Many rural black teachers understood that foundation programs would provide resources that were not available from southern whites, and the organizational means to expand services to the community. The Tunica County, Mississippi, Jeanes teacher reported that her goal in 1928 was "gravel from the main road to the schoolhouses," in order to allow access to buildings.[44] Many teachers worked on finding sufficient resources to make the schools habitable. The Jeanes teacher in Brooks County, Georgia, asked the teachers to have children "bring drinking cups and towels. We are trying to get every school to build pit toilets. . . . When I began visiting Ione school last year, there were only wooden shutters—now they have new glass windows and the school is part ceiled."[45] However, the same teacher also brought in a white county nurse to examine the children and organized an extension class and summer school for her teachers. The Elbert County Jeanes teacher wrote a letter about her work: "I labored under some very adverse circumstances. My health failed. But the county teachers cooperated so nicely that we put our planned programs over."[46] She succeeded in setting up a health clinic and organized a countywide commencement to provide an opportunity for community involvement.[47] The teachers perceived that foundation support might provide an opening to address the most basic needs in rural schools, but also came to understand that foundation networks and stronger administrative systems provided opportunities for far more.

Faison reported that in his new role, he would be responsible for forty-three schools and 1,431 pupils. Given the number of schools that already existed when he was appointed in 1913, it is clear that rural black communities took responsibility for their own schooling long before foundations took an interest. Of course, we know very little about the schools, which likely ranged from classes that met sporadically in makeshift spaces, to one-room schoolhouses that existed for four months or more, to an academy like Zion. However, there was no administrative structure to connect these schools across neighborhood lines or, indeed, even to connect neighborhoods. Given the rural nature of Anson County, with no major town or population center, it likely had developed no administrative system at the beginning of the twentieth century. However, to the extent that a formal infrastructure did exist, it would likely be white and based on the spoils of a political system dominated by democratic politics and relative disinterest in the county's black schools.

Most southern states provided no data about the number of administrators appointed at the local level and excluded black administrators from reports until the 1930s.[48] However, the negligible amount of black school administrators included in the data obscures the growth in administrative capacity that was encouraged in rural black communities through philanthropic funding. Administration was strengthened by the appointment of state agents, school consolidation that streamlined authority structures, and systems of ongoing data collection that ensured that local schools were meeting minimum standards for both the curriculum and for teaching. The Jeanes teachers were instrumental to the development of this capacity in rural areas and were, indeed, the primary administrators there.

The foundations came to recognize the extensive role these teachers played in administering the schools of the county. By 1918, the North Carolina state agent reported that, "in most cases the Jeanes Teacher occupies the place of leadership in the county and must work with people of both races. . . . A few Jeanes teachers are assistant County Superintendents in reality, for they look after everything pertaining to Negro schools."[49] Early reports from teachers referred primarily to industrial education and club work. A teacher in North Carolina reported in 1916 that more than four thousand children had taken part in a parade at the county exhibition, where every school had an industrial-education exhibit, while another reported that she had helped to create school farms at six schools.[50] Another teacher organized Thursday afternoon teachers' meetings during the vacation to focus on sewing and reading.[51] These reports focused on curriculum but also foreshadowed the evolution to greater administrative oversight. From these examples alone, one teacher had reached more than four thousand students; another had solidified leadership in six schools, while the last promoted not just sewing but also reading to all of her county teachers. These efforts might lead to endeavors that were not industrial, like fundraising and academics. In general, the applications indicate that day-to-day work was largely the responsibility of teachers. That was bound to offer openings to extend the work beyond merely promoting industrial education. Indeed, teacher reports rarely indicated white participation except for special events, including town meetings, commencements, or field days that were dedicated to showcasing the work of black schools.

The teachers answered to foundations, usually through the state agent but sometimes directly, and typically supported basic foundation objectives. However, most teachers quickly transcended the basic goals of the position—

the original "home and school improvement" goals defined in 1909—and took on greater responsibility. They focused more on community development through schooling, which required organization and cooperation with other agencies at the state and county level.[52] This was true across the South and could be seen in both the applications for Jeanes teachers that the state submitted to the foundation as well as in teacher reports. One application pointed out that the new teacher was expected "to cooperate in all school, home, and community activities."[53] Lina Brookins, who began teaching in Yazoo, Mississippi, in 1921, provides a good example of how extensive that work could be. Her contract in 1928 indicated that she was responsible for 120 teachers in ninety-two schools for a five-month school term, though she was paid for six months of work, likely reflecting club work and extended responsibilities outside of the regular school year, for which the county provided 51 percent of her ninety-dollar monthly salary.[54] In 1932, when she was to be appointed for her tenth year of work, the funding application said that she would visit the schools and report conditions, help organize PTAs, assist teachers in planning their work, follow up on the summer school for teachers to see whether methods were put into practice, and assist with organizing teacher reports.[55] The teacher in Lincoln, Mississippi, was expected to supervise classroom instruction and "encourage the standardization of schools . . . and a definite community cooperation."[56] Applications from Georgia teachers indicated that teachers would be responsible for "supervising instructions, organizing PTA organizations . . . planning and conducting teachers' meetings . . . [and] supervising and directing colored schools."[57] The scope of the work went beyond basic home and school improvement to extensive oversight of schools.

Some applications described school supervision in detail. For example, in Jasper, South Carolina, the teacher was expected to "assist in filling vacancies with prepared teachers; supervising work of teachers in all schools; assisting in raising money for school purposes, including . . . longer school terms."[58] Applications and reports indicated that once a county appointed a teacher, it quickly delegated all responsibilities for the local black schools. Local whites clearly accepted the extent to which these teachers assumed almost full responsibility for administering rural black schools. White citizens often had so little concern for rural black schools that many Jeanes teachers could develop their work in any way that they believed would be beneficial. Of course, there were limitations, and superintendents had the right to approve or deny requests, or put a stop to activities. That formal supervisory role affected education work across the South. In some communities, the white superintendents kept strict boundaries on the work, limiting teacher efforts to develop programs beyond industrial education, and many provided just enough oversight to prevent the expansion of schooling.

Some teachers met regularly with the superintendent, and those meetings could serve both to create parameters that limited teacher initiatives and connect rural black schools to governance structures. The obvious problem was that as formal oversight of local schools increased, teachers risked handing over their control of schools to local whites who were hostile to black education. Many teachers also saw the value of promoting a stronger public system of schooling generally, and meetings with the superintendent could provide a formal venue for the teacher to promote community needs and engage in education policy as a professional. One report explicitly acknowledged these connections. The application for a Jeanes teacher from the superintendent in King George County, Virginia, was clear that the teacher would provide general supervision of instruction and teach some courses but also serve as a kind of political liaison: "The class-room teacher looks upon the supervisor as their means of making contact with the school board, and our local school boards permit the colored supervisor to sit-in at our meetings and represent his people."[59] A description in Tennessee acknowledged a direct line to the state, noting that the teacher would supervise schools under the direction of the state department of education.[60] While it may not seem particularly surprising that teachers who were part of the public school system reported to officials located in either state or county education agencies, it is important to note that these formal connections existed primarily because of foundation initiatives. The expansion of county and state oversight required stronger administrative systems, and foundation agents, like the Jeanes teachers, could create formal ties between isolated rural schools and governance structures at the state and local level.

Many local whites came to recognize the important function of these teachers and allow them to participate in local governance, a key illustration of the central role that schooling might play in political development. These connections between teachers and governance structures formed relatively early in some areas, which were more progressive in their racial attitudes, but took decades to develop in other regions if they formed at all. In Anson County, North Carolina, the teacher was clear in 1932 that she would make recommendations to the county superintendent and the board of education.[61] Jennie Robinson, the teacher in Virginia's Westmoreland County, reported in 1939 that she met monthly with the white supervisor regarding suggestions for classroom teachers, attended supervisors' conferences, state and district teacher conferences, and meetings organized by white citizens to address health and welfare issues.[62] Mayme Coleman reported from Caroline County that she had met with the superintendent to develop a program to improve instruction, which included four district teacher meetings that promoted better reading, spelling bees, arithmetic demonstration, and a plan to continue sessions monthly.[63] These applications were submitted annually, often for teachers who had been appointed for a number of years. The position descriptions reflected both white expectations and work that teachers were already performing. These reports are not isolated and indicate formal connections between rural teachers and governance systems at both the state and local level. The reports also underscore the latitude these teachers had. While these examples indicate formal connections to the local superintendent, each Jeanes teacher also had power to make reports on behalf of the rural teachers that they supervised and provide extensive oversight in their respective counties.

The experience of the teacher in Spartanburg County, South Carolina, in 1915 is illustrative. She sent a letter that promoted community organizations and cooperation to all of the teachers in the county but also noted that the county superintendent has "permitted me to ask ten of the schools to work for School Libraries." The language indicates that she was not supposed to embark on the development of new policies or organizations without some approval. However, she was likely free to work independently with county teachers on other initiatives that she outlined. For example, in 1918 she wrote to her teachers, "I know that you have entered into the year's work with an aim to make your school a community center and to use every educational force to encourage thrift, economy, and patriotism." [64] This effort at community organization was likely acceptable to local whites because the teacher presented it as an effort to promote in the black community values that local whites supported. As the Virginia state supervisor of black schools pointed out in 1919, "there is undoubtedly a very general feeling among the people that the splendid patriotism of the Negroes is deserving of some recognition and while financial limitations may stand in the way of our doing much that we would like to do, yet in increasing the efficiency of the work of this group of women we have a chance to make a very large contribution to the progress of the Negroes at a relatively slight increase of cost."[65] To the extent that blacks were allowed schools, local whites wanted blacks to take responsibility for supporting them and be happy with what was provided.

The teachers understood that acceptable forms of citizenship might be rewarded, though discussions about the meaning of economy or patriotism were largely left between the Jeanes teachers and the community. Most of the teachers recognized that their success depended upon writing reports that were similar to the example of Faison's 1913 letter. It was important to use language that was not just acceptable to southern whites but also seemed to promote the goals that the white community condoned for schooling. At the same time, the teachers also recognized, as did the state agents, that their reports were designed accordingly and did not necessarily reflect the breadth of community and education organization. The relative inattention of local whites made this possible. The relative isolation of rural black schools redounded both autonomy and power to the teachers.

The applications and reports indicated that these teachers could play a significant role in enhancing the organization of rural communities. Indeed, their work is a better indication of rural school administration than what might be illustrated by traditional measures. The state agents had recommended in 1929 that a stronger county unit of school administration and finance be developed with a formal program of general supervision of all schools in a county by Jeanes supervisors. "The desirability of connecting negro education with general education policies and procedures, which seems to have been the ultimate goal hitherto in mind, is given expression in this suggestion. Certainly in some of the states, probably all, this form of cooperation would now find favorable response."[66] By 1937, Floy Mitchum, the teacher in Spartanburg County, South Carolina, was able to organize a school-based health and safety campaign that resulted in a set of integrated services, including the county health department, local physicians and dentists, the highway department, nutrition workers, and extension workers focused on farm and home. As part of this campaign, workers inoculated preschool children, promoted dental work, added dental hygiene to the school curriculum, called on the highway department to stress safety, and enlisted the help of parent-teacher associations, with the aid of farm and home agents, to address a range of sanitary conditions.[67] These teachers were important leaders in their communities, not just by virtue of their role within the schools but also because the program itself created opportunities for the teachers to make formal connections between schools and government agencies.

The expanded role of the Jeanes teachers was also not lost on the foundations. The state agents explicitly addressed this issue at the 1925 state agents' meeting: "Originally . . . their purpose was largely to relate the Negro home a little more closely to the Negro school, to help instruction, and to teach simple industries. Now in some instances these teachers are used largely to direct the Negro school system of the county. [This] raised the question of whether or not the Jeanes county teachers had departed too much from their original work . . . to take on the work of county school administration for Negro schools."[68] The subsequent discussion revealed that the state agents found this to be a desirable outcome because the teachers, "even when given direction of the whole Negro school system, were rendering invaluable service in selecting well trained teachers, holding worthwhile teachers' meetings, promoting a building programme, and otherwise improving the school spirit among the Negroes in the counties."[69] Indeed, applications for Jeanes Fund aid, often filled out by the teachers themselves and then signed by superintendents, were clear about these expanded roles. One teacher noted that she would "encourage the standardization of schools. Encourage more efficient teaching and a definite community cooperation."[70] It was clear that effective teachers were important to foundation goals and to the success of the state agents. In fact, their work was essential to the extensive collaboration that foundations sought and facilitated the development of stronger local governance capacity. The teachers could help to integrate the work of multiple agencies at the local level, and to foster a positive relationship between the state-level office and both rural black and white citizens.

Teacher reports indicated the difficult community politics that they faced in their work. The teacher in Telfair, Georgia, detailed her three greatest difficulties: "Getting children to attend school regularly. Majority of children without books and no way to get them. Getting parents to see importance of schools and cooperate." At the same time, she had accomplished a major change in the teaching force, having administered a test that allowed her to replace the teachers who scored in the lowest third with certified teachers. However, the teacher was also getting significant pushback from the community. She explained that she was attempting to "break up former community factions by calling the patrons together and allowing them to elect their trustee board. And we are also prohibiting a teacher to work in a school where a close relative is a Trustee. This, we hope, will give us better patronage and cooperation from the patrons at large."[71] An advantage to greater standardization was that the standards provided Jeanes teachers the legitimacy they needed to restructure communities and schools. However, they had to tread carefully.

Teacher efforts to collect and share data about local schools were important to foundations and useful to rural black communities. The development and implementation of new policies required extensive data, which was in line with the scientific giving that characterized the twentieth-century foundations. Foundations collected information on every detail of the southern program, including successes and failures by state and locality, by state agent, by individual Jeanes teachers, in teacher-training programs, and in school-building construction. However, weak administrative structures at the state and local level, as well as a lack of state reporting requirements across the South, inhibited data collection in the early years. The Jeanes teachers could provide information about local areas. For example, teachers who organized Rosenwald School Day programs to raise funds and advertise the schools to the broader community, were required to "score" their schools on a set of measures that included school grounds, buildings, equipment, and organization, and then mail the information to the state department of education within three days of the celebration.[72] In a circular letter regarding a Jeanes conference in 1918, a state agent asked teachers to be prepared to make a three-minute presentation that included the number of schools in the county, length of the term, number of schools visited, churches and homes visited, community leagues organized, and amount of money raised.[73] Of course, these platforms provided an opportunity for teachers to share important information, particularly the gross inequality of rural black schools, and develop working relationships with field agents who participated in regional conferences.

For local teachers, data collection was not particularly difficult because of their extensive efforts at community organizing. These teachers had opportunities to meet with a majority of parents, visit homes, and develop organizations that reached large numbers of local citizens. Most teachers reported organizing parent-teacher associations, mothers clubs, homemakers clubs, girls clubs, boys clubs, and other types of agricultural clubs. The summary of reports for 1914–1915 in Georgia noted that in nineteen counties comprised of 533 schools, the Jeanes teachers visited 1,588 homes, formed 101 parents clubs, and organized 1,020 girls into canning clubs and 563 boys into corn clubs.[74] The Jeanes teacher in Leake County, Mississippi, recognized the value of these groups when she responded to a question about the "special things" she had set out to do during the year and noted the "organization of people in the various communities into groups."[75]

While the foundations promoted industrial education in rural black communities, national vocational-education programs benefitted that cause. One form of vocational education included agricultural-extension work, which provided agents to rural communities to disseminate information about best practices in rural farming and increase revenues through better farm productivity in both black and white communities. Increased revenues might result in a bigger tax base and help local governments to raise the funding necessary to create schools.[76] The GEB was instrumental to the development of agricultural-extension programs that would be funded through the US Department of Agriculture, and facilitated the passage of the Smith-Lever Act in 1914, which helped to disseminate information through publications and practical demonstration, and reflected shared ideals about rural reform between the government and the private sector.[77] The Smith-Lever Act supported the use of extension agents throughout the South, and the Jeanes teachers often served in these positions, paid an extra month or two of salary beyond the school year for the work. A primary task was to organize agriculture clubs and homemakers clubs, which would ostensibly promote agricultural and industrial training but actually enabled teachers to extend their reach into the homes of all members of the community, where they might develop shared ideals about community life and education reform, and raise considerable funding for school improvement.

Government-funded extension work expanded the role of the Jeanes teachers and augmented the Jeanes budget, cementing the teachers more deeply into the community and contributing to the important role that they played in subsequent decades. The federally funded programs reflected increased attention to the political concerns of the populist coalition and was reflected in the country life movement and Roosevelt's Country Life Commission. The commission provided an early opportunity for the federal government to respond to agrarian interests, which increasingly influenced politics, particularly in the South. Indeed, federal promotion of agrarian policies like extension work and vocational education, especially in cooperation with foundations, provides an interesting illustration of the overlap between political coalitions active in agrarian reform.[78] Such programs, generally designed for white communities, reflected a conscious effort by the executive and legislative branches of the federal government, and southern politicians, to be responsive to rural concerns. This work was easily extended to the South's homemaker clubs in rural black communities because southern whites perceived them to be another form of industrial education. As Senator Smith, for whom the Smith-Lever bill was named, explained, the fund "not only furnished farm demonstrators and aided the boll-weevil fight, but by its use boys and girls canning clubs were formed."[79] While most states were unwilling to hire more than a handful of black extension agents, early Smith-Lever funding was used to provide additional remuneration to Jeanes teachers in states like North Carolina to support the creation of agricultural and homemakers clubs in rural black communities. The teachers were often paid for an extra month or two beyond the school year for this work, though clubs were organized year around and in a self-defining manner.

The overlap between the development of federal extension programs, the GEB agenda, and the Jeanes agenda made sense at the time given the interlocking directorates of the philanthropies and their influence. The GEB had completely funded the US Department of Agriculture extension work prior to 1914 and then provided $155,275 for homemakers clubs in southern states between 1914 and 1919.[80] In 1916, the director of the Jeanes Fund expressed appreciation to the GEB for the "great extension work which has been made possible by the donation from the General Education Board."[81] While federal law prohibited the comingling of Smith-Lever funds with philanthropic funding in 1919, the GEB agreed to continue funding homemakers-club work and replace Smith-Lever funding in North Carolina, which it did until 1922.[82] However, by the time the federal government prohibited either federal or GEB funding for the program, extension work for the Jeanes teachers across the South was institutionalized in both practice and policy, and the teachers continued to use club work as a primary form of community organizing throughout subsequent decades.

Agricultural and homemakers clubs helped to promote an expansion of the education system in rural communities. For example, while matching funds for foundation gifts were often procured from private donations, clubs provided a formal organizational means to both sell agricultural goods and reach out to rural families. The teacher in Lutie County, North Carolina, reported in 1918 that she had enrolled 3,622 mothers and girls in clubs, and had visited 246 homes. The teacher in Brunswick had organized 5,566 into clubs and had visited 464 homes. In total, North Carolina teachers reported visiting 8,347 homes that year and raising $12,575 for "School and Home Improvement," specifically as part of the homemakers-club work.[83] The teacher in Pender County reported that she had enrolled one hundred members in her corn clubs "at some places money raised for new schoolhouses, painting, etc."[84] Once matching funds contributed to a school being built, terms being extended, or teacher salaries being raised, it would be hard to take away these additions to the infrastructure. In this context, the amount of money provided to or raised within the black community might be significantly less than that in the white community but have relatively greater impact. For teachers who received funding from federal programs, it was also an early indication that perhaps the federal government might be enlisted in the future to address the needs of southern black communities.

The benefits of this work, however, transcended merely raising revenues. The superintendent in Beaufort County, North Carolina, said of the 1917 club work that "by no means the least benefit derived is the spirit of cooperation and confidence aroused among the folks."[85] The teacher in Lowndes County, Georgia, reported on club work in 1917 and connected it to broader goals:

"We have accomplished more in our Club work this year than ever before. We are trying to complete two buildings before our Fall term begins, one one-teacher school and a Central Training school."[86] Over time, these clubs took on more than just industrial work. The teacher from Bamberg County, South Carolina, reported on club work in 1937: "Improved attendance in all schools—has been one of the aims of the year. The Mothers' Clubs, many of which are affiliated with the State Women's Federation, have given their cooperation to this goal."[87] Reports long after federal involvement ended indicate that club work was essential to the provision of integrated services in rural communities where both cooperation and coordination helped to alter the political landscape.

The teachers capitalized on the opportunities for community development made possible by these programs. When local citizens coalesced around rural and industrial-education themes, these groups also could enhance literacy, share news, and promote more academic endeavors. In Noxubee County, Mississippi, the teacher reported that thirty of sixty-three county schools had been visited, and "at the homemaker club meetings, newspapers are read and reports made."[88] Health and homemaking not only brought the community together, the endeavors also promoted education and linked the community to values beyond local concerns. Like voluntary organizations, these school-based clubs were nonprofit, provided mutual aid, regularly enacted rituals stressing shared values and identities, and performed genuinely civic functions in that they participated in public occasions, in support of education and community service, and in legislative and policy campaigns.[89] The clubs helped the teachers to extend their work beyond schools and into the community.

Teacher reports make clear the important role that teachers could play over time in promoting community consensus with regard to black education and progress. The majority of reports from teachers highlight the connection between schooling and community organization. Their work might be centered on schooling, but schools would be a vehicle for reorganized communities. That work brought teachers in contact with the majority of local families and provided a platform to promote education ideals. In Dale, Alabama, the teacher was expected to help with the organization of schools and engage in club work, "thereby working with teachers, parents and pupils."[90] Most job postings stated explicitly that community organization through schooling was a central duty, and many mentioned that this would afford the opportunity for teachers to be not just in schools but also in homes. Of course, this reflected paternalistic white concerns that black communities needed to be managed, and for many whites this was simply an effort to promote cleanliness. Yet, schooling was the institutional site from which to achieve such a goal, and black teachers who were eager to advance progress in their communities were asked to carry out the task.

Teacher work evolved over time in ways that made schooling central to the community. A teacher in Elmore, Alabama, planned not just to supervise classrooms but also to organize the PTA and direct "all phases of community activities."[91] By the 1930s, these teachers were much more explicit about the scope of their work in terms of promoting shared ideals and community goals. One teacher was clear that the development of such shared goals was important to progress and discussed her plan to "develop a dynamic philosophy of education on the part of supervisors and teachers to promote child growth."[92] The teacher in Surry County, Virginia, wrote a lengthy report on her work that included plans to provide hot lunches and enlist the help of local health agencies in schools. She also added that in honor of Negro History Week, she had organized one-act plays that raised money for both the local teachers' association and a donation to the NAACP.[93] This was clearly not a foundation objective, yet the teacher's role as community organizer provided an opportunity to promote a political cause, one that clearly represented shared community goals, and she felt no concern about sharing it with the state agent or her foundation benefactors.

Community development that was outside the boundaries of industrial education could only be accomplished if the teachers had some degree of autonomy. That autonomy was possible both because of the structure of the position and because white supervisors often articulated that they lacked both time and interest in providing greater oversight of the work. When Virginia Randolph was appointed as the first Jeanes teacher in Henrico County, Virginia, in 1909, she wrote extensive reports to the Virginia state agent and to James Dillard as president of the Jeanes Fund. In 1915, she discussed her progress in the county, as well as the problems that she had with one of the fund's field directors, Arthur Wright. "I wish you only knew the true condition of things and every superintendent would look after their supervisors and Mr. Wright's position would be abolished."[94] Randolph recognized that the fund required field agents because so little attention was paid to local work. She bristled at the field agent stepping in, perhaps because the superintendent had given her more autonomy. Her note also indicates a direct line to the foundation. Beyond those structural advantages, even if interested in teacher work, local white superintendents were not likely to participate in their community enterprises. When the state agents met for their annual conference in

1929, the South Carolina state agent reported that effective teachers should have particular traits, including common sense and sound judgment, the initiative to formulate objectives, the executive ability to carry them through, and effectiveness at keeping government authorities informed of school needs and requirements.[95] State agents wanted teachers who would take responsibility for notifying the white superintendents who likely paid little attention to their work, which implied a lack of general oversight or assistance.

At the same time, federal and state agencies utilized these teachers to support a range of causes. State agents recognized that collaboration with Jeanes teachers would redound important local benefits, which both bolstered the teacher's role in the local community and made the state's agents work indispensable to numerous governmental agencies. The North Carolina state agent was explicit in his 1918 letter to teachers. "Organize in every community where possible clubs of girls and women in groups of ten to twenty, and urge food producing and food saving. . . . [This] may help next fall in organizing many permanent Leagues for the promotion of all phases of real community work—schools, health, food, better homes, war-work, etc."[96] Teachers worked with parents through parent-teacher associations, cooperated with health and welfare departments and with home and farm demonstration agents, and assisted with state and national campaigns.[97] For example, the state of North Carolina had appropriated funds in 1922 to address tuberculosis in black communities. While the amount provided was not sufficient for a twelve-month campaign involving the cooperation of multiple state and local agencies, the state board of health used the funding to pay for an additional month of salary to each of the state's Jeanes teachers.[98] One year after the work commenced, the supervisors had "reached 311,005 by word of mouth; distributed health educational literature to many thousands more; given illustrated lantern slide lectures to 15,000; raised $5,253.13 in the seal sale and established the Modern Health Crusade in a number of colored schools in each county, enrolling a total of 16,500 crusaders since September, 1920."[99] The report concluded with a statement extolling the campaign's success. "You will be interested to know that the deaths from tuberculosis among the negroes have declined 21.4 percent in the last two years, according to reports of deaths sent the Bureau of Tuberculosis."[100] Effective teachers could mobilize groups for a range of social policy initiatives that also included vaccination campaigns, the war effort, and other goals determined outside of the black community. However, community building was a dynamic enterprise, providing a platform around which citizens could come together, at the same time that it provided opportunities to share information and exchange ideas. The Jeanes teachers' work in community healthcare and social work outside the classroom, and specifically their work with the homemakers clubs provided important opportunities to effect social change.[101]

Faison's report that he had held a fair to showcase industrial education to Anson County blacks resembled reports from almost every teacher in the South who regularly organized community events. However, while industrial education might have been an explicit agenda item at these events, fairs or commencements also served a larger purpose. A teacher in Georgia reported that she had "successfully brought [teachers] together in frank discussion of their problems in a series of monthly meetings, which culminated in field day and joint commencement. These features brought together trustees and patrons and also marked the beginning of county wide interest in schools and their problems."[102] Most teachers organized commencement exercises and other school-based venues that would promote community organization, while showcasing black accomplishments for local whites. In Alabama in 1916, "Little fairs and exhibits were held in many communities, to which the public, both white and colored, came. The co-operation of leading white people has been no small factor in making the club work a decided success."[103] These organizations promoted rural uplift and community cooperation, which promoted successive change, even though the work was presented in the context of industrial-training initiatives. While this created strict parameters around the behavior of the black community in policy settings, it also provided them with opportunities to engage within and beyond their communities.[104]

While rural blacks had no access to local party organizations, they could sometimes develop instead cooperative ties between community school-based organizations and the state agents and private agencies that might promote their needs. The existence of public-private collaboration between philanthropists and southern states provided important opportunities for rural blacks to participate in policy development, often circumventing the local political structure. It was not uncommon for rural black citizens to initiate arrangements directly with northern foundations and their agents. The archives contain many examples of rural black citizens and teachers who corresponded directly, which in turn provided access to state education organizations. One incident from Mississippi is particularly instructive as reported by the state agent for Negro schools. The newly elected state superintendent of schools in 1935 had little experience with rural black schools, "knew practically nothing about them . . . [and] for months had not time to get out and visit Negro schools. . . . At once, a group of Negro leaders in the State were contacted. It was suggested to them that they ask for a conference with the new

State Superintendent at the Vicksburg Negro school. . . . The State Agent and the State Superintendent and his wife . . . [visited] the Field Day exhibit of the Jeanes teacher of that county . . . [and] . . . became enthusiastic in his support of the Negro work. The following year he arranged for State funds to be given to the counties as a part of the salaries of the Jeanes Teachers."[105] A black resident in Center Cross wrote to the Virginia state agent requesting that a county training school be established, and the state agent contacted the superintendent there to initiate reform, the result of the letter and accompanying petitions.[106]

In another example, the Alabama Rosenwald Fund agent reminisced about his experiences building schools. He recalled a visit to the town of Bexar, a small village with almost two hundred black children in Marion County. The residents there "represented a class of old settlers left over from slavery days, and they had made but little if any progress at all educationally or otherwise. Some of them had never seen a state man or one who represented the 'higher ups' as they called us." He was able to persuade them to try to build a school with the help of the Rosenwald fund, in spite of them being "at a loss when we told them they would have to raise seven hundred dollars. That sounded like a million to them."[107] However, they were successful in their efforts, and a county training school was established. Their relationship to the field agent led to the development of a local school that would prepare teachers for the area, and the agent's encouragement that help would come from outside of the county inspired them to raise the money necessary for the school.

The foundations required matching funds, which were to be provided by both local taxes and private donations. However, the Jeanes teachers were quite successful at raising those private contributions at the local level. Almost every report from the Jeanes teachers to state agents and foundations included information about how much money had been raised for school improvements. For example, in the 1919 summary of reports from Jeanes teachers in nine states, almost every entry included examples of fundraising in black communities. In Mississippi, a teacher reported that "most of the schools are injured by storms and should be condemned," but "money is being raised to establish a county training school."[108] The state agent in North Carolina reported in 1916 that rural black communities in the state had raised a total of $15,293 that year for school improvements, in addition to contributing labor valued at over $6,000.[109] Rural blacks often paid property taxes and then made private donations for services that the taxes should have supported. The unjust tactic of double taxation to prove "Negro self-help" was grossly unfair but was also encouraged and managed by the local Jeanes teachers because the money contributed in significant ways to both building and sustaining community infrastructure. As the infrastructure grew and public sentiment toward education evolved, it would be more difficult to take away these gains. As one GEB report stated, "It has been the policy of the Board gradually to withdraw support of activities in public education after having demonstrated the value of these activities, and to let the public school funds assume the support of such activities."[110] Matching funds that were provided through both taxes and donations created an additional revenue stream, managed by the state agent and the local Jeanes teacher, which helped to ensure that the agenda of the black community would become institutionalized. Over time, as the organizational capacity grew, the ability of local partisan politicians to limit the development of educational opportunities for local blacks might decrease.

In Pickens County, South Carolina, the Jeanes teacher described the process by which a Rosenwald school had been constructed. She explained that she had been reading a Christian index journal and noticed a headline: "'Better Rural Schools.' . . . Where Mr. Julius Rosenwald was deeply interested in Better Negro School buildings and would give dollar for dollar in the erection of modern negro school buildings. [sic] I wrote him immediately for further information. He referred me to Mr. C. J. Calloway, Rosenwald's Agent. . . . From him I received all needed information. Filled with encouragement I began to advertise my project. . . . I tried to organize a school improvement association. I succeeded with three men and four women. The men were afraid to venture, so I had to assume all the responsibility. I bought two acres of land at a cost of $50.00. With my school-improvement association we planned a school rally and raised $62.00. This paid for the land, which was encouraging."[111] This teacher was able to bypass the local government structure and work directly with foundation agents to extend the school term and promote minimum salaries for teachers. Once the community donated funds, and there was some agreement from philanthropists to provide a budget, it would be difficult for the county to deny the extension or revoke it at a later date, thereby institutionalizing the goals of the black community.

The last example also underscores the gender dynamics, where women were often more successful in organizing schools because they were perceived as nonthreatening by local whites, especially given their role within the context of schooling. As the example illustrates, this point was not lost on the black community. Some local whites may have been interested in expanded educational opportunities for rural blacks. However, as we have seen, white reformers and superintendents often wanted these teachers for reasons that were anything but academic, and often perceived that these community-based organizations had little power. Yet, the foundations knew that the teachers were instrumental to reform. The GEB acknowledged after just a decade of Jeanes teacher appointments that if support for the Jeanes program was withdrawn, the "building of new schoolhouses, the improvement of teachers, and school improvement activities would be seriously hampered . . . it is more than a coincidence that the sixty percent of the counties of the South ranked by state agents as strong in negro education have Jeanes agents . . . and that an examination of the map of the southern states shows that in sections of the South where Rosenwald buildings are thickest, Jeanes agents in considerable numbers are also found." [112]

While foundations and their agents recognized that local teachers were instrumental, they were also aware that the teachers often had an alternative education vision for their communities. Most reports from Jeanes teachers were quite explicit about industrial education, noting progress made in promoting the curriculum in rural communities and the extensive club work that was organized to promote it. Industrial education, however, could be used to organize rural families, especially through club work that both created networks within and beyond the community and helped to raise significant sums of money for school improvement. The intangible benefit of reporting primarily on industrial education is that it ingratiated rural black communities to the broader political structure. Teachers may have supported and promoted industrial education, though it is possible that they omitted significant information in their reports about academic work, especially in the early years of these appointments.

Because of the lack of oversight of these schools, it was unclear how pervasive the industrial curriculum was, even in schools overseen by experts who were paid with philanthropic funds.[113] Hollis Frissell was clear about this issue in 1899 when he warned members of the Conference for Education in the South that many institutions in the South were "industrial" in name only, while devoting themselves primarily to a classical education.[114] In a fully segregated school system where local whites, even those involved with schooling, often cared little about black education, it is unlikely that there was significant, effective oversight of the curriculum in rural classrooms.[115] The GEB had notified state superintendents in 1914 that the state agents ought to focus on improving the underlying conditions of rural schools, rather than directly supervising them. States were encouraged to get the agents involved in organization, taxation, length of schools terms, salaries, and the training of teachers.[116] These state-level initiatives rarely included oversight or supervision of local schools.

The state agents acknowledged in 1923 that their own jobs had become significantly more complex. For one thing, state agents had become institutionalized within many state departments of education, bringing greater bureaucratization and all of the work that can come with that transition. In addition, the scope of the state agents' work had grown as the program for southern education evolved so that agents were supervising broad initiatives like building programs and state standards. They recognized that it was important to visit schools personally as often as possible. However, "several of the agents confessed that they had done very little to find out about the teaching that was actually going on in the class room."[117] The Jeanes teachers and the organizations that they established ended up having considerable control over what actually was taught in the schools.

In a set of 1919 reports from across the South, teachers discussed industrial training in almost every entry while simultaneously including information that implied that it was not pervasive. In Mitchell County, Georgia, the teacher reported that there were forty-seven schools, and twenty that included work in industrial training.[118] In this example, similar to others across the South, it appears that at first glance there was real progress in implementing a foundation-driven curriculum. However, in reality less than half of the schools participated, and, for those that did, it is not clear what it meant to "include work in industrial training." The GEB visited various Mitchell County schools and noted concern regarding the curriculum. "One of the schools had no industrial work, and at least two of the schools are teaching Latin. . . . A loom was found still crated in one school, and in another school no use had ever been made of the loom provided. It appears that no one feels charged with the duty of giving these schools very close supervision."[119] In North Carolina, the state agent for Negro schools conducted observations of both the Smithfield and Stonewall Training Academies. He pointed out that at Stonewall the phonics drills were "very good," and spelling was "well taught," and the subjects of history, geography, arithmetic, and civil government were taught, but also noted "as yet this school has very little equipment for industrial work."[120] At Smithfield, he observed similar disciplinary studies and industrial training that included cooking, sewing, and laundry work for the girls. He also reported, however, that the school should implement "some definite industrial work for the boys."[121]

The state agents met at a conference in 1925 and discussed the curriculum differences between black and white schools. Each of them reported on whether the standards in their state differed between schools for blacks and those for whites. Some recognized that there were disparities but attributed them to funding differences. Only two states, North Carolina and Louisiana, reported that the number of people who worked for the state department was sufficient to supervise high schools that were developing in black communities. Mississippi was explicit about the differences between black and white schools, but seemed not to find it problematic. The state agent reported, "Negro high schools had a different course of study, but this course had been made by the Negroes themselves."[122] As later chapters will illustrate, Mississippi took no responsibility for overseeing high schools in general, or rural black schools specifically, and abrogated responsibility for developing standards to the state's universities.

Foundations and other reformers expressed concerns that black teachers were of very poor quality in the South, and these concerns were generally overstated. However, the issue illustrates the complicated nature of education reform in the South. State standards defined in terms of industrial training promoted an unequal system that not only affected what was taught but also what teachers would be paid. Indeed, teachers like Faison who were trained with a more classical curriculum had to agree not to explicitly build on that work and, instead, wear the mantle of an industrial educator, which certainly brought less prestige and lower standards for certification, making it more difficult to argue for greater equality or even to teach it. Yet, there were teacher shortages in many areas, and a successful campaign for universal education extending through high school would dramatically increase the population of enrolled students. A demand for more trained teachers was generally a valid cause.

Teacher certification was important to the standardization and rationalization of a comprehensive public school system but could not be implemented without training programs that ensured that rural black teachers would qualify. Many of the highly qualified black teachers had been trained in private academies, perhaps like Zion, but many of those were shut down or absorbed into the public school system in the early twentieth century. Many southern states did not have state normal schools to train black students, and those that did had an insufficient number of slots. Foundations promoted teacher-training programs and encouraged states to develop standards with regard to teaching. Both objectives promoted new layers of bureaucracy and formally connected rural black teachers to the public system. However, while the early agenda of the foundations did not explicitly promote high schools for rural blacks, it did promote teacher training in county training schools, summer schools, and through the work of Jeanes teachers.

The foundations promoted the creation of county training schools that would educate future teachers. As the earliest high schools for rural blacks, these schools were formally under the supervision of the county superinten-dent. However, the supervision and ultimate responsibility fell to the state agents and Jeanes teachers. Many counties supported the schools because they brought with them foundation funding for industrial education that might lessen the local burden and placate the black community. In order to receive funding for such a school, the county had to provide adequate funding to lengthen the school terms, raise teacher salaries to a minimum, and adhere to requirements around curriculum and certification. Those counties that had such schools were required to meet these minimum standards and de-velop a bureaucracy that ensured oversight and community support. As such, decisions to create a training school with foundation support could also bring measurable changes to the infrastructure. The Jeanes teachers were essential to achieving these goals in counties that had such schools, and these schools played an early role in teacher training and in expanding the public system.

A relatively less expensive method for teacher training was a network of summer schools, typically taught at normal schools throughout the South and funded by the GEB, student fees, and local contributions. Industrial training was a centerpiece of the curriculum, but the schools did far more. For exam-ple, the 1919 Statesboro Summer School in Georgia reported forty-four teach-ers from the county, thirty-one teachers from neighboring counties, six from other parts of the state, and one from out of state, with five instructors. The curriculum included "methods in grammar composition and reading methods in elementary and advanced arithmetic."[123] The Waynesboro summer school in Georgia, for seventy-seven teachers with eight instructors, noted that many of the teachers subscribed to educational magazines for the first time because they were encouraged to do so at the school.[124] In Monroe County, Georgia, the summer school utilized the Georgia Teachers Manual as an outline for the eighty-five teachers enrolled.[125] Finally, the Morehouse Summer School in Atlanta had 406 teachers and twenty-one people instructing these teachers, and along with the standard industrial curriculum also included French, US history, educational measurement, primary methods, observation, and child psychology.[126] These schools, especially when offered at institutions that attracted teachers from across the South, like Hampton or Tuskegee, were essential for standardization in two important ways. First, teachers received similar and consistent training in content and pedagogy. Second, and more importantly, the summer schools promoted the development of teacher networks across rural, county, and state boundaries. The Jeanes teachers participated in these summer schools and then trained their county teachers by example and encouraged their participation in future programs.

Foundations recognized that Jeanes teachers were important to teacher training and extended their work through state-level elementary or rural education supervisors. Many states appointed Jeanes teachers and foundation field agents to state-level positions. For example, Kentucky employed a black man to supervise the teaching in the high schools, and North Carolina employed two men to work with the county training schools. Georgia appointed a state-supervising Jeanes teacher beginning in 1919.[127] Mississippi was not enthusiastic about creating a state-level position to oversee the efforts of the Jeanes teachers but did appoint one teacher in 1923 to supervise primary work like cooking and sewing in the county training schools across the state, an easier job given that so few of these schools existed.[128] The Rosenwald Fund asked Mississippi to create a position in 1930 for an "Elementary Supervisor of Negro Schools" and offered to finance it on a fifty-fifty basis, though the state had little interest.[129] In 1932, the state appointed Florence Alexander with GEB assistance.

Annie Holland's story is illustrative of the possibilities that might exist for black educators working within foundation-based programs and the ways in which schooling could connect rural black communities to the state. Holland originally had served as a Jeanes teacher in North Carolina and was promoted to state supervisor for elementary schools for the Division of Negro Education, responsible for visiting schools and supervising Jeanes work in rural communities.[130] She developed state policies for black teacher certification and school accreditation that were more academically focused. Foundation agents promoted standardization and bureaucracy to strengthen black schooling by connecting it more formally to the broader public school system.[131] Foundations appointed black agents who could influence policy decisions, including W. T. B. Williams, a field agent for the Jeanes Fund; Clinton Calloway, first director of the Rosenwald Fund; George Davis, Rosenwald Fund field agent in North Carolina; Florence Alexander, state Jeanes supervisor in Mississippi; Helen Whiting, state supervisor in Georgia; and Annie Holland.

The archives in many southern states, regardless of whether such state-level appointments existed, present evidence that expectations for black education became more consistently aligned in the early twentieth century with academic training and greater standardization around teacher training, efforts that were strengthened by the bureaucratic structures that developed through foundation programs implemented by local teachers. By the 1930s the agents required teachers to be more involved in efforts to standardize teaching. In Sylvania, Georgia, the superintendent specifically noted that the Jeanes teacher would be required to visit schools and to produce "reports on teachers."[132] By 1935, the teacher in Telfair County, Georgia, reported that her most essential achievement related to staff changes in the teaching force. She had "made an unbiased study, through observation and personal contact, of each individual teacher in and out of the classroom. At the end of the term we gave a county exam, on seventh-grade level, and the incapable ones inevitably fell in the lowest third. We plan to replace these with certified teachers."[133] In Aiken County, South Carolina, the teacher reported that one objective was "to use the State manuals in teaching," and the Barnwell County teacher reported that district group meetings were held, attended by members of the state department of education, and resulted in using state manuals that "are proving most helpful."[134] The teacher from Charleston County made even greater progress, organizing her teachers into six groups called "Elementary Progressive Study Clubs," which were studying bulletins of the Elementary Manual Series, and in Florence County the state had sponsored group meetings in which bulletins from the Elementary Manual would be used.[135]

Foundation efforts increased state bureaucracy for teacher training and certification and led to a significant increase in black certified teachers in the South. These efforts would not have been successful in rural black communities without the work of the Jeanes teachers. However, the programs that helped to standardize curricula and create minimum standards for teaching did not lead to a centralized system with authority vested in foundations or states. Instead, greater standardization in a system working toward greater centralization provided teachers with a platform to exercise authority, at least in the short term. This was especially true for Jeanes teachers who served as the primary administrator in many rural schools.

CONCLUSION

Foundations worked in the South to develop administrative capacity at the state and local level and promoted top-down initiatives, which lend some support to class-hegemony critiques of philanthropy. However, foundation programs also included space for more dynamic relationships with local communities. In fact, the foundations could not implement programs at the local level without those relationships. This had important implications for interest-group agency and its relative power in policy development. Philanthropic goals may have been national rather than local in scope, but their implementation at the local level was a basis for both policy and political development.[136]

While many rural black communities sough to retain control over their local schools, both public and private, the Jeanes teachers also facilitated an expansion of public schooling, including greater centralization. The information available in applications for these teachers, and in reports from both teachers and state agents, indicates considerable overlap between foundation and teacher objectives, even if the teachers simultaneously hoped to achieve something greater for their communities. Teachers were actively involved in school administration, school funding initiatives, teacher training, and curriculum development. Their role in each of these endeavors indicates the central role that they played in not just providing education at the local level but also developing an education infrastructure that, by extension, enhanced local governance capacity. Their work was essential to developing a state system of universal education that extended into local communities. These teachers also provided leadership and an organizational structure that was nonexistent prior to the position.[137]

Like Faison, many perceived that this strategy would bring both personal and community benefits. While the South can be defined by its localism, schooling helped to link rural blacks to the political and social structure outside of their communities, helping to overcome the extent to which the local nature of the political system, especially in education, has often worked to the detriment of racial equality.[138] The more that black schools became part of the public sphere, the more likely it was that the public sphere and its institutional arrangements could be transformed.[139] Schooling provided opportunities for community organizing, expanding political opportunities, and the development of shared cognitions about education among members of the black community, factors that are crucial to the more formal insurgency that would later develop.[140]

The existence of a successful Jeanes teacher contributed to the establishment of translocal networks that connected rural schools to education leaders outside of the community who could collaborate with local schools to promote reform.[141] However, foundation programs could extend these networks to more formal connections between local communities and governance systems. Southern whites perceived that industrial training defined the organization of black schools. As such, the organizational repertoires of schooling were considered nonthreatening and were often supported by southern whites.[142] Jackson Davis, acting as field agent for the GEB, was asked to describe the accomplishments of the Jeanes teachers: "They succeeded in organizing the people into school community associations and bringing to bear the united sentiment of the community in favor of better school buildings, longer terms and more practical work in the schools by introducing simple industries. . . . The schools lost their isolation."[143]

The concept of "agency" can be defined along a continuum that includes anything from subtle forms of resistance to group insurgency.[144] However, black teachers were able to engage with the organizations that were developed in local areas, and in doing so exercised agency more broadly defined. Their work helped to establish centralized administrative capacity in the lower tiers of government. It is not possible truly to understand black agency in the South without understanding the institutional venues in which it operated. Schooling helped to make political opportunity structures more permeable. The actions of individual reformers were important, but school and foundation programs connected local schools to the broader political structure.

While foundations had power but no political authority, rural black reformers had neither. However, the organizational capacity created in the form of schooling became an important venue for organizing at the local level and negotiating the reform dynamic. It expanded the participation of local interest groups, allowing rural black reformers to participate in the creation of an education infrastructure, and not always in ways that philanthropists expected, even if these efforts took place within strict parameters defined by white supremacy. The amount of latitude these teachers had vis-à-vis the state varied both within and between southern states. It would be an overstatement to claim that blacks were able to mobilize in a significant way during this time period. However, at the local level, black reformers were able to organize more formally when reform was school based and assumed to be in the context of industrial education. This provided rural blacks with relatively greater opportunity to participate in discussions about education policy and to promote their own vision for education reform as part of a broader group of political actors with competing visions for change. However, that participation differed significantly by region. As subsequent chapters show, states such as North Carolina developed stronger administrative structures while others, such as Mississippi, did not. These differences affected not only education development but also the ability of rural black teachers to participate in policy development in both the short and long term, sometimes in ways that were unanticipated by representatives of state and local political systems, as well as by foundations and their agents.

CHAPTER THREE

"There Are at Least Two Souths"

By 1919, almost every southern state had appointed a state agent for Negro education, and counties throughout the South had appointed Jeanes teachers and undertaken Rosenwald school campaigns.[1] Yet, there were significant disparities with regard to education progress that persisted throughout the first decades of the twentieth century. In 1927, the GEB ranked the fourteen southern states in the provision of rural black education. The highest seven states in the South, in order of their composite ranking were Maryland, Oklahoma, Kentucky, Texas, Virginia, Tennessee, and North Carolina; the lowest were Arkansas, Florida, South Carolina, Louisiana, Mississippi, Georgia, and Alabama.[2] The foundations also produced more detailed reports that highlighted variation between counties within states and indicated that inequality at the local level could be accounted for by the "unequal distribution of wealth, poor systems of taxation, and improper distribution of school funds . . . white public sentiment on the question . . . the presence or absence of Negro school leadership, and, in some sections, the measure of economic dependence of the Negro."[3] Each of these variables affected education reform but, taken together, indicated the political context in which northern foundations worked. In general, foundations sought to create an education infrastructure and developed an array of state and local programs to achieve it.[4] However, the form of those programs and the ability of these alternative governance structures to accomplish meaningful and sustained reform required engagement with state and local governance systems. Ultimately, North Carolina politicians actively sought collaboration, while Mississippi politicians did not.

By the end of the nineteenth century, many states across the nation were promoting stronger public school systems with greater state and county oversight.[5] Foundations hoped to bring the South more in line with these national trends, but each southern state presented a unique context. Most southern states had no developed public school system at the end of the nineteenth century. The South had been relatively unaffected by the common school movement in the early part of the century because interest in public schooling was generally shaped by white supremacy and particularly by the experiences of slavery, the Civil War, and Reconstruction. Most southerners were committed to states' rights, local control, and preservation of the racial state. Philanthropists had been promoting public education in the South beginning with Reconstruction, and many states considered legislation to expand schooling. However, many southerners after Reconstruction remained deeply suspicious that institutions based on northern ideals would lead to greater taxation, a loss of local control, and might be detrimental to white supremacy. Efforts to expand southern education during Reconstruction and after were abandoned when Jim Crow became the southern norm. Reformers from both the North and the South, concerned about the South's economic and political development, recognized the need to promote a public system of education that would be separate and unequal. Southern politicians and reformers who embraced education reform recognized that foundation funding would be important to the cause. However, many southerners were not enthusiastic about the cause.

Foundations provided funding for state agents in almost every southern state, appointed Jeanes teachers wherever counties welcomed them, and developed plans for schoolhouse construction across the South. However, the foundations also tailored programs to fit the needs of each state and locale and to fill the policymaking voids that resulted from a range of contextual reasons, including white supremacy, lack of political will, weak administrative systems, and inadequate finances. These contexts defined the collaborations that would develop between northern foundations and southern states, and the differential power of foundations, state and local politicians, and even private citizens. Interstitial collaboration is more than just an organizational structure joining governmental and nongovernmental interest groups. It includes the range of programs, the strategies to overcome the strict parameters on education expansion in the South, and the relative power of interest groups and institutions. Foundations integrated political actors from a range of institutional and organizational affiliations, who could work within and parallel to existing governance structures to promote new education policy. Those structures varied considerably by state and influenced foundation success and, by extension, the growth of administrative capacity in state and local governance.

Most of the groups engaged in southern reform recognized the differences across states and local communities and sought to tailor plans accordingly. For example, the work of the Commission on Interracial Cooperation exemplified the associated action between foundations and other interest groups. It was organized to confront white supremacy, including lynching, but was also an important tool for the foundations, which funded the work. The commission organized committees—in each of the states and in eight hundred of nearly 1,200 southern counties—composed of education reformers that included the state agents for Negro education.[6] In addition, the commission also established close relations with church groups and prominent clergy, business leaders, college groups through conferences of professors and students, and "strong state committees of women, all in positions of influence and leadership in their respective civic and religious groups."[7] The commission fostered collaboration and better communication between the two races without confronting the racial state.

In 1922, the commission reported feeling discouraged by its inability to work in some areas of the South: "There are at least two Souths. In the upper South, including Virginia, Kentucky, Tennessee, North Carolina and South Carolina, there has been no opposition to the commission's activities. . . . Oklahoma and Texas resemble more closely the lower South—Georgia, Florida, Alabama, Mississippi, and Louisiana—where progress in promoting better race relations is very slow. . . . In a few communities of these lower states, the work has met with open hostility."[8] The decision to designate states according to their place in the "upper south" or "lower south" makes sense, given that the report indicated a correlation between location and reform, but is insufficient for understanding regional differences and the relationship of foundation work to education reform and political development. Most people would likely perceive that the majority black populations across regions of the Deep South profoundly affected politics and race relations in that region, while the upper South's demographic patterns and proximity to the North made it relatively more progressive on issues of race.

North Carolina and Mississippi represent obvious extremes in the two regions. It is outside the scope of this book to do an exhaustive history of both North Carolina and Mississippi. At the same time, important characteristics of each influenced the role northern foundations would have in each state's education development. At the beginning of the twentieth century, both states were predominately rural and committed to white supremacy, states' rights, and local control. Further, state and local governance systems in both were administratively weak and dominated by one-party rule, leading to an education policy void for rural black communities. These states were also different from other states within their regions, owing to industry, political leadership, and regional politics. There was a demarcation between the "Upper South" and the "Deep South," but for reasons that were far more complicated than the distance between any state and the Mason-Dixon line. Indeed, the differences between North Carolina and Mississippi were greater than the similarities but more nuanced than such a simplistic designation suggests. For example, the Mississippi River had a significant impact on the political divide in Mississippi between the plantation owners in the Yazoo-Delta region and small farmers throughout the state. Differences within regions could provide an important dimension to understanding political development in the South at the level of individual states. However, a comparative study of North Carolina and Mississippi provides an opportunity to understand in greater depth how those differences affected education reform, political development, and foundation efficacy.

One factor that had considerable influence was the nature of the plantation economy in a particular region. The plantation economy was related to geography, and the pattern of these large agricultural economies determined regional demographics and influenced politics.[9] Plantations were not just large slaveholding farms but also agricultural centers that included significant capital investment, an emphasis on a particular commercial crop, significant landholding, a large labor force, and careful centralized management.[10] The largest segment existed in a crescent that began in the Delta region of the Mississippi River and extended east through the Deep South and then up into the North Carolina Piedmont. The plantation economy was related to geography but not merely geographic, and the pattern of these large agricultural centers determined regional demographics and influenced politics.[11] The planter class in these regions generally sought to retain economic and political power through lower taxes and limited government.

In those states with a large number of plantations, primarily in the Deep South states like Mississippi, black citizens were in the majority in many regions. The plantation economy was instrumental to the strength of Jim Crow, and a primary concern was maintaining control over the southern black labor force. Most whites within it believed that providing anything more than rudimentary, industrial education to rural blacks would upset the racial state. However, many planters also wanted a class of laborers who would be content enough not to migrate out of the region. Hence, planters were not necessarily opposed to collaborating with foundations to provide limited educational opportunity to rural blacks. Again, there were differences within groups about the role that education should play in the South, and it is not useful to make sweeping generalizations about foundations, southern whites, or rural blacks. However, state context influenced the views and relative strengths of disparate groups. It affected foundation influence and defined interstitial collaboration.

This chapter considers the context for education reform in North Carolina and in Mississippi, and considers both the general attitudes of politicians and citizens regarding race, education, and economic progress, and each state's administrative structure, including tax legislation for schooling. While the consensus established at the Conference for Education in the South led to the general goal of universal education supported through public taxation, in the two subsequent decades foundations developed particular programs to achieve those goals for every southern state. By 1920, the main contours of the southern program existed in every state, including state agents, Jeanes teachers, and Rosenwald schoolhouses. However, in spite of these similarities, there were significant differences in foundation efficacy.

In North Carolina, the state called on northern foundations extensively to promote a state-defined vision of universal education. The state's education reformers played a prominent role at the annual Conference for Education in the South. This was not the case in Mississippi, where most politicians refused to cooperate and were noticeably absent from national discussions about southern education. Interstitial collaboration is clearer in these varied contexts. Foundations developed different strategies to implement their programs in each of the states in order to address gaps in state policy and practice with regard to rural black education reform. In North Carolina, public-private collaboration was extensive and effective at the state level. State actors sought foundation support to expand schooling and, with it, the administration of the state. Mississippi was a closed system where foundations collaborated more with foundation agents located in universities than with state actors and accomplished far less. The context in each state makes clear why different strategies were necessary, though ultimately ineffective at creating publicly financed state systems of education across the South.

BUILDING A PARTNERSHIP WITH NORTHERN
FOUNDATIONS: NORTH CAROLINA

Lautrec Cranmer Brogden, state supervisor for rural education in North Carolina, submitted a report to the General Education Board (GEB) in 1913 that provided a detailed account of his work in both the state department of education and the field. He attached an addendum to the report that specifically addressed progress in the creation of new tax districts and the consolidation of schools.[12] That same year, the state appointed Nathan Newbold to be the state agent for Negro education with the hope that he would extend Brogden's work into rural black areas of the state. Both men reported to state superintendent of education James Joyner, who had been working closely with the foundations since his appointment in 1902. Reports from Joyner and the agents who reported to him reflected Joyner's belief that it would not be possible to serve all of the students in a community without a stronger administrative system supported by a local tax base. Those goals defined work in North Carolina's Division of Public Instruction.[13]

Indeed, Joyner had helped to formulate an education agenda in North Carolina that embodied the consensus reached at annual meetings of the Conference for Education in the South. This included a series of school and tax campaigns that were partially funded by the GEB and the Southern Education Board (SEB). This was the beginning of decades of extensive and collaborative foundation support of North Carolina education initiatives beyond that provided to other states. The state sought foundation assistance in developing almost every aspect of its education vision and that collaboration continued for decades.

North Carolina's relationship to northern foundations began formally in 1901 during the tenure of Governor Charles Brantley Aycock, infamous for his views on white supremacy. His openness to northern participation in addressing the state's problems set the stage for decades of deep collaboration. Aycock's gubernatorial campaign had benefitted from the 1898 elections, in which Democrats had taken control of the state senate and passed both a constitutional amendment that disfranchised black voters through literacy tests and the first significant Jim Crow law requiring separate seating on trains and steamboats.[14] In his campaign, he pointed out that his predecessor, Republican governor Daniel Russell, had won the office in 1898 with the votes of 125,000 blacks who had "put him in office over the votes of the *white* men," with the result that "negroes became intolerably insolent; . . . ladies were insulted on public streets; . . . [and] burglary in our chief city became an overnight occurrence." According to Aycock, it was "the negro behind the officer, and not the officer only, that constitutes negro government."[15] He demanded disfranchisement as "necessary because we must have good order and peace while we work out the industrial, commercial, intellectual, and moral development of the state."[16]

Aycock's campaign for white supremacy might have looked quite similar to such campaigns across the South at the beginning of the twentieth century, but the policies that resulted were different in important respects. He was also known as the "education governor." He took seriously his quest to improve all aspects of state development, and universal education for all citizens was central to his overall goal for economic progress, even if it was conceptualized and promoted in the context of white supremacy with an unequal education for black and white citizens.[17] Aycock explained in his inaugural speech that "wealth increases as the education of the people grows. Our industries will be benefitted; our commerce will expand; our railroads will do a larger business when we shall have educated all the children of the state."[18] Aycock was also explicit that his goals included black students in the state. His speeches were filled with references to racial differences, yet the language about education typically referred to the "whole people," because industrial development required intelligence, "not just of the few, but of all."[19] In a speech that focused on promoting racial peace, Aycock proclaimed, "I am brave enough to sacrifice my own popularity—my future if need be—to the speaking of the rightful work and the doing of the generous act. I have therefore everywhere maintained the duty of the State to educate the negro."[20]

There was a clear irony in Aycock's support for black education because it came at the same time that the state completely disfranchised its black citizens. Indeed, the expansion of schooling both to accommodate higher enrollments and additional grades often required a local tax levy that could only be approved through the vote. It is possible that Aycock believed that his speeches might placate black citizens who considered leaving the state in response to recent laws supporting disfranchisement and hoped that the reality of black schooling would never match his rhetoric.[21] However, suffrage laws in the state also created political problems for the governor because North Carolina had the second highest white illiteracy rate in the nation. If the state disfranchised black citizens with a literacy requirement, it would need to ensure that whites would retain the vote. He was explicit about this issue in his speeches to the state legislature. Aycock assured voters across the state that he would address their concerns through expanded educational opportunity, but he understood that reform required an extensive campaign, additional funding, and broad political support. He easily won the election by advocating white supremacy, black disfranchisement, and public education for both races, but had to figure out how to deliver all three and solidify democratic rule in the state. He included in the campaign for public education the men who were active in the Conference for Education in the South, many of whom were state allies who continued to promote education for both races for decades after Aycock left office.

Aycock called upon the foundations to help him achieve his goals. His interest in education was part of his broader vision for the political development of North Carolina; it was a vision that dovetailed with the views of northern philanthropists and conference reformers. The fact that North Carolina sought foundation support is significant given southern attitudes and politics at the beginning of the twentieth century, where sectional interests, often defended in terms of states' rights and commitment to local control, were strong determinants of policy development. However, the state zealously embraced the idea of the New South championed in speeches and editorials by Henry Grady, editor of the *Atlanta Constitution*. Grady called for the South to exist "not through protest against the Old, but because of new conditions, new adjustments and, if you please, new ideas and aspirations."[22] Politicians and businessmen in North Carolina were expansive in conceptualizing political and economic aspirations, including a willingness to work with public and private funders from outside of the state. Aycock's education vision developed in this context and was shaped by a set of characteristics that influenced the state's relationship to northern largesse.[23]

North Carolina agriculture and industry was determined by its geography, which in turn created demographic patterns that were distinctive from those in the Deep South. The state borders the Atlantic Ocean and has a large tidewater region that was known for tobacco and cotton production and was the location of a majority of the state's plantations. Moving west across the state, the tidewater becomes a coastal plain, and then the Piedmont region, extending nearly three hundred miles across the center of the state with moderately fertile land. The western part of the state is mountainous and rich with timber, with far less land devoted to agriculture. The black population was quite large in the plantation regions of North Carolina, which included the east coast and sections of the Piedmont. Though slaveholding was prevalent in the Piedmont by the start of the Civil War, the relative size of the farms and individual slaveholdings was much smaller than in the eastern part of the state, with its large tobacco plantations. In the western counties, a significant portion of the black population had migrated out by the beginning of the twentieth century.

While slave labor and the tenancy that followed were essential to agricultural production in regions of North Carolina, the plantation ruling class was both smaller than that of other southern states and represented more diverse business interests. Like many of the southern states in the late nineteenth century, North Carolina experienced economic hardship when the worldwide price of cotton declined precipitously and farmers faced crop devastation brought by the boll weevil. However, unlike many southern states, North Carolina addressed the problems with relatively greater success. Many farms continued to produce cotton, but farmers on the coastal plain switched to tobacco farming. Southern states had to redefine the relationship between agricultural production and labor after the Civil War and, like many states, tenancy arrangements became the norm. In North Carolina, these arrangements accounted for 45 percent of farming units, and the average size of a farm unit decreased by more than half.[24] The arrangements were designed to favor landowners and maintain their power over the labor force, but in North Carolina many tenants were relatively better off than those in other southern states. They suffered economic hardship and the oppression of the racial state, but fewer migrated out than in other states.[25]

North Carolina planters were relatively successful at diversifying business interests around the agricultural unit. For example, plantation owners invested in textile mills beginning in the antebellum era and then after the Civil War, reaping significant profits by the end of the nineteenth century. In fact, the Piedmont was strategically located for textile production, with railroad access to markets, waterpower, and cheap labor. Owners of cotton plantations in the state recognized the possibilities and constructed forty-nine mills by the 1880s.[26] Similarly, the owners of large tobacco plantations, like the Dukes, invested heavily in tobacco manufacturing. In addition to business growth in these agricultural domains, investors also promoted the furniture industry, capitalizing on the hardwood in the west and conifer in the east, and built more than a hundred furniture factories in the state.[27] By the early twentieth century, the state had moved from harvesting cotton, tobacco, and lumber to full-scale production that vertically integrated operations.

While outside investment was frowned upon by many southerners, including those living in North Carolina, many of the state's planters and politicians recognized that their aspirations depended upon it. Mill owners initially tried to minimize the use of external capital, but this became increasingly difficult. The cotton-mill campaign in the 1880s centered in the Piedmont and led to additional investment by northern entrepreneurs, especially from northeastern cotton-mill owners.[28] However, the state was also attractive to investors given its close proximity to northern markets, a more advanced transportation system, waterpower necessary for moving agriculture from harvest into production, and a more cosmopolitan outlook that promoted education and urban development. Industrial growth resulted from state policies that consistently promoted business.[29]

Industrial growth also required an infrastructure that would support economic expansion. Efforts to improve the state infrastructure through road construction provide solid evidence of the New South successes of state reformers. The state was predominately rural at the beginning of the twentieth century, with about 90 percent of the population living in rural areas, mill villages, or towns of less than 2,500 people. Reformers and industrialists were devoted to the development of a transportation system. The amount of railroad track increased from 891 miles in 1860 to more than 3,650 by 1900.[30] In addition, the Southern Good Roads Association boasted a large North Carolina membership through regional associations and published a bimonthly periodical in which North Carolina efforts and successes figured prominently.[31] Association members successfully lobbied the state general assembly to create a state highway system through gasoline taxes and auto licensing fees managed by a state highway commission.[32] With the assistance of federal funds and the use of convict labor—an idea that originated in North Carolina but spread throughout the South—North Carolina built 7,680 miles of hard-topped roads by 1925.[33] The roads connected the eastern and western parts of the state and opened markets with the North. These accomplishments were essential not just for economic development and the diversification of industry but also to state building.[34] The progress further developed the state's relationship to northern capital.

The Republican Party had remained relatively powerful following Reconstruction, and their strength was buoyed by the popularity of the National Farmer's Alliance, which claimed more than ninety thousand members in the state.[35] The national leader of the alliance, Leonidas Lafayette Polk, was born in North Carolina, where he also became the state's first agricultural commissioner. The People's Party, which developed from the alliance, recognized that it could have power only with the support of sympathetic Democrats or blacks in the Republican Party. While the People's Party developed a fusion ticket with Democrats on the national scene, in North Carolina's 1894 and 1896 elections, fusion took place with Republicans.[36] As such, state politics in the 1890s developed in a context of greater compromise, relatively greater openness to black participation, and probusiness ideals that tried to address populist concerns.

Conditions existed for education reform to take root in North Carolina, given the desire for industrial and economic expansion, connections to northern industry, and the nature of partisan politics. There had been interest in developing a system of public schooling after the Civil War, but the local tax structure that developed was not sufficient for addressing rural needs, the result of poor economic conditions and a reluctance to impose taxes in a region opposed to the creation of state bureaucracy and central control. However, the fusion ticket between populists and Republicans promoted education reform in 1895 with more aid to public schools, an increase in statewide property taxes for education, larger appropriations to county commissioners for local schools, and elected rather than appointed boards of education.[37]

The 1895 assembly also assured eastern counties with a majority of blacks that the elected county commissioners could manage the election of sheriffs, appoint deputies, and supervise police affairs. Some scholars have described the racial caste system as relatively more "laissez-faire" than that of the rest of the South between 1870 and 1901, when the last black congressman in the South lost his seat in North Carolina, and have attributed this to a more diversified agricultural economy and a relatively smaller and unique plantation economy.[38] These factors might have shaped relatively progressive attitudes about public education and economic expansion, albeit within the context of a grossly unequal racial state. However, in spite of the possibilities, education had remained a local matter in the state, and by 1900 few educational institutions existed for either blacks or whites. Further, the political landscape that had allowed blacks to retain citizenship rights beyond that of other southern states began to unravel.

The Wilmington Riot in 1898 made clear that in spite of fusion, there were important differences between the Republican Party and the People's Party with regard to race relations. The depression of 1893, the farmers' revolt in the mid-1890s, and then the 1898 riot shaped the populist impulse in the state and created an opening for a return to white supremacy. It also propelled the state toward the kind of "New South" development that scholars like C. Vann Woodward would deplore, in which economic success was achieved in the context of better and more just paths that were not taken.[39] Aycock's campaign for white supremacy was a direct attack on the Republican Party, and populists sought distance from the Republicans on this issue. Aycock spoke of the amendment that disfranchised black citizens as one that proceeded along "wise lines" because it demanded sufficient intelligence for voting, whether gained through inheritance or education, but "requires of the negro the qualification by education because he has it not by inheritance."[40] He believed that a separate education should "find all of the strongest and best in competition one with the other until the fullest power of each shall be developed. In doing this, we shall get the largest contribution to society [and fill] each man full according to his capacity, whether that be much or little."[41]

Education reform evolved from the perspective of white supremacy and was influenced by the state's connection to outside money and northern markets, but was distinctive because it was developed by a group of public intellectuals who were well versed in social-scientific theories of the time about race and progress.[42] Aycock spent his formative years at the University of North Carolina at Chapel Hill, where he had been close to a number of men who were instrumental in state education reform throughout the late nineteenth and early twentieth century, including Charles McIver, James Joyner, and Edwin Alderman.[43] These men were part of a broad current of "selectionist" reformers, who used a statist approach to governance that celebrated the role of educated leaders in determining and reproducing those parts of society that would drive national progress.[44] They were committed to white supremacy, state expansion, and public education. However, their views about white supremacy were somewhat more progressive than reactionary, and deeply paternalistic. They believed that universal education was the right of all citizens, the key to promoting the kind of competition between societies and nations that would promote progress, and important for evolutionary purposes. Their ideas resulted in beliefs about black education that were complex. Blacks were inferior, but a strong public system of education would ensure that each reached his or her full potential, which would in turn contribute to the state's prosperity. Their focus on the relationship between education and progress coexisted with a more insidious belief that a neglect of black education would cause the "child race" to degenerate even further and potentially bring degradation to whites.[45]

The North Carolina reformers were white supremacists, but their views translated into education policy that was generally more inclusive. McIver's correspondence regarding Aycock's education reform initiatives is illustrative:

I am also sure that North Carolina is not going to put herself in the attitude before the world of depriving a race of its vote on the ground of illiteracy and ignorance and then upon the heels of that pass another amendment which looks toward keeping them in illiteracy and ignorance. A state has a reputation to sustain before the world of states exactly as a man has among his fellowmen. . . . Ignorant and illiterate negroes and white people not only will not place her where she belongs but they will make it impossible for men who live in the state to get their just recognition in the forum and markets of the world.[46]

They did not believe that education for whites and blacks should be equal, but they agreed that state progress required that education be extended to all.

The group of North Carolina reformers was influential in both national discussions about education reform and in developing state initiatives in the late nineteenth century. They worked together to establish graded schools in rural communities throughout the state, participated in a campaign for greater state aid, sparked a debate about the role of the state, and spoke to fundamental disagreement about local control and the role that education should have in the changing economy.[47] Many of these men also participated in the Conference for Education in the South, which included more members from North Carolina than other southern states.[48] While Aycock's gubernatorial term lasted only four years, the connection he had to other reformers who remained influential in the state and in national discussions about education ensured that his universal education vision continued.

The 1902 conference featured a report on progress in North Carolina from Dr. Charles McIver, president of the State Normal and Industrial College in Greensboro and one of the state's principal education authorities. He was also the newly appointed district director of the Southern Education Board, where he remained active until it disbanded in 1914. McIver focused particularly on the need for local taxes, and underscored his belief that any outside campaign to improve the schools should be undertaken in cooperation with the education authorities of the state. He explained that newly elected governor Charles Aycock had given "hearty endorsement to the movement" and expressed "appreciation of the spirit in which the Southern Education Board desired to aid in [the state's] educational development."[49] North Carolina reformers helped to shape the agenda of the conference and the formation of the SEB and the GEB.[50] McIver called on participants to recognize that members were "serious minded citizens who perceive the difficulty and the majesty of Republican citizenship, who really love their country throughout all its length, and who count it the glory of good citizenship to seek to translate ideals into institutions." Indeed, he related national ideals to local work, recognizing in particular that teachers in the modern state would be a "social force, the philosopher and friend of legislators and politicians miraculously turned statesmen."[51] North Carolina reformers believed education central to state progress.

Aycock's theory of white supremacy was insidious and hateful, but its intellectual roots distinguished him somewhat from other race-baiting politicians in the South.[52] North Carolina reformers drew on early anthropologists to define African Americans as a "child race," which lagged behind whites but was not doomed to extinction. They believed evolution and social reform were linked.[53] As a result, they made a case for black education that was based on "ethics, class interest, and soft eugenics," believing that with industrial training and guidance into proper competition, the race could progress.[54] Aycock's early education initiatives developed from the consensus reached at the 1901 Conference for Education in the South, and he spoke the language of conference reformers and foundation representatives when he was in their presence. Members of the SEB were enthusiastic about Aycock's vision, but also believed that the state might be pushed to do even more than what Aycock advocated. The SEB recognized the state's limitations and the problem of Aycock's virulent white supremacy. They wanted black citizens to participate proportionately with the whites in schooling but recognized that any attempt to compel such proportionate participation would in all probability defeat foundation efforts and limit the expansion of black public school education.[55] This reflected foundation beliefs that education reform could not be unilaterally imposed on the South. At the same time, North Carolina was a willing partner in promoting education and a stronger state.

Northern businessmen, including those who were involved in developing the large foundations that emerged at the turn of the century, joined New York City business magnate Robert Ogden on his famous Pullman railroad tours that took place annually between 1901 and 1906, The 1901 tour, which included a number of stops in North Carolina that preceded the annual conference to be held at Winston-Salem, displayed a landscape of both poverty and promise in the state. Aycock, who had recently been elected governor, took advantage of the 1901 visit and was particularly eager to showcase the state's industrial potential and seek outside funding for his efforts. Further, his views on education were particularly compelling to northern businessmen, many of whom were participating in the railroad tour as part of the annual conference. These men recognized the potential in Aycock's vision, especially reflected in the success of wealthy and powerful industrialists in North Carolina like the Dukes, who were originally plantation owners but had joined the "captains of industry" who defined American industrialism in the late nineteenth century. Aycock toured his state with Ogden's group, was the keynote speaker at the 1901 conference, and addressed the group again in 1902.

Aycock promised the foundations that he would increase funding for public schools, reorganize the offices of the state superintendent, and strengthen the authority of the state by requiring that county boards of education report to the state superintendent and accept his interpretation of the school law. When Aycock took office, there was a limited and ineffective administrative structure, making it difficult to pursue sweeping changes.[56] Aycock wisely perceived that foundation support would help the state to create stronger governance structures, essential to his vision for both economic and educational development. He eagerly courted the northern businessmen, appealing to their interest in the role that education might play in promoting a stronger state.

Aycock's speech at the 1901 conference was compelling and instructive. The opening to his speech appealed to reformers' nationalist beliefs and extolled North Carolina's place in the union. "It was in this state that the first battle was fought against British tyranny. It was in this state that the first Declaration of Independence was written. . . . This state was one of the last states to leave the American Union, but when it did leave it was first to offer the sacred blood of its sons upon the altar of our country, and it laid down its irons last. . . . It is our Union, it is our country; we are one people, in purpose, and in high aim, and in noble aspiration, one in a settled purpose."[57] He called upon members to join him in a new era of education in the state, in which every girl and boy would have an opportunity to be educated; he enumerated the state's educational progress and then called on the conference to assist with putting schoolhouses into every rural district in the state so that no child, white or black, would remain illiterate. Aycock's speech was followed by a resolution that passed unanimously to make education "the foremost task of statesmanship," achieved through better school systems throughout the South.[58] In spite of his southern roots and support for states' rights, Aycock's views reflected national ideals about universal education, and his particular initiatives, beginning with the appointment of the men who would serve in his administration, pointed toward greater centralization at the state and county level and increased standardization of schooling.

The following year, Aycock addressed the conference again and called on members to engage local communities in reform: "The real work of this Conference is to be done in the rural districts, where you have got to go to the people because the people will not come to you." Aycock acknowledged that his program would be at great cost and understood that many citizens viewed taxation as a dangerous power, but he argued, "Taxation that goes for the upbuilding of the public schools is the very freedom and liberty of the people."[59] He recognized that the state's current tax system was prohibitive to the expansion of schooling. The state levied a general property tax that was applied based on a uniform and fixed rate, for which each county received its per capita share to support both local government and schools. However, the state also imposed constitutional limitations on the rate, making it difficult to raise sufficient revenues to support both state and local government, as well as the schools. School districts at the beginning of the century could vote for a local levy, or "special tax district," for additional support to the schools, but the general assembly also regulated local taxation by placing constitutional limitations on the state and county tax rate.[60] In addition, the state legislated a poll tax to be collected at the county level, designated for schools and the poor, and allowed counties to augment it with their own local poll tax as long as the total did not exceed constitutional limits.[61] The poll tax contributed a significant sum of money for public schooling, nearly one-half the amount in 1898. However, in 1896, one-half of black men over the age of twenty-one paid the poll tax.[62] This would decrease once disfranchisement laws went into effect under Aycock and exacerbate complaints from local whites, who resented their tax dollars going for the support of black schools.

Aycock was in favor of increasing local taxes. He explained to northern philanthropists that this was a better model than the benevolence of private donors because the southern people were proud. "We recognize that it would not uplift us if some kind-hearted people came along to pay for our instruction. . . . I have quit talking to the towns of our State—I go straight to the country, and I desire to impress it upon you that your workers should go to the country and stimulate the people to vote for local taxes for the public schools and help them in every way until the rural districts shall regain what they have lost and become what they used to be—the strongest part of this Southland of ours."[63] His comments indicated that he understood his vision might be a hard sell in local areas, and foundations might be effective where the state's politicians were not. His speech also made clear that he considered education reform to be a state responsibility, which might be supported by national ideals but certainly should not be directed there. He promoted those national ideals but retained his belief in states' rights, which was clear in his reflections on his conference participation: "We do not probably entirely agree, but we respect more than ever the opinions of each other. . . . Philanthropists in the North may think they can educate the negro without the help of southern whites, but they are mistaken. We favor universal education and intend to accomplish it. If our friends in the North, earnest men and women, choose to aid us in our work we shall receive their aid with gratitude . . . we need help, but we can do the work unaided and will rather than humiliate ourselves."[64] His presentation resonated with conference participants and appealed to foundations, which shared his interest in developing a public, tax-based system of education in North Carolina. In subsequent decades, it was the state that effectively called on foundations and not the foundations calling on the state to promote a stronger state and county administrative structure to provide oversight to a public system of schooling.

Aycock's education vision did not have the support of all or even many of his constituents. He made some progress because he based his arguments in white supremacy. When Charles McIver spoke at the fourth conference, he made clear that a call for universal education would not make all citizens "equally intelligent or cultured or skilled," because all children would not be educated alike but aided in discovering the work for which they were best fitted.[65] These men were clear that state progress depended upon an educated workforce and that included black citizens. Yet, Aycock's vision remained a hard sell to white political leaders in the state Democratic senate, who had been elected on a platform of white supremacy and black disfranchisement, opposed universal education, and politically maneuvered to block reform efforts. Many white citizens at the local level were also opposed to universal education and a more centralized state. Immediately following Aycock's election, opponents introduced several bills in the state legislature that would improve white schools at the expense of black schools. The most popular bill, and one that received unanimous approval from the state senate judiciary committee, was a constitutional amendment authorizing the citizens of either race in a school district to vote a tax upon themselves for the benefit of their own schools. Aycock threatened resignation if the bill passed, though he was more concerned about the possibility of the negative attention it would bring to the state than he was the fairness of the funding plan.[66] The state's reformers also recognized that the law might not be constitutional. McIver reported that Judge William Hoke of the state's superior court, who refused an appointment to the supreme court bench of North Carolina, did so out of fear that he might be called upon to rule on the amendment and hoped not to have to decide against the validity of the law.[67]

Aycock sought to canvass the entire state on behalf of education but recognized quickly that infrastructure obstacles would limit his efforts. The state was large, had no centers of population, and 80 percent of people were working in agriculture and widely scattered across inaccessible rural areas. The policy making void in North Carolina was the result of counties that refused to cooperate, a legislature that was not necessarily on board, a weak administrative structure, interest in local control, and fear of a centralized state. At the same time, many people in the state still believed in an unequal but universal education that would lead to state progress and were more open to using outside funding to achieve it. The SEB saw the potential for reform in the state and provided funding to support a campaign for public education.[68]

The SEB also had its own education-campaign committee, chaired by North Carolina reformer Dr. Charles D. McIver, who was experienced with the work. As a young teacher in the state, McIver had canvassed rural areas and helped to convert the Farmer's Alliance toward greater support of education. McIver suggested that Aycock convene a state conference, to which forty-three North Carolina educators were invited, to organize the state's campaign. One result of the conference was a "Central Campaign Committee for the Promotion of Public Education in North Carolina," which was led by Aycock, the state superintendent of education, and McIver.[69] Funding from the SEB ensured an office at the state capitol and an executive secretary to run the campaign using methods similar to those used by the foundations. A special committee was formed to furnish information to state newspapers, while another committee enlisted the help of every North Carolina preacher, who was asked to deliver at least one sermon a year on the subject of public education. Further, district conferences that included county superintendents, school officers, and other public-education employees were convened, with railroad fees for participant travel covered by the SEB.[70]

McIver was clear that broadly based cooperation within the state was essential to the campaign's success, which was "participated in by political leaders, educators, editors, clergymen, lawyers, physicians, businessmen and farmers."[71] The first conference included the presidents of the state public and denominational colleges, superintendents and public-school officers, and Wallace Buttrick, executive officer of the General Education Board, who proposed to match all private subscriptions for public schools in Guilford County with a matching gift from the GEB, as long as the local contributions took the form of a special tax levy.[72] Aycock never had the best interests of the state's black citizens in mind and certainly did nothing to promote greater equality for the race over either the short or the long term. However, by the time he left office, the state had agreed to increase every education appropriation and adopted all but one recommendation of the state superintendent of public instruction. This included additional staff in the state's office of public instruction, a more centralized process for schoolhouse construction that included a state loan fund, rural libraries, increased compensation and conference travel funds for county superintendents, and more favorable local tax laws.[73]

This work continued throughout subsequent decades. In 1918, Joyner wrote to the GEB to ask for funding to survey education conditions and needs in the state; he also asked for a grant of $2,500 to conduct a vigorous campaign for an amendment to the state constitution that would require state and county taxation to fund a minimum school term of six months for both blacks and whites and a special local tax to increase the salaries of teachers. Joyner acknowledged in his request that it was no longer typical for the board to appropriate for educational campaigns but also pointed out that he had personally requested the funds in a meeting with the head of the GEB and had provided documentary support for the campaign.[74] Joyner had regular access to foundation representatives and a long-term relationship to support his efforts. The board approved this funding. The legislative act that appropriated $1,000 for a statewide survey was augmented by the GEB with an additional $18,000 in funding and the staff necessary to conduct the work.[75] With foundation help, Joyner continued to make progress, with new legislation to support the expansion of schooling and additional positions appointed to the state board of education. However, it would be difficult to have an impact on rural black schooling when those schools were not connected in any meaningful way with the larger public school system.

Aycock's initial vision for universal education was developed in tandem with the annual conference, and support to realize that vision came in the form of intellectual and financial support from conference members, the SEB, and then the foundations. Aycock initiated foundation support, setting up decades of collaboration between foundations and the state. An important component of these collaborative efforts was more than financial in nature. The state also borrowed from foundations the organizational capacity necessary to promote extensive educational and administrative reforms throughout the early decades of the twentieth century.[76] Aycock's early efforts defined a relationship that would develop and deepen. Education reformers in North Carolina envisioned a comprehensive plan for universal education that was connected to goals for a stronger administrative state, ideals that mirrored foundation beliefs. While Aycock's tenure ended in 1903, the state continued to work with the foundations to alter fundamentally the nature of education and the administration of local communities. The state of Mississippi, however, would take a much different approach.

LIMITS TO FOUNDATION COLLABORATION: MISSISSIPPI

While James Joyner and the rest of his staff focused on promoting tax reform and stronger administrative structures in rural areas, and worked extensively with the foundations to achieve these goals, W. H. Smith, a rural school agent in Mississippi who was also on the payroll of the GEB, barely mentioned such initiatives. In fact, Mississippi did not appoint a state agent for Negro education until 1916, so Smith's interest in rural areas focused primarily on the needs of white schools. His 1914 report to the GEB merely mentioned in its concluding paragraph that he would promote community organizing at the local level that might, over the longer term, lead to consolidation, local taxes, and agricultural clubs. Smith's report indicated that the state would not take a lead role in promoting those objectives in any of the counties, white or black. Indeed, the state lacked the political will and administrative capacity necessary to promote most foundation initiatives, particularly those that would serve rural black communities. Mississippi politics prevented any meaningful discussion about rural black schools at the state level except to argue against providing it. The state failed to develop an education vision—beyond extending education where possible in white communities—let alone a comprehensive program for education reform in collaboration with foundations.

The SEB was clear in 1903 that, in Mississippi, "The influence of the University over the high schools has grown from no legal enactment but from an aggressive and tactful leadership in cooperation with the Teachers' Association and school officials."[77] As an alternative to state-initiated collaboration, foundations worked closely with faculty at the state's universities. Beginning in 1908 the GEB hired and funded Thomas P. Bailey, a professor of secondary education at the University of Mississippi who facilitated many of the early foundation efforts in that state. The appointment was similar to those that existed throughout the South to help formalize the relationships that developed between foundations, business, universities, and states in the early twentieth century. However, Bailey played a more prominent role. In a report on Mississippi high schools he explained that the schools were not standardized and typically existed as the upper grades of graded schools. Further, the state "has no high school Board, and the supervision of the high schools is entirely in the hands of the university; it is a matter of custom and not of law; nor does it seem advisable to increase high school machinery or to impose a system externally. I work with the principals in a personal way . . . work for the cooperation of all healthy educational agencies."[78] These early reports confirmed foundation perceptions that Mississippi had an education-policy void characterized by a lack of state interest and oversight. Foundations realized early on that collaboration would not necessarily include state political actors. As such, while collaboration might lead to improvements in education in particular communities, it would not likely result in a stronger state education system or, more generally, in a stronger administrative state. This fundamentally changed the form of collaboration between the state of Mississippi and northern foundations.

One incident illustrates the relative limits of public-private collaboration in Mississippi. In 1919, the university professor who had replaced Bailey, John C. Fant, reported that he was participating in a better-schools campaign that had been authorized by the Mississippi State Teachers' Association and asked the GEB to provide funding to support the campaign.[79] The foundation did not consider this a good investment, claiming that it had already provided sufficient funding to support men in the state who were engaged in education reform, including the professor and the school agents, and did not think it "wise for the Board to take any steps which might influence the opinion and action of the voters."[80] Their position was somewhat odd, however, given the board's extensive support of school campaigns in North Carolina. One reason for their reluctance was a series of 1914 congressional hearings in which members of Congress vigorously debated the appropriateness of public-private collaboration in the federal government after discovering that the Department of Agriculture had been receiving funding directly from the GEB for staff hired to engage in agricultural-extension services. The hearings, which took place just after the Ludlow strike in Colorado against Rockefeller subsidiaries, featured Mississippi senator John Sharp Williams. Williams supported private funding for vocational education in the form of extension services but also expressed the sentiments of many of his colleagues when he said it was "a very bad thing to get the employees of the Federal or of the State or of a city government in the habit of relying upon rich men and corporations for aid and assistance, because it brings around . . . a certain, perhaps dominating, influence upon the officials themselves that might be and probably would be finally detrimental to the public service or to self-respect and interest of the masses."[81] Because the SEB was not endowed as a foundation, there had been less political baggage associated with its earlier campaigns across the South, like those in North Carolina. However, the SEB had been absorbed into the Southern Education Foundation in 1914, and the GEB took subsequent responsibility for coordinating and promoting foundation objectives across the South. As such, the GEB may have perceived education campaigns in Mississippi to be a political quagmire. It is also true that foundation objectives changed over time, meaning that better-school campaigns seemed useful in the early twentieth century but may not have been considered as beneficial almost two decades later.[82]

However, the GEB was also involved in a range of campaigns and fact-finding missions in North Carolina at the same time that Fant requested the money. The foundation might have considered providing funding to Mississippi, and then defined the award in a way that addressed the delicate politics of outside influence. It was in 1919 that the GEB provided extensive funding and expertise to revamp the entire education department of North Carolina. A campaign for better schools in Mississippi that was initiated by the State Teachers' Association hardly seems a controversial cause, especially since it was a local effort rather than a foundation initiative. It is more likely that while the GEB needed men like Fant as part of an integrated program, state-driven initiatives were more in line with foundation goals and more likely to lead to longer-term benefits. The state legislature had not approved or initiated a campaign to improve schools, and the teachers' association ignored the issue of race. Further, Senator Williams's statements in the congressional hearings reflected a deep distrust in the state about collaboration with northern foundations. In fact, Mississippi had not participated in a meaningful way in the Conference for Education in the South, a move that weakened the state's connection to the national discourse on education and the reformers who promoted it. As such, foundations were present in Mississippi, but collaboration looked quite different. It involved a range of actors, but state and local politicians were not always at the table.

Mississippi politicians simply did not consistently aspire to the expansive conceptualization of New South development following the Civil War that North Carolina did. Because the state developed no related educational vision, it is not surprising that Mississippi was a less-visible participant in the Conference for Education in the South. While North Carolina legislated a state-education fund in the antebellum era, Mississippi made no provision for public schooling until Reconstruction, and its first real effort to expand public education took place only in 1890. While the state relied on county governance systems for tax collection, it was at this time that it formally recognized seventy-five separate school districts, reaching up to 20 percent of school age children in the state, that were funded by local taxes.[83] The state had less of a presence in many of the alternative governance structures that developed at the federal, state, and local level in the early twentieth century.[84]

Many Mississippi politicians considered men with New South perspectives to be traitors to a southern way of life, and the most virulent of the politicians who promoted a more traditional version of southern life had mentored James Vardaman, who was elected governor in 1904.[85] Mississippi politics and culture promoted demagogues like Vardaman and Theodore Bilbo who knew how to exploit the economic tensions between plantation owners and small farmers and between white and black citizens. The most divisive issues existed between those counties with a majority white population and those with a majority black one, leading to conflicts that had a significant impact on education reform. The politics of that divide shaped the influence of the plantation economy, and even transcended what it meant for Mississippi to be part of the "Deep South."

Mississippi borders three states, as well as the Gulf of Mexico to the south and the Mississippi River to the west. The river, which forms the border with Arkansas and Louisiana, is one of the state's important geographical distinctions. It is a powerful waterway, hard to control, and the cause of frequent and sometimes devastating floods. However, centuries of such flooding deposited a coating of rich alluvium, a fertile soil composed of silt, clay, sand, and gravel that resulted in the development of the alluvial plain commonly referred to as the Yazoo-Delta region. The rich soil in the region enabled crops to flourish and was especially conducive to cotton.[86] The state also has nine other major rivers, and more than a thousand lakes, ponds, and reservoirs.[87] Natural deposits such as petroleum, gas, gravel, sand, lignite, limestone, and clay can also be found in the state. Its mild climate, rich forests, relatively level topography, abundance of water, and fertile soil fitted it superbly for agricultural production. Such favorable conditions—and the high prices being paid in England for cotton at the turn of the century—led to the genesis of the Cotton Kingdom and made Mississippi, particularly the Delta region, the center of southern cotton production.

The Delta region was developed in the late nineteenth century by land speculators who recognized its agricultural promise and established large plantations and a large black labor force to clear and cultivate the land. A majority of Delta counties had a black population that exceeded 80 percent of the total at the turn of the century, and the remainder had a black population that was in the majority. Delta landowners amassed fortunes on the backs of black laborers and developed an aristocratic culture that redounded significant wealth and power to the region. Farmers outside of the Delta resented the successes of the planter class. Additionally, state politics often benefitted the Delta to the detriment of other regions. The region and its planter class dominated state politics throughout the nineteenth century by virtue of its wealth and participation in important political bodies, like the Mississippi River Commission.

The Mississippi River was good for agriculture, but it also posed an environmental threat that had to be managed. By the mid-nineteenth century, farmers in Mississippi, Louisiana, and Arkansas had been working to control the river's extensive flooding, which threatened New Orleans and the developing agricultural lands in the Delta. Engineering debates focused on whether a system of levees or one of more extensive floodways was necessary to tame the river. Federal legislation established the Mississippi River Commission in 1877 and provided some funding and oversight for levee construction within its mandate to improve the river. However, river control prior to the devastating flood of 1927 remained primarily a local matter, managed by county levee administrations that were often mired in self-interest.[88] An appointment to the regional levee board was important personally and politically. If managed effectively, it could redound significant benefits to individual planters and considerable wealth to the region through remuneration for legal work, construction, engineering, and other associated labor.[89]

The politics of levee administration contributed to the political divide between Delta planters and the rest of the state. Plantation owners on both sides of the Mississippi were distrustful of federal involvement but at the same time believed that the huge costs of managing the river should be borne by the federal government. Mississippi Delta planters recognized the pragmatism of federal involvement, which would be far more cost effective than local control. In fact, the planters were more open to outside money generally. Railroad investors promised to connect rural plantations to more cosmopolitan areas and to provide agricultural transportation that was safer and more dependable than the river, and planters were willing to bring in outside capital, both public and private, to develop the state's infrastructure and benefit the region.[90] The result was new railroads that connected Delta cities and provided them with transport to Memphis or New Orleans. The rest of the state did not enjoy the same benefits, which compounded anger in other regions toward the Delta's wealth and influence.

The self-interested and pragmatic behavior of the Delta aristocracy also manifested itself in their fight against the boll weevil, which devastated cotton crops throughout the South at the beginning of the twentieth century and arrived in the Delta in 1909. While the rest of the state was encouraged to diversify crops, sometimes to the detriment of reaping the benefits of a successful cotton season, the Delta planters chose to respond in their own way. They actively thwarted information campaigns intended to educate farmers about the boll weevil, fearing that such knowledge of the insect's pending arrival and potential for damage might drive away black labor that existed through tenancy arrangements.[91] A successful cotton-crop year in the Delta could result in significant financial gains for its inhabitants, and diversification of crops was considered too costly, regardless of the threat, because it would upset the labor market and turn fields away from cotton production. Instead, planters assumed that because the Delta was different than the rest of the state, the region would not be affected in the same way and would more easily weather the storm. Fortunately, against all odds, this gamble was successful. The Delta produced so much good cotton despite the infestation that it mitigated the disaster. Farmers in the rest of the state, however, who felt they had no choice but to collaborate with agricultural-extension agents who were funded through the US Department of Agriculture and the GEB to diversify crops, suffered. While the Delta continued to prosper, the rest of the state encountered economic uncertainty. Indeed, Cotton King success meant that farmers in the state, especially in the Delta, engaged in an annual chase for riches, were reticent to diversify crops, and had little incentive to invest in industry.

Any real effort to industrialize in Mississippi was unsuccessful before the Great Depression. While an isolationist attitude was a notable contributing factor, Mississippi did not attract industry as well as neighboring states for a multitude of other reasons. The state's primary natural resources were extractive, and sources of power were few and far between until the late 1930s. Further, the network of rivers and lakes were not conducive to hydroelectric power or transportation. Businesses that considered investing were reluctant to move families and businesses to a state that had no real urban areas, no conservation program, limited educational opportunities, a limited infrastructure with a lack of good roads, an ineffective governance structure, a labor supply in danger of migrating out of the state, and extreme racial segregation. Further, efforts to industrialize seemed unnecessary before the arrival of the boll weevil, and the state repeatedly failed to make effective use of outside investment.

The lumber industry, which was important to the state's economy, provides a telling example. Most speculators went into the state to extract timber but, after the trees were cut down, migrated out to other regions of the country. While North Carolina had built a furniture industry around their timber resources, and a corresponding forestry program, Mississippi did not use their own resources to integrate production from forest development to finished product. Tax programs may have contributed to the problem, over-taxing lumber mills up front in anticipation of their move out of the state, leading to a few years of labor and exploitation without responsible consideration of longer-term conservation and industry sustainability.[92] Thomas Bailey, the university professor appointed by the GEB in 1908, reported on the connection between lumber production and educational development in southern Mississippi: "What is to become of the country when the timber has been cut out? Agriculture and horticulture, say some. Evidently, but these industries are by no means keeping pace with the destruction of the forests. . . . In some portions of the pine belt, the land is poor and full of stumps, debris of trees, and honey combed with mud holes and swamps." He noted that the teachers in these areas typically migrated out to other regions, making it difficult to develop rural schools. He also recommended that a deliberate effort be made to "combine the industrial and educational forces of the state into a harmonious whole that shall re-make the state at once industrially and educationally."[93] However, lumber production in Mississippi reached its peak in 1925, and the state failed to sustain the industry through legislation.[94]

Mississippians were suspicious of centralized government and commerce, traditions that politicians expressed in the state's 1890 constitutional convention. The new constitution relied excessively on an elective system for government administration, divided power in ways that led to a diffusion of responsibility and a lack of common direction, grouped unrelated functions in one office with related functions scattered throughout independent boards and departments, and provided no mechanisms to coordinate state agencies. It led to an administration that was inflexible, inefficient, and wasteful.[95] These administrative issues made it more difficult for outside investors and foundations to conduct business in the state. Further, a series of laws severely restricting corporations, including the railroads, would have lasting detrimental consequences for both the state economy and infrastructure. Given the wave of industrialization that swept the country, industrial growth in Mississippi between 1890 and the Great Depression lagged behind other states; reports of a significant percentage gain appeared large only because it was built upon such a small base. Because the majority of workers were dependent on the soil, many viewed industrialization with extreme distrust and suspicion; it was a Pandora's box, or "an open invitation to disaster."[96]

The support for an agricultural economy, the general distrust of a stronger national or state governance system, fluctuations in the economy, and a fear of outside interests created a context in which it was difficult to expand public education at all, even if it included only white citizens. North Carolina linked state progress to national progress, and believed education central to both, but Mississippi's views were far less ambitious. Mississippi wanted economic prosperity, but did not explicitly link it to stronger state governance or enhanced educational opportunity. The state superintendent for education issued a biennial report in 1907 that included reports from each county. Almost every county superintendent lamented the lack of a state normal school to train teachers, insufficient funding, unequal school terms, and a lack of roads or transportation to end the isolation of small rural districts. Complaints about the poor quality of teaching highlighted the state's failure to develop teacher training and standards for certification and curriculum. The state superintendent made clear the limitations of public education in the state, noting that county superintendents were appointed by popular vote, served part-time, and typically answered to the demands of their white constituents. He requested the appointment of a rural school inspector for the thousands of white schools throughout the state, a minimum salary for county superintendents that would require each to commit to full-time service, a standardized course of study, and a state normal school. However, the report did not translate into new legislation. The superintendent from Hancock County told of an effort to use a school budget surplus to build schools, though the county board of education vetoed the effort and reduced the local tax levy instead.[97] State politicians, including members of the elected school boards, were eager to appeal to rural white voters, and education was often not a priority.

The state also failed to collect sufficient revenues to support a public system of schooling. Like North Carolina, at the beginning of the twentieth century, Mississippi's largest source of revenue was the state property tax, followed by the privilege-licensing taxes and the poll tax.[98] School districts received poll-tax revenues to support a legislated four-month term, and state property-tax allocations augmented that amount when poll taxes were insufficient to cover the school term, or when poll taxes were sufficient but residents wanted a term longer than four months. In practice, the poll tax was never sufficient to cover a legislated four-month term and always required significant appropriation from the state property-tax revenues.[99] While estimated revenues from the annual poll tax in Mississippi in 1897 exceeded $525,000, less than half that amount was collected, making clear that the tax was used primarily to disqualify black voters in the national elections and control local elections. A report on state taxation in 1900 made clear that "the poll tax is more important in the state as an adjunct of suffrage than as a source of revenue."[100] In addition, the state allowed school districts to levy taxes to continue school for a full session of nine months and counties to levy additional funds for a nine-month term for districts within their boundaries. However, like North Carolina, the state enacted revenue laws in 1898 that placed a limit on the total amount raised through local tax levies. In order for rural blacks to levy additional taxes, they would need not only to have the franchise but also to be part of a recognized school district. Unfortunately, Mississippi blacks in the early twentieth century typically attended makeshift schools and, without the franchise, did not pay a poll tax and could not vote on a local tax levy. It was a system that made it easy to exclude black schools from efforts to create a public system of schooling in the state. As one report made clear, "The separate school district law has given the opportunity for the development of good schools in the most favored localities."[101]

Residents of the state were particularly averse to increases in the property tax rate after their experiences during Reconstruction, when state and county land taxes, combined with the poll tax, led to the forfeit of over 6.4 million acres of land and an organized tax revolt.[102] Like many regions in the South, the county was the fiscal unit of the state beginning in the antebellum era, responsible for the collection and submission of all state taxes. An elected sheriff was responsible for collection and an elected tax assessor for the valuation of property. However, citizens believed that Reconstruction policies had been unfair, and the state strictly limited the rights of local elected officials to increase taxes beginning in 1876. Over time, these elected positions were believed to curry favor. Further, unlike many other states that relied on property taxes, Mississippi did not have a state board of equalization, which led to gross inequalities in property assessment from county to county.

While Delta planters were opposed to any acts that would threaten either their elite role in society or their independence, including greater taxes, control of labor, or a stronger government, they also recognized that labor control depended upon keeping the black community content enough not to migrate to other regions. As such, the Delta planters tended to advocate a minimal system of education for rural blacks. One report from Thomas Bailey to the GEB explained those politics in the Yazoo region:

> The lot of the Negroes would be far worse if the whites had not found that Negro labor will be more likely to be satisfied and not emigrate if fairly decent school advantages are given. The Negroes for the most part, are 'white men's Negroes'—polite, deferential, careless about their social and political status. As soon as the steep slopes of the city are properly graded and terraced, it will be found that the black population will be driven down to the river or some other undesirable part of the town. As a sort of a commentary on this situation, I may state that a Negro was lynched at Yazoo City last Easter morning![103]

In this context, education might be offered on a limited and grossly unequal basis to rural blacks, and with powerful detractors.

In Greenville, Mississippi, located in Washington County in the heart of the Delta, the school superintendent sought a few acres of land in 1909 in order to expand the school building and offer industrial training for blacks. The response of the trustees was indicative of white attitudes about the relationship between education and economic progress in the state: "That's all nonsense, Bass [the superintendent]—your [sic] trying to teach the negroes morality and industry through gardening. You are wasting your time. Of course, if you insist on it, we'll give you what you want; but nothing will come of it and it will be likely to rouse opposition."[104] At the same time, Bass persisted, perhaps because of either his own benevolence or recognition that a stable labor force required it. He had to tread lightly though because a local chapter of the Daughters of the Confederacy was "ever on the lookout lest Bass shall show too much 'unionism' in his school and, 'therefore' too little reverence for the Confederate cause and its sainted dead. Some of the members persisted in telling people that Bass intended to have a special celebration of the centennial anniversary of Lincoln's birthday."[105] While some Delta inhabitants may have understood the relationship between education and economic development, the context made overtures at reform exceedingly difficult.

Outside of the Delta, there was occasionally minimal support for rural black education. The superintendent of Laurel, which was located in Jones County and predominately white, had developed a plan for rural black schooling and, by 1928, more than $75,000 had been spent on the program, with about $23,000 provided by the city and another $60,000 provided through the private donations from the owner of the local lumber mill. While seven thousand blacks lived in Laurel, the mills would soon close down and leave many of them without employment.

> These negroes will drift to northern cities where they are not wanted. We understand the negro, and feel that he has had a part in creating our wealth and industrial development. We want to keep him because we are friendly to him and understand him, and as a matter of plain justice, we want to provide for his future. . . . Negroes can be settled in communities and with suitable direction and help will be able to make a most considerable contribution to our further development, which must now become agricultural. . . . We believe our purposes can be accomplished if we are patient, because, as you know, the negro is easily influenced and directed by people who understand him and are genuinely interested in his future.[106]

There were Mississippi whites who believed in limited education for rural blacks, because they had some sense of the long-term benefits, even if the state had never articulated an education vision. Poorer whites in the state, however, especially those who lived outside of the wealthy Delta region, resented that they did not share sufficiently in the state's economic progress and were against these efforts.

Southern demagogues like Mississippi's Theodore Bilbo and James Vardaman knew how to respond to the needs of the large, poor white voting bloc in the state. The white direct primary law in 1903 further disfranchised black citizens and expanded and empowered the state's poorer white voters. This was a powerful step in Mississippi because it undermined the strength of the Delta planters by extending political power to white farmers in other regions of the state.[107] However, a successful politician would need to appeal to that mass of white voters and bridge the regional divide. Men like Vardaman and Bilbo were successful because they made race the issue that could connect the state's disparate voters. They created a psychology of crisis from the persistent poverty, the boll weevil, and fluctuating cotton prices, and then vilified blacks as the cause of the state's problems.[108] Both men promised to address the race issue through strict disfranchisement, but Vardaman promised repeal of the Fourteenth and Fifteenth Amendments, and Bilbo the repatriation of black citizens to Liberia at federal expense. Both men appealed effectively to the passions and prejudices of the general electorate, especially poor whites in the state who might never achieve the economic success of Delta whites but could always count on their superiority to blacks.

Vardaman served as Mississippi's governor from 1904 to 1908 and as US senator from 1913 to 1919. He was enormously popular during the first two decades of the twentieth century, hailed as the Great White Chief and found at political rallies dressed completely in white as he launched his attack on black citizens. He goaded white citizens with campaigns intended to protect the goodness of southern white women and promoted a culture conducive to lynching. His campaign literature for his gubernatorial and senatorial elections demonstrated a commitment to the values of early twentieth-century progressive reformers, detailing his support for such measures as the eighthour workday, the Good Roads Act, and child labor laws. However, the campaign materials always called attention to racial issues, often in the opening line. "Don't you approve Vardaman's work in securing the defeat of the negro for Registrar of the Treasury?" began one publication, while another highlighted that he had "defeated confirmation of two negroes to important offices. Tried to defeat others" and had "separated white employees and negro employees in Washington."[109] His campaign literature also boasted his support for the Agricultural Extension Act, for which he explained that he "kept the disbursement of this money in the hands of the white people of Mississippi."[110] Throughout the early twentieth century, his views struck a chord with Mississippi voters and brought him enormous popularity.

Vardaman also boasted about plans to expand public education but was clear that it would be for whites only. He wrote articles in which he proclaimed, "The negro as a race, in all the ages of the world, has never shown sustained power of self-development. . . . He has never created for himself any civilization. . . . In truth, he has never progressed, save and except when under the influence and absolute control of a superior race."[111] He connected his disdain for what he perceived as a lack of racial achievement to his beliefs about Mississippi education, asserting that the provision of education for black citizens not only would serve no long-term benefit but also would likely be detrimental to the race. He believed that black students ceased to be able to learn after reaching puberty and then regressed.[112] Ultimately, he expressed his concern, which appealed to many of the state's citizens, that black education was a waste of both time and money. "We are furnishing them with schools which run from four to nine months in the year, and the white man pays for the bill. . . . But this progress is not making a better citizen of him. You cannot understand it, but I tell you in all solemn candor he is a thousand times more criminal today as a race than he was in 1861. . . . Your education will only serve to make a less desirable citizen."[113]

Indeed, the politics of education reform was important to the state's political campaigns and served Vardaman well. Education funding was a flash point in politics and race relations. The rural nature of the state and the wealth available in cotton meant that most families in the Delta relied on private schools and tutors to educate their children. When the district director of the SEB presented information about Mississippi and Louisiana to members of the 1902 Conference for Education in the South, he pointed out that Mississippi had the lowest white illiteracy rates in the South.[114] In addition, the residents of that region received much larger education appropriations from the state, given its large black population, than whites who lived in counties with relatively fewer numbers of blacks.[115] The Delta families were relatively more educated than other regions of the state and better able to develop a public system of schooling for whites at state expense. The presentation of data about school funding in the biennial report of the state superintendent of public education in the early 1890s makes clear the seriousness of this issue to Mississippi residents. Rather than report on total revenues and expenditures by county, the state superintendent presented the data in terms of race, high-lighting the effects of the poll-tax law in ten white and ten black counties. "In the white counties the whites are three-fourths of the population; in the black counties the whites are one-fifth of the population. The ten white counties received $87,226 from the state distribution. Of this sum they paid in polls $30,166, or 38 percent of the whole. The ten black counties received from the state distribution $170,353, of which they paid in polls $32,459, or only 19 percent of the whole. The white counties paid practically the same amount in polls as the black counties, while the black counties received nearly twice as much from the State distribution."[116]

The superintendent from Jefferson County claimed that county residents were ambivalent about public schooling, but their concerns related to race:

> The eastern portion of the county favors it, while in the western part where there are few white children, the people are very much opposed to it, be-cause there are not enough white children in one section, under the law, to make up a school, and the negroes reap all the benefits. If the whites could be exclusively taxed to support the white schools and negroes taxed in the same way to support the colored schools, then we would not have the least trouble in the world to keep up white school for eight or nine months an-nually. The negroes are totally unfit for self government.[117]

This quote makes clear not only the difficult politics of school reform but also the general agreement that black education was not a worthy cause. When Vardaman ran for public office, he capitalized on those resentments by point-ing out in his campaign speeches how unfair it was that whites paid the larger part of the school tax, but the Delta counties, heavily populated with blacks, received a greater share of the proceeds. Delta schools had longer school terms and better schools for its white residents than districts outside of the Delta, ensuring that education issues would exacerbate the tensions between Delta planters and the rest of the state. Vardaman proposed in his campaign that blacks not be educated at all, and advocated policies that would pro-vide education funds to each race based on the amount that each paid into the fund.[118]

It is unclear whether Vardaman actually believed all that he proclaimed, especially given that his policies and actions, which often related to more pro-gressive reforms, sometimes did not quite match his oratory.[119] However, his views mattered less than their appeal to his constituents and his influence on subsequent politics and practices in the state. Much of the support for men like Vardaman and Bilbo in the early decades of the twentieth century came from the men and women who composed the farming and laboring classes of the state and supporters of the now-defunct 1890s Populist Party. Vardaman's radical views appealed to an electorate that had become resentful and distrustful of Delta planters and of the influence of the outside world on Mississippi's southern way of life. Their deeply held views on the issue of race were detrimental to education reform, state development, and participation in the integrated efforts that would define those endeavors. At the same time, the Delta planters supported the racial state and sought control of the labor force, but they also resented the demagoguery that upset race relations and risked triggering a migration of the labor force out of the state.

Vardaman's white-supremacy campaign exceeded and differed from that of Charles Aycock. While Aycock's view of white supremacy included a belief in the positive possibilities of universal education, even if unequal for blacks and whites, Vardaman argued that any money spent on the education of blacks was destined to be a waste. Vardaman also exploited his constituents' fears about northern influence. He espoused this in both his campaign speeches and in congressional debates. In a discussion about foundation programming, he claimed that, "Aid could be accepted from local interests directly concerned in betterment work, although outside assistance would be banned."[120] He argued similarly in congressional debates on the Sims Amendment, which was intended to repeal part of the Panama Canal Treaty that exempted American coastwise vessels from paying tolls. While shipping interests had spent considerable sums of money promoting their version of the bill, Vardaman's critique of the amendment centered on his concern that the Carnegie Endowment for International Peace had spent $30,000 to disseminate literature in favor of the act.[121]

These beliefs also affected the state directly. During his tenure as governor, Vardaman prevented the University of Mississippi from accepting a gift from the Carnegie Corporation. The chancellor had tried to address the problematic circumstance of the university's lack of a library and had negotiated with the Carnegie Corporation for a gift to endow one. Vardaman, who exerted unusual influence over the board, forced the university to reject the offer. A possible explanation is that he believed corporate wealth threatened academic freedom in higher education.[122] However, his behavior is consistent with his general reluctance to collaborate with business interests and his fear of how those interests might influence the state more generally.

Of course, Vardaman was just one man in Mississippi governance, and his popularity peaked following World War I. He was pragmatic in seeking federal assistance from programs such as the Federal Farm Loan Act of 1916 providing farmers with long-term, low-interest credit, the Flood Control Act of 1917, and the Smith-Hughes Act in 1917 providing federal funds for vocational education as long as it did not redound benefits to Mississippi blacks. He was committed to states' rights but also promoted progressive legislation as a US senator that protected the rights of white citizens. Support for education generally would have fit with his progressive ideals, but only if those efforts did not either benefit the state's blacks or antagonize his base of supporters. Indeed, Vardaman and subsequent governors promoted education legislation that benefitted whites, including consolidation efforts, but their initiatives generally did not lead to a strong state system of public and universal education.

Vardaman's distrust of outside interference in a Mississippi way of life struck a deep chord with his constituents. Many Mississippi politicians, particularly the powerful Bourbon politicians in the state, sought to get him out of office because his views threatened Mississippi progress. However, his tenure as governor and then senator was followed by the similar trajectory of Theodore Bilbo, who served as a state senator from 1907 to 1911, lieutenant governor from 1912 to 1916, two terms as governor from 1916 to 1920 and from 1928 to 1932, and as a US senator from 1935 to 1947. Vardaman and Bilbo effectively rallied the masses of white citizens in the state who were adamant about states' rights and committed to white supremacy and the rule of the Democratic Party. Their views reflected their constituents' suspicion that education reform might benefit blacks and that collaboration with outside groups might influence an established way of life.

Field agents for the GEB recognized the difficulty that any outside group, especially the foundations with connections to northern business interests, would have in Mississippi. Early reports from the GEB-funded university professor Thomas Bailey included discussion of the deeply entrenched attitudes held by a majority of the state's white citizens: "With three fifths of the population negroes; with a pretty general prejudice against immigrants; with an unusual amount of political agitation of a demagogic kind; with the advancing danger of the boll weevil and danger of disaster to the lumber industry—with these conditions, I say, the educational conditions in this state need very careful and tactful handling. There is a great danger of reaction, if we move too fast. The Carnegie Foundation, Carnegie libraries, the General Education Board, and all other similar agencies are more or less distrusted by a large number of ill-informed people." He continued with a plea for the foundations to understand that many people in the state were humanitarian but that nothing would happen until everyone had a better sense of how the "negro problem" would be solved over the longer term and made clear that this was largely because the "negro question underlies all other questions connected with the South."[123] Politicians exercised mass appeal and influenced the extent to which Mississippi would, at any level of government, be willing to align itself with alternative governance structures that involved outside interests.

Bailey connected education and race issues to state development:

> I am persuaded, when I look around at the detached, sporatic, and spasmotic [sic] efforts in educational and industrial directions that this state needs integration as much as it needs differentiation in its efforts to educate the people in the very widest sense of the term. . . . Integration is the word . . . to note the waste of uncoordinated energy and the groping in the dark of good men from the South and from the North, moves me to say that the Educational Conference for the South might become the agency through which this work of co-ordination could be done. But the co-operation of the masses of the people would have to be obtained, especially of the farmers and the preachers and politicians, and, if I mistake not, these classes have little concern with the Conference and are often inclined to mistrust it.[124]

Bailey's views were instructive and made clear that foundations would need to approach reform differently in Mississippi.

Mississippi's racial attitudes precluded the belief that education might positively impact the development of its black citizens. While North Carolina reformers at least paid lip service to the relationship between education and race betterment, even if those effects might take generations to produce, Mississippi reformers were more likely to promote education only to the extent that it benefitted whites and kept blacks in the state as docile workers. Even education experts shared these views, such as the chancellor of the University of Mississippi, who wrote to the GEB in 1909 to discuss his plan to educate black female students: "You fully understand that the servants in southern homes are nearly all negro girls . . . none of them have any adequate instruction in the important subject of Hygiene and in sanitary matters. . . . Indeed, contagious deseases [sic] of every character prey upon the negroes . . . Coming in contact, as they do, with each other as well as with the white people through their domestic relations they rapidly disseminate their contagious diseases." The chancellor suggested that a female high school inspector be employed through GEB funding who would visit city schools for blacks to promote health and sanitary conditions. "No subject is of more vital concern to those of us who must carry the burden of our 'brother in black' than the subjects of health and sanitation."[125] Vocational education for both races became a popular Mississippi campaign issue at the turn of the century, yet white supremacy prevented any real effort to promote the full capacity of the working population of the state by expanding educational opportunity. The chancellor claimed that his suggestion originated in a "very sincere desire to help the ignorant and unfortunate."[126] White citizens in North Carolina espoused similar views but also held a broader political vision to expand educational opportunity, even if unequally.

State agents in Mississippi may have been on the payroll of the foundations, but they worked in a political context that made it difficult to be effective, assuming they were interested in promoting foundation programs in a meaningful way. State and local politicians, especially in the executive branch, showed no real interest in developing an education vision with or without foundation support. They simply did not allocate the funding necessary to support educational change. This was true at the state level, where appropriations were relatively meager, and at the local level, where most citizens refused to tax themselves.

In 1911, W. H. Smith, Mississippi's state agent for rural education, responsible for white schools, prepared a bulletin for teachers, trustees, and citizens throughout the state. He had been appointed with foundation funding and included in his report a discussion of the annual Conference for Education in the South, which he had recently attended at Jacksonville, Florida. His presence at the conference provided an opportunity for Mississippi educators to be more involved in the conference's work, but it seems clear from his report that, although conferences by now had been underway for a decade, he remained largely unaware of their far-reaching work:

> Reports of conditions in each state were made and thoroughly discussed and feasible lines of action indicated. Considerable time was spent in working out forms for reports and inspection blanks in an effort to unify the work and to get such statistics from the field as would indicate as clearly as possible actual conditions, and reveal the fundamental problems in our work. . . . The results of these conferences will evidently be far-reaching in effect on the rural school problems. Consolidation, a better system of supervision, and a vital content for the courses of study for rural schools are seemingly the fundamental problems and are to receive the greatest possible emphasis in our efforts.[127]

The state agent was unconvinced about the suggestions made and perhaps even unaware of the agenda that had developed for the southern states, especially toward the creation of stronger administration systems. His report instead sounded somewhat bemused about the comprehensive efforts, even if he was also inspired. He noted in the bulletin his intention to advise the legislature that district supervisors of rural schools be appointed, and that he would bring the matter to the attention of business and commercial clubs.[128] However, his efforts never came to fruition. While rural white schools continued to improve, neither rural black schools nor state governance showed meaningful improvement, a fact that foreshadowed the relationship that the state would have to foundations and comprehensive southern reforms in subsequent decades.

CONCLUSION

The foundations sought to integrate stakeholders from a range of institutions in both North Carolina and Mississippi order to fill the void created in each state by the lack of political will, weak governance systems, or both. The foundations sought to fill that void regardless of whether the states actively sought their participation. They were but one part of a larger reform dynamic that depended upon collaborative relationships not just with foundation agents at the state and local levels but also with state and local political systems. For southern education reform to serve a broader state-building agenda, states would need to be involved in the endeavor. As this chapter illustrates, the social and political milieu defined the extent to which either state would be willing to collaborate with northern foundations.

State differences highlight some important points with regard to southern education reform and political development. First, they underscore the extent to which the South was not monolithic. Regional differences are essential to understanding the impact of foundations on both education and political development. Second, the foundations were but one of many interest groups, both public and private, that were engaged in a process that contributed to the development of the modern state. Success depended upon the foundations' ability to work with other political players through an array of governance systems designed to promote education. Each state defined both its own role in the southern reform dynamic and the form that collaboration would take. Ultimately, the nature of that dynamic, which reflected forms of interstitial collaboration in each state, influenced the administrative structure in which policies and practices regarding the public education of both races would be promoted. North Carolina politicians and reformers established a strong state presence in the reform dynamic. Mississippi politicians were less eager to participate.

The racist attitudes of southern whites, education reformers, and even the northern philanthropists is not new to the literature. Indeed, a body of literature has appropriately focused on and provided substantial evidence of racism, especially by today's standards, that defined the agenda in the South.[129] However, while the racism was hateful in every form, it was also varied in character and led to divergent policy outcomes. North Carolina reformers were concerned about the relationship between education and evolution, and between education and state progress. They were white supremacists but wanted each citizen to perform at the best of their ability, even the state's black residents, who were considered a "child race." North Carolina politicians and reformers decided to collaborate extensively with foundations. As the next chapter will illustrate, with the assistance of northern foundations, the state developed a school system that included both races and a bureaucracy that connected rural black schools to the public sphere.[130] While rural black citizens were clearly excluded from the social and political structure, and disfranchisement meant that normal avenues to political power in the South were not open, the decision to collaborate with foundations had a significant effect on state development and on the relative power of rural black communities. These differences affected the longer-term development of schooling, the organization of rural black communities, and political opportunity structures in rural areas. As the chapter on Mississippi will illustrate, the state's reluctance to participate with outside interests was detrimental to both foundation success and the state's long-term educational and political development.

CHAPTER FOUR

The "Splendid Support" of Private Interests

In 1931, the Institute for Government Research of the Brookings Institution issued a report, "State Centralization in North Carolina," commending the legislature for a series of acts that redefined the relationship between the state and its political subdivisions and centralized control over a number of government functions. The report details the evolution of policy and practice in the state in three domains.[1] The inclusion of public schooling as one of those domains makes clear its relationship to political development in North Carolina and appropriately recognizes the significant increase in education bureaucracy and infrastructure that had developed in the previous decades. However, what was notably missing from the report was the role of northern foundations, which were a central and ongoing feature of the long evolution from a state system based in local control to a more fully developed, centralized bureaucracy. Collaboration between the state and northern foundations was central to education reform beginning in 1901, fostering the creation of a state-run system of schooling that was central to political development more broadly conceived.[2] In the case of North Carolina, one consequence of organizational change was a more formal role, even if circumscribed by white supremacy, for rural blacks in education.[3]

The Southern Education Board (SEB) recognized early on that the context for promoting reform in North Carolina was considerably different than that in most southern states. When the board conducted its first field study of each of the southern states, the 1904 report on North Carolina opened with the most significant finding: "Initiative, control, and support of Public School Education in North Carolina are by the State as distinguished from the local community. This fact marks a characteristic difference between the States of the North and most of the States of the South." This was not meant to imply that its citizens were not committed to local control. Indeed, that same report acknowledged that the centralization of power was "partly theoretical, as far as local educational direction is concerned, for the State Superintendent often finds it difficult to get county boards and local officials to carry out the improvements he desires: it is largely a matter of persuasion rather than direction, as southern tenacity of local independence is very strong in spite of reliance on State support." At the same time, the state superintendent was having unusual success with "direction through persuasion." Ultimately, the SEB recommended the GEB could be most effective in promoting education for rural blacks through "such forms of cooperation with the State as may be agreed upon after conference with the State Superintendent, whose views and convictions on this question are eminently sound and just."[4] Education reformers in the state were active participants in the Conference for Education in the South and shared the objectives of the SEB. This included the state superintendent, James Joyner, whom the SEB considered an important ally in southern education reform, as well as other prominent leaders like Charles McIver and Edwin Alderman.[5]

Alderman's address at the 1902 Conference for Education in the South made clear that education would serve a pivotal role in transforming North Carolina into a more modern state. He claimed that southern reformers had concluded that national progress and poverty were mutually exclusive, that public education was an investment and not an expenditure, and that it was necessary to reconsider the meaning of the state:

> I can remember myself when the State was looked upon as a sort of machine for the protection of life and property, and its highest and holiest duties were symbolized by justice and penal laws, by the hangman's rope or the policeman's club. But the change has come. Today the State is the collective will of the people expressing itself in laws and institutions.[6]

For Alderman, schooling was the most important institution, integrating the will of the people with those changing conceptions of the state. Alderman's address was also a reflection of the education vision that Governor Aycock promoted beginning with his election in 1901 and continuing with his appointment of James Yadkin Joyner as state superintendent of education, whose tenure lasted until 1919 and ensured the continuation of Aycock's views. Joyner collaborated extensively with foundations, which resulted in lasting changes in the state's administration of the education system. He was an ex-classmate, friend, and ideological ally of Aycock's from the University of North Carolina and the first person to hold the office of state superintendent who had professional training and experience as an educator. He was also a member of the SEB.

Joyner connected his goal of universal education to democracy and good government. He believed education to be both the highest government function and the chief concern of a good government.[7] Like Aycock, he was a white supremacist who was devoted to public education and statism.[8] He believed schools to be the birthright of all citizens, supported by a tax on all citizens, and specifically sought higher teacher salaries for better-trained teachers, a stronger curriculum, higher attendance rates, and longer school terms.[9] These objectives required support from local communities, especially in the form of increased taxes. He spoke to the "success and wisdom" of local taxation because it could stimulate "local pride, self-help, self-reliance, and independence."[10] He also recognized that the office of the superintendent had lacked power because it was perceived by state residents to be a political appointment. Surrounding himself with other professional educators, Joyner sought public support for education initiatives and embarked upon a statewide campaign to change public perception and promote reform. Foundations supported these efforts. The campaign resulted in essays published in newspapers across the state, requests to clergymen to preach about the importance of public education, and rallies throughout the state to raise money for school reform, for which the GEB agreed to provide matching funds.[11]

Joyner sought to alter the administrative structure of rural communities when he took office in 1901. There were no requirements at that time that county superintendents answer to the state superintendent, but the state revised the public-school law so that the governance of each county included a board of education, and the superintendent of each reported to Joyner, providing regular reports about school terms, rates of attendance, and the curriculum.[12] The legislation also detailed the process for certifying teachers.[13] Aycock and Joyner sought a more bureaucratized system for schooling and then worked diligently to elicit foundation support to create the infrastructure necessary.[14] By 1910, Joyner had developed a draft statement on rural education and began a statewide campaign to gain the support of education leaders, both black and white. He received additional foundation funding to add a supervisor of teacher training and a supervisor of rural schools, positions that were filled by 1910.

The expansion by 1910 of the state department of public instruction did not lead to direct gains in rural black education. Joyner's work focused at the state administration level and on the development of an infrastructure, and the rural school agents focused on public white schools first. Both foundation reformers and southern white educators believed that white schools would need to be improved before it would be possible to focus on black education. That was a plan that not only appealed to racial attitudes but also reflected an understanding that it would not be possible to increase local taxes, standardize schools, or strengthen black education unless whites perceived the benefits of a public system of education. There was no meaningful effort to expand black educational opportunity before 1910, even though reformers paid lip service to a system of universal education that included blacks. However, by that point, there was a firmly established relationship between the state and northern foundations and between the state and local white communities, leading to more collaborative work and measurable gains in education. After getting agents in place to address the education needs of rural whites, the state moved to addressing those of rural blacks.

While the county superintendent was responsible for all schools in the county, both white and black, few counties had formal schooling for blacks. Blacks developed their own education institutions, which often existed outside of the local governing structure. Many superintendents were simply not interested in supervising or improving these schools. North Carolina eagerly sought a state agent for Negro education, for which the GEB would provide matching funds. The agent was expected to represent the state's interest and have access to all local districts in order to "direct state, county and local effort in developing an effective system of public schools for the training of the negro children of the state."[15] Nathan Newbold was appointed to this position in 1913, where he remained until 1950. When Newbold was selected, Joyner explained to the GEB that "the selection of the man would be subject to your approval, and that I had no authority to offer him the position at this time; but . . . I should like for him to consider the matter and let me know how he would feel about it in case the position should be tendered him, and that I would take the matter up with you."[16]

While Joyner had found a good candidate for state agent, in providing the salary, the GEB gained control over both the selection and the work. The GEB designed the state-agent program to allow foundation control in all of the southern states, which provided greater opportunity to influence state administration. However, Joyner was eager to cooperate. As Joyner outlined the position, the state agent would oversee rural reform efforts in the state and, in Joyner's words, would "organize industrial teacher training courses . . . to train negro teachers to work in all the rural schools for their race in the state, teaching the growing youth the things they should know to be practical useful dwellers in the country, and to make better more thrifty citizens for the state."[17] Joyner must have perceived that Newbold's success would be important to sustaining the strong ties that existed between foundations and the state. The appointment also represented a direct means for the state to act on the beliefs that Joyner and his colleagues held about white supremacy and public education. Joyner directly supervised Newbold's work, rather than having him report to the state supervisor for rural schools, L. C. Brogden, who had been focusing on white schools. Newbold was given wide latitude to promote black education in the state, and the scope of his position and the size of the office expanded over the next decade. The state seemed not to limit in any way Newbold's work, and Joyner's initial correspondence indicates that he considered the new position important to education reform and one that would promote foundation objectives in the state.

Newbold guided reform in North Carolina's rural black communities for almost four decades, and the foundations considered his work a model for successful foundation practice. The state agents for Negro education were important to the comprehensive implementation of foundation goals. Every agent had the potential to provide important service and good press with little expense, especially where the state refused to legislate funds for education. However, philanthropists and reformers alike recognized that incremental steps might lead to lasting reform, and it appears that this was the case in states like North Carolina, where each step became institutionalized as part of the state system of schooling.

Newbold's appointment led to the development of a Negro education department that functioned within the state department of education but also operated discretely. When he accepted the position in 1913, he explained that he would "give special attention and encouragement to the upbuilding of the negro rural schools and by helping to introduce into them all kinds of useful and profitable industrial and vocational subjects; to promote better farming, better community conditions, better morals and cleaner home life; to endeavor in every possible advisable way to make better workers, and better citizens of the negroes of North Carolina; to do this work by aiding the County Superintendents and other white citizens interested in our educational development to produce the desired results.[18] The appointment of Newbold was essential to maintaining the collaboration that had already developed between the state political system and northern foundations, but it would extend that work more directly in the area of rural black education.

Foundations successfully implemented the full range of education programs in North Carolina in the first three decades of the twentieth century. The state Division of Negro Education had a staff of nine people by 1925, successfully layered onto existing state education organizations. That office included Rosenwald field agents, both black and white, a black state-supervising Jeanes teacher, and a black supervisor of high schools. By 1932 Jeanes teachers worked in thirty-nine of one hundred counties in the state, where they developed a comprehensive system of agricultural clubs and extension work that reached a majority of rural families in their jurisdiction.[19] More Rosenwald schools were built in North Carolina than any other state in the South. Foundations also funded a series of educational campaigns in the state and supported efforts at tax reform and a reconceptualization of public school administration.

Ultimately, education reform in North Carolina illustrates the importance of associated action to early twentieth-century reform and the power of schooling as a site to enhance governance capacity at the state and local level and expand political participation in rural communities. The state's success at implementing new programs depended, however, upon an expanded form of associated action that included rural black citizens. White reformers from both the North and South perceived that schools would provide the best venue for connecting rural communities throughout the South to formal governance structures, ultimately improving state and local governance capacity. Such a structure provided better avenues for promoting national ideals through schooling. Those ideals did not include efforts to challenge the racial state in the South. Even in North Carolina, where politicians promoted universal education, public schooling was intended to maintain white supremacy. Yet, neither foundations nor southern politicians could anticipate the way that national conceptions of race might change over the twentieth century. A public system of education, managed through state legislation and administered at the county level, would provide a better venue over the longer term for challenging inequality in public education. Indeed, the development of schooling in local communities could open political opportunity structures in the short term, and perhaps challenge the larger social structure over time.

ACHIEVING FOUNDATION GOALS FOR RURAL BLACK EDUCATION IN NORTH CAROLINA: THE STATE

Newbold approached his work with conscientious enthusiasm, visiting counties across the state and providing detailed reports to Joyner and the General

Education Board on a monthly and annual basis. He came to know personally the county superintendents, Jeanes teachers, and education leaders of both races, and kept in regular contact with the foundations that supported his work intellectually and financially. In an early report, he noted that he would make clear to residents of the state that black schoolhouses were a "disgrace to an independent, civilized people" and that "these schoolhouses, though mute, would tell in unmistaken terms a story of injustice, inhumanity and neglect on the part of our white people . . . intolerable, indefensible, unbusinesslike and, above all, unchristian."[20] Newbold was untiring in his support of expanded educational opportunities in rural black communities, work that was made easier because he served in a state that considered education for both races a central component of its economic vision.

North Carolina may have been more open to universal education, but that vision was still developed in the context of white supremacy. Like most southerners who promoted expanded education for blacks, however, Newbold held views far more complicated than what his efforts implied. In the first year of his work, he said that black citizens of the state were showing greater willingness to help themselves and expressed gratitude that they now understood that the white community should not be expected to furnish schools without that sacrifice. He also expressed relief that white attitudes toward black education had improved, but with a comment that said more about his attitude toward black citizens than white ones: "All of us are beginning to understand that a clean, healthy, intelligent negro is a better neighbor and a better citizen than a dirty, diseased, ignorant one just as this is true of any other race. Many white people gladly contribute to aid the negroes in building schoolhouses."[21] His first letter to superintendents across the state indicated that he would focus on industrial training, which would "include all the principal subjects incident to country life, such as; sanitation, cooking, sewing, housekeeping, laundering, gardening and orchards, farming, manual training, poultry, dairying and stock raising, attention to small things."[22] Newbold expressed education values that were similar to those of many white reformers who believed universal education should happen in segregated schools that focused on industrial education for blacks.

In spite of his views about an unequal curriculum, however, Newbold made incredible progress toward the establishment of a centralized education system that included rural black schools, progress that also affected his attitudes toward rural black citizens over time.[23] Some of this success was the result of working in a state that had a vision for universal education and was eager to collaborate with northern foundations to achieve it. While the 1904

SEB report advocated that white schools be promoted as a first priority, it was also clear that blacks could participate in those benefits, with the degree of participation depending somewhat on local demographics and public sentiment. "As a matter of absolute justice [black citizens] ought to participate proportionately with the whites. But we are confronted 'with a condition and not a theory.' An attempt on our part to compel such proportionate participation now would in all probability defeat all our efforts and work to the injury of negro public school education."[24] The state cooperated with foundations wherever possible in developing its system of education. Their interest in collaboration extended to every level of governance, and to every aspect of Newbold's work.

In 1913, the state developed an industrial course of study and training in order to prepare a large number of black teachers as rapidly and efficiently as possible. Rather than recapitulate the consensus of the Conference for Education in the South, which certainly guided the work, the program was developed through a state conference that promoted cooperation across interest groups.[25] The agenda included white and black teachers and reformers, state politicians, representatives of the GEB, the Jeanes Fund, the Slater Fund, and members from the US Bureau of Education. From its inception, education reform in the state was an inclusive and collaborative process—even if white participants had far greater power—and the basis for a paternalistic form of cooperation that was intended to mollify the state's blacks.[26] Newbold's success can be attributed to the state's general interest in collaboration and his specific skill at working with a variety of interest groups, including rural blacks.

Newbold developed deep relationships with communities across the state through regular visits to counties and rural schoolhouses. He understood the importance of collaboration at every level of government, in line with the strategy of his benefactors, and knew that a modern, centralized school system, which might strengthen bureaucracy throughout state and local governance systems, depended upon those networks. For example, an early initiative was Rural School Day in 1913, a meeting organized for both leading black and white educators. The program included a general discussion of actual conditions county by county and a proposal to develop an education plan tailored to each. "To succeed with these plans the indorsement [sic], cooperation and leadership of the county superintendent, the county board of education, and the best people in the county both white and colored should be secured."[27] Newbold tailored efforts to the region on a county-by-county basis in the spirit of cooperation and accommodation, an approach that helped to ensure his success.

The archives include many examples of teachers who corresponded with Newbold directly, and often in confidence. It appears that he was careful to protect these confidences and tried also to provide support. For example, the Palmer Memorial Institute, a private academy for black students, was having financial difficulty like many private schools in the state. The principal recognized that foundations might provide for the long-term financial stability of the school, and in a 1914 series of letters she sought funding to turn the institute into a county training school. She also wrote to Newbold, presenting the institute as a training school for rural teachers, a presentation that was more about what the institute could be than what it was at that time. In her request, she strategically pointed out the extent to which the institute supported and implemented the industrial-training curriculum of the state. "We find it necessary to get a few business men of high standing to write letters to him [Rosenwald]. Will you please sir write and tell him of how you have watched the work grow, what you believe it is worth to the county and how deserving it is of help. Please make this letter as strong as possible."[28] Newbold followed up with the requested letter for funding, and the Palmer Institute became a public high school by 1925.

Another incident is worth discussing in detail because it particularly well depicts rural politics, the Jeanes teachers, and Newbold. The teacher in Greene County asked Newbold for advice about how to procure funding for a county training school. Newbold advised her to create sentiment for the institution, secure a centrally located school building on five to ten acres of land, and solicit income from the county, which would make it possible to secure money for teachers' salaries and the possibility of Rosenwald funding if a new building was planned.[29] With a promise from the county that it would provide $750 in matching funds, the teacher raised funds from private black donations. In fact, the superintendent joined her in a meeting with the black community, and contributions amounted to more than $1,400. But even after the black community exceeded its fundraising goal, the county denied the request:

> But when we went before the Board of Education to ask the $750 and deed the 10 acres of land over to the county, the Board of Education led by Mr. Debnam turned us down. . . . No answer save this: that the colored people of Greene County received a great deal more than they paid. After the meeting Mr. Debnam sent for me and spoke in strong language his disapproval of my ever bringing the subject up. . . . His answers are neither pro or [sic] con. His silence has caused a few of our strongest colored men

to back out where as it has strengthen [sic] quite a few to press on. . . . Please advise. . . . This letter I send as a personal one, and if there is any way you can get to the bottom without letting Mr. Debnam know that I told you all about it, I'll thank you.[30]

The superintendent seemed to have initially supported the plan and then refused, and the teacher felt comfortable sending a confidential letter to Newbold about the incident with a request that he intercede on behalf of the community.

Newbold also received a letter from the superintendent regarding the same matter, who said that the matter of a black training school had become embarrassing:

> We haven't the money, and there appears to be no feasible way by which it may be gotten from the public chest. . . . I have taken pains to show [the teacher] . . . that the negro schools in this county cost in round numbers $1000 more than the negroes contribute. . . . I think that you'd do well to call a halt to the matter, or make some move by which the matter may be handled in a way more satisfactorily.[31]

Newbold wrote back to the teacher, advising her to tell the superintendent that she would be glad to let the matter rest until another year. "I am sure you know you cannot afford to antagonize the school authorities as they are better informed as to the financial conditions than any one else." In a letter written the next day to the superintendent, Newbold stated that it would be no trouble "for us to put a quietus on the training school matter in your county, if you think it wise to do so." However, Newbold also informed him that in order to do this conclusively, the county would have to provide detailed information about county support for Negro education, as well as a written statement from the teacher.[32]

Newbold had encouraged the teacher to drop the issue, in spite of verbal promises and success at raising the requisite funding from rural blacks, but he did not let the issue drop. By requesting additional information, Newbold could show that the county support was clearly less than adequate or the needs of the black population were sufficiently met. Finally, his requirement that the superintendent request a letter from the teacher promoted dialogue between the two of them. Greene County followed up with two proposals for Rosenwald schools the following month, and the teacher sent a thank-you note to Newbold: "You certainly spoke my sentiments when you said that the

Board of Greene Co. were my friends, and the friends of my race . . . frankly speaking I would rather keep their friendship than that of all the County—for this reason; Their attitude towards my work and its success mean more than a great many county people: they can help or they can hinder."[33] She had gained two school buildings but lost the county training school for the time being. She would have to overcome these differences in order to promote future success.

Newbold also followed up with letters to foundations and to Dr. Thomas Jesse Jones at the US Department of Education, in his capacity as agent of the Phelps-Stokes Fund, to ask for funding for the Greene County Training School. Newbold outlined the situation in Greene County and explained that he was uncertain whether or not there really were insufficient county funds: "I had supposed that perhaps the recent lynching in that county had created such conditions that the school board felt that it would not be justified in attempting to establish a Training School at this time, but the superintendent tells me that this affair has had no effect whatever on the school conditions in this county."[34]

Newbold quietly cajoled counties that were not interested in education reform, making rural blacks in that county feel that they had his support, while never forcing whites to do more than they were willing to do. Newbold's approach made him popular with county school boards and rural whites, as well as rural blacks, because he was accessible to both groups at the same time that he was careful to reinforce constantly the authority of local whites. Nonetheless, every relationship that he fostered helped him to develop a vast network of people throughout the state, which gave him greater power to promote sustained reform than direct state authority might have. These relationships expanded the authority of the state agency that Newbold directed.

Efforts to promote broad participation within the state were important, but Newbold also learned to include reformers and philanthropists from outside the state whenever possible. It is significant that soon after being appointed he organized a conference that included black educators from across the state, who were provided an opportunity to engage in discussion with leading reformers and foundation representatives. However, he also developed these efforts within the parameters of the racial state. Joyner's message to black educators at the conference was instructive: "Universal education does not mean giving all the same kind of education, fitting them for the same thing, but giving every man the training in the sphere of life to which he is adapted."[35] Joyner's speech on industrial education was followed by a proposal for black teacher training presented by Newbold, which resulted in a paper that was distributed to all of the attendees, and then shared with the US Bureau of Education.[36] Newbold sought outside guidance and advertised the state's work, ensuring ongoing support from foundations and experts. That form of associated action also meant that schooling would serve as a means to connect the state in formal ways to national conversations about education, while promoting greater standardization and administrative oversight in local areas.

It is significant that Newbold also immediately sought assistance from northern foundations and the federal government to promote his work. He developed forms of collaboration that included political actors from every level of government, from the federal down to the local, and was adept at capitalizing on his relationships to foundations and to national education leaders. Indeed, the US commissioner of education shared Newbold's proposal for teacher education with the Department of the Interior's Division of Rural Education. The specialist in that division corresponded directly with Newbold to provide bureau bulletins to inform the work in North Carolina and complimented Newbold on the course design.[37] Newbold's actions promoted federal-state collaboration in rural education development and ensured the support of a range of agencies.

In 1914 Newbold visited Anson County, where J. R. Faison had been appointed as the Jeanes teacher. Faison had been in the community for more than a decade leading a private academy for Anson County's blacks that would be absorbed by the public school system. Newbold met with the Anson County superintendent, who expressed particular concern that the rural schools there received more from the county school fund than they paid into it. He pointed out that the black schools in Anson County received $2 on average for every $1 paid into the school fund, though he was also effusive about his support for black education. After Newbold and the superintendent met with black residents, the superintendent said he believed black citizens were appreciative of county progress: "They had never understood so well before, and that they intended to cooperate with their teachers, the county superintendent, and the Jeanes supervisor to secure better schools."[38] Newbold acknowledged that some of this talk was pure bombast, but also believed that many of the black citizens were in earnest and believed it a "god-send that two white men should come out to talk with them, and to advise with them as to means for their uplift."[39] Newbold noted that the meeting led to a number of black citizens stating that they were "surprised to learn the true state of affairs, saying they had felt that their schools had not received their just share of the school funds in the past. They heartily promised to contribute of their own means to help their schools."[40] This example makes clear the strategies employed by both black and white local residents. The superintendent, who likely gave little support to the schools, was effusive about positive race relations, which Newbold correctly perceived as "bombast." At the same time, Newbold brought both races together, and they publicly committed to working together to expand schooling. It is also likely that black attendees also spoke with similar bombast, understanding that public proclamations of appreciation for the superintendent would result in better race relations, a strategy that was clear in detailed reports from Faison to the state that lauded the county superintendent for his support. There were gross inequalities at the local level, yet additional help would not be forthcoming unless blacks were willing to cooperate with local whites, and this often meant compromising their values in public spaces.

Newbold's efforts reflected the paternalism that defined the efforts of most white reformers, and brought with it a sense of true "noblesse oblige." In his first year as state agent, he distributed copies of *The Human Way*, an address on race problems published by the Southern Sociological Association in 1913. The book devoted a chapter to university efforts in addressing southern race issues and pointed out that "millions of dollars had been spent on black education in the South between 1870 and 1910," and "the negro is beginning to pay a fair proportion, especially in North Carolina." The chapter also quoted the late commissioner of education, William T. Harris, who had said, "the Southern white people in the organization and management of systems of public schools manifest wonderful and remarkable self-sacrifice."[41] The book promoted the idea of the school as a social and welfare agency that would be responsible for the "uplift of the negro," and "where the course of study fits its pupils to take their place in the life of the community . . . progress in this depends on greater intelligence, justice and righteousness and demands our good will, our helpful guidance."[42] Newbold asked superintendents of county school districts to read the publication and then distribute it to Jeanes teachers in counties that employed one and the president of the Negro County Teachers' Association in counties that did not.[43] He advertised to both races his desire to promote better schooling in rural black areas and his language was simultaneously deeply condescending to rural black teachers and families and conciliatory in allaying the fears of local whites. He also worked diligently to convince rural communities of the importance of educating its black citizens, employing the language of white supremacy in a manner that established common ground with local whites. He made clear to both races that he sought educational progress.

Newbold was devoted to working with foundations to build a school system in rural black communities that was institutionalized as part of the state system of education through an expanded state bureaucracy. However, he did not force local whites to cooperate. When the Elizabeth County Board of Trustees informed Newbold that they would not continue with the appointment of a Jeanes teacher, Newbold provided a list of five reasons why they should reconsider, including that they would "gain the co-operation of the educational authorities of the county in giving the colored people the *kind* of education and training that the southern people have for years believed they should have," which included sanitation, cleanliness, domestic duties, gardening, and manual training.[44] The trustees found his argument compelling. In another example, a teacher offered to work for free in a county that was unwilling to provide funding for a Jeanes supervising teacher. She explained to Newbold that she knew that "colored people need help and they are suffering and I really feel that I can help them. I am really anxious about this thing and interested in this work of my race. You [the state agent] can do this and will you do it for me, please?"[45] Newbold asked the superintendent to support the supervisor, given that she was willing to work for free, but the superintendent did not agree and expressed his doubts that any work should continue in the county.[46] This example highlights important dynamics. The teacher knew that she could rely on Newbold to intercede on her behalf, and was not afraid to plead with him openly. Newbold followed through, even though he knew that the superintendent did not support the teacher. Finally, Newbold cajoled the superintendent but ultimately left it up to the county to decide whether a teacher could volunteer her time to administer black schools there.

Newbold's responsibilities as the state agent were quite broad to begin with, but as his extensive networks evolved so did the scope of his position. His relationship to foundations also became less bureaucratically hierarchical and allowed for more personal discretion over time. In 1919, he outlined his basic responsibilities, which included the supervision of Jeanes Fund work, including recruitment of supervisors and all administrative budget and personnel aspects of the program; oversight of the homemakers club program; oversight of eighteen county training schools, including the recruitment of principals and teachers, the solicitation of funding, budgeting, and general administration; all aspects of the Rosenwald school-building campaign, which included more than two hundred state projects in 1919; oversight of summer schools for teacher training; and all additional requirements for rural education, including the collection of data, the preparation of reports, conferences with black and white education leaders, and visits to local communities.[47] He essentially served as the state superintendent of education for the segregated black system.

Newbold's success was due to the significant support of northern foundations. G. H. Ferguson, a white director in the Division of Negro Education, wrote a paper in the 1930s on the previous decades of education reform in North Carolina that discussed the evolution of education thought in the division and explained the basis for its success. His report highlighted the significance of collaboration at every level of the work, from the national down to the local level. In particular, he felt the division was made more effective and meaningful by the "splendid support," financial and otherwise, given by private interests outside the state, that included the SEB and a long list of northern foundations like the GEB, the Rosenwald Fund, the Jeanes Fund, the Slater Fund, and the Phelps-Stokes Fund. "The representatives of these philanthropic funds, through visits and correspondence, gave a vision, a perspective, and stimulation which was most significant, even down to the local level."[48] It was clear that Newbold was in a much better position than other state agents to promote educational progress. The GEB recognized Newbold's progress in a comprehensive 1927 report on educational progress in the South, "Virginia's one agent and secretary can hardly compete with North Carolina's division of nine people exclusively in Negro education, in a task of similar magnitude."[49] Indeed, by the end of the 1920s, Newbold had greatly expanded the division, which was supported with both foundation and state appropriations.

Newbold's achievements were due, in part, to how adept he was at garnering foundation support that went beyond just funding. By 1915, after only two years in the position, he was already pleading successfully with the foundations to provide greater support in North Carolina. In one request, he outlined how he had capitalized on foundation efforts to leverage uncooperative counties to expand educational opportunity. He pointed out that in addition to the original eighteen Jeanes teachers who would continue their work, he had also persuaded twelve additional counties to meet the criteria for a teacher, and had developed interest in five more.[50] He encouraged the Slater Fund to continue its support of the black teacher-training schools located at Method, Smithfield, and Stonewall, and to develop a cooperative relationship with training schools located at Parmele, Clinton, and Powellsville, efforts that yielded additional financial support to those schools. Finally, he restated his five-year goals for the state, which included a Jeanes teacher and homemakers club in every eligible county, a training school in every county where one was needed, black teacher-training departments in higher-education institutions, and a schoolhouse built in every needy district. "I do not want to rob any other states, but I think you already know that I am anxious to develop this work in North Carolina just as far as it is possible. . . . I realize that to accomplish this task we shall need much outside assistance, as well as to create a great deal of interest and enthusiasm within our own borders."[51] He also recognized that continued outside assistance depended upon efficient work that led to education progress in line with foundation goals. Yet, Newbold also recognized that many local politicians and educators did not share his goals for rural blacks.

In Durham County, North Carolina, the superintendent had allowed schools to be built that did not follow the architectural plans of the Rosenwald Fund, lacking windows of the appropriate size and number and an industrial room. In Wilson County, the construction called for a new room to be added to an old two-room school, which presented a "very unsatisfactory appearance. None of the rooms are properly lighted and the industrial room is entirely too small."[52] Indeed, Newbold realized that Rosenwald buildings were often not of high quality or exhibited shoddy and incomplete work. Beginning in 1916, the state Negro teachers' association provided funding to hire a black educator, Charles Moore, to work in Newbold's office as the Rosenwald agent for school buildings.[53] The association knew the importance of building rural schools and giving black education leaders an instrumental role in reform. Moore's salary was paid by the association through voluntary contributions by members of the black community. In addition, the association set up a rural extension department made up of eight black education leaders to oversee Moore's work.[54] Moore would be responsible for holding "meetings with his people arousing them to contribute toward the building of new schoolhouses."[55] Newbold described his work to foundations in a more expansive manner, perceiving early on the importance of having an experienced and respected black educator available to promote the work in local areas. Newbold reported to the GEB that Moore would "visit the various counties of the State and to give aid wherever possible in creating a more wholesome school sentiment and to help, as far as possible, to create a cooperative spirit between the white school officials and the negro schools. His work has been very successful. He visited practically all of the counties . . . made speeches, did personal work, and, I feel sure, has helped to promote our general work."[56] Newbold also used construction problems to get the Rosenwald Fund to support the position, thereby institutionalizing it more formally as part of the bureaucracy that had been established through foundation support, and then got the GEB to provide funding for a second, assistant field agent, through resources transferred from the GEB to the Rosenwald Fund.

While some agents might have hidden construction problems from their benefactors, Newbold used those problems to request greater oversight, which required additional support. He explained, "While I feel more or less embarrassed in making any sort of further request for North Carolina, I do so sincerely hope some provision may be made to provide us extra help in the matter of inspecting the Rosenwald building."[57] Newbold recognized that it was politically difficult for him to come down on local politicians for shoddy and incomplete work. He understood that some of the problems were the result of insufficient county oversight, while others were a deliberate attempt to sabotage funding appeals. He sought additional agents, supported by foundations and located within Newbold's office. These agents could keep the difficult political battles with local communities off his desk and out of state politics.[58] His request provided a formal means to delegate to foundations the difficult process of navigating the political tensions that surrounded local issues, thereby deflecting criticism away from state and local politicians. Further, many local governance systems simply lacked the capacity to implement reform, but when foundations took over an issue they might also supply focused administrative effort to the cause. Newbold's strategies were particularly successful with regard to schoolhouse construction. The Rosenwald Fund built 813 schools in North Carolina, more than any other state in the South, accommodating 114,210 students.[59]

Newbold had made considerable progress in the first ten years of his appointment with a successful program of Rosenwald building construction, an increase in the number of Jeanes teachers, and a reorganization and expansion of his Division of Negro Education. Newbold anticipated next steps in developing the state's education system and sought the support of foundations, their agents, and other educators across the South. At a Rosenwald conference in 1923, Newbold proposed a number of items for the agenda, including a discussion of whether "anything [could be] done to standardize teachers in Rosenwald Schools."[60] By 1927, the state began a campaign to increase and strengthen secondary education for rural blacks, but recognized both the political difficulty of the work and the limited resources for accomplishing it. By this time, Newbold's office was receiving almost $20,000 annually from the state to support three staff people. The state superintendent of public instruction in 1927, A. T. Allen, lobbied the GEB for additional funding to support the expansion of black high schools. Specifically, the state requested funds to support the salary of W. A. Robinson, who had been the supervisor of Negro teacher training and high schools in the division since 1921, originally paid by the state's high school fund. [61] Newbold's experience with the Rosenwald agents who were located in his office made clear to him that even greater collaboration was essential to reform. Ultimately, with GEB funding, Robinson had significant influence over the development of black high schools in the state. From his position in the North Carolina Division of Negro Education, he joined the National Association of Teachers in Colored Schools and initiated a successful five-year campaign for the all-white regional accrediting agency, the Southern Association of Colleges and Secondary Schools, to assume responsibility for the accreditation of the state's black high schools. [62]

Foundation agents who were located in the state's Division of Negro Education could be relatively more effective in addressing the needs of local communities. Two Rosenwald agents were located in the division by the end of the 1920s, William Credle, who was white, and George Edward Davis, who was black. The two men traveled throughout the state promoting Rosenwald schoolhouse construction, inspecting school plans and building sites, and collecting data for both the state and northern foundations. While the two traveled together, each often worked separately with his own race. In 1929, the Douglas Board of Education refused to spend money for a Rosenwald school after previously committing to it. Credle held a conference with the board to get the support necessary, while Davis spent time with black members of the community helping to raise private donations. [63] In another example, Credle reported that he had been in New Bern to talk with the superintendent about a new black school building, where "ambitious real estate agents with some assistance from members of the School Board are trying to coerce the Board into buying a lot of undesirable land, a part of which would be used for school site, the remainder to be sold by the town for Negro home sites. The land that they have to offer is desirable for neither of these purposes." [64] He had the authority to deny funding, and was able to cajole local politicians into modifying plans so that the schools would be more in line with state and foundation models.

In the town of Matthews, the white superintendent was reluctant to allow an auditorium in the planned school for the town's black population. Credle met with the supervisor, who approved the auditorium, after Davis met separately with black citizens to ensure they would provide $1,020 in contributions. [65] The Ayden City schools needed a decent schoolhouse for blacks but could not get agreement for construction because the district was short of funds, already had a high tax rate, and did not believe that the white school was sufficiently adequate to justify a new school for blacks. Credle worked out an arrangement for the district to borrow money from the state's Literary Fund, to be added to Rosenwald's $1,500 gift, along with private contributions of $2,500 that Davis organized with the town's black citizens.[66] Fundraising efforts were easily measured, but Newbold also recognized that black educators like Davis and Holland could be instrumental in developing ties to the black community to gain their support for foundation initiatives.

Correspondence between Newbold and the GEB took place through the state superintendent of education early in his appointment, in line with the way in which the position was defined, but quickly became less formal. After that, Newbold often sent his correspondence directly to officers of the foundation. A letter to Abraham Flexner, the secretary of the GEB in 1919, was telling: Newbold requested a raise of $10 per month for his stenographer, illustrating that he interacted on the most minor of topics.[67] His plans for the new Division of Negro Education in 1921 were sent to Flexner, stating that he was "enclosing a copy of this outline and shall appreciate it very much if you and Dr. Buttrick [the president of the GEB] will read it over carefully and give me the benefit of your judgment."[68] The following year Newbold's handwritten note to the GEB, which suggested confidentiality, indicated concern that "friends connected with the General Education Board there were apparently not pleased with my petitions for the negro people of North Carolina. . . . In all earnestness I beg you to eliminate from our requests to the General Education Board any and all items that may in any way be embarrassing to you and your associates."[69] Buttrick's reply indicated the depth of the relationship. "[Your letter] disturbed me a good deal because, dear Newbold, there are few men in the world whom I love as much as I do you. Not only have I a deep affection for you, but I have great respect for you and great appreciation of the work you are doing."[70] A month later, the GEB increased his annual salary, and Buttrick wrote, "No man in the world is more deserving of such recognition than you. Your work has been beyond praise; your devotion has not been less than Christ-like; you are greatly beloved by the Negro people, who give you their unlimited confidence; you enjoy the respect and confidence of the white people."[71]

The state department of public instruction was reorganized in 1921, the result of a 1920 study by a state education commission, funded with a $1,000 appropriation for the work but supported further with an $18,000 grant and accompanying staff from the GEB to conduct the work. The report recommended a reorganization of the state department of public instruction, which called for separate divisions with an increased level of state support. The result was that the department of Negro education was reorganized as a separate division, and Newbold was given greater authority and staff, with state funding for approximately 50 percent of the personnel costs.[72] The black members of the staff effectively promoted rural black education initiatives. This included George E. Davis, who was supervisor of Rosenwald buildings, Annie W. Holland, supervisor of elementary schools, and W. A. Robinson, who was the supervisor of high schools.[73] The size of the division, however, likely affected not only the scope of the activity but also its ability to create the bureaucracy necessary to sustain itself organizationally.[74] Programs that developed in collaboration with private entities became embedded in the public system and contributed to political development, similar to the institutionalization of centralized schooling in the North. It is also likely that the reorganization of the state's Division of Negro Education, and Newbold's inclusion of black educators as members of that office, helped to raise awareness of a need for greater academic standards for the state's black citizens and contributed to Newbold's willingness over time to consider that separate education could also be more equal.

Newbold's relationship to northern foundations clearly facilitated the implementation of the fund's goals in North Carolina and furthered the state's education vision. However, work in rural black communities depended upon rural black citizens. Not only did individual blacks exercise agency, a fact well documented in the literature, but southern blacks were a catalyst and a force for change in North Carolina.[75] The state's administrative structure for implementing universal education included rural black citizens, both formally and informally. Formal policy development and implementation could be detrimental to black progress by promoting a curriculum that limited educational attainment. At the same time, the development of a broader and inclusive state bureaucracy for schooling strengthened governing capacity at the state and local level and created opportunities for rural blacks to influence the developing school system.[76]

ACHIEVING FOUNDATION GOALS FOR RURAL BLACK EDUCATION IN NORTH CAROLINA: THE COMMUNITY

The foundations implemented programs in North Carolina that promoted administrative growth, including state agents for Negro education, county training schools, teacher-training programs, and the Jeanes teachers. Even though foundations funded most of these programs, at least initially they operated within the state political system, while existing parallel to it. However, rural blacks were central to implementing programs locally. The public schools that developed out of this work in North Carolina served as an institutional site for rural blacks to engage in reform, and to challenge the political structure at the state and local levels. Education reform helped to establish centralized administrative capacity in the lower tiers of government; it had the potential to undermine the strength of sectional interests, and led to forms of community organizing that might evolve over time.

North Carolina reformers agreed that the organization of rural communities was an important cause. G. H. Ferguson, the assistant director of Negro education in the state, summarized in his 1921–22 annual report observations he made visiting twenty-one county training schools, which Ferguson found to be seriously handicapped by a lack of financial support and a mediocre teaching force. However, he also expressed concern about supervision: "Before these schools can develop into the organized units which we hope for, the county superintendents . . . must give more personal attention and professional advice to these units of work. The principals in many cases lack the ability to organize their school so as to use the school day most profitably. The bulk of work everywhere seems to be in the lower grades. The irregular attendance, unusual crowded conditions, and inefficient teachers have developed a system of retardation which almost destroys high school possibilities."[77] Ferguson perceived that standardization might help to improve schools by providing for minimum standards. In the meantime, the Jeanes teachers were one means to address the limitations of governance in rural areas.

The initial gifts for Jeanes supervising teachers in 1909 in North Carolina were overseen by the GEB, a function that became the job of the state agent when Newbold was appointed in 1913. The GEB also provided funding for a state supervising Jeanes teacher beginning in 1915, who would be located in Newbold's office, and augmented annually the Jeanes Fund contributions to the North Carolina program, where the number of teachers grew consistently between 1909 and 1932.[78] Counties that were interested in appointing a Jeanes teacher in the early years of the fund could make a request directly to the president of the Jeanes Foundation, but after 1915 all requests were made to Newbold, who corresponded with the foundation. Newbold considered these positions to be central to education reform: "From the beginning of the work of the Division of Negro Education, it was realized that the key person to the development of local schools was the Jeanes teacher."[79] Newbold was aware that his success depended upon local progress.

The negligible number of reported black school administrators obscures the growth in administrative capacity and bureaucracy that was developed in the state's rural black communities through foundation funding, which included the appointments of state agents and Jeanes teachers, school consolidation that streamlined authority structures, and the development of systems for ongoing data collection. Indeed, these programs were established in North Carolina quite early and continued to grow in subsequent decades. State standards and bureaucracy were important for political development generally and for public schooling specifically. Better data made clear the needs of rural communities and were instrumental to developing education policies; standards empowered local teachers to supervise both teachers and curriculum, and stronger administrative structures connected isolated schools and communities to state and county systems of governance.

Soon after beginning his appointment as state agent, Newbold received a long and detailed letter from J. R. Faison in Anson County detailing his work in the rural schools. At the time, Faison had held the position for one year, overseeing forty-three rural black schools that were in very poor condition. One of Faison's first acts had been to organize two school-betterment associations, a number of school clubs, and an industrial fair. Faison was clear, however, that the "most effective has been accomplished by the associations. For instance, one of the associations supplemented a teacher's salary in order to procure a proficient instructor. The other association has planned to move their school house to the center of the district, where the pupils may have good water and a larger playground."[80] Faison pointed out that the teachers had been organized into a teacher association prior to the appointment of a Jeanes teacher in Anson County but considered it a duty to "perfect this organization and make it permanent."[81] This correspondence is notable in a number of respects. First, it was clear that rural blacks had been organizing public schools in Anson County well before foundations began their work and would likely have continued promoting schooling regardless of foundation involvement. However, while foundation work was not the catalyst for rural black education, it did provide organizational sites for more formally expanding the schools. Second, Faison, in his capacity as Jeanes teacher, corresponded directly with the state agent about school activities. In that correspondence, the teacher highlighted the ways in which the Jeanes position was meeting the objectives established by the foundation and the state. The position provided for opportunities for the school to connect not just to the state administration, but also to residents of the community and, conversely, for the state to connect to Anson's blacks. Finally, the letter makes clear that Faison's position as Jeanes teacher might make it possible to use the foundations to achieve far more than industrial education.

In addition to the job description as defined by the Jeanes Fund, these teachers were also responsible for the homemakers club program, which was particularly effective in North Carolina. The homemakers clubs existed throughout the South after the Smith Hughes Act passed in 1914. However, in North Carolina, the state initiated a program in 1913 with the US Department of Agriculture's Bureau of Plant Industry.[82] The USDA explained to Newbold that the Bureau of Plant Industry was collaborating with the GEB, which had agreed that Newbold would be appointed state collaborator for the bureau, complete with franking privileges.[83] In addition, the US government would provide $1,000 to extend the time of "about ten of your best county rural school supervisors with the understanding that they are to do club work among their people," which might include "garden, canning and crop work among negro girls and boys," as well as their parents, with the "idea of improving home and living conditions."[84] Newbold restructured the offer and got permission to double the breadth of the work, providing smaller gifts to twenty counties and requiring more of a contribution from county funds and private donations but more than doubling the breadth of the work.[85] The USDA also consulted Newbold on whether "Home Making Clubs" would be an appropriate name and asked for suggestions with regard to badges and emblems.[86] The plan was for teachers to spend at least ten days each month for five months promoting club work as defined by the Department of Agriculture and the GEB.[87] However, even if the USDA had not provided the funding, Newbold had already explored alternative sources to extend the teachers' work into the community. He had also asked the state board of health for money to provide to Jeanes teachers to support an extra month or two of work for public-health initiatives.[88] As a result, the Jeanes teachers often received an eleven-month appointment in the state, and sometimes even a twelve-month one.

Teachers reported on their work in the schools but often focused on the club work that was central to creating community. A teacher reported that she had created four Betterment Leagues and had taught cooking and sewing in the homes of league members.[89] Teachers organized literary and industrial clubs for boys and girls, emphasized physical fitness in their club work, held lectures on health and other subjects, and promoted measures for better sanitary conditions. One teacher pointed out she had organized two cooking clubs but also said, "We have held several community meetings, organized and worked the road in the communities." Another teacher was more specific, explaining, "A general interest of the communities having the work was manifested through the women's clubs in the schools."[90] Another report lauded one of the teachers for having generated sufficient interest to send in eleven applications for Rosenwald buildings.[91] Through club work, teachers had greater access to members of the community, a platform for bringing the community together for education issues, and opportunities to raise money and facilitate the creation of a public system of schooling. After federal participation through the USDA for club work ended in 1917, the GEB continued to provide funding until 1922. However, by this time, the club work was institutionalized in each community, and most teachers continued community club work as part of their regular appointments.

Newbold believed that his own position should be used to promote community development for rural blacks, but these efforts depended upon the Jeanes teacher in each county. He developed a bulletin in 1918 that would foster "Negro Community Improvement Leagues" to promote community uplift and serve as the local organization responsible for collaborating with state agencies, including the board of health, the state home and farm-extension service, and the state insurance department. Newbold's report called for "establishing *one* strong community organization among the Negroes thru [sic] which shall be carried forward all the propaganda for community development, educational, health, home, farm, protection of property, etc., will be the means of helping the people to realize their possibilities along the various lines of growth, better than it could possibly be done through a multiplicity of organizations."[92] He knew the Jeanes teachers would promote this work if there were additional funding to employ them beyond the school year. Because the GEB and the federal government had already been funding Jeanes teacher summer work for Homemakers Clubs and extension work, Newbold was able to include his plan for community leagues in the teachers' regular job descriptions.[93] In that way, he used GEB funding not only to pay teachers throughout the summer, but also to have them assume responsibility for streamlining community organizations that could more easily cooperate with a range of state agencies.

The Jeanes teachers submitted monthly reports to Newbold, and he compiled them into a "progress report" that was shared with all state-supervising teachers as a means to provide suggestions for improving the work.[94] However, this process created stronger networks between black teachers across county lines and between rural black communities and state and local government agencies. Newbold considered those networks important, and facilitated them with his visits to local communities. When he was in Hertford County in 1914 to see an industrial exhibit and presentation attended by 150 people, the county superintendent announced that "two or three contiguous counties would unite and hold a joint institute for Negro teachers . . . such a union to continue for three or four weeks with several instructors."[95] The state encouraged such opportunities. In another visit to Sampson County in 1915, Newbold attended an exhibit organized by the farm demonstration agent, which included a meeting of the black teachers and citizens of the county, the domestic science advertising department of the Southern Railway, the white supervisors for the county, the state director of the Farmers' Institutes, the county health office, and the superintendent.[96] On a basic level, these meetings strengthened networks across the state. Beyond that, however, such meetings created formal venues in which rural black teachers and community members could participate in discussions about education policy with a range of government actors. These programs also served to integrate government agencies and strengthen governing capacities.

Teachers may have already developed their own networks, but foundation programs formally connected them to government agencies and the foundations themselves, and those groups were more likely to take seriously foundation-supported and state-sanctioned teacher or community groups than groups organized separately by rural blacks. In February of 1916, all of the supervising teachers in both North and South Carolina attended a meeting at the Slater State Normal School that was also attended by members of the North Carolina State Department of Education and county superintendents. The meeting included James Dillard from the Jeanes Fund, B. C. Caldwell from the Rosenwald Fund, and Jackson Davis, the first southern state agent in Virginia, who also worked for the Jeanes Fund and the GEB. Newbold organized state meetings that often included foundation agents, but foundations also organized such meetings.

While rural blacks were generally discouraged from organizing politically, black teachers could organize the community for the purpose of industrial education.[97] The early reports from the North Carolina Jeanes teachers indicated that community organizing was an important part of their work. Most teachers reported mothers clubs, homemakers clubs, girls clubs, boys clubs, and other types of agricultural clubs. Local white citizens did not perceive these school organizations as threatening and typically ignored the groups' work. However, this form of organizing provided rural blacks with opportunities to participate in discussions about education policy and to promote their own vision for education reform as part of a broader group of political actors with competing visions for change. The Jeanes teacher in Yance County reported in 1924 that she had "visited forty-seven homes during the month. In these visits I made it a point to visit the homes of the children who completed the seventh grade year to get the parents to see the importance of sending them to high school somewhere."[98]

Almost every teacher report included the amount of funds raised, typically through community organizations, to expand schooling. In 1915, teachers organized 355 clubs with a total membership of 3,854 women and girls, who raised $6,639 from poultry and the sale of canned vegetables and fruits.[99] In Iredell County, the teacher reported that a "patron gave four acres of land to the school," and the "proceed from the gardens will go towards extending the school term. He has promised to give four more acres if they are needed."[100] In 1916, Newbold reported that teachers had raised $15,293 for school improvements.[101] However, while many of these reports reflected efforts to solicit direct donations, some teachers recognized the connection between this work and governance. Faison reported in 1914 on fundraising in Anson County: "I am using three methods in raising money, one is through popular subscription, another by having teachers to give entertainments, and still another by free will offering and taxation. . . . The last two plans have thus far worked best in my county. Through these plans several teachers' salaries have been supplemented and one assistant teacher has been employed."[102] These organizations reached large numbers of rural black citizens in the name of industrial education. However, the club work raised money for education reform that went well beyond simple industrial work and enhanced the education infrastructure.

Health and homemaking brought the community together, promoted education, and linked the community to values beyond local concerns. It became evident to state agents early on that community organizations established by these teachers could have considerable influence and reach. Community building was a dynamic enterprise, providing a platform around which citizens could come together, at the same time that it provided opportunities to share information and exchange ideas about issues that encompassed far more than just agricultural work. Newbold was explicit in his 1918 letter to teachers when he asked them to organize in every community clubs of girls and women in groups of ten to twenty, and urged food producing and food saving. He hoped it would lead to permanent leagues for the promotion of all phases of real community work including schools, health, food, better homes, and war-work.[103] Indeed, in North Carolina, the Jeanes teachers were able effectively to mobilize groups for a range of social policy initiatives that were often defined outside the black community. At the same time, these efforts integrated government functions in ways that were relatively more inclusive of the black community.

In North Carolina, the Jeanes teachers were the primary administrators for black schools, and were also more likely to have a formally established line to county superintendents, the state, and foundations. Significant authority was vested in these teachers over time, and position descriptions were explicit with regard to the administrative oversight that these teachers would have. In 1932, Alamance County hired a teacher who was expected to have general supervisory duties but also to advise in the selection of teachers, conduct teacher meetings, and supervise the classification of pupils into grades, while in Catawba County the teacher would not just provide advice about selecting teachers but also have responsibility for employing them.[104] In later applications for Jeanes aid, the Anson County superintendent asked the Jeanes teacher to define her own job and make recommendations concerning the work.[105] The role of the Jeanes teacher in Bladen would be even more expansive: "Recommending teachers, holding teachers' meetings, visiting schools, distributing instructional materials, holding group conferences of teachers, organizing and helping Parent-Teacher Associations, encouraging girls and young people's clubs."[106] It was not just that these teachers took on far more than the job originally required. County officials who wanted little to do with the black schools abrogated their responsibility to them, giving the Jeanes teachers greater latitude to administer the black schools in their counties, often with reporting lines to the state agent, foundation representatives, and a range of state and local government agencies.

Private donations, whether from foundations or fundraising efforts within black communities, had greater significance than just the benefits of additional revenue because these gifts had the potential to influence the developing school system. GEB contributions to public school enterprises in North Carolina came to only $371,171 between 1902 and 1926, and the GEB was criticized for providing a relatively small amount for black education compared to its overall appropriations for general southern education.[107] However, foundation gift policies impacted both the infrastructure and its centralization. The Rosenwald school building campaign began in North Carolina in July, 1916, with a promise of $6,000 and instructions to build twenty schools and ensure the "money should be stretched just as far as possible."[108] The Rosenwald Fund agreed to supplement contributions from school officers and the community, on the condition that the public school fund or individual donations raised were in an amount equal to or larger than that given by the fund.

Additionally, the fund would also provide up to $300 for any one schoolhouse in 1916, an amount that changed in subsequent years based on the size of the school, but would not release the funds until the total amount was raised for construction.[109] In the beginning, the Tuskegee Extension Office administered North Carolina Rosenwald Funds, but within two years the work came under the purview of Newbold, who seemed to be quite effective at getting the most out of each dollar that the fund gave to the state.

Rosenwald provided a greater amount of appropriations to North Carolina than either the GEB or the Jeanes Fund, and the money it provided brought with it the greatest amount of contributions from local tax dollars and private donations.[110] For example, in 1917, Newbold provided a list of the twenty-four counties that had requested aid, totaling $5,600 in gifts, commitments for $9,273 of county funds, and private black donations of $6,470.[111] Newbold recommended that the fund provide $4,375 instead of the $5,600 being requested, so that counties would have to provide $10,075, with pledges staying the same.[112] The teacher from Wake County made clear in a 1924 report the sacrifice required for many of these private donations: "In May, several citizens mortgaged their property and borrowed from the bank in Zebulon $3,500. They had to do this as it is hard to raise money at this time of year. The parents have pledged this money and will pay those who borrowed the money in November. Zebulon has on hand at present $4,100. This is what they were required to raise."[113] Forcing additional community donations was inequitable given the burden already placed on the black community, but Newbold managed to get a little bit more from each. In the end, local funds raised in North Carolina, either privately or publicly, led to more teaching appointments, schools, and larger county budgets. These infrastructure gains were typically difficult to reverse.

North Carolina's state tax laws in the early twentieth century made it difficult to implement Aycock's vision for universal education. Foundation funding policies provided one means to collect local revenues and institutionalize schooling, even on grossly unfair terms. However, efforts by state actors in collaboration with foundations and outside organizations, like the Interracial Cooperating Commissions, made the state "pioneering, and in some respects, revolutionary" regarding the public schooling system.[114] Fortunately, the state had a history of relying on taxation to support schooling. Legislation had passed before the Civil War to fund public education from a state permanent school fund and county taxes. However, after the war, the new state constitution provided for four-month school terms in segregated institutions, but with strict limits on the combined state and county tax that could be provided for schooling. The tax ceiling meant that many counties were not able to find sufficient funding to meet state-mandated school terms. The poorer counties called on the state for additional funding, and the richer counties resented having to support those counties through a state equalization fund that was to be distributed in inverse value to the ratio of taxable property in each county. The arguments against the state equalization fund reflected not only a distaste for income redistribution but also a recognition that equalization managed by the state implied greater centralization of schools and a potential loss of local control.[115] Ultimately, the state did not raise the ceiling on local tax rates but consistently increased the state equalization fund and allowed counties to levy special taxes.[116] Even with these laws, however, local whites found ways to increase local taxes without benefitting black schools. In Moore County, the superintendent of Aberdeen schools reported that not one cent of the local tax was expended on black education because a special act of the legislature set tax rates of $.65 and $1.95 for schools but drew the district lines so that every single negro house and property was excluded from the local levy.[117]

By the early twentieth century, responsibility for schooling was established as a county issue, but it was not possible to levy sufficient local taxes except through special issue-specific tax districts that failed materially to change the ability of state or local governance structures to provide additional and sufficient revenues to the public schools.[118] The state continued to increase the equalization fund early in the twentieth century, though it was hard to provide sufficient funding to address the problem. Many residents resented increases to their property taxes and argued in court that limits on state and local property taxes should take priority over state mandates for greater standardization, including legislation to extend school terms. However, public opinion evolved toward greater support of schooling, and the state's courts concurred.[119] Beginning with Aycock, the state developed legislation for tax equalization across the state and slowly moved from implementing education reform only when special tax districts were approved to a system in which priority was given to state-mandated laws. For example, while high schools in 1907 existed only in regions that had successfully voted special taxes for their purpose, by 1917 counties were required to establish and fund high schools in accordance with state law and were precluded from denying tax assessments to do so. When the state mandated a six-month school term in 1919, most counties could not handle the burden of providing for high schools and the extra two months of schools. Both the problems of equalization and legislated caps on state and local property taxes impeded efforts to standardize schooling. The counties were expected to fund the legislated school term, but many had insufficient revenues to do so; others initiated special tax districts to extend those terms and add other amenities including high schools. As a result, local taxes increased, but so did the state's pledge to collect additional state taxes to augment county revenues.

Fortunately, in 1918, just before the school term was extended to six months, the state adopted a constitutional amendment that provided for the levying of a state income tax, which raised enough funds to allow the legislature of 1921 to abolish the general property tax.[120] The state also designated the poll tax for general county and state purposes, rather than as a basis for school funding, and repealed the law that made it a prerequisite for voting.[121] Many state politicians believed that tax legislation, especially as it granted greater authority to the counties to raise taxes in order to meet state mandates, was central to universal education. The state's interest in tax reform dovetailed with foundation efforts to create state systems of schooling funded through local taxes. The foundations supported efforts to increase state and local property taxes and any legislation that might increase revenues that went to the equalization fund. Fortunately, many state residents agreed, and those who opposed such efforts lost their battle in the courts. In the end, legislation to reform the state's tax code for public schooling gave counties control of schools in a more standard system as mandated by the state.

Newbold's role gave him opportunities to increase revenues for black education at the same time that it gave him political influence among black and white community members in a larger number of communities. He used the parameters of funding decisions to maximize both the number of schools that could be built and the leverage that could be gained with the possibility of funding. Rosenwald hoped that the rural building campaign would be conducted in cooperation with Jeanes teachers and the state agent wherever possible, which operationalized the role that the Jeanes teachers would have in the building campaign in North Carolina.[122] The system of providing small grants that required matching funds ensured that private donations would be institutionalized as part of the local budget, often creating comprehensive changes to the infrastructure. While "double taxation" was grossly unfair, in North Carolina in particular, where the teachers were so effective in raising money, the practice led to significant increases in local tax levies in order to sustain the expansion of the public system and the institutionalization of reforms, such as higher teacher salaries, term extension, and new school construction. Unlike other states that expected ongoing private donations, teacher fundraising efforts in North Carolina often led to long-term structural changes in education financing that were embedded in county budgets.

The GEB support for the development of county training schools, which might extend through the twelfth grade, is also illustrative. Newbold sent a letter in 1914 to the state's county superintendents requesting potential sites and setting minimum expectations. Each school should have a "fairly satisfactory annual income from permanent sources, a good building reasonably well equipped, a curriculum of nine or ten grades at least, and be located where it can meet a real need. A public school of three or more teachers might be developed into a training school of this type."[123] Many counties supported the schools because northern largesse promoting industrial education might lessen the local burden and placate the black community. In addition, since black teachers taught in black schools, training schools could meet a minimum need with foundation support. However, Newbold was clear about the connection between teacher training and a comprehensive school system and believed that elementary schools for blacks could not be improved without high school graduates capable of teaching. The state superintendent for education used that argument to request GEB funding to support the expansion of black high schools. "In other words, so long as the teaching profession stays on the level of the elementary school, we will never be able to make the elementary school what it ought to be. The best work that can be done right now to build up the whole situation for the negroes, as I see it, is to strengthen the high schools."[124] The GEB had promoted a more subtle agenda, believing that the "first results of an enlightened community interest and a sincere effort to improve the elementary rural school will be a demand for better teachers . . . [and that] the public high school for negroes will be an inevitable outgrowth."[125] Newbold, in fact, was willing to go beyond what the foundations hoped to achieve in terms of high school education and the foundations came to support that work.

The county training school initiative addressed the concern about teacher training in rural North Carolina. These schools were supposed to provide basic K–12 schooling, though most counties did not provide schooling for rural blacks beyond the seventh grade, and schools went only as high in grade level as the county was willing and able to provide. The county training schools were established as venues for teacher training because the state more closely oversaw the work in these schools. A teacher trained through grade seven and possibly higher with state oversight was considered far better than a teacher who had no training at all or one who had been more academically trained in a private academy. One of Newbold's most ambitious plans was to develop within five years of beginning the program a county training school in each of the state's one hundred counties. As of 1916–17, he reported that only six of these schools were in operation, and only one went as high as ninth grade (granting six certificates that year). However, six other counties had formally requested state assistance in establishing such a school, and "several other counties indicated interest," leading Newbold to feel optimistic that he could achieve his goal.[126] In order to receive funding for such a school, the county had to provide adequate funding to lengthen the school terms, raise teacher salaries to a minimum, and adhere to requirements around curriculum and certification. Once the commitment was made, it would be hard to take away these gains. Newbold's plan for a school in each county could have a measurable impact on the entire system of schooling because these schools could be developed as models for their counties, disseminating the state curriculum and best pedagogical practices. These schools were formally under the jurisdiction of the county superintendent, but ultimate responsibility belonged to the state agent, who was located elsewhere, and supervision on a daily basis fell to the county Jeanes teachers.

A 1920 letter to a superintendent in a county wishing to establish one of these training schools illustrates how private donations for schoolhouse construction might lead to significant gains. Newbold explained that the county might start with the new Rosenwald school as a center. He then described the resources that would be necessary to establish a county training school given an overarching goal of teaching "good farming, gardening and the like." The county would need to devote at least five acres of land, a salary fund for teachers, and provisions for at least eight grades, with the hope that additional grades could be added year to year, with an ultimate goal of twelve years of schooling. Newbold pointed out that if these conditions were met, he would ensure $500 from the Slater Fund to aid in paying teachers' salaries, possible funding from the GEB for salaries, and a "well trained man to teach Vocational Agricultural [sic] under the Smith-Hughes Fund."[127] A commitment for a rural Rosenwald school provided Newbold with an opportunity to create an education package for a community, one that promoted better teaching, a standardized curriculum, and higher tax contributions from the county, all of which would exist as part of the state system of education.

Newbold's letter to the superintendent also illustrates the extent to which he had access to funding from a variety of sources, a point that was not lost on rural blacks and whites and enhanced his influence and power. Rosenwald funding often came with the requirement that school terms be extended and minimum teacher salaries be provided. Indeed, by 1923, of the 236 Rosenwald schoolhouses constructed in the state, 163 had a six-month term, and seventy-three had a greater-than-six-month term, with eleven reporting a full nine-month term.[128] Indeed, Credle and Davis, the Rosenwald agents located in the North Carolina Division of Negro Education, reported regularly to the Rosenwald Fund about the relationship between schoolhouse construction and school terms, detailing the number of schools in session, the number that had extended terms, and whether the extended terms resulted from private subscriptions or special state or county aid. These schools were the precursor to the development of regular high schools in black communities and to teacher training at the college level. As such, their numbers diminished in the 1920s as regular district high schools were created and higher-education institutions grew. However, they played an early role in expanding both teacher training and the public system.

In the end, the Rosenwald Fund believed that North Carolina had shown "greater interest than any other southern state in providing good school buildings for its Negro students."[129] The state built the most schools and provided the largest proportion of matching funds. The fund's proportional share in the state was lower than that of every other state, because North Carolina was more effective at levying local taxes and legislating additional funds. However, the Jeanes teachers were also successful at raising private donations. While reform efforts were directed and partially funded by northern philanthropists, the state was more successful at transferring private initiative, including funding, to the public enterprise. The Jeanes teachers were essential to these efforts, and a more centralized system of schooling developed in the process.

Newbold sought a better state administration to manage and improve training, which became a state priority through 1925 because of the concern that there were so few teachers who were adequately trained in rural areas.[130] However, a related problem was the number of schools in which there were no teachers available to teach at all. In 1919, there were 433 teaching positions vacant in the state, not including open positions that county superintendents failed to report, which likely brought the number closer to five hundred. Newbold estimated that, on a conservative basis, as many as 250 rural schools were closed as a result, and fifteen of twenty-six schools in one county were closed for the year as a result of having no teachers.[131] Newbold explained to the state superintendent in 1923 that a conservative estimate of the number of new teachers needed for black schools in the state was approximately six hundred annually, a number for which at least five state normal schools for blacks would be required.[132]However, in 1923, only three state normal schools existed. Newbold's report illustrated the problem of training teachers at two levels. The most obvious was that without a sufficient number of trained teachers, a state curriculum would be moot. The second problem, however, was one of supervision and oversight. An expanded school system and greater centralization would have an impact on the number of teachers needed, as well as teacher training and certification.

The state certification requirements in 1921 included a provision that principals must graduate from a four-year normal school. However, there were no four-year schools for blacks in the state at that time.[133] Simultaneously Newbold was working to create a centralized system of schools with supervision and oversight provided at the local level, where rural schools lacked sufficiently trained black principals to take on the task. The deficit of their own training combined with the indifference of white superintendents meant that many schools saw no effort at all to supervise the curriculum, recommend improvements, or train teachers. Of course, the person who could take on this work in local areas was usually the Jeanes teacher. Newbold hired G. H. Ferguson in 1921 as assistant director of the Division of Negro Education, for whom teacher training would be a primary responsibility. Ferguson made frequent visits to the public and private colleges, organized educational offerings in line with certification requirements, set up a two-year normal school course to train teachers for elementary schools, collaborated with private schools, and arranged for the salary of one teacher at every private institution to be paid by the state for teacher training.[134] With Ferguson's help, the state developed a new state curriculum in 1921, which would be implemented in new normal school courses, defined as two years above high school.

Ferguson believed that the key figure in the development of local schools was the Jeanes teacher. Annie Holland was promoted from the role of county Jeanes teacher to a state-supervising role in Newbold's office. In 1924, she established the North Carolina Congress of Colored Parents and Teachers, which "soon became the most effective community agency for improving facilities and instructional staff."[135] Holland further promoted the important role of local teachers, making their work even more connected to rural black education policy development. These teachers had significant power in North Carolina, where the state acknowledged that by 1918 their positions in many counties were akin to that of the "assistant superintendent."[136] Indeed, the teachers were able to participate in more formal ways within the state bureaucracy than they were in most southern states. At the 1931 at statewide conference on Negro education, discussion focused on the ability of rural blacks to present requests formally to local authorities. Conference members proposed that institutions of higher learning in the state share information with local communities about school laws and data. During this discussion, the Jeanes teacher from Dublin County noted that the standard black high school "is being menaced because it is not included in the regular school district. Our problem is what is to be done." Her comment reflected the extent to which the schools were marginalized but also the opportunities created by foundations to connect rural schools to the state. Newbold explained that the North Carolina State Board of Equalization had provided money to the Dublin black high school, which meant that it was indeed part of the system, a public assertion that made clear his goal to expand schooling and strengthen administrative oversight.[137] In a later session, the principal of the Waters Training School in Winton noted that 440 students were transported to school every morning. . . . Our county board is very generous if they have the money. We keep at it and when things are blocked, we appeal to Mr. Newbold and he aids us."[138] Indeed, the Division of Negro Education was an effective state agency that seemed not to be unduly influenced by local politics and was a resource for citizens across the state.

The state worked to enhance teacher training through a variety of other measures, including summer schools, county training institutes, and community clubs. For example, many communities developed "reading circle work" that was organized and supervised by county superintendents and Jeanes teachers to increase skills of rural teachers. For the year 1923–24, fifty-six counties reported that this work was ongoing, with 1,907 of 2,260 teachers participating.[139] However, local areas did not always support these efforts. One Jeanes teacher wrote a confidential letter to Newbold in 1919, asking for his assistance in persuading the county superintendent to support the reading circle work that Newbold had requested she organize. She explained that the superintendent did not wish for her to adopt any aspects of the state curriculum that went beyond the basics, in spite of the fact that it was for the training of teachers, and noted that "he feels that Reading, Writing, Arithmetic, and Language is all should be given, and directed me to teach those branches." She also noted her concern that she had already taught a county training institute prior to learning of his displeasure about the enhanced curriculum and considered herself to be in a very awkward position.[140] This example illustrates that even when the state was able to implement teacher-training programs outside of regular schooling, counties were frequently unwilling to support this work or were uncomfortable with the possibility that programs might be used to enhance academic training. However, it is notable that this teacher continued the work and had a direct line to Newbold to support it.

Further, since the superintendent did not support the work, the teacher became solely responsible for teacher training and supervision.

The emphasis on industrial training in the curriculum remained relatively unchanged between 1910 and 1925, though steps were taken to expand the curriculum, often because rural blacks had a more formal voice in policy decisions. Annie Holland, in her capacity as supervisor of elementary schools, was responsible for visiting schools and supervising Jeanes teacher work in rural communities. Her report for 1923–24 provides evidence that while industrial training was still the focus of rural schoolwork, the state was working slowly toward raising academic standards. She noted that there were 2,503 Negro rural schools in the state, with an average school term of just over six months, and that standard tests were given to rural black students in six counties, but that she personally had supervised the testing of 1,619 students. Her report on the curriculum focused on health work in the schools and industrial work. However, she also pointed out that, "for the past two years we have emphasized reading in our rural schools, because the pupils are so backward in this subject. As a basis for stimulating both teacher and pupils, tests have been given. Standard tests have not been used to a very great extent on account of the cost of material."[141] Newbold may have hired black educators in his office for politically expedient reasons, but they used these roles to promote a better education system for rural blacks.

Holland worked carefully within the parameters of the reform system but, when the time was right, was able to promote higher teacher standards, which would lead to better elementary and high schools in the state. Her 1926 outline for supervising teachers included additional teacher-training programs, standardized tests, parent-teacher associations, school libraries, and provided for six units of work, the first of which was "to improve the quality of teaching," and the last of which was to "direct the teaching of industrial work."[142] She also noted that community cooperation could be developed through parent-teacher associations, community clubs, and school benefit events.[143] She had considerable influence in that state as evidenced by the comments made by the North Carolina state agent for Negro education in 1930, who advocated "the same course for Negro high schools that the white high schools had."[144] While an important element of the reform agenda early on was the creation of a trained and certified teaching force that was in line with the industrial-training agenda, by the 1930s expectations in North Carolina, where greater centralization had been achieved, were more consistently aligned with a call for greater academic training, especially for certification purposes.

George Davis, who served as a black Rosenwald Fund agent in Newbold's office, also promoted policy and practice that would expand black education benefits beyond industrial training, influencing architectural plans that could make schools the center of black communities. Credle reported on general improvements to the state's school system that resulted from Rosenwald funding, citing three hundred new schoolhouses for rural blacks, constructed in easily accessible areas with sufficient space for playgrounds and agricultural work. Credle justified these improvements to black schools, explaining that the architectural requirements not only improved rural black schoolhouses but also had an impact on the construction of schools for whites with regard to window placement, ventilation, painting, and other attributes. For both blacks and whites, these improvements to the buildings and grounds made it more likely that trained teachers might be persuaded to teach in rural areas.[145] Credle's advocacy for playgrounds and auditoriums as important community benefits reflected Davis's interest in including these amenities in rural black schools. Davis had reported from Belmont, North Carolina, where "auditoriums in these schools are doing much also to cultivate the aesthetic and social life of the brown group. . . . Many of our larger towns are providing play grounds and recreation centers for Negro groups. This attitude is doing much to integrate their lives into the community and to encourage them in self-development. It is safe to say that in rural centers Rosenwald Schools are leading to these results more than all other agencies combined, even producing results more beneficent than the churches of the rural centers."[146] In areas where local whites were reluctant even to build a school for their black citizens, the inclusion of expensive amenities likely had to be carefully negotiated. The inclusion of both black and white field agents was important to these efforts, and Davis's interest in the relationship between school and community development was influential.

Newbold's work with foundations, along with the influence of black educators like Holland and Davis and Jeanes teachers across the state, may have changed his perspective and his policies over time. In 1921–22, Newbold was granted a one-year leave to study at Teachers College, Columbia University. An excerpt from a draft of his thesis states, "It is no longer possible for any reactionary to say that the state is a pauper and prove his case. With a showing like this no responsible white citizen of North Carolina will be willing to say the state is too poor to provide adequate public school facilities for its white children, and for its Negro children as well."[147] His statements imply frustration with both the state government and with state residents who continued to oppose the provision of adequate education facilities, usually on the basis that localities were too poor. While he may have worked within the parameters of the state reform program, he also came to feel that rural blacks had not been treated justly in the state. Newbold expressed his evolving sentiments in 1922 in a letter to William Credle:

> A good many years ago I found that a number of people held the opinion that we should offer different courses of study for the training of negro teachers from those offered white people. I found myself inclined that way, however, my past eight years' experience have rather convinced me of the fallacy of this point of view. The only difference, I may say, is in degree or rate of progress. For instance, if you consider it from the stand point of an ascending scale with a possible basis of three points in a very large way, the whites as a whole may have reached two on this scale, while the negroes are still struggling with one. . . . I would refer you to the Army Tests. . . . These will show a very wide difference in the figures taken by the Intelligence Test of the whites and negroes in the draft.[148]

He believed that black achievement was behind that of whites, but also blamed this lack of progress, at least partially, on the state and its residents for providing inadequately for their training. The conflict between different groups involved in reform helped to change the conversation in North Carolina. Newbold came to believe that rural black citizens had not been treated fairly. Foundation programs helped black teachers and reformers to promote progress in rural communities and to have some wider impact in the development both of state ideals and the policies that came from them.

CONCLUSION

By the end of the Jim Crow era, North Carolina became a US pioneer in the centralization of state power that was a precondition for an effective reorganization of the state. The Brookings Institution report, using North Carolina as its shining example, recommended that political centralization was essential to providing the services necessary in a modern economy and to eliminating inefficiencies.[149] The report provides considerable detail about the evolution of public law with regard to school terms, high schools, and special tax laws to meet legislative requirements around schooling. It is, of course, silent on the gross inequalities that existed within the school system with regard to race. However, as practice and policy evolved, the North Carolina Supreme Court supported reform. While many citizens objected to the provision of numerous special tax districts to comply with minimum school terms, minimum teacher salaries, or the provision of high schools, the court ruled that the state legislature had the right to establish uniform standards for schooling, and that counties were rightfully required to levy sufficient taxes to meet these standards.[150] The language of the Granville case is particularly interesting because the court stated clearly that, "the large powers of regulation and control conferred upon our State board, extending at times even to legislation on the subject, the inclusive nature of the terms employed, 'to all the children of the State, between the ages of 6 and 21 years of age,' together with the steadfast adherence to this patriotic, beneficent purpose, throughout our entire history, it is manifest that these constitutional provisions were intended to establish a system of public education adequate to the needs of a great and progressive people."[151] The problem, however, was that as the court continued to support these mandatory tax levies, the comparison in taxes paid from county to county became considerably wide.

While foundations had worked through the state superintendent, the state agent, and Jeanes teachers to lobby for additional taxes on a county-by-county basis and strengthened state bureaucracy for the provision of minimum services, by 1931 the disparities by county were too great. For example, the Brookings report explained that until 1931 there were two school terms in North Carolina. The first was the six-month term mandated by the state, and the second was the extended term that rested upon a vote of the people in any district and operated under its own set of laws and provisions. Multiple tax districts existed to provide for standards that went beyond legislated services, like consolidation, rural schools, high schools, and graded schools. Ultimately, the state decided to centralize completely public school as a state function in order to overcome the disparities between counties in all of these domains. Specifically, the McLean law was adopted, which provided for a "general and uniform system of public schools" that would be "mandatory and that legislation will be enacted by this General Assembly to make it effective, so that the public school system for the constitutional term of at least six months shall be general and uniform in all the counties and shall be maintained by the State from sources other than ad valorem taxation on property."[152] The state law stated clearly that the amount due to any county from the state should be sufficient for general control, instructional service, operation of the plant, and auxiliary agencies.[153] Most important, the legislation expressly provided that the provision of public schooling for a term of six months would be in accordance with state standards. The provisions for public schooling were enacted along with new legislation that centralized state policies on taxation, roads, and local government finance. In the end, these sweeping changes represented a complete reorganization of state government, which was the result of agitation for changes in the organization and the administration of the state that began early in the century.[154] Foundation support was important to achieving these goals.

After 1932, when North Carolina had centralized more formally the administrative structure of the school system, teacher roles became more proscribed in local areas. This illustrated the extent to which centralization could be detrimental to black participation, even if it created the possibility that black schools would become more equal to white schools over time.[155] The state agent acknowledged this explicitly and worked to ensure that the teachers were still essential to the organization of rural black communities. He worried that greater centralization might limit the power of Jeanes teachers in local communities, and he advised them to continue their work until the next legislature could make provisions for their continued usefulness.[156] They were advised to assist the superintendent in selecting and placing teachers, to plan monthly countywide teachers' meetings where classroom work was outlined, and to aid in the examination of pupils for advancement. Newbold explained that the reorganized school system would group three to eight or more single schools into one administrative rural unit, which could be a distinct advantage for the black rural schools because it would encourage cooperation and consolidation within large areas, promote the emergence of high schools, and serve as a centralized unit for providing information on community improvement. He noted that there were fifty black school districts in Wake County prior to 1932 with more than six thousand children, but under the new plan there would be only eleven.[157]

The Brookings report predicted that the long evolution from bureaucracy to new organizational structures would have some unintended consequences. When the state commenced efforts to reform public education at the beginning of the century, reformers considered a range of strategies. One possibility was that the state could consider implementing a set of top-down initiatives that centralized control through state standards for teacher pay, the curriculum, funding, and reporting. This was hardly a feasible alternative when Aycock's team began working with northern reformers because it required political buy-in and might require a significant increase in state funding for education. While some state reformers might have been enamored of this idea in 1900, most foundation reformers and state politicians recognized that such a structure would need to evolve from a system developed from the ground up. Only then would residents feel some ownership over and connection to the public system of schooling, and support the increased funding it would require.

The state achieved a more centralized administrative structure by 1932, but that evolution required a number of interim steps. First, rural districts had to be sufficiently organized in order to join a state system. Foundations saw community organizing to be essential to the development of rural life. They promoted this in rural black communities through the work of the Jeanes teachers and local programming. Rural blacks participated because they understood that school organizations could redound educational benefits and provide a platform from which to promote community needs. The foundations recognized that stronger community organizations would create pressure for greater administrative capacity. It is not clear that black residents were concerned about administrative capacity, but possibly they perceived that community organizations formally connected to national and state networks would provide a platform to publicize education inequality and promote the outside interference necessary to address those injustices. A more well-developed school system and stronger community organizations in rural black communities almost invited greater oversight from both the county and the state. However, for rural black teachers, enhanced administrative capacity also provided them with greater authority to supervise rural schools and to participate in the bureaucratic structures that offered greater professionalism and leadership. Of course, once local communities developed their own organizational structures and were connected to state and local organizations beyond their community, their expectations for school reform increased. Foundation reformers and state politicians also recognized that increased bureaucracy was a first step toward enhancing organizational capacity at the state and local level. Foundations did not have the power to reorganize government, but their programs promoted that cause.

Efforts to create a centralized school system could not be imposed from the top down. While such efforts demanded infrastructure changes like increased funding, school administration and oversight, and teacher training, they also required rural participation. Bureaucracy in these domains helped to connect small, rural schoolhouses to a universal system of public schooling, where it was possible to begin to address the profound inequalities that existed between the two races, even if that was not the foundations' original intent. However, the evolution of Newbold's conception of black education indicated that as national and state ideals changed over time, centralized schools would be in better position to support that. Efforts to implement reform by region, and to accommodate local white attitudes, meant that early attempts did not immediately lead to a strong centralized system or any reconsideration of the purposes of black education. Over time, however, centralization evolved and connected rural black schools more formally to a state system. By that time, black educators had made inroads with regard to influencing the development of state educational policy, even if within strict boundaries. Many southern states worked collaboratively with northern foundations, but none had established as deep and enduring a partnership as North Carolina. That collaboration may have been generated by top-down initiatives but depended upon rural black citizens for its success. Over the longer term, black reformers were central to bureaucratic structures, but they also capitalized on their participation in ways that expanded formal black agency relative to other southern states in a difficult and risky compromise that ultimately took power away from them and vested it in the state.

CHAPTER FIVE

"Working with Them a Step at a Time"

While the Brookings Institution had developed an extensive congratulatory report on North Carolina government in 1932 for its successful efforts at centralizing state functions, including public schooling and related tax structures, a similar report on Mississippi in that same year came to almost opposite conclusions. The state's chief defects included the "division of power among elective officers and other agencies leading to a diffusion of responsibility and a lack of common direction and responsibility for the conduct of state administration." The heads of the many disconnected departments, bureaus, and agencies were typically elected and could not be coordinated by the governor. The report specifically recommended that a new state board of education be appointed, rather than elected, to succeed the work that was being carried out in fourteen boards and eleven professional examiner groups, which included a state board of education, a state board of vocational education, a state board of examiners, and a high school textbook commission.[1] The report's rebuke was not news to anyone familiar with Mississippi and was ineffective at promoting any significant change in governance at the state or local level, particularly with regard to the administration of the school system. In fact, previous attempts to address the state's governance issues had been similarly ignored. White supremacy and weak political development limited Mississippi's willingness and ability to collaborate with northern foundations, and an effective reform dynamic never developed in the state.

The political context in Mississippi created an educational policy void with regard to rural black schooling that was relatively greater than that found in most southern states. The state's politicians were reluctant to collaborate with outside groups and failed to develop stronger administrative systems within the state to promote change. Foundations responded by doing the obvious. They developed forms of collaboration that were peculiar to Mississippi. The foundations encouraged state participation where possible, but also sought alternatives.

White supremacy defined the social structure in both Mississippi and North Carolina, but it manifested itself differently in Mississippi. When the GEB ranked the southern states according to their educational progress, Mississippi was listed with the lowest seven states. However, foundations tried to understand the ranking with greater depth and generated data at the county level to determine which counties were favorable or unfavorable to reform and to delineate the reasons for an unfavorable rating.[2] Mississippi counties considered "unfavorable" typically cited a lack of funding as the primary reason. And it is true that the Mississippi economy suffered, especially in the sense that the agricultural economy depended upon an annual crop and fluctuated from year to year. Poverty was a fact of life in rural Mississippi. At the same time, it is essential to recognize that the lack of funding for education reform was also a product of the racial state. Mississippi politicians, and most of the state's white citizens, were unwilling to allocate funding for education or social services generally when they believed black citizens would reap benefits. One letter to the state superintendent of education was illustrative. The superintendent announced that his county had voted a local tax in order to receive state aid to extend the rural school terms to eight months. The request for term extension was intended for white schools, however, and the county superintendent was concerned about the legality of the plan. "Please inform me at once as to whether or not, under the law, darkies will be entitled to terms of equal length as white schools."[3] As this example illustrates, the foundation rankings lacked nuance, failing to recognize the possibility that, in spite of claiming that money did not exist, neither the state nor counties would have been willing to provide support if it did.

The foundations understood that a primary threat to education reform was the racial state. Efforts to expand education in the Delta community of Greenville, were telling. The county superintendent signaled a relatively humanitarian interest in black education, but was pessimistic about progress because of the "hopeless provincialism of the people."[4] A foundation report indicated that Greenville was in a region that was "liberal toward the negroes and anti-Vardaman in sentiment," but also made clear that "no one can work intelligently on the problem of Southern education who does not appreciate the immediate necessity of making this Negro question one of national concern."[5] Of course, the federal government was not willing to take on the issue of race in the South. Foundations worked around that lack of government support, which began at the national level but extended to state and local communities in Mississippi. However, there were limitations to what might be accomplished in the lower tiers of governance.

When the Rosenwald Fund offered to help with the construction of the Duck Hill School in Montgomery County, Mississippi, in 1923, the black residents embraced the opportunity, contributing $1,456 from their own pockets to supplement $700 that was awarded by the Rosenwald Fund and $344 in private white donations.[6] The Duck Hill School replaced a small makeshift school that was likely similar to many throughout the South, operating in a space not designed for schooling and lacking basic amenities including desks, textbooks, heat, and water. Five years after the school was constructed, one of the Duck Hill School teachers wrote directly to Julius Rosenwald asking for additional assistance. She expressed concern that she might seem ungrateful for asking for another favor on top of the original gift but felt it was necessary because "our white friends will not help us to a great extent." The new school had not been usable without desks, so residents ordered furniture from the Sears-Roebuck catalogue with money from their own pockets, for which seventy-five dollars was past due. She asked Rosenwald if he would personally cover the cost of the debt, which both the county and state refused, to ensure his "dream of a modern grammar school for colored . . . for which we shall be doubly grateful."[7] It is significant that this teacher wrote directly to Julius Rosenwald, and it is not clear whether he forgave the debt. However, the example illustrates the obvious fact that rural blacks were tenacious in their fight for expanded educational opportunity, and in Mississippi, where there was little support for those goals, foundations were unable to collaborate effectively with the state. As a result, reform initiatives often took place outside the boundaries of state and local governance systems through individual efforts that were difficult to sustain and had little impact on the state's administrative systems.

The state's weak administrative systems were the second important impediment to reform. A foundation field agent assessed the Mississippi work in 1919 and found that the first Mississippi state agent for Negro education had been working effectively, but "conditions have not been favorable. The County Superintendents, as you know, are elected by the people and in the 82 counties of the state, 50 have elected new superintendents, the changes being for the worse in most cases."[8] Most white citizens opposed the expansion of educational opportunity for rural blacks and those who were in favor were unlikely to pursue it. Further, white supremacy was an important reason for keeping power in local communities and inhibited any real effort to strengthen governance systems. While foundations found it effective in many southern states to locate their agents within state departments of education, this was far less effective in Mississippi. The weak state administration meant that local politics dominated state education policy.

Foundations developed forms of interstitial collaboration that would allow for cooperative ties to fill the policy-making void and expand schooling at the local level. They promoted the same programs in Mississippi that they did across the South. The state department of education received funding from the GEB to appoint both a state agent for Negro education and an assistant state agent, beginning in 1916. There were Jeanes teachers appointed in twenty-seven of the state's counties by 1932, and the Rosenwald Fund facilitated the construction of 633 elementary schools.[9] However, foundation-funded field agents were relatively less effective than in North Carolina, and the state failed to develop a more centralized system of education that resulted in greater standardization of the curriculum, teacher training, or certification before 1940. The state and counties lacked the administrative capacity to provide oversight to a public system of schooling, and tax law failed to provide adequate financial support to the schools. Foundations in Mississippi developed relationships to state and local politicians where possible but, as an alternative, also worked closely with the professor of secondary education located at the University of Mississippi, who was funded by the GEB to promote rural education programs in the state. They also worked with local citizens, where possible, to promote expanded education opportunity for rural blacks.

In spite of these efforts, foundations would have a difficult time in Mississippi influencing black education reform specifically and political development generally. Of course, rural blacks would also have relatively little opportunity to participate in foundation-based school reform. Mississippi failed to establish the formal bureaucracy and organizational structures to create rural black schools and connect them to a state system of schooling. Those schools remained relatively isolated from both formal governance structures and many of the informal networks that had been established throughout the South. The schools were at the mercy of county superintendents who ignored their every need, yet provided just enough oversight to limit their development. The story of black school reform in Mississippi illustrates regional distinctiveness and the limits of foundation efficacy. Interstitial collaboration was necessary to reform, allowing foundations to provide alternative strategies to implement programs that were tailored to regions, but those programs could only be effective when collaboration included state and local actors, or when foundation programs could be institutionalized in state and local governance.

Foundations recognized Mississippi's limitations and sought to collaborate in ways that might be effective within this set of difficult parameters. They continued to promote rural schooling and, at the least, attempted to demonstrate to rural blacks that help was available beyond the borders of Mississippi. Rural blacks, in this context, remained central to their own educational development and assumed the majority of the responsibility for improving their schools. Their efforts remained isolated, and their actions were often covert, presaging the extent to which an end to black oppression in Mississippi would require the force of both local effort and outside intervention. In the meantime, the schools would provide a central organizing venue for such grassroots participation in the early decades of the twentieth century.

PLEADING FOR GREATER COLLABORATION IN MISSISSIPPI: THE STATE

The lack of interest in establishing stronger state governance systems in Mississippi was a problem for political and economic development in the State, and particularly detrimental to education reform. Foundation efforts to provide funding to the state so that it could appoint field agents in the state department of education are illustrative of the difficult context. Mississippi agreed in 1908 to appoint, at GEB expense, a state supervisor of rural schools, who would promote public schooling, including changes to tax laws, provision for a system of county and district supervision connected with agricultural high schools, and conferences with county superintendents and principals of agricultural high schools to encourage consolidation and local tax levies.[10] The focus would be on white schools, similar to other rural school agents appointed throughout the South. Mississippi agreed to the appointment and followed it with two legislative acts that affected the expansion of rural white schools.[11] This was an important achievement given skepticism in the state about expanding educational opportunity at taxpayer expense.

Skepticism about education reform related to a range of issues. In part, it was due to the nature of the agricultural economy and a belief that education would not necessarily make a material difference in farmers' lives. The state's reliance on agriculture inhibited the development of an education vision that might serve as a basis for political and economic development. Beyond that, Mississippi citizens were vehemently in favor of state and local rights and suspicious of any plans that might transfer power to a more centralized system. A more significant issue, however, was the fear that reform might benefit blacks. While the state recognized a need to expand and improve rural white schools and was more willing to work with foundations toward that goal, it also stopped short of initiating or supporting comprehensive changes that included greater centralization, a redefinition of state and local oversight, and a reconceptualization of the tax code. As a result, the state did not collaborate with the foundations to alter fundamentally rural education unless the programs would lead to progress for whites only. For example, the state also agreed to appoint Susie Powell to be the white supervisor of school improvement with foundation funding, who canvassed the state and had considerable success developing white community organizations and school-improvement leagues. She developed her plans in consultation with the GEB and, by 1912, was able to hold a statewide school-improvement contest, with awards given in each congressional district for sanitation, beautification, and the largest number of new local associations.[12] However, many whites were unwilling to move beyond these modest initiatives to a more comprehensive overhaul of the public system of education. And, if foundations were not able effectively to collaborate with state politicians and reformers to alter the public system of education for whites, it was unlikely that any progress would be made with regard to developing one for blacks. Indeed, foundation programs for rural blacks that were successful in other states were relative failures in Mississippi.

The widespread politicking and corruption throughout the state extended to black education reform. In 1914, GEB secretary Abraham Flexner wrote to the Mississippi State superintendent to encourage the appointment of an agent whose primary focus would be rural black education. The foundation's request highlighted problems with the state's education infrastructure: "It seems to us above all that the most useful service that can at this time be performed by the rural school agent lies in the direction of bringing about improved underlying conditions . . . by underlying conditions we meant such things as organization, taxation, length of school terms, salaries, training of teachers, etc., [and that the state superintendent ought to be the] judge as to the relative urgency of the several items forming your program . . . the outcome of which would be a common movement towards a common end."[13]

Mississippi provided an extreme example of the problem of inefficient government led by local and partisan rule. The state also exhibited the disadvantages of an uneducated workforce, with high rates of illiteracy in its majority black population, many of whom were isolated in rural communities. The foundations recognized that the state agent was an important position to address these issues. However, it took two years more for the state to appoint someone permanently, and that appointment was tainted by corruption and state politics. In 1916 the state appointed John Ellis, who would be assisted by R. S. Grossley. Ellis had been a relatively progressive superintendent in Lauderdale County and had the support of the state superintendent of schools. However, soon after his appointment became official, he was indicted for transactions that had occurred while he served as the Lauderdale superintendent and was urged to plead guilty to what some perceived to be a trumped-up charge that emanated from an outmoded law that "every progressive county superintendent of the state violated, if he did a construction job."[14] Many assumed that his plea would end the legal battle, though he was called into court and sentenced to four years in prison, and then pardoned by the governor a few weeks later.

Bura Hilbun was appointed along with William Strahan in 1917 and served until 1928. Hilbun was subsequently indicted and sentenced to five years for claiming to have used Rosenwald funding to build rural schools that were never constructed. The governor pardoned him before he finished his sentence.[15] Willard Bond, the elected state superintendent of schools, selected William Strahan and Percy Easom to replace Hilbun, put Easom in the role of assistant, and announced the appointments in the newspapers in advance of gaining GEB approval. The GEB actually had concerns about both of these men, and questioned the state's model of having two agents appointed instead of one, but preferred Easom to Strahan. Bond acknowledged that he "had probably hurried in his action" but explained that "hesitancy on his part to make known his preference of Mr. Strahan as Mr. Hilbun's successor would have resulted in great pressure being brought to bear upon him to appoint some political follower of the present Governor."[16] The GEB relented in their criticism by "adhering to the fundamental principle of the Board in recognizing that this is the state's work and these are the state's men. We get further in the end by working with them a step at a time, than by imposing conditions which may impair the feeling of local responsibility."[17] Easom remained in the office for two decades, in spite of a lack of state funding for the position.

The foundations had some success collaborating with state superintendent Willard Bond. Bond was elected to the office in 1916 under Governor Bilbo. He had written a confidential note to the GEB regarding his difficult reelection campaign in 1923: "I suppose you have heard of the very bitter campaign through which I have just come as a candidate for reelection to the office of state superintendent. My opponent used the high cost of textbooks, what we have done for negroes, and many other things against us. He even accused me of being fair to Catholics."[18] He was eventually defeated in his reelection bid for the office in 1935 and replaced by J. S. Vandiver. One of Vandiver's first acts was to meet with the GEB to discuss specifically the public-private collaboration that Bond, his predecessor, had promoted between foundations and the state, and noted his desire to get rid of personnel in the Mississippi Department of Education who were funded by the GEB and had "participated actively in the campaign against him."[19] He wanted the names and salaries of the persons paid with funds provided by the GEB and the dates their current appointments expired. The GEB encouraged him not to take such action, and also informed him that its support of special divisions within state departments would be withdrawn.[20]

The discussion with Vandiver is just one of many illustrations of GEB efforts to improve governance in the state in a difficult political climate. As the example indicates, education policy in Mississippi in 1935 still depended on elected officials and the spoils system rather than on professional expertise and a more centralized state, in spite of efforts to address these issues over the previous decades. The lengthy stories of these appointments, indictments, and interactions with northern foundations reflect not only difficult state politics and the presence of corruption, especially in promoting black education, but also the general lack of administrative oversight. Nonetheless, the foundations persevered in their efforts to promote better coordination, stronger administrative systems, and universal education.

In fact, while state agents were effective in other southern states, they were not in Mississippi. By 1916, the state relied upon foundation funding to support a state supervisor for rural schools, a supervisor for school improvement, a state agent for Negro education and an assistant state agent. Yet, the foundations felt frustrated by the lack of progress in developing a public system of education, especially with regard to rural black citizens. The state made progress in expanding white schooling but did not materially change the state system of administration.

Foundation representatives called a meeting with the state agents for Negro education in 1925 to figure out why so little had been accomplished. The two men prepared a detailed description of their work. They explained that they were, essentially, "assistants to the Superintendent, at his will," and expected to focus on state initiatives that included Better School Week campaigns, county superintendent conferences, and county trustee meetings, work that was often only tangentially related to rural black education. They argued that the unrelated work provided a "wedge in launching the educational program for the negroes." They also outlined their specific responsibilities to the foundations, which included the Rosenwald Building Program, the teacher-employment bureau, and supervision of twenty-four county training schools, twenty-three Jeanes teachers, and a network of nineteen summer schools. But none of these initiatives was a primary focus. The men hoped to create a summer-school manual and lamented that the Rosenwald program required three trips to the site of each construction project, while the county training schools were "weighing heavily on our hearts at the present time," and the Jeanes teachers received only a "minimum amount of time which, of course, is a regret to us."[21]

Indeed, none of the agents were particularly effective at translating foundation objectives into state initiatives in Mississippi. First, the lack of state support meant the agents had no funding to support even minimal initiatives. In 1929, the state agent made a plea to northern foundations for an award that would not be earmarked for specific projects but instead deposited in a state fund for leveraging local communities, used to improve the school plant, and put "to great advantage in stimulating school authorities to provide more adequate equipment."[22] The foundations were understandably reluctant to provide such a slush fund. Second, the agents were reluctant to participate in the collaborative relationships and programs that were developing throughout the South, because it might hurt their relationships with local communities. At best, they might be politically maligned; at worst, they might be indicted. Finally, it is not clear that the agents had a positive view of rural black education anyway. It is likely that the state agents had mixed feelings at best about what was possible or desirable, in spite of their willingness to occupy these foundation positions.

An obvious problem was that the heavy reliance on elected positions made it difficult to work with local school boards, though it is just as likely that the state agents themselves had ambivalent feelings about the work. The first state agent for Negro education, Bura Hilbun, articulated this problem in one of his earliest reports after meeting with the superintendent of Carroll County. "I find often that the County Superintendent would do more for the negroes were it not for the fear of his losing his hold on the people in a political way."[23] It appeared that this agent had some good intentions, which the GEB acknowledged when it claimed that "the situation in Mississippi is not exactly satisfactory, but I am convinced that Mr. Hilbun is trying hard to push his work along."[24] Hilbun explained that his work was "considerably handicapped, because of the attitude of the board of supervisors in assisting in paying the salaries of the state teachers. . . . I sincerely hope that having failed twice in the attempt to get the Legislature to allow the superintendents the authority to write pay certificates on the county school fund for their teachers, that next time we will be successful."[25] Hilbun's initial correspondence indicated some real interest in promoting black education, yet he was in the office only a short time, and his records were not as robust as that of the agents who succeeded him, making it difficult to evaluate his work. He was also alleged to have misappropriated foundation funding, which potentially calls into question both his efforts and his motive.

The foundations recognized that there were whites in Mississippi who perceived that some education was essential to sustain a black labor force, providing a wedge to promote progress, no matter how meager. Bolivar County, located in the Delta where the ratio of blacks to whites was four to one, had proposed to establish a county high school for black youth, the first of its kind not only in the region but also in the state, and the Bolivar Board of Supervisors had donated $25,000 to the cause.[26] The effort, however, was a strategic one. "Negroes have been leaving the state in large numbers, and I do not doubt that the proposed school represents an effort on the part of the white people to hold them here by increasing their educational advantages and otherwise causing them to be more contented."[27] In 1919, a landowner in Leflore County, also in the Delta, had desired to "do something nice for the negroes on his plantation" and asked for assistance from the county superintendents and the state agent.[28] As a result, a model school was built at the cost of approximately $20,000, with a plan to extend the plant to include a laundry and blacksmith shop to support industrial work. The state agent hoped that other plantation owners would be inspired by the school to construct industrial-training plants on their own property, because plantation-based schools encouraged plantation tenancy arrangements. As one state agent said, "A good schoolhouse for your tenants will help you to hold a better class of tenants, and at the same time, of course, it will help the tenants themselves."[29]

A number of plantation owners supported these efforts to prevent the black tenant population from leaving. The *Chicago Defender*, the popular national black newspaper, reported in 1920 that a large, two-story residence had been purchased to be schoolhouse in New Albany, Mississippi, because the board of education realized that "more ought to be done for the members of our Race in an educational way in order to keep them satisfied in the South."[30] According to the article, black parents had been sending their children to other states to be educated and then leaving their jobs to follow them. The *Defender* reported in 1925 that the US secretary of labor planned to focus on bettering schools in the South because "the migration of the past eight years has taught us the lesson of the terrible cost of educational negligence."[31] Black citizens recognized the threat to wealthy landowners and could capitalize on that fear in those areas, like the Delta, where whites were more likely to address, even if minimally, the needs of their tenant population. Unfortunately, there were also planters who remained ambivalent about the cost benefits of providing greater educational opportunities to black laborers. Mississippi demagogues like Vardaman and Bilbo achieved political power because they understood that whites across the state shared these sentiments. They capitalized on those beliefs and promoted the most extreme beliefs about white supremacy with regard to education.

State politicians often worked actively against efforts to expand black education, particularly when those efforts were funded by private foundations, reflecting not just a personal interest in negotiating the political context to win the next campaign but also a deep concern that good governance in Mississippi depended upon limiting outside interference. Further, while many black citizens came to recognize that outside interference might be the only way to end oppression, they also believed that they were the best managers of their own schools. Of course, this was a concern in every black school in the South but an even more difficult issue in Mississippi, where neither the state nor foundations had developed an education infrastructure that rural blacks found compelling. Even the state agent understood this tension: "I find in some counties that there is a little bit of fear in the minds of some of our white people, also our colored people, with reference to going into a building proposition of any kind. They fear that some outside authority will get hold of the school. This is entirely a false assumption."[32] While the main impediment to change came from Mississippi's white citizens, black citizens in that context were suspicious of aiding in the development of a more centralized school system, which would be managed by politicians who often did not support even a minimal education for rural blacks. As a result, it was difficult for foundations to develop a set of allies in the state.

It is unlikely that even the state agents really supported the expansion of black schooling. They were relatively ineffective in promoting rural black education, and foundations understood that working in Mississippi would require new strategies. The GEB had funded a professor of secondary education at the University of Mississippi beginning in 1908, who would be in a position to help to promote education reform and strengthen cooperative ties between foundations, universities, and elite state actors. The professor's principle work would be to determine where conditions were favorable for the establishment of public high schools, create public sentiment for their establishment, and then place the high schools under local leadership, at the same time that he and the university planned to "exercise a fostering care over such institutions."[33] While these university positions existed throughout the South, the program took on greater significance in Mississippi, which had a history of delegating education policy for the high schools to the universities.[34] The GEB reported at a 1909 conference that "Mississippi had no means of reaching high schools apart from those associated with the University."[35] The university office operated as a separate agency, with 101 high schools in the state affiliated by meeting university admission requirements by 1912.[36] While the high school curriculum was typically developed and promoted in state boards of education, in Mississippi the curriculum was often developed by the university professor and shared with the GEB.[37] Of course, there were no black high schools so the position served primarily the state's white high schools. However, the most detailed information about the State's rural schools, including those serving the black community, often came from the university professor rather than the foundation-appointed agents in the state department of education. The university reports to the foundations provided a wealth of information and an insightful analysis of the social and political context.

The university professor was a step removed from local or partisan politics, but also lacked power relative to other political actors who were located within formal governance structures. Thomas Bailey was the first appointee in Mississippi and felt that his connection to the GEB was fortunate because educators perceived him as more than merely a representative of the university or the state—a characterization similar to that describing the benefits of having state agents for Negro education located in state departments of education throughout the South.[38] Unfortunately, a university professor did not have the power of a political position, like the state agents, though the appointment provided some means to implement reform outside of normal governance structures. Foundations fostered this relationship but also recognized its limitations. After more than a decade of working closely with Bailey and then John Fant, his replacement, the GEB asked the state to reconsider whether high school supervision should take place in state departments of education, but the state was not interested in exploring the idea.[39]

John Fant replaced Bailey in 1910. Under Fant, a stronger connection developed between schooling and the university, which helped to promote a more standard curriculum in the absence of state mandates. Fant's views were similar to those of the northern foundations. "Increased crop yields are essential to the development of rural civilization, as the people must have larger means if they are to be able to build and maintain better schools, better roads, and better country conditions generally."[40] He recognized that education was important to rural prosperity. GEB representatives visited the state in 1914 and traveled to a number of schools with Fant. They were pleased with his efforts to relate the schools to country life and offered to join him in developing better farming methods toward increased production.[41] Both Bailey and Fant acknowledged in their reports a need to address the "negro question" in the state and expand educational opportunity for both races. However, their position as professor of secondary schooling limited their ability to address the needs of the black community until black high schools actually existed. Nonetheless, the position was important to foundation efforts.

Fant's reports to the GEB were more similar to Newbold's state-agent reports than those of the Mississippi state agent were, and his correspondence makes clear the close relationship that Fant developed with foundation representatives. He reported that he had enjoyed visits from foundation leaders, like the secretary and president of the GEB, which resulted in a change to the University of Mississippi admission requirements. The new requirements would reflect formally what Fant believed had existed already "in spirit, in close co-operation with the work of such schools as those which [the GEB representatives] visited in the state." [42] He attached to his letter a copy of correspondence that he had with the university chancellor explaining that the university would modify enrollment requirements in order to recognize vocational subjects, which would place the university more in harmony with the universities of the West and into "close articulation with the county agricultural high schools of the state." [43] These charges also meant that Fant was moving requirements into greater conformity with those of the foundations, even if these early efforts included only white schools.

Fant had some power to promote the kind of collaboration that was lacking at the state level. He had met with the state's county superintendents in 1914, and the profitable meeting looked as if it might result in new legislation for the schools.[44] He had proposed to the superintendents a new scheme for the certification of teachers, which was unanimously adopted by the group and forwarded to the legislature for enactment into law. In a detailed report on high school development, he noted that in spite of local interest, high schools "suffered for the lack of central guidance and control, and of a systematic plan of development. The first agency of this sort has emanated from the state University."[45] However, the foundations' most important ally in Mississippi was focused primarily on white schooling, though his efforts in that regard improved the state's administrative systems and connected local schools to a public system that might be transformed over time. The state agents were also not effective at expanding black education in a meaningful way, but believed that their presence at the least created the wedge that foundations needed to promote local change. However, Fant was supposed to coordinate the state's high schools, and for rural blacks high schools did not exist, although he continued to promote their development. The foundations were more sympathetic to the parameters of his work and appreciative of his extensive efforts on behalf of broader goals.

The university also understood that it would, unfortunately, have to conform to the racial state. In the early days of his work with the university, Chancellor Kincannon made clear what would be allowed in the state. He had initially received a resolution of confidence from the trustees of the university. Soon after, however, Governor Vardaman appointed a number of new trustees known to have unfavorable views of the chancellor's work. The university asked him to resign shortly thereafter.[46] It was unclear how much influence the state administration had over the university in subsequent years, though in 1922 the GEB received a letter of complaint from a faculty member who was concerned about the relationship between political favors and one of the GEB appointments at the university. "There is very satisfying evidence that the appointee of the Chancellor's to my department received his appointment for his work on the state textbook commission, which, you will find, obtained the reputation among book companies of being the most crooked adoption in the United States. The Governor and Chancellor deserve to be exposed, and it is my intention to take the matter up immediately for the approaching session of the Legislature. . . . I suggest that you start an investigation as to how your appointment has been used in Mississippi."[47] It seems that, at the least, the possibility for interference likely affected many university decisions in the early decades of the twentieth century and culminated in Governor Bilbo's infamous attacks on academic freedom at the University of Mississippi in 1930.[48]

Fant promoted schooling for rural blacks where possible, however, and frequently discussed rural black communities in his reports. In 1917, he reported on efforts to join other southern states in promoting the establishment of county training schools for rural blacks, and he invited a GEB field agent to Mississippi to discuss a proposition for promoting these schools. He was the GEB agent most active in efforts in Bolivar County to provide a public black high school in order to encourage blacks to stay in the county. In 1919, he requested funding from the GEB to promote a campaign for better schools in the state, and in developing a plan for that work he also consulted the state's black teacher associations, which had raised $250 for the effort. As Fant said of the donation, "They, of course, will profit indirectly in the results."[49]

Fant's work became central to foundation aims, but the GEB also understood that he had limited power, and his efforts might not lead to sustained reform. The foundations did not provide him with extensive funding, and that included denying his request for the school campaign in 1919. However, the request indicated the scope of Fant's work. His proposal included considerable data about Mississippi's black and white schools, and he planned to have educational speakers canvas the state, which he hoped would result in better buildings, longer terms, and better-paid and better-qualified teachers. For the foundations, there were political problems associated with giving funds for such a campaign in 1919, but it was also not clear that it would lead to the kind of sustained reform that was worthy of foundation investment, given the political context and the poor state infrastructure.[50] In spite of Fant's efforts to define a far-reaching, well-organized campaign, the foundations likely believed it did not make sense to provide significant investment to an undertaking that did not feature direct state involvement.

The reports to the GEB written by Bailey and then Fant, which began in 1908, consistently highlighted administrative impediments to reform. County superintendents were actually required to have educational training and were responsible for filing annual reports with the state about numbers of schools, personnel, budget allocations, and enrollments. However, when Professor Bailey filed his first report, he underscored the lack of oversight in rural counties:

> To show how little has been known about the Mississippi high schools, even by the University, I may instance the report I sent in last Sept. of the number of high schools in the various counties. . . . There were no records that I could appeal to. Even this year it will be hard to get reports from some of the schools. . . . I fear that all these southern data will need careful criticism. . . . The Co. supts. [sic] are often incompetent, and the qualified ones are too much crowded or too much engaged in getting ready for another campaign. Again and again do I find their judgment at fault in regard to the schools they visit.[51]

Fant expressed similar frustrations after he replaced Bailey: "I have not been able by a good deal to cover the entire state by personal visits, but have attempted to do so by correspondence and the use of suitable literature. Even in this way I have not been successful in reaching all the high schools of the state; as a good many of our county superintendents of education and principals of school have failed to respond to repeated requests. So far as I know they are *unable to write*. [emphasis in original]"[52] These reports underscored foundation concerns and made clear that significant investment might be for naught.

Fant recognized, like the foundations, that the lack of reliable data made it difficult to design and implement programs. This was another intractable problem because, again, nobody was really interested in actually solving it. Indeed, while conditions in Mississippi were not a secret, more data would highlight the gross disparities that most white Mississippians lauded and call out the counties that were doing more for black citizens than many whites found palatable. It is incredible that even county officials claimed not to be able to produce basic information about their black schools, though they must have known of every school in their district. The lack of general information and oversight made it difficult to implement foundation objectives, or to promote greater standardization as part of a school system for blacks.

In one example, a black teacher wrote to the state agent requesting funds for school equipment, and the agent's first response was that he would need a "little more information with reference to the size of your school, when it was built and just what equipment you have, and what you need."[53] In spite of the fact that the school was a four-teacher Rosenwald building that had been constructed just two years earlier, the state claimed not to have records available to evaluate the request.[54] In another example, the state agent wrote to the superintendent of schools in Forest, Mississippi, and reported that the principal from the black school there had stopped by the state offices to ask for additional aid to pay the salary of a fifth teacher. "From what he said about conditions, it seems that there is really a need for this additional teacher, but this department has very little money for negro schools."[55] The state agent provided no evidence to support the principal's request and, again, offered no encouragement to the teacher, even after he had traveled to the state offices. Another letter to the Rosenwald Fund by one of the state agents is telling: "On September 8 you wrote us in long hand asking for some data which should be gotten from our Department of Statistics . . . the blank is herewith enclosed with comment on yellow sheet attached. May I suggest that you use the same figures, possibly swelled a little bit, in this case. I am sorry that this cannot be given exactly. As you know, we are trying to get things in shape and in the future we hope to be more prompt in granting all requests."[56] He acknowledged that the data were estimated and that this administrative issue required correction, but nothing was done to change it.

In fact, the lack of data likely served the objective to limit black schooling. Indeed, written documentation and extensive data could be detrimental to the goals of both state and local politicians. In 1929, the state agent for Negro education wrote to the superintendent of Tunica County to warn her that it appeared there would be an investigation of work done in Tunica's black schools in recent years. The agent warned the superintendent to "be sure to keep all records and letters that you now have in your possession. You may be called on for these if this investigation should get under way."[57] The letter neglected to refer to the issue at hand or offer advice, except noting how important it was that a review of documents might take place. An elected official might be tempted to dispose of documents that were favorable to black schools, while a corrupt one might be tempted to do so for other reasons. In another example, the state agent reported to the superintendent in Coahoma County that he had been "accosted" by a reporter after he had visited an agricultural high school there. He had given the reporter "such facts as I remembered them, carrying in mind that nothing should go in the paper that would be detrimental to the cause your school represents."[58] He advised the superintendent to "work this whole matter on the quiet," and promised not to discuss his own findings, even with members of his own department. In closing, the state agent reminded the superintendent that if she decided to "have some of the representatives of out-of-state funds visit you, you may feel free to call on me for any kind of service you may want me to render."[59] The implication here is that the superintendent promoted rural black education and hoped to have foundations visit her county, perhaps to showcase progress, or perhaps to make a case for additional funding. Regardless of the reason, it was clearly important that the information not be widely shared.

The lack of reliable data was just one of the limitations of the weak administrative structure. A related issue was the lack of state policies with regard to the curriculum, pedagogical practice, or the training and certification of teachers. Fant explained that trustees in one county had been authorized to establish a high school course of four or fewer years with at least a seven-month term but that no provision had been made for state direction, supervision, or support of such work.[60] The state superintendent of education acknowledged in 1915 that state oversight was lacking and provided an outline to the GEB regarding a proposed administrative structure that included cooperation with local and state agencies to provide oversight. The GEB, however, recognized the limitations of the proposal and encouraged the superintendent to visit Baltimore, Maryland, in order to see their model county school before implementing any plans in Mississippi.[61] Nothing came of these initial efforts, which remained a source of frustration for the foundations and their agents.

When Fant appeared before the state school code commission in 1917, he asked the GEB to provide materials about the "best means for creation of a state board of education, its character, personnel, duties, term of office, etc. I am inclined to think that our State Superintendent of Education should be elected by this Board and not by the people as at present. Also, we want to reorganize the county board of education."[62] Fant found it difficult to work with county boards that were appointed by an elected county superintendent and expressed his frustration about the lack of legislation in the state with regard to high schools. In response, the GEB forwarded their own report on public education in Maryland, which they believed provided an outline of best practices in state education administration, and promised to send as many copies as Fant might need for the hearing.[63] Unfortunately, while it was clear where the problems lay, the state made no progress in addressing these issues over the next two decades, a problem that foundation field agents and the university professors regularly lamented. For example, Fant expressed dismay in 1918 that the new school code, which would have reorganized education administration in the counties, was not passed.[64]

While states like North Carolina were moving to more centralized systems, promoting standardization and a stronger bureaucracy, Mississippi failed to move in a similar direction. At a very basic level, the lack of attention to infrastructure issues, such as good roads, impeded education development.[65] It was difficult to promote reforms like school consolidation and better oversight without roads over which to transport students and teachers. It was even more difficult absent state education policies and procedures. The superintendent of Bay St. Louis wrote to the state agent about administrative requirements for black high schools, information that appeared nowhere in the state's education bulletins and about which he had limited understanding that was based on observations of the black schools in his county He asked for state guidelines for four-year, three year, and two year high schools and provided a one-paragraph description of what he understood to be the minimum requirements for each type with regard to library and laboratory equipment, number of teachers, suitable buildings, and school terms.[66] The state agent responded, "The requirements set up in your letter for the various types of high schools for negroes are as nearly correct as I can make them. These requirements have not always been adhered to strictly but they are just about in accordance with the usual practice."[67] In 1929, when the principal of the Booneville, Mississippi, Colored High School wrote to the state agent for Negro education seeking information about what was required to transform the school into a county training school, the agent responded that the state had no literature pertaining to the establishment of county training schools.[68]

The agent sent information about required courses and textbooks, but was pessimistic in his correspondence that adequate funding or a sufficient concentration of black residents existed to expand the school anyway, implying that the request was irrelevant. The black resident knew that county training schools, a foundation initiative, existed, but the state refused basic information about the program. The information requested in both of these examples would be fundamental to a developing school system, yet the state made no real effort to guide that development.

The lack of both data and formal policy continually frustrated the foundations, though the state did not address either issue. The Rosenwald Fund wrote the state agents specifically to request better information to guide funding. "Would it not be possible for each superintendent to furnish you a county map showing the location of the Negro schools in the county, indicating where he desires to build the new school and the territory it is to serve. This is definitely required when an application for a seven teacher school or larger is filed. It occurs to me that it would be well to do this same thing for smaller schools wherever possible."[69] The letter to the state agent indicated the level of frustration and the difficulty of making funding decisions. The state agent responded that he was encouraging county superintendents to develop their own map of these schools, which delegated the task without creating any real expectation that it would happen.[70] The state agents were certainly aware of the issues, but worked in a context in which there was inadequate interest to address the problem. Indeed, it was politically expedient not to do so.

When the Rosenwald Fund supported state-based research programs in 1926, some state agents made requests to explore issues like the relationship between class size and learning, or higher education financing. The Mississippi state agent wanted help setting up a proposed plan of county organization for school administration and supervision, and a system of surveys to gather county information that would lead to better administrative and supervisory practice.[71] Fant had made this same request almost ten years earlier, and Bailey when he was first appointed before him. The state agent's 1926 request for help strengthening the state administration of public schooling was the continuation of a conversation that had started with the first university professor in 1908, and which continued to go nowhere.

The state did not take advantage of foundation interest, choosing not to borrow the organizational capacity that might have helped to shape the administration of public schooling. Foundations, instead, worked to leverage change through alternative means.[72] However, the attempt to bring along a reluctant state was fraught with difficulty, even if the state agreed to participate in some foundation programs.[73] Indeed, in those rare instances where the state seemed aligned with foundation goals, state agents sometimes tried to leverage local communities. The agent reported in 1920 that he hoped to "see if an appropriation from the Slater Fund would be worth while [sic] to stimulate the school [Bay St. Louis] to do better work."[74] There were limited funds for this kind of initiative but little evidence of it being used. Soon after being appointed in 1928, the state agent reviewed the extensive lists of existing state funds and discovered that an educational development fund could be used for "stimulating school authorities to provide more adequate equipment for negro schools. . . . I can, by offering to give help toward the purchasing of a sewing machine or a stove, stimulate the school authorities to put in water works or revamp the entire Home Economics building. Without this fund as a stimulus, I would never be able to get such building improvements done."[75] These efforts were limited, and leveraging either the state or local communities was a piecemeal effort, often not sustained.

Efforts at leveraging were woefully inadequate, especially because neither the state nor local government systems provided sufficient funding for basic schoolhouse amenities like furniture. Even where Rosenwald money could be procured for school construction, there were no additional funds provided to furnish the schools, in spite of the fund's requirement that equipment be included in the cost of schools. The two-teacher Rosenwald school in Mt. Vernon had never been equipped, and the principal hoped that the state might provide some funds to furnish it.[76] The state agent not only denied the request but also offered no suggestion of how the school might resolve it. The Mount Olive School in Franklin County, a Rosenwald schoolhouse, was not able to use community donations to procure matching funds for new teachers or term extensions, because three years' worth of donations were being used to pay off a debt to the Bank of Franklin for a loan to equip the school when it was originally built.[77] Indeed, most schools went without the basic elements fundamental to a functioning school.

Funding issues were an example of the complicated nature of state and local politics, as well as the racial state. There was no pretense that any of the efforts to leverage individual communities would result in more comprehensive changes to the state system of schooling. Instead, efforts often focused on particular projects with no broader vision in mind. As a result, local programs rarely resulted in any substantive change to the state's political development generally, or the education system specifically. The state's reliance on elections exacerbated the funding problems. The Southern Education Board provided a detailed study of Mississippi's education system when it first began its work in the South and considered the ways that administrative inefficiencies were detrimental to school reform. The report recognized that in other states, like North Carolina, a school district could levy a local tax by majority vote of qualified electors as long as it did not exceed state limits on local levies, even if it was only a special tax district for cause. However, Mississippi's local tax levies required the vote not just of counties, but also by the board of supervisors, elected officials not likely to win reappointment by raising taxes.[78] There were economic problems, but white citizens also did not want their tax money spent on black schools and likely would not elect someone who advocated doing so. Further, for both North Carolina and Mississippi, legislated state taxes did not include a portion designated specifically for schools, meaning that the county could decide how much of the allocation of state taxes would be used for education.[79] Politicians often floated the idea of letting taxes collected from whites be used for white schools and those collected from blacks be used for black schools. Of course, aside from the gross inequities and constitutional problems of such an allocation of property taxes, whites in those counties with a majority black population would likely not have been in favor of such a plan.

In 1916, Governor Bilbo created a joint committee of state house and senate members to survey chronic deficit problems in both state and local governance. While personal property assessments had been rising in the years preceding the study, decisions to reduce local tax levies compounded the problem. Bilbo's committee acknowledged the issue, but "condemned as burdensome" tax rates that exceed thirty-five mills. The state also designated the poll tax as a source of education revenue in the state, two dollars on every inhabitant between twenty-one and sixty years of age. In spite of Bilbo's efforts, however, state revenues exceeded expenditures in only six of the thirty years between 1902 and 1931, and constitutional restrictions on local taxes exacerbated the problem. The 1932 Brookings Institution report on Mississippi made clear the need for tax reform: "The local property tax burden is unevenly distributed; it is heavy in some counties and light in others. It is burdensome in some sections of a particular county and relatively easy to bear in others. This is due to the creation of a multiplicity of special road, school, drainage and levee districts, which are piled one on top of the other within the counties, and to the variations in governmental efficiency and economy among the counties." Some counties had unusually high local taxes because of debt that had been incurred both to manage deficits and invest in the infrastructure. The problem was compounded by a lack of appropriate and adequate taxation on state business enterprises. However, as the Brookings report pointed out, "the fundamental cause of complaint arises out of the inequitable distribution of the tax burden. Exemptions, avoidance, evasion, inequality of assessments, pyramiding of tax levies by the creation of special taxing districts all work to throw an intolerable burden on those classes of property which are taxed."[80] The report also indicated that even when tax reform was legislated, it was not enforced. Unfortunately, little changed following Bilbo's commission, and the legislature failed again to enact any considerable part of the Brookings recommendations.[81] The state's citizens continued to complain about the tax burden. Indeed, the state failed to develop centralized administration and remained out of the mainstream with regard to national governance and taxation trends. Rural Mississippi consisted of a "multiplicity of counties, districts, cities, towns and villages . . . [that] . . . vary widely in their resources."[82] The administrative structure of the state, accompanied by an inequitable system of taxation, made it difficult to centralize and coordinate functions, especially in education.

A final report of the Rosenwald Fund illustrated that the lack of adequate funding limited the progress of almost two decades of work in Mississippi. This was a problem of both local taxation, compounded by an unwillingness to provide local revenues to black schools, and a need for private donations in areas with very high rates of poverty. In 1917, there were 3,400 black elementary schools in the state. Over the next two decades, while Rosenwald provided funding for the construction of 633 additional schools, accommodating 77,850 students, only 3,500 rural black schools existed at the end of the campaign.[83] Most of the construction replaced "some shacks with good schools" but failed to increase materially the number of schools.[84] One teacher's request highlighted the problem: "Could we tare [sic] the old building down and leave 4 rooms standing for primary rooms and trade school and use the material in new building?"[85] The extreme poverty of rural black communities and the lack of state and local funding made it impossible for foundations to use the same approach for awarding funds to local communities. At the same time, pouring significant sums of money into the state to solve the problem was antithetical to foundation aims because it ran the risk of expanding rural black education at private expense, with no means to make it a public enterprise.

Funding problems persisted throughout the early decades of the twentieth century in Mississippi, because the state failed to develop a tax system or an equalization plan to address local needs. State equalization plans in Mississippi typically focused on making school budgets more consistent across the state, an attempt that sought to address revenue disparities created by property valuation problems as well as white citizens' anger that counties with larger black populations had more money for schools. State politicians were reluctant to address these concerns due to fears that a state commission might be detrimental to tax structures in their communities. For example, Bilbo's administration got approval in 1916 to create a state tax commission in an effort to relieve unequal burdens of taxation but failed to provide adequate funding or assistance to the work. Legislators hoped to repeal the state tax commission law in 1918, a measure that ultimately failed and resulted in tax legislation that did not fundamentally solve the state's revenue problems.[86] A comprehensive study of the state's revenue code in 1932 explicitly stated that the seriousness of the revenue problem at the local level had materially increased since 1918. Bilbo's commission condemned property tax rates of thirty-five to fifty mills as burdensome. However, by 1932, there were gross disparities in tax rates between counties, given the multiplicity of local tax levies, and many counties exceeded 100 mills.[87] While Bilbo had attempted to address deficit problems, by 1932 the deficit had grown to $8 million, and the state established a sales tax to address the ongoing revenue shortfalls, which increased state revenues by 25 percent by 1934.[88] Equalization plans in the state typically meant greater inequalities for rural blacks. In 1926, the state had set up a program of equalization of educational opportunity that provided for a minimum school term of eight months for whites, and six months for blacks. And, by 1937, more than ten years after the legislated equalization plan, the state was expending $28.90 per white student and only $3.06 for each black student.[89]

In 1930, the state agent wrote to one of the state's judges regarding a proposition to compel counties to provide their pro rata share of the cost of Rosenwald school construction. The agent hoped that the state would add a paragraph to the tax code, empowering county boards to levy a tax on all property, limited to one mill, which would be paid into the county treasury to the credit of the school fund and used for the purpose of building rural schoolhouses. The state agent made a strong case for the amendment: "This sort of legal provision would obviate the necessity of an election. It is left to the discretion of the board of supervisors, which board would undoubtedly not put on such a tax except where such a tax was popular. The tax would not be popular in counties sparsely settled with negroes. In our counties heavily populated with negroes, it would be applicable, and at the same time a definite restriction is made as to the amount of this tax. There could, therefore, be no danger that this provision would ever become a heavy burden to the people."[90] This amendment would ensure that blacks would be compelled to pay additional taxes for their schools on top of the private donations they were already providing, and this system of double taxation would limit the responsibility of local and state governance. Double taxation in the form of private donations was even more unfair in Mississippi than in states like North Carolina, where local taxes and private donations were also the norm, because private donations from local blacks in Mississippi were rarely institutionalized and replaced by local taxes in subsequent years. It was crucial that a process be in place to transfer costs to the local government or it would be impossible to sustain reform over the longer term.

Efforts to extend school terms through GEB or Rosenwald funding in the state highlight the complexity of these issues. Schools that wanted to take advantage of the term-extension program had to guarantee that teachers were earning a minimum salary and provide matching funds from the community. The state gave little direction and oversight to foundation-based efforts, and the program was implemented in individual schools rather than more comprehensively through programs that addressed regional, county, or even district needs. The Rosenwald Fund provided incentives but often had to deny requests because most local communities could not meet minimum requirements, like teacher salaries. In 1929, the state provided limited funds to bring teacher salaries in some districts to a minimum level in order to get foundation funding, which resulted in a few term extensions. However, the state did not systematically apply the program across consolidated areas, meaning that many requests for term extensions remained unmet. In 1930, a teacher in Leake County submitted an application to extend the school term in the community of Walnut Grove. The state agent pointed out to the teacher that the chief requirement was that the teachers' salaries be a minimum of fifty dollars per month before the foundation would extend the school term. While some school districts found donations to raise teacher salaries to this minimum, Leake County did not. The state agent did not write to the county superintendent requesting county funds, nor did he inquire whether the black community might be able to provide private donations. Instead, the application was forwarded directly to the Rosenwald Fund by the state agent, who must have known that the fund would have no choice but to deny it. "All the salaries in your school are less than this amount except the principal's salary. For that reason your application cannot be approved."[91] Indeed, the state agent delegated the task of saying no to the foundation, and then passed that denial on to the teacher without recourse, illustrating not only the lack of assistance available from the state or local whites to help rural black communities but also the difficult and disappointing interactions the teachers had with the state, including the state agent for Negro education.

The Rosenwald Fund required school term extensions to be guaranteed for three years, and agreed to provide 50 percent of the cost for the first year, 33.3 percent the second, and 25 percent for the third. In Tunica County, the superintendent had submitted an application with her support to extend the term of the Rosenwald school there to six months, with a note promoting her work with the black schools. "I attended several Rosenwald Day celebrations and the programs were real good, quite gratifying, and evinced a feeling of appreciation, something we think is not typical of the negro."[92] However, the state could only get foundation approval for the sixth month if the county already ran the school for a minimum five-month term. Ultimately, the term was extended in 1930, but the funding was not included as part of the ongoing county budget. While Tunica County successfully applied for and received funds the county turned down the award in 1931 because "there is not a chance for me to extend the school terms this year. I appreciate your offer to aid, but we are, as everyone else is, 'low' in funds."[93]

The Rosenwald Fund was likely frustrated by the number of requests that had to be denied by the fund, or subsequently given back by the counties. The Harmony Consolidated Schools had asked the Rosenwald Fund to lengthen the school term, but the fund denied the request because teachers there did not earn a minimum of fifty dollars per month. At the urging of the Rosenwald director for southern schools, the state agent agreed to provide funds that were not locally available to increase teacher salaries and then sent a letter to the superintendent of Harmony Schools informing him of the funded initiative.[94] This illustrates that the fund did have some power to compel the state to do a little bit more than it was already doing. However, this is an isolated case, rather than a more comprehensive effort.

A more difficult situation with regard to requests to extend school terms occurred when only one teacher salary was lower than fifty dollars, which might result in that teacher simply being let go in exchange for an award to extend the school term. While the Rosenwald Fund might have discouraged such practice, it certainly was not out of the ordinary.[95] This practice reflected the complicated nature of schooling in Mississippi. Because compulsory-school laws were not enforced, enrollments were not consistent throughout the school year in the many counties that were organized around agricultural production. The state agent explained the problem to the director of the Rosenwald Fund: "Regarding the minimum salaries of teachers, please allow me to suggest again that it happens in both white and colored schools in Mississippi in the spring of the year when enrollments run down that some of the teachers are dropped from the list. . . . The one teacher whose salary was less than $50 was discontinued. This is not a practice in this county with colored schools alone, for several white schools had to drop off some teachers when the enrollment went down."[96] The agent blamed it on a statutory law that governed the number of teachers a school was allowed, based on enrollments. However, it is a rather spurious argument given that enrollments in black schools were so much higher than those in white ones. Further, the state agent neglected to address the important issues, which were a lack of state legislation to standardize school terms or teacher salaries and a lack of attention to compulsory-school laws.

While rural blacks might have asked their superintendent to support a request for term extension, the county rarely cooperated with blacks to see that the basic criteria could be met. Even in term-extension programs, for which counties were contractually obligated to assume longer-term costs for additional months of schooling, the private donations from black citizens often did not translate into a revised budget that would affect the schools prospectively, or result in formal tax levies or county matching funds. In Leake County, a number of teachers received only thirty-five dollars per month in salary, so residents needed to provide donations of fifteen dollars per month for each teacher. However, unless this arrangement was made in cooperation with the county, there was no guarantee that the terms would be extended indefinitely, and no guarantee that the term extension would continue beyond the three-year contract. That would require a state policy on minimum salaries and a county budget that provided for it, or a guarantee of private donations indefinitely. Indefinite private donations, however, were no different from a tax levy, except that they would not be formally institutionalized in the budget. At the same time, the Leake County request also led to an unusual response from the Rosenwald Fund, which wrote a separate letter to the state agent expressing some concern. The state had used its full foundation appropriation in that year for term extensions, and the fund conveyed that it would be unwilling to approve any additional projects. "The applications for term extension are generally scattered over wide areas, making it very difficult for the states and for us to keep in close touch with these miscellaneous projects. We have decided that no further commitments will be made in term extension until the problem has been carefully studied and demonstrations made in a few model counties"[97]

The foundation planned to grant requests for term extension by units, like counties, rather than for individual schools, hoping that extended terms could be both institutionalized and concentrated in broader areas.[98] Indeed, it was not always clear that the agreements made between the Rosenwald Fund and local governance systems were kept in Mississippi, because there were inadequate systems at the state level to monitor progress. The state agent disbursed a set of checks to the superintendent in Indianola, Mississippi, but included a reminder in the letter accompanying the checks. "I hope you will not disburse these funds until you have checked over carefully the schools to see that the terms of the agreement have been kept."[99] Both the agents and the state provided relatively minimal support. For example, the foundations always expected that initial grants for programs like term extensions or Jeanes teachers would gradually decrease because over time state and local government would increasingly share in the cost of their programs. However, Mississippi was one of the states where the counties still provided less than what the Jeanes Fund provided for the Jeanes teachers, almost two decades after the program began.[100] However, in an effort to promote some progress, the foundations were often willing to overlook these shortcomings in the state.

The foundations tried to get the state agent to be more involved in oversight, but it was largely an exercise in futility. An incident in 1930 is telling. While a basic part of the state agent's job was to work with counties to promote foundation initiatives, including schoolhouse construction and Jeanes appointments, the agent seemed reluctant to promote those programs. He asked the Rosenwald Fund to send applications for construction directly to various county superintendents, rather that work through the state agent's office. The fund responded as might be expected. "You are asking us to send several application blanks to the superintendent. We are mailing them directly to you, feeling that this is a matter to which you should give very close personal attention to see that everything is worked out in very careful detail before the applications are approved."[101] In a postscript to the letter, the state agent was also asked to bring the Mississippi program more in line with the southern program. "We would much prefer to extend schools above six months instead of above 5, since 6 is to be the minimum for next year."[102] Foundations tried to implement programs but felt continually frustrated by the lack of cooperation.

The foundations tried to create greater state oversight through the use of state agents for Negro education, agents for Rosenwald schoolhouse construction, and a state-supervising teacher for black schools. Nathan Newbold had requested such additional foundation-funded positions in North Carolina early in his appointment, which included black professionals like Annie Holland, as the state supervisor of schools, and G. E. Davis, the black agent for the Rosenwald Fund. However, in Mississippi, the Rosenwald Fund wrote to the state agent on more than one occasion with a promise of 50 percent funding if the state would hire an elementary supervisor of Negro schools.[103] Because the state did not provide matching funds or procure the funds from another source, the Rosenwald Fund suggested that the GEB provide the other half of the salary, and explained, "Such a state supervisor could be most helpful to the Jeanes workers and to counties in which there are no Jeanes workers. You would be surprised to know how little supervision the county superintendents give and how little value some of it is where they do give it."[104] The Rosenwald Fund also provided 50 percent of the salary of a field agent to oversee schoolhouse construction in Mississippi. These appointments were intended to provide opportunities for the sort of collaboration that would lead to sustained change, but in Mississippi these appointments came much later and were not embraced by members of the state department of education. It was clear that state-sanctioned cooperation would not develop.

It is unlikely that any of the white Mississippi agents on foundation payrolls were particularly enthusiastic about universal education, which probably explained their lack of enthusiasm about working with foundations or developing better systems of oversight. A teacher's guide for the county normal schools published in 1932–33 was distinctive in illustrating this lack of commitment. The guide was not practical in the sense that it promoted an agrarian lifestyle or any of the commonly held beliefs at that time about rural black education. Instead, the pamphlet focused on education theorists that included Aristotle, Comenius, Locke, Rousseau, Pestalozzi, Herbart, Spencer, Dewey, Thorndike, and Gates. The book does not mention industrial education and bears no real connection to what actually happened in rural Mississippi schools.[105] Indeed, the discussion of curriculum areas like math, reading, algebra, and geometry was quite incongruous with rural schools and teacher training. One way around the regular requests to standardize schools was to create something based in educational expertise, even if it did not actually address any of the needs of rural schools or take on the complicated political questions about their purpose. The state could say it was providing guidance and even pretend it was aligning the schools with current educational thought.

Early efforts to address standards for black secondary schools sought to capture what happened in practice, rather than to provide meaningful oversight. The state superintendent had written to twenty-five black secondary schools to ask for reports on their work, which he planned to translate into "some definitive standards whereby such schools might be governed. I found it a hopeless task to reconcile the different conditions revealed in their reports."[106] The politics of this issue could be seen in a letter from the state agent to the superintendent of schools in Brookhaven. The agent had sent accreditation forms used by white high schools and indicated that the superintendent should use similar forms for black schools. However, he explained that a "good many of our negro schools are going to be left off the list in the years to come if we do not change the requirements laid down for approving them. I feel now that we would get in a pick of trouble if we should use different standards for the negroes from the ones used for the whites. You may, however, feel assured that my attitude in the matter will always be a cooperative one."[107] Foundations and other outside agencies may have been pushing the state to improve administrative oversight of schools, but doing so would require the state to confront the issue of race.

The state also failed to develop any centralized plans with regard to teacher training and certification. This was a structural problem not just because there were no real standards for certifying black teachers but also because teachers who sought employment across state lines needed certification. When the superintendent in Decatur, Alabama, wrote to the state agent in Mississippi in 1929 inquiring about the need to grant a professional license to a black teacher who had been trained in Mississippi, the state agent responded that "under the laws of Mississippi no such license can be granted to college graduates from any colleges except those on the All-Southern list. This means that it is not possible, under the law, to grant to any negro teachers such a license because no negro institution in this state is accredited by the Southern Association of Colleges and secondary Schools."[108] In other words, after being pushed to strengthen the administration of its public schools for more than two decades, Mississippi still had no schools accredited for the training of black teachers and no standards for certifying them.

The state was encouraged to develop a stronger system of standards, but continued to dig in its heels. In response to the pressure, the state superintendent in 1929 developed a plan to improve instruction in rural schools through what he defined as a more "democratic" process, but one that again deflected oversight. The state proposed a system to the GEB that would put the onus on black teachers in county training schools: "Would you, then, think well of a scheme of supervision worked out by the teachers in the county training schools as a result of group conferences in which the state supervisor participated in preference to one arbitrarily imposed by the state supervisor.[sic]"[109] The GEB agents thought the idea of a "democratic program of supervision" seemed unclear and reminded the state superintendent that it was important to develop a formal program for supervision: "Nevertheless, it seems essential that a scheme of supervision or improvement of instruction be set up that can be carried on by the principal in charge, by the county superintendent, or by some other supervisory agent in the absence of a state supervisor. I feel that it would be very essential for you and Mr. Easom [the state agent] to agree upon the objectives to be carried out in a plan of improvement of instruction in county training schools, and agree also upon the method to be used in achieving these objectives."[110] Of course, the state agents had already made clear that the state would not assume responsibility for developing standards and centralizing schools.

The state agents established summer schools to provide additional training to rural black teachers, as most of the southern states did during this time period. The teachers also benefitted when summer schools were located at the Hampton Institute or any location outside of Mississippi given attitudes that prevailed in the state. The first Mississippi state agent recognized the benefits of state-run institutes and sent a circular letter to all county superintendents encouraging the participation of their county's white and black teachers in summer training schools. The letter explained that four summer normal schools for black teachers had been established at Jackson, Meridian, Natchez, and Hattiesburg, Mississippi, with the hope of adding two more in other regions of the state. The idea was sold to the county superintendents by suggesting plans for the schools, which would run for four weeks and, "hold an examination so strict that a colored teacher cannot cheat, teach arithmetic only as far as percentage, and other fundamental subjects in like manner, give strong courses in hygiene and sanitation, practical agriculture, home science, all year garden, good morals, and personal cleanliness, have all teachers examined for malaria, syphilis, tuberculosis, hook worm, etc. . . . negroes will pay a fee."[111] And, if that was not enough to get support from county superintendents, one final plea was made: "The time has come when we should either do something for the negro or quit wasting so much money on him."[112] This method of relying on racial perceptions to advance foundation programs was somewhat similar to Newbold's strategies in North Carolina. Yet, the Mississippi agent's tone felt more critical and was rarely coupled with conciliatory gestures to the black community. The results, unlike in North Carolina, seemed never to benefit the black community.

It was a depressing approach to expanding teacher training and highlighted the racist nature of Mississippi politics and education reform. Some teachers arranged their own institutes, but that work would not typically have the support of state and local government. Black citizens were on their own. Indeed, it was difficult to get any cooperation from the superintendents for summer schools. The state agent pleaded with the Holly Springs superintendent to have his teachers participate in a state summer school organized in the region. The superintendent, however, planned a separate institute that would be for Holly Springs's teachers only. The state agent explained to the superintendent that it would not likely be possible for the state to have the co-operation of adjacent counties unless Holly Springs participated, but the superintendent refused, unless his teachers could arrive after the first weeks of August, meaning that they would miss at least a quarter of the state's program. Instead, the superintendent proposed that the state allow him to schedule his own institute for the Holly Springs teachers, using the funding available for summer institutes to supplement what he planned to collect by way of tuition.[113] While educators may have recognized the benefits of summer institutes, county superintendents also wanted to retain control of both the curriculum and the fees.

While it was always beneficial to create formal venues for bringing rural teachers together, it remains unclear how much these summer institutes accomplished academically. In one telling exchange of letters, the superintendent of Coahoma County was asked about the low grades that teachers had received through the summer school. He responded that the summer school had tried "to hold up a standard of work there as high as they are capable of coming up to, and very few that really went on through and took the examination failed."[114] Of course, it would have been easier to evaluate the strength of the summer schools if the state had some standards for teacher training and certification, guidelines for summer schools to which counties adhered, and data that detailed classes taught, teachers enrolled, and assessments. The summer institutes, however, were a microcosm of the state's progress in all aspects of education reform for rural blacks. Over three decades of foundation work during Jim Crow, state leaders in Mississippi refused to collaborate in a meaningful way and neglected to address issues that were central to the development of a state system of schooling, which included greater standardization, a comprehensive overhaul of the tax system to support schools, and schoolhouse construction and consolidation. Foundation programs were relatively ineffective at expanding black schooling or, by extension, state and local governance, even if schools had some success in organizing rural black communities. The Division of Negro Education in the state was heavily influenced by state and local politics and was mistrusted by black and white citizens alike. As such, black teachers had fewer opportunities through foundation programs to promote the goals of the black community in rural areas, and the relationship between black agency and foundation programming was not as formal or extensive as it was elsewhere. Yet, black agency in school reform persisted.

ACHIEVING FOUNDATION GOALS FOR RURAL BLACK EDUCATION IN MISSISSIPPI: THE COMMUNITY

In early 1929, Mag Hanna, a teacher in Conway, Mississippi, wrote to the state agent for Negro education to complain about local government policies for rural black schools. The new county superintendent was "cutting the colored schools short this term." Hanna pleaded for help to extend the school term because "we as a race of people can not advance in education without a chance to do so."[115] The state agent responded that it would not be possible to remedy the situation for the whole county without the support of the white superintendent and the "good white friends of Leake County." Instead he provided an application to get money from the Rosenwald Fund to extend the school term, a process that would require raising enough money in the community to guarantee teachers a minimum salary.[116] While it would seem impossible that anyone outside of the local governing structure could be consulted on matters of educational policy in rural Mississippi communities during Jim Crow, this teacher not only protested but also bypassed the local government to get an application for funding that could potentially have a significant impact on the county's public schools. Rural blacks in Mississippi were far more marginalized than those living in North Carolina. However, in spite of this relative marginalization from state and local political structures, rural black teachers understood that foundation programs might mitigate the strength of local politics. The lack of meaningful collaboration between foundations and the State certainly limited what was possible. Nonetheless, rural blacks continued to be a catalyst for education reform, organizing in local communities to take advantage of whatever opportunities might be available.

The presence of foundation funding in the state provided opportunities that would not otherwise have existed for rural blacks to elicit outside support for their work. In 1918, the Colored Teachers Association met in Bolivar County, with more than one hundred teachers in attendance, and asked the county superintendent to invite the state agent to join their meeting. He had also had a similar meeting with the county association in Panola.[117] Regardless of whether the state agent was responsive to rural black community needs, these venues provided a platform for rural black teachers to promote their schools and give a more comprehensive description of rural black education. These meetings might also disseminate that information to outside interests.

It appeared that the state did not organize regular meetings with the teachers or provide venues for rural black teachers to organize. Mississippi teachers were already doing that, regardless of whether foundation funding was available. However, the teachers took advantage of opportunities to promote their agenda and hoped the state agents would provide reports of these meeting to foundations to learn about not only the needs of rural black communities but also the community's interest in participating formally with foundation programs.

The Jeanes teachers in Mississippi played the same role that they did in other states, acting as the de facto superintendent of black schools in the country. In spite of the fact that their positions were similarly defined, the lack of stronger administrative systems at the state and local level made it difficult for foundations to have an impact on work in local areas. It also made it more difficult for rural blacks to use foundation programs to promote the goals of their communities or to develop a strategy for doing so. Jeanes teachers across the South sought simultaneously to promote community goals and to work closely with foundations. For many, this included facilitating the building of an education infrastructure and a more centralized school system.

In Mississippi, however, greater standardization was a double-edged sword. On the one hand, standards would limit the ability of rural black teachers to shape the schools, especially if those standards undermined the academic curriculum by promoting industrial education. On the other hand, Mississippi county superintendents limited rural black schooling, and standards might promote minimum expectations with regard to school terms, teacher salary, and buildings.[118] Local whites prevented local black efforts to expand education not only in an indirect way by simply ignoring the needs of rural black schools but also directly by denying their requests to improve the schools and thwarting their attempts to reach out for help. There was no compelling reason for blacks to integrate with the public school system until there was some guarantee that the public sphere might be more congenial to blacks. In many areas of the South, local school systems would not be, but a system defined by the state might be more easily changed in the longer term. However, Mississippi blacks likely perceived that real change would come only with outside interference, not outside the local community but outside the state.

The Jeanes teachers' first resource should have been the state agent for Negro education, but assistance from that office was often discouraging. In 1929, the black principal of the Noxubee County Training School wrote to the state agent regarding equipment needed for the home science department and repairs needed to the roof of the principal's house. The state agent's response provided some flavor of the relationship that existed between that office and rural black teachers:

> I shall hold this list of Home Science equipment and make my offer to provide funds for this department in your school, contingent upon the school's attitude in general, and particularly upon the efforts put forward in the next few weeks toward re-roofing your house. Now, if you want to get special aid from this Department for your Home Science work, it is up to you to show us that there is a good attitude on the part of your community toward the school, and that you are going ahead with your roofing of the building. I took this matter up with both your county superintendent and Mr. Anderson.[119]

The teacher responded to the state agent's directive. "I am very glad also, that you recomended [sic] same, as the problem placed in my hand which you were aware, was very disreable but differcult [sic] . . . I do not hesitate in saying, For me to attempt to do anything without his favor or the superintendent is like 'beating the air" and suggesting plausible impossibilities."[120] Rural black educators were aware that they had neither state nor local support.

Correspondence from the agents was often both condescending and discouraging to rural blacks. One black principal received a letter from the state agent announcing that one of the foundations had awarded money to his school. Instead of offering congratulations, the agent admonished him. "It is now up to you to make of this department what these outside funds expect you to do. It is wholly a waste of money and effort to place equipment of this character in a school and not have it properly cared for every minute of the day . . . I am sure both Mr. Favrot and Mr. Caldwell [foundation field agents] will be interested in paying a visit to your school the next time they are in the coast. I hope they will find everything in first-class shape on their visit."[121] When a teacher from Meridian, Mississippi, asked the state agent to support a supervisor in Lauderdale County, and offered herself as an applicant for the position, he responded only two days later that the question was "largely up to Supt. Ivy and Supt. Riddell. If they want to take you on and give you a trial, perhaps I can pay a part of the salary."[122] He committed to nothing, was actually less than encouraging, and made no indication that he would speak to the superintendents. At the least, he did not engender the feeling that he was there to intercede on behalf of rural black citizens, in spite of his position.

The inequalities, the lack of support, and the condescension often bordered on the ludicrous. When the Jeanes Fund provided one desk and chair as a special appropriation for one of the rural schools, the state agent sent it to Lauderdale County with instructions for the superintendent to decide which of the rural black schools should receive the gift. The stipulation was that it could not go to a school that had ever received outside funding, with the hope that it would have a "stimulating effect on your teachers to do higher and better things in the future."[123] Given that black schools rarely had equipment provided of any type, from chairs to textbooks, it is unlikely that one teacher desk would have the kind of stimulating effect and result in the appreciation that the state agent thought it warranted. In general, correspondence between black citizens and state agents was often tense and patronizing. Local blacks did not speak freely about the problems in their local communities, unlike some of the correspondence that existed in North Carolina. While all of the state agents in the South deferred to the wishes of the local superintendent, the Mississippi agents rarely indicated that they might try to influence the outcome in a way that benefited the black community.

The teachers received responses from the state agents that differed substantively from responses that teachers typically received in North Carolina. This was the norm for Mississippi teachers, who were likely discouraged by their interactions. One teacher wrote the state agent about a lack of funds to keep the school open. "As our school will close in a few days on account of funds, is there anything that you can do to extend our school term? We were told that you could help in some way. . . . Thank you in advance for what you may do."[124] The state agent immediately responded but not with any advice for remaining open during that academic year. Instead, the school was provided with an application for term-extension funds, which were to be taken to the county superintendent to fill out and submit, with a promise that the application would be shared in the future with representatives from the Rosenwald Fund.[125] This school likely closed, and it is unclear whether the term was extended in future years. If the state agent felt that the superintendent was favorable or that improving rural black education in a particular county was politically feasible, the response was more tempered. The superintendent in Franklin County, Mississippi, was impressed by the efforts of rural blacks to raise a significant amount of funding not just to extend the terms but also to purchase equipment and repair the school. The superintendent wrote a plea on behalf of the school, which ultimately resulted in an award from the Rosenwald Fund to extend the term.[126] One positive outcome in both examples is that the agent provided information to the schools about outside assistance that was available. He offered to rural blacks a possibility of funding and advertised that there were outside groups that supported expanded education.

They may have been marginalized by state and local politics, but rural blacks learned quickly that outside groups recognized their plight and were instrumental to change, in spite of the fact that, to date, outside influence was woefully inadequate to the cause.

Even when the correspondence was not condescending, there was little real assistance offered. Mag Hanna's request for equipment is illustrative. When he informed the state agent that his two-year-old Rosenwald school had no equipment, the agent responded to him with a request for more information, but all subsequent correspondence on the matter went only to the county superintendent. The agent informed the superintendent that the state might give $100 if the black community raised $200, yet made no request of the county to help meet the need. "We would like him [Hanna] to make up his funds and turn over to you [the white superintendent], or rather put it in the bank and show deposit slips therefor, whereupon we would donate $100 and cooperate with you."[127] The teacher in Tippo, Mississippi, located in Tallahatchie County, wrote to the state department of education requesting information about getting a Rosenwald school for approximately five hundred black students in the area: "We are not so well informed as to the method and plans as to what Mr. Rosenwald requires of us and what he will do."[128] The agent provided the instructions and typical awards for different sizes of schools and then suggested that the teacher confer with the superintendent. However, while the state agent had already discussed the prospects for a school in Tallahatchie with the county superintendent, neither the superintendent nor the state agent were forthcoming about whether the project would be generally supported, how to proceed, or how much money might be available from county sources. While the state agent's letter implied all-around support for the project, it made no commitment and gave no indication that the county superintendent would make efforts to promote the school construction. The correspondence made it difficult for black citizens to determine next steps, especially if they wanted outside support.

Indeed, rural blacks must have found it frustrating, to put it mildly, to work with the state, yet nonetheless many continued to seek methods to articulate their needs. Sometimes, however, citizens realized that the process of asking for and receiving outside funding was not worth the effort. The state agent wrote to the black teacher at the Watts Rosenwald school in Lamar County and notified him that his salary from the county would likely be terminated. The agent suggested that the teacher's job might be saved if the Watts school consolidated with the Lee School and moved closer to the line between Marion and Lamar Counties. Consolidation might make it possible to use federal funds from Smith-Hughes and county funds to support a larger school that accommodated black citizens from both counties.[129] The agent suggested they tear down the schoolhouses at both Watts and Lee and then use the funds from the sale of the materials toward the construction of a new consolidated schoolhouse with aid from the Rosenwald Fund.[130] The black teacher from Watts was put in a difficult predicament. It is likely that neither he nor his students nor those in the other community wanted to lose their local school, though consolidation at a new site would not only allow him to retain his job but also expand the education infrastructure. The two communities of Watts and Lee proceeded to negotiate consolidation because it could enlarge and improve the facilities and establish a "united, moral and physical background of power and influence among themselves sufficient to warrant and maintain the cooperation of both local and state authorities; to build and support an outstanding Smith-Hughes school for the communities."[131] Both communities recognized the benefits of consolidation, including the possibility that it might lead to outside funding.

The representatives from each of the black communities agreed on an appropriate site and proposed it to the state. However, the state agent overruled their plan, deciding that the new school would be built at the site of the present Lee School, because it was located on a county road, would be accessible to students in another township, and the land was owned by the patrons, which meant that there would be no additional cost for land purchase or for an entirely new school.[132] In the end, the consolidation plan really meant only the loss of the Watts School, even if the Lee School expanded. The agent also suggested that the residents merely add two rooms to the existing school, instead of building a new one, and a vocational building of two or three rooms, a suggestion that minimized the original offer. The difficulty of travel between the counties would hinder the plan, but the state agent justified his decision with the belief that "no doubt roads will improve," implying that those who traveled the roads to the school would improve them. It was clear that the state had no plans to help with building better roads; the onus would be on the black community to accomplish those improvements.[133] His letter closed with the statement that the patrons could, if they preferred, build whatever they wanted, but at their own expense. The Watts citizens pulled out of the plan for obvious reasons, and were soundly criticized for their decision.

Infrastructure problems made it difficult for rural blacks to develop and administer their schools, and particularly impeded what the Jeanes teachers could accomplish in the state. Those teachers understood that foundations hoped for a stronger infrastructure, including new schools, better data, teacher training, consolidation, and community organizations to connect schools and homes. However, it was difficult at best for those goals to be realized in rural Mississippi, especially because small schools were scattered over wide rural areas, often without adequate transportation routes. The superintendent in DeKalb, located in Kemper County, was encouraged to consolidate the black schools even though "it will not be possible now to spend much money on transportation of negro children. Perhaps it would not be possible to spend any public funds."[134] A lack of good roads made education development more difficult to achieve. Students had difficulty getting to schools, and Jeanes teachers were unable to visit schools and provide oversight, or promote more comprehensive reforms.[135]

Rural blacks wanted better facilities and stronger schools, but the costs of promoting the expansion of schooling might actually outweigh the benefits in both the short and longer term. In the short term, they risked hostile reprisal that might limit future progress. In the longer term, a state committed to white supremacy and hostile to black education might formally take over the supervision of their schools. Rural black teachers had to make difficult choices about how to collaborate with foundation programs, and especially how to benefit from them. This was the case for black teachers throughout the South, but Mississippi presented particularly painful challenges. The state's black citizens must have found it especially difficult to be blamed for the failure to achieve education reform, as they often were. At one point, the state agent wrote to a planter in Kemper County to encourage Rosenwald schoolhouse construction. He suggested that the planter underwrite the cost of building a Rosenwald schoolhouse but "charge each tenant his pro rata of the cost of such a building. This is being done in other communities, particularly so where there are large numbers of negro tenants. . . . A good schoolhouse for your tenants will help you to hold a better class of tenants, and at the same time, of course, it will help the tenants themselves."[136] The state agent clearly supported the belief that the lack of an education infrastructure for rural black schooling was the fault of black citizens whom he perceived as unwilling to underwrite the cost of their own education. This is an argument that played out in political debates about how to rewrite the tax system in a way that would not require white taxes to be allocated to black education.

Black citizens understood that state and county politicians were unwilling to provide any funding to support their schools, yet continued their efforts. The superintendent of schools in Sharkey County told the black residents that the plan to build a shop was too expensive and would not be supported. In response, the black principal wrote directly to the state agent for a "plan of the cheapest shop with which you can furnish us," in order to take the cause back to the superintendent.[137] However, when those efforts were unsuccessful, as they often were, rural blacks forged ahead and worked on their own. The citizens of Poplar Hill raised $738 for a new school and wrote to the state agent several times requesting assistance from the Rosenwald Fund. "I am writing to see if we may have our Rosenwald appropriation which was allowed more than three years ago, but we did not get it. Still our school (Poplar Hill) was checked up as a Rosenwald School on Mr. Hilbun's books. We received the plan for a two-teacher school several times from Mr. Hilbun, but he would always say raise a little more money. We had $738 in the Jefferson County Bank, but my people got impatient and built a very good two-teacher school, but we want to change the plan into a Rosenwald School as we first started."[138] The state agent responded that he had no idea that Poplar Hill had been checked up as a Rosenwald school, and there were no records to prove it, though he hoped that he might visit the school in the future to find out whether it might become available for aid.[139] Of course, in this example, black residents for years sought aid, which failed to materialize, and the state agent who had responsibility for Rosenwald schoolhouse construction failed to maintain adequate records. However, they built the school anyway, without the funding that had been promised.

The existence of the foundation program, even though the assistance did not materialize, provided encouragement to Sharkey blacks to build the Poplar Hill school. This is not to say that black citizens were not the catalyst for their own education system, but to acknowledge that foundation programs focused and shaped local campaigns. In the case of Sharkey County, the residents received a construction plan for a two-teacher school and hoped to receive money. Sometimes it was better to proceed on their own anyway. In Copiah County, the black residents of Shady Grove donated $1,000 in cash and another $200 in land and labor, which was to be matched with an equal contribution from white residents, another $400 in district tax allocations, and an award from the Rosenwald Fund. The building was completed based upon the Rosenwald Fund plans for a three-teacher school that would serve 225 students in Shady Grove. However, when the application was sent in for funding, the Rosenwald Fund turned it down because the school was constructed without adhering to the plans, in particular building only nine-foot ceilings in the rooms instead of the ten-foot ceilings required. The state agent asked the director of the fund to overlook the nine-foot ceiling and give aid only based on a two-teacher school, with a promise to rework lighting to make it "fairly adequate." If the ceiling height could be "overlooked," the state offered to help with a fourth room to be added to the back, also with a nine-foot ceiling height, in order to make it a three-room school.[140] The fund flatly refused aid, and the agent informed the superintendent that the anticipated award would not be forthcoming. It is unclear whether these problems developed from a lack of oversight in rural communities or more explicit efforts to limit reform, but outcomes were disappointing for rural blacks. The foundations were also in a difficult position. On the one hand, the black residents had constructed a school at their own expense and may not have realized the ten-foot-ceiling requirement. On the other hand, while the Rosenwald Fund may have wanted to provide money, it was a slippery slope because shoddy construction was a problem throughout the South, and Rosenwald hoped to establish schools that met minimum standards.

These stories provide depressing evidence of the effects of white supremacy on rural black education. Teachers who were in contact with the state agent rarely received encouragement. On one level, this was the result of a state system that was defined by a lack of both funding and the administrative structures necessary to oversee public schooling. On another level, however, the correspondence must have been frustrating because, at the least, teachers lacked the means to leverage outside support to expand schooling. There was no clear set of objectives for them to try to meet. Further, the foundations recognized that, absent state participation, it would be almost impossible to implement policies that would fundamentally alter the landscape, making foundation programs relatively ineffective. At the same time, foundation presence in the state provided some encouragement to rural black education leaders. It made them more aware of the potential for outside help, and the extent to which it was unlikely that comprehensive and systemic change would ever come from within. The existence of foundation programs in Mississippi made clear to rural blacks that there were people who believed in universal education and a need to improve schools.

Rural blacks became aware of foundation programs through teacher journals and their own networks, but also through networking opportunities that were created through foundation programs like summer schools, as well as state and regional meetings of the Jeanes teachers. The 1929 edition of *The Bulletin*, the official publication of the National Association of Teachers in Colored Schools, explicitly promoted the possible benefits of foundation support. The edition announced the annual meeting of the association, which would take place in Jackson, Mississippi, that year. It also included an article, "Negro Education in the South," written by the general field agent for the GEB, that would likely be read by the many Mississippi teachers that planned to attend. The article provided encouraging detail about education progress across the South and a comprehensive description of foundation programs that were available to rural communities.[141] In addition to addresses by Mississippi's governor and state superintendent, other featured speakers included black historian and writer Carter Woodson, the president of the Jeanes and Slater Funds, a GEB agent, and a representative from the Federal Board of Vocational Education.[142] The state may not have been interested in developing formal ties to foundations, but the foundations were eager to develop stronger connections to the black community, which they understood was essential to their work.

The information about foundation programs was widely shared among rural black teachers, as is clear in requests to the foundations: "I have been elected principal of the Progress School out from Prentiss Mississippi. We have the school building, and since we see on the back of the Teachers' Journals where we may get Rosenwald aid on Teacher's Homes, I am asking you upon the request of our County Superintendent of Education to please send me the information."[143] This teacher was clear that he had discovered the information about the possible funds, but also knew that he would make no progress without invoking the superintendent. He knew that programs had been developed to assist rural black communities, even if it was no easy task to connect with those programs. Additionally, while teachers were active in rural black communities before the foundations began their work in the South, specific foundation programs helped to expand that work. The Mississippi meeting of the National Association of Teachers in Colored Schools was designed to feature foundation work. The lack of formal state involvement meant that new programs would not easily be implemented in the state, and blacks would have fewer opportunities to connect formally to political structures outside of their communities. At the same time, foundation programs encouraged greater networks between counties and states through regional meetings and summer schools and within communities through support for agricultural clubs that promoted local organizing. It also made clear to black teachers that their quest for expanded opportunity was a reasonable one and that support would likely never come from Mississippi whites.

The applications for aid from the Jeanes Fund provide numerous examples of the way in which foundation programs supported local efforts to expand schooling in Mississippi. These applications detailed the amount of county funding provided to each teacher, the length of the school term, the credentials of the teacher who would be hired, and a job description for the particular county that was written by the superintendent. Some of the submitted applications did not include the job description, providing some indication of the extent to which county superintendents paid little attention to the work of the teachers.[144] Other Mississippi applications provided clear evidence that the teachers served as the primary administrator of rural black schools and promoted greater centralization and standardization. In some, where teachers had been appointed for a number of years, the applications may have been written by the teachers themselves. A teacher in Pike County was expected to supervise classroom instruction and "encourage the standardization of schools."[145] In Oktibehha County, the teacher would be "supervising, standardizing, and otherwise improving" the schools.[146] The superintendents in Lee and Leake Counties articulated that the teacher would be the supervisor of the black schools, and in Kemper County the teacher would be the "general supervisor and advisor to the negro teachers of the entire county."[147] The Lauderdale County teacher was hired as the elementary supervisor but was expected to visit and inspect regularly, "at least once month [sic], forty selected negro schools and as many of the remaining fifteen schools as circumstances and conditions may permit."[148] Sometimes these applications explicitly connected the Jeanes work to other foundation efforts to improve rural schooling. In Yazoo, the teacher was expected to visit schools, organize PTAs, and follow up the work of summer schools "to see if they are putting into practice the methods they have learned."[149] Especially given the lack of both county and state oversight, these descriptions make clear the central role that Jeanes teachers played as the primary administrators of black schools in counties where the program operated.

The county support for the Jeanes teachers varied considerably, as did the scope of each teacher's work. In Leake County, the Jeanes teacher had about 40 percent of her salary provided by the county for an eight-month school term, was expected to supervise thirty-seven schools and sixty teachers, serving 3,500 black students.[150] In Leflore County, which provided 55 percent of the salary for a seven-month term, the teacher supervised 102 schools with 180 teachers, serving 7,200 students.[151] However, in that same year in Monroe County, the teacher was given two months of salary each from both the Jeanes Fund and the county but was serving a system of forty-eight schools, sixty-one teachers, and 2,885 students in a six-month term.[152] It is unclear where the remaining two months of salary came from, possibly from private donations since the application did not include a county allocation.

It was also clear in the applications, however, that many of the teachers extended their educational work beyond general schooling issues in an effort to meet the broader needs of the community. The Monroe County Jeanes teacher would not only help to improve teaching but also visit homes and churches to promote educational and industrial work and good citizenship.[153] The teacher in Pike County would work not only to improve elementary teaching methods but also to "reach the homes through the mother's clubs."[154] Finally, the teacher in Carroll County would promote "school, home and county cooperation."[155] Foundations promoted this work, through the design and financing of their programs, which strengthened the role of schools in rural communities.

Teacher reports indicate that foundation programs like homemakers clubs, agricultural clubs, and PTAs strengthened connections between the schools and the families served, even in Mississippi, where foundation programs were weaker. The superintendent in Warren County spoke about the breadth of the work, where the teacher would "visit all the schools, organize and direct clubs along right lines; help teachers write their teaching problems; distribution of literature to teachers and pupils; improve exterior and interior of schools, encourage better living conditions among patrons."[156] Of course, white reformers were patronizing, especially given the assumption that foundation support of a Jeanes teacher was necessary to improve the living conditions of rural black families. At the same time, these programs encouraged whites to sanction schools as formal sites for community organizing.

Ann Britton was a twenty-one-year-old graduate of Tougaloo College when she was hired to teach in Washington County in 1935. This Delta school had eight classrooms that typically held two classes at a time, an auditorium, and indoor toilets, which were unusual features for rural black schools. These amenities were perhaps understandable given the location of the school in the Delta, where a larger population of blacks and greater support from some of the planters made for relatively newer schools. Britton's third-grade class met in the schools' auditorium, which was shared with another second-and-third-grade class. Soon after she began her work, she was elevated to the position of Jeanes teacher in Washington County, which had been the job of a male teacher there for a number of years. She was expected to improve the curriculum, assist with teacher assignments, issue textbooks, and compile term reports. She reported that when she had replaced the other Jeanes teacher, more extensive duties were added, including "issuing, checking, and compiling textbooks, transportation for black children in the county, conducting in-service workshops, and visiting all the county schools." The most interesting information she shared, however, was about the students. She reported that the summer school was the only way most of the pupils could go to school because of their work in the fields. "At that time, every pupil did not have proper clothes. They could go to school in the summer session with less clothing."[157] These teachers understood the problems of delivering education in rural, agricultural communities and were eager to develop educational programs that could meet the community's needs. Absent enforced compulsory-schooling laws, agricultural clubs and community organizing could serve to make schools the center of the community and provide a more compelling case for attendance, especially when agricultural demands got in the way.

Foundation programs also created opportunities for Mississippi teachers to meet and share information. When the Mississippi Jeanes teachers met in 1919 to discuss their work, one of the teachers said that there were eighty-five schools in the county, but half were in churches and a third in lodges; the majority of schools had been damaged by storms, and the teacher suggested they be condemned. The teacher in Madison County reported that many of the seventy-one schools in the county were closed due to a lack of teachers, and from Noxubee County the teacher reported that most of the sixty-three schools in the county were held in churches and shacks.[158] Teachers had opportunities to share local conditions with other teachers and in a venue that included foundation representatives. The reports from these meetings, which took place at least annually, provided a formal venue to expose the plight of rural black Mississippi schools and reach out for additional support. At the least, it made clear to teachers what might be available and what existed in other southern communities within and outside of the state.

Beyond the regular conferences of Jeanes teachers, foundations provided some limited scholarship funds for Mississippi teachers to travel to the Tuskegee Institute for summer school in general teaching instruction and to the Hampton Institute summer school to focus on librarian work.[159] The foundation asked that funds be provided to outstanding teachers who wished to render special and advanced service. Lillie Bryant, who taught in Pike County, had completed three years of regular studies at Jackson College and then seven years of instruction at the Tuskegee summer institute with foundation support.[160] The summer school curriculum informed their supervisory duties, but the opportunity to interact with Jeanes teachers from other states was likely more beneficial. It brought Mississippi Jeanes teachers in contact with other teachers who were also supported by northern foundations and likely provided helpful information about the range of programs that were being implemented across the South and the role that teachers played in them. The black teachers who attended foundation summer schools were encouraged to subscribe to teachers' journals and generally given access to information and networks to which they would not necessarily have had access. Of course,

national black teacher organizations also held conferences and national meetings and organized without foundation support. However, foundation supported networks provided institutional venues that formally connected rural
black teachers to alternative governance structures, an imperative in oppressive, locally controlled areas of Mississippi.

Sometimes the lack of state or county support led teachers to organize
their own summer schools with the hope that it would be funded and supported by the state. The teacher in Charleston, Mississippi, wrote to the
state agent in 1930 to inquire about holding a summer school for the region's
teachers. The teacher explained that there were 124 teachers in Tallahatchie,
with additional teachers in nearby Tate and Panola counties, who would be
interested in attending. The Tallahatchie teachers had planned the summer
institute and estimated that more than one hundred teachers would attend,
without any financial assistance from the state. "We are not asking for money.
We are asking only for authority to have it here. This is the only hope to build
up the negro teachers of Tallahatchie County."[161] The state agent responded
that they did not have the authority to hold the school and, in fact, the number
of summer schools in the state would be reduced rather than expanded for the
next session.[162] However, while black teacher organizations already existed,
foundation programs encouraged teachers to organize with outside approval,
sometimes in new ways with the hope of strengthening connections to outside
organizations that were interested in rural black education.

The archives also contain many examples of rural black citizens and teachers who corresponded directly with the foundations and agents outside of
Mississippi. A black teacher in Merrill, Mississippi, wrote directly to the
Rosenwald Fund to ask for assistance in 1929. The teacher hoped to have
a new school constructed and pointed out that the land already existed, but
the community had no idea how much money might be made available and
what would be required to procure funds. In another example, the teacher in
Renova, Mississippi, wrote directly to Julius Rosenwald to ask for funding
for repairs and equipment.[163] In this case, the Rosenwald field director wrote
back to the principal and referred her to the state agent.[164] It is not likely that
the state was helpful, though the teacher may have perceived that the state
might be more likely to respond when the request came through the Rosenwald Fund, rather than directly from the rural community. While this was not
often the case, it is significant that there were lines of communication opened
between teachers and foundations during this time period. Their requests
provided information about local communities that states were not collecting
or sharing.

In another example, a resident of Dundee, Mississippi, had written to Robert Moton, principal of the Tuskegee Institute, to complain about the short term of the schools in Tunica County, Mississippi. Moton brought the complaint to the attention of the Rosenwald Fund, and the fund then contacted the Mississippi state agent. At this point, the state agent merely wrote to the resident who had complained and told him to take the matter to the white county superintendent.[165] However, the Rosenwald agent simultaneously wrote to the resident informing him of their action, thereby opening a direct line of communication between the community and the Rosenwald Fund.[166] The programs that were set up by northern foundations signaled to rural black communities that help might be available through alternative means.

The foundations understood that their hands were tied in Mississippi and likely found it difficult not to provide money for requests that were clearly deserving. In 1930, a citizen of Mantee, Mississippi, wrote directly to Julius Rosenwald. This particular letter was an incredible example of the strict parameters in which blacks promoted their own education, and is actually worth sharing in greater length:

> Not knowing just how to write you my wishes however I make this adventure. Myself specially [sic] and a few others wishes one of your schools built here. On land given by me. . . . I can get plenty help to work but they are like myself they have but little money. Pleas [sic] help me build a school here (a rosenwall) [sic] I will do the work. And will deed the land to any set of authority your honor will dictate that it will take to secure your asstence pleas [sic]. We are poor but want a good school like they say you build and I pray you to direct your authority of this state to grant me such aid as will warrant me to get this school. I sure want the school. So since you've just newly mairrid [sic] I pray you to let us be among the first of your good gifts for a schools. We are weak finantially [sic] but sure want the school. There is a large number of children will gladly go to the school if we could obtain it. Yet we are all poor, anxious of your help, your servant . . .[167]

The letter illustrates a great deal about rural Mississippi life. First, it makes clear the role that rural blacks had in promoting their own educational opportunity. The letter's author, Mr. Gaston, was willing to deed his own land to the state and provide the labor. Second, it indicates that rural blacks, even those with a minimal education, knew a great deal more about foundation programs than might be expected. In this case, he even referred to Rosenwald's recent remarriage, following the death of his wife three years earlier. Third, the lack of any type of support available to rural blacks was clear. Mr. Gaston appealed in the only way he thought might be successful. Finally, these citizens understood that foundation money might lead to a loss of local control but were willing to turn over authority in exchange for a facility. The director of the Rosenwald Fund referred the letter to the state agent and told Mr. Gaston he was sure that the state would cooperate with the community and offered suggestions to get the proper equipment.[168] It is unclear that anything was provided to the community in the end. However, the Rosenwald Fund letter in response to the request was sent directly to the black resident and copied to the state agent. While money might not be forthcoming, it did give the black patrons of the school a platform to air grievances. Over the longer term, it might be possible even to work toward some way to address the community's needs.

The perseverance of the state's Jeanes teachers led to notable achievements, which they discussed in detail in their final reports to the state and to their foundation benefactors. One summary report for 1928–29 made clear the scope of their efforts in the state, in spite of the strict parameters in which they worked. There were twenty-three Jeanes teachers appointed that year, overseeing 1,374 schools, where they raised $78,022 in donations.[169] The teacher from Adams, Mississippi, reported that she had overseen thirty-three schools and thirty-seven teachers, in session for 120 days per year. She acknowledged that many of the schools met in area churches but reported that money had been raised to build two schoolhouses, which would be held until deeds could be obtained for land.[170] In Amite County, the Jeanes teacher reported that she had seen one Rosenwald school completed at a cost of $2,500, but her special accomplishment had been to "set out to encourage better health conditions, sanitation of school rooms and grounds, also to teach those industries that will be most helpful."[171] The teacher from Bolivar reported that the county supported about a three-month school term, and funds from other sources added another month to the school year, but the community was "now raising money to build several schools and have now in bank several hundred dollars for the above purpose."[172] These three examples illustrate some important issues. First, the teachers made choices about what to report. It was important to advertise the scope of the work and the benefits of foundation funding to local communities. At the same time, these final reports were strategic, highlighting the need for longer school terms and new schoolhouses. It is likely that the teacher in Bolivar hoped for Rosenwald funding for her school but also knew it depended upon maintaining minimum school terms, which was not provided for in the local budget.

The teacher from Kemper County was proud to report that citizens planned to work during the summer to complete a new Rosenwald school. Her comment illustrates the ambivalence of rural blacks about the implications of accepting outside funding: "My people have been suspicious of the Rosenwald Aid but it has vanished now."[173] The teacher in Lamar County successfully consolidated two schools "after four years of persuading" and planned to have the school terms extended in the next year.[174] All of these reports indicate the important accomplishments of the Jeanes teachers in expanding and supervising the local school system. They also illustrate an awareness of the criteria for funding, the implications of accepting it, and the potential to improve rural schooling with outside support.

Beyond the progress in expanding education infrastructure, however, these teachers were able to use these positions to strengthen community organizing in spite of the relatively more oppressive environment in Mississippi. In 1917, twelve counties had GEB funding to support homemakers club work.[175] With this funding, Jeanes teachers organized 565 clubs with an enrollment of 5,930, visited 1,079 homes, and "raised enough money to build school houses in several communities."[176] Even when community organizing was not explicitly funded through the support of club work, teachers considered it central to their job responsibilities. In Leake County, the teacher reported that one of her goals was the "organization of people in the various communities into groups. . . . I was very successful in carrying out the things set forth above. There was great interest manifested among the patrons, teachers, and pupils, and the work was really a pleasure."[177] Another teacher detailed nine objectives for her work that were in line with foundation and state wishes. These included hygiene, building and repairs, equipment, organization and classroom management, industrial education, longer terms and larger enrollments, prompt opening and closing of schools, field rally and student days, and teacher certificates of merit. However, when she was asked to provide information about her special accomplishments, she focused on one, reporting that "work was very well centralized and through co-operation much good was accomplished."[178]

The teacher in Walthall County was also explicit about her teaching responsibilities, noting that she encouraged her teachers to make lesson plans for at least two subjects. However, she also organized teachers meetings, which she reported as a success with almost 100 percent attendance.[179] In Warren, Mississippi, which seemed to have a relatively developed school system, the teacher reported that there were fifty-eight schools and eighty-eight teachers, and that she had overseen the completion of one Rosenwald school that year, bringing the total number of Rosenwald schools in the county to twenty-two, with an eight-month term. Her primary focus, however, went beyond her success at expanding the infrastructure. She was proud that she had improved rural communities through a better homes movement.[180] The Jeanes teacher in Winston also organized school-improvement clubs and community clubs, "which cooperated in every effort."[181] Mississippi Jeanes teachers recognized the central role that schools might play in the organization of communities, with many of them believing this to be as important as building schools and improving teachers.

Applications and reports to the Jeanes Fund indicate the wide disparity in the infrastructure of schooling between counties and towns in Mississippi, including school terms, tax support, the existence of a high school, and the existence of well-constructed schoolhouses. It became clear to teachers, however, that the state would be more responsive when local communities raised more money, and community organizing facilitated that goal. In 1930, the newly appointed Jeanes teacher in Choctaw County joined a school system with terms that were less than four months a year. The superintendent wrote the state agent that the new teacher was so successful that the parents in three of the schools that she supervised had agreed to raise funds for half of her salary. As such, the superintendent followed up with a request to almost double the school terms in both Ackerman and Weir, two of the Choctaw school districts.[182] The state agent filed the application and said that at the end of the term he would be willing to forward additional funds if any balance remained in the Jeanes account.[183]

It is truly remarkable that in a Deep South state, schooling might offer an institutional means for rural blacks to engage with private donors whose agenda was not in accordance with Mississippi whites. Rural blacks were able to covertly promote action with the imprimatur of whites because that work was within the context of schooling. Some teachers might have been less likely to mobilize because of their dependence for employment on local communities.[184] However, from the perspective of the public-private relationships that developed in that state, a number of teachers were actually on the payroll of the northern philanthropists and, while these teachers might still fear economic reprisal, they had relatively more power—not only access to information outside of the community but also connections between the institution of schooling and forces outside of the local arena. These teachers were in a position to organize local communities during Jim Crow. Unfortunately, in the face of the massive resistance that came with *Brown v. Board of Education*, most of these teachers had to choose between their professional education work and the fight for expanded rights. Fortunately, by this point many had facilitated grassroots efforts to promote expanded educational opportunities in rural Mississippi and had helped to expose the plight of rural blacks in Mississippi to groups that existed outside of the formal governance structures of the state.

CONCLUSION

Research has shown that public support is ultimately more fragile in those relationships in which collaboration is promoted by private rather than public interests.[185] The lack of state initiative, or even participation, in Mississippi ultimately resulted in greater opportunity for white opposition to education for rural blacks, a longer process of policy development, fewer opportunities to promote reform from the outside in a meaningful way, and less sustained reform. Given that the majority of whites at every level of state governance were not in favor of education for rural blacks, it would seem obviously detrimental to rural blacks to take power away from the local black community and place their schools in a public sphere, dominated as that sphere was by white supremacy. At the same time, it is extremely difficult to redefine the public sphere through individual acts in local communities. Even more than in North Carolina, rural blacks in Mississippi had much to lose in a centralized school system overseen by an agency that was influenced by state and local politicians who opposed universal education. In the short term, black schools may have benefitted from controlling their own operations, but in the longer term inequalities continued to grow. Rural blacks sought cooperative ties between community school-based organizations, state agents, and private agencies that might promote their needs, and many came to realize that outside efforts would displace the influence that local politics had on education reform. Indeed, black publications in the early part of the century increasingly called upon greater federal oversight of the entire education system so that blacks would be treated more equitably.[186]

Throughout the first half of the twentieth century, Mississippi made little progress creating an education system for rural blacks or improving the state's governance structures, lagging far behind the rest of the South in the years before World War II. Mississippi's state agent for Negro education published an article in 1937 that explained that the state had the highest percentage of black citizens of any state in the union, and almost three hundred thousand of them attended school. At the same time, there were only eighty-three high schools, including public and private, to serve the state's black citizens, and only one higher education institution for the training of teachers, which as a land grant institution was supported by both the state and the federal government. The agent also noted that of the 3,753 public schools for black citizens, "1,440 were conducted in churches, lodges, old stores, tenant houses, or whatever building is available." However, while he lamented the shoddy state of rural black schools, he also laid blame at the doorsteps of the rural black community. "The colored people themselves need very much to be aroused on the question of the importance of proper training of their children. They have not yet learned to put first things first. They want schools, but they have not learned how to discriminate between real schools and mere makeshifts, nor how to provide school facilities within the bounds of their own resources." He also called on white people, however, to take a more genuine interest in the "right sort of education for our colored populations. . . . The Negroes are here and will stay here. It is, therefore, our responsibility to give them a fair chance to become an intelligent, self-supporting and self-respecting people. . . . From a Christian standpoint, from an economic standpoint, and from the standpoint of the future welfare of our state, we should give more serious consideration to this question."[187] Indeed, after decades of reform initiatives in the South, the state was only beginning to question the relationship between education and political development, and the state agent's call to action in 1937 reflected the extent to which most people in the state felt that such an exploration would be detrimental to their conception of a separate and unequal racial state.

In fact, a decade after the 1937 state agent's report, another report on black higher and professional education in Mississippi outlined similar problems and highlighted the intractable problem of political development in the state. The report detailed the factors that limited higher education, including state finances, a need for coordination, the influence of partisan politics, the lack of a unified state program of teacher education and certification, and the organization and administration of institutions.[188] For fifty years, reports from both the state and private interests lamented the poor condition of education, and particularly the state's administrative structure. The lack of a more centralized and coordinated system between the state and local communities had a palpable effect on the education of all Mississippi children, from kindergarten through college. These problems had a profound impact on educational opportunity for rural blacks in the state throughout most of the twentieth century.

The state's inability to overcome local racial politics and to develop a state system of education affected every foundation effort. Given state politics and the lack of any central administration, foundation programs that had been successful in other states languished in Mississippi. Foundations were unable to create an administrative structure conducive to education reform that was racially inclusive, or to develop a reform dynamic that would strengthen the administration of an unequal school system or governance capacity more generally. The foundations sought alternative ways to achieve goals. They cooperated extensively with the foundation-supported university professor and with black teachers and their organizations when it was possible. They created forms of collaboration in Mississippi that looked quite different from collaboration in North Carolina, and which failed to yield significant progress. The Rosenwald Fund acknowledged the difficulty of doing business in the state in one of its final reports. The fund reported on progress across the South in schoolhouse construction from 1917–1932. While most of the progress had been made in the elementary schools in Mississippi, the state had also moved forward in providing black high schools. "Today there are over 100, with 10,000 enrolled. However, if all the students graduating from the eighth grade of the elementary school went to high school and stayed there, Mississippi would have to increase its high school facilities for Negroes eight times."[189]

Foundations could have a huge effect on a state like Mississippi. The state shared many characteristics of others in the Deep South, with a powerful plantation economy, a significant black population, and state governance structures that were the most blatant reminder of why foundation support was necessary for education reform. However, the unwillingness of state politicians to collaborate with the foundations and other business interests outside the state's borders put a limit on what might be accomplished there. The lack of cooperation highlighted the extent to which foundation power depended upon other institutions. In the end, education and governance systems changed very little in the first decade of the twentieth century, and rural blacks knew that a change to the oppressive environment in which they existed would require grassroots efforts and formal intervention from the federal government.

CHAPTER SIX

Conclusion

On March 4, 1948, Gladys Noel Bates filed the first civil rights lawsuit in the state of Mississippi. Bates, who was born in the state in 1920, became a teacher in Kosciusko in 1938 and then moved with her husband to the Smith Robertson Junior High School in Jackson, where she was also active in the Voters' League, the Jackson Teachers Association, and the Mississippi Teachers Association. Bates wrote a letter to the superintendent of schools in Jackson to complain about the unequal pay between black and white teachers. The superintendent claimed to know of no pay differential but also believed that, even if one existed, he would be in no position to address it because the teachers had signed a contract. Thurgood Marshall, as chief counsel for the NAACP, advised Bates that there was a case for discrimination, but she would need $5,000 to file the lawsuit. The Mississippi Teachers Association increased dues by $1 that year for its 5,600 members in order to raise the funds, although the political environment required the association to claim that the dues would support a "benevolent fund" for teachers who fell on hard times. They raised the money, and the NAACP took the case.[1]

The decision not to share plans of the lawsuit was a wise one. Bates and her husband lost their jobs, their home was burned down, and teachers who were overheard speaking in favor of the lawsuit were fired. It was difficult even to find a lawyer in the state who would file the legal papers. There were two black lawyers in Jackson who were qualified, but both worked as postmen and had young children; their participation would put both their families and livelihood at risk. Instead, an elderly black lawyer from Meridian, who was in his eighties and could barely walk, "gained enough courage and strength" to ride the bus to Jackson to submit the paperwork.[2] Ultimately, Bates lost the case and moved her family to Colorado, where she and her husband continued their teaching careers.

Like *Brown v. Board of Education*, the more well-known and successful civil rights case just six years later, organizing in black communities often focused on schooling even though Jim Crow laws meant that almost every domain of southern life was segregated and unequal. Rural blacks in the South perceived that education was central to their quest for greater equality and understood the risks associated with pursuing it in most regions. Bates's actions were incredibly brave. While the NAACP had been building a set of precedent cases across the South in the first half of the twentieth century that would eventually result in *Brown v. Board of Education*, not a single desegregation case was filed in Mississippi before 1961. It is particularly notable that it was in the domain of schooling that black citizens of that state took a legal stand on the oppressive inequality that existed in every aspect of their lives. Indeed, rural black reformers across the South recognized the value of promoting an education system not just as an end in itself, especially given the value placed on education as the antithesis to slavery, but also as a means to create avenues for greater participation in the political and social structure. Foundation-based education programs were intended to maintain the South's racial structure, but rural blacks recognized that effective foundation programs could potentially expand schooling and, by extension, enlarge opportunities for participation in policy and political development.

The emergence of the modern foundation in the early twentieth century was significant for school reform, particularly in the South. This book has focused on three of those foundations that perceived education to be central to addressing a set of national concerns. Foundation reformers sought a strong national state, and they believed that goal could be best served with efficient state and local governance systems, a rehabilitated and integrated South, and public schooling that provided an institutional site to reach children and families in rural areas. State building, particularly at the state and local level, was just one of many areas that concerned philanthropists in the early twentieth century. However, it was the most important of their concerns. The South presented problems that were detrimental to a stronger nation, including weak economic and political systems, a large number of illiterate citizens in both white and black areas, and an uneducated labor force. The philanthropists were interested in municipal reform efforts across the nation, but the South presented a particularly extreme version of local and partisan control that led to inefficient government.

Education was a key social policy initiative for foundation reformers, who hoped to create a school system that would serve both races, even if unequally, and would be publicly funded and administered. Indeed, schooling would not only educate students and serve as a conduit for disseminating national ideals into the rural South, it would also provide a means to strengthen both state and local governance. It was an organizing feature of rural communities in the first half of the twentieth century for both foundation reformers and rural black citizens, and was important to political development. Foundation programs had the potential to strengthen government capacity through new tax structures, better data collection, and systems that integrated a range of agencies and government functions to provide greater oversight.

Foundations developed programs to implement across the South. By 1920, every southern state had appointed a state agent for Negro education and Jeanes teachers in many local counties. Over the next decade, Rosenwald schools were built across the South. Foundations collaborated with state and local politicians, reformers from the North and the South, and local black citizens. Their programs led to an infrastructure to accommodate industrial education, considered the most appropriate curriculum for rural blacks because it would maintain both the labor force and white supremacy. At least in the short term, consensus on this issue fostered cooperation with a broad range of political actors. However, while industrial education was common to the southern agenda in every state, the reform dynamics that developed in Mississippi and in North Carolina reflected the unique political contexts that affected long-term prospects for universal education and the development of state and local governance. Foundations developed education programs that could accommodate the political context and responded to variation in racial attitudes across state and local communities. Interstitial collaboration filled a void in state and local governance with regard to education policy, reflecting a set of unique relationships that developed in each state among foundations, universities, state and local officials, and local citizens.

Most southern whites worked actively to prevent the kind of changes to the social and economic structure that might come from greater educational opportunity, yet attitudes toward rural black citizens also varied somewhat, affecting state and local decisions about education policy.[3] In general, white southerners were concerned about a public, centralized system of education for either race that would increase taxes and take control away from local communities. Beyond that, some southern whites considered any money spent on education for blacks a waste of public resources, while others believed that a school system designed to provide an unequal and industrial education that would serve the existing economic and social structure was appropriate. Foundation reformers recognized this variation among education reformers, yet neglected to address in a meaningful way important questions about education and race. Mississippi's university professor Thomas Bailey acknowledged as much in the first decade of the twentieth century. He pointed out that foundation efforts would amount to nothing without some attempt to confront in a meaningful way the "negro question" in the South.[4] Foundations avoided directly addressing this larger question and promoted universal schooling that was influenced heavily by local tradition. As a result, they simultaneously extended rural black schooling and limited educational attainment in rural black areas by offering lower-quality education programs. They also recognized that as rural black schools became more formally connected to the political structures outside of the communities and to a state system of public schooling, local tradition would have far less influence. Their programs promoted greater black participation in policy and political development in some states where schooling influenced governance capacity at the state and local level.

Interstitial collaboration not only filled policy-making voids in rural black education development but also changed the shape of governance in ways that provided greater power to rural black citizens, even if within strict boundaries. A universal system of schooling required organizational capacity, which expanded through programs aimed at schoolhouse construction, Jeanes supervising teachers, county training schools that promoted teacher training and state certification standards, stronger administrative systems, and an increase in local tax revenues. Rural black teachers and citizens were instrumental to these efforts, illustrating the extent to which these individuals took responsibility for expanding educational opportunity for themselves. In the short term, local control and initiative was important to educational development and black agency. It not only provided important professional opportunities for rural black teachers but also opportunities for both foundations and rural black teachers to develop innovative ideas that could be replicated across the South. Rural black teachers were able to exercise a degree of control over their schools in many regions of the South throughout the early twentieth century, within narrow parameters. However, the development of an infrastructure to deliver education enhanced the administration of the state and of local communities in ways that could connect rural black citizens more formally to the larger political structure and would lead to greater centralization of rural black schools. Indeed, foundations sought such centralization, at both the state and county level across the South, as an important means to organize rural communities and enhance governance capacity at the local level. There were obvious political benefits to centralization, but ultimately it took away from local teachers the power that had come with the localized implementation of foundation policies. Many black teachers were willing to accept this risk because collaboration might lead to more schooling and the kinds of outside interference that would be necessary to overturn the unjust and unequal segregated system.

Centralization was difficult to achieve. Southern whites were generally disinterested in black schools and foundation programs were not always successful at promoting stronger administrative structures. Foundation experiences in North Carolina and in Mississippi led to different outcomes. While foundations depended upon collaboration with political actors at every level of government, conditions for collaboration varied across state and local areas, and its efficacy depended on the unique reform dynamic that developed in each state. Foundation officials cooperated with a range of political actors in an array of programs that were intended to fill gaps in state policy and practice regarding education development for rural black citizens. Where states were unwilling partners, foundations hoped that their programming would promote administrative systems and institutionalize basic education standards, including school terms. They initiated programs that would enhance both education and governance, and hoped that state and local politicians would institutionalize reform over the longer term. Their power derived from collaborative relationships that were promoted at every level of governance. However, where meaningful collaboration was absent, foundations were less effective. Their potential was realized in North Carolina, but not in Mississippi.

The reform dynamic that developed between foundations and the state in North Carolina was conducive to foundation efficacy, in terms of both schooling and political development. Many North Carolina whites perceived great possibilities for economic progress in the reunified nation after the Civil War, and politicians embarked on an extensive reform of government and the economy at the end of the nineteenth century. The state worked closely with foundations to realize those goals. Foundation programs in North Carolina were designed to expand an education infrastructure for blacks that was industrial in nature and considered more acceptable by local white citizens but also more centralized, with stronger administrative systems that helped to promote political development at the state and local level. The reform dynamic strengthened governance capacities both locally and more broadly, and foundation programs were instrumental to those efforts.

Foundations established their program for rural black education reform in

North Carolina by creating and developing a state-level agency, the Division of Negro Education, directed by Nathan Newbold for more than forty years. Newbold carefully accommodated the range of political and racial attitudes at the state and local level, yet the office was relatively impervious to political influence. While he was constantly aware of the political environment and tried not to force the agenda on rural communities, neither local majorities nor private interests captured public authority for the developing system of universal education. Newbold was effective at organizing cooperation with an array of institutions and agencies at the state and local level, as well as with local white and black citizens. His ability to coordinate such a diverse group influenced positively public perceptions of the work in both white and black communities. The reform dynamic in North Carolina led to stronger governance structures and a more centralized system of universal schooling. It was essential to creating a universal system of schooling supported by local taxes.

Foundations cooperated extensively in North Carolina with white field agents like Nathan Newbold but also with those who were black, such as Annie Holland, B. C. Caldwell, W. A. Robinson, George Davis, and the Jeanes teachers in local areas. Black educators, like the Jeanes teachers, were important to the development and greater centralization of the state's public school infrastructure. They were able to participate in a limited way in developing education policy and shifting schools in North Carolina more into the public sphere. The developing bureaucracy in that state created the space for grassroots organizing, and school oversight often included black administrators like Jeanes teachers, who helped to formalize rules, promote standardization, and expand levels of authority. Their participation in foundation initiatives potentially gave these teachers an important role in expanding the local administrative structure for schooling and in influencing both state and local decisions about rural black education. These deeply collaborative efforts in North Carolina created a reform dynamic that resulted in an expanded public school system for rural black citizens in that state, with more than eight hundred new Rosenwald schools, a Jeanes teacher in more than half of the counties, state standards for teaching and certification that included black teachers, an expanded local tax base, and stronger administrative systems.

Ultimately, North Carolina developed a more centralized and bureaucratic governance system with greater authority vested in the state, especially with regard to education, and foundation work helped to create these shifts in the authority of schooling. The 1932 Brookings Institution report, *State Centralization in North Carolina*, made clear that state officials had successfully redefined the relationship between the state and its political subdivisions, and specifically commended North Carolina for formally centralizing control over a number of government functions, including schooling.[5] The report recognized that significant progress had been made in creating an education infrastructure. Schooling strengthened governance structures at the state level by creating a stronger and more centralized education bureaucracy, and at the local level by organizing communities and connecting them to that state structure. Schooling created links between rural communities and the political structures outside them; this gave some rural blacks the means to participate as political actors beyond the borders of their local communities and space in which to mitigate the oppressive nature of the local political system.[6]

Foundations had a very different experience in Mississippi, where they unsuccessfully tried to implement programs that would promote rural black education reform and stronger state and local governance systems. They appointed two state agents for Negro education at a time, and intended that those appointments would lead to a state agency devoted to universal education. However, the agents were far less effective at promoting the work—a result of both personal attitudes about black education and the difficult political context of Mississippi. Political interests at both the state and local level heavily influenced the office. Staff turnover in the Division of Negro Education was more common in Mississippi, yet all of the agents appointed during the first decades of the twentieth century were relatively ineffective at promoting collaboration between the office and other institutions and interest groups in the state. The Mississippi Division of Negro Education remained beholden to state and local political interests throughout the first four decades of the twentieth century. The state agents there were perceived as friendly to local whites but indifferent and even hostile to local black citizens.[7]

Mississippi preferred to remain isolated from outside interference, prioritizing its traditions and culture. Unfortunately, a significant part of that culture was white supremacy. The political context in Mississippi created an educational policy void with regard to rural black schooling that was relatively greater than that in most southern states. The state's politicians were reluctant to collaborate with outside groups and failed to develop stronger administrative systems within the state to promote change. It was difficult for foundation officials, state and local politicians, and rural black citizens to promote education reform given the administrative context. Further, racism and weak political development were related, making it challenging to overcome either. In the end, both factors limited Mississippi's willingness and ability to collaborate with northern foundations. Foundations developed some limited forms of collaboration that were peculiar to the state, but there was little progress in expanding rural black education or in developing a stronger administrative state.

Mississippi politicians eschewed foundation support, and for most of the first half of the twentieth century foundations did not have powerful allies in the state with whom they could collaborate. Mississippi schools remained relatively more isolated than those in rural North Carolina. Black teachers organized on their own, through formal networks like the Mississippi Association of Teachers in Colored Schools, and tried to take advantage of any opportunities made available through foundation programs. However, foundation work in that state did not contribute to political development in the ways that it did in North Carolina. The Brookings Institution's 1932 report on Mississippi came to almost opposite conclusions than the one issued for North Carolina that same year. The state's chief defects included a division of power between elected officials and other agencies, a lack of common direction, a weak executive branch, and no clear lines of responsibility for governance. The report, one of many that were similarly critical in the first half of the twentieth century, focused specifically on the weaknesses in the education system, pointing out the ineffective system of state and local governance in Mississippi.[8] State officials never responded in a meaningful way to any of these reports.

Rural black citizens in Mississippi struggled to expand educational opportunity on their own and with foundation support when possible. Foundation programs promoted grassroots organizing in the state, beyond what blacks there were already doing independently. However, even with foundation support, rural blacks organized more covertly than in North Carolina, and local white citizens still thwarted their efforts in education reform. Most of their schools remained isolated from the public system of schooling and from the broader political structure, and foundations did not have the same reach in local communities that they did in North Carolina. Rural black teachers also managed their own schools in Mississippi and participated in networks through their own black teacher organizations and through meetings that were organized by foundations. Yet, foundation programs did not create more significant formal avenues that connected these teachers to governance structures in which policy and political development could advance. Indeed, Mississippi's reluctance to participate in a reform dynamic was generally indicative of the lack of formal governance structures in the state. Administrative work did not connect rural communities to a public system of schooling. Mississippi politicians at both the state and local level worked to exclude black schools and limit their reach. For Mississippi's black citizens, foundation programs highlighted the extent to which outside intervention would be necessary to change the social and political structure of the state.

Education reform was based in industrial education in both North Carolina and Mississippi, yet both black and white reformers differed in their longer-term conceptions of black education and equality. Colonialism around the world in the early twentieth century generated a discourse about the South that challenged national progressive ideals.[9] In the aftermath of the Civil War, foundations believed they would need to rehabilitate the South. Prominent North Carolina reformers believed in both white supremacy and the idea that universal education would contribute to race progress. North Carolina reformers were not necessarily motivated by more benevolent or just attitudes toward rural blacks. Scholars have described a form of "managed race relations" in some areas of the South, where whites allowed social reform, but only enough to reduce racial tension.[10] Many whites in North Carolina created paternalistic organizations aimed at sustaining segregation and disfranchisement, while simultaneously promoting limited reform and better race relations.[11] They rejected the rigid oppression and violence characteristic of the Deep South, instead providing limited black educational opportunity, with the expectation that blacks would react with appreciation and complete deference. At the same time, there were also local whites who were not committed to these more paternalistic ideals and remained resistant to universal education. It was helpful in North Carolina to let foundations assume some responsibility for local education reform. It was easier for foundations to take on difficult political issues at the local level and provide the organizational capacity that only emerged in the state during the early part of the century. However, state reformers could not completely control what happened once foundation programs shifted authority for the education system away from local interests and into the hands of state-managed institutions and simultaneously promoted the participation of local black citizens.

In general, even if foundation officials and their agents encouraged the participation of rural blacks as a means of addressing community grievances in a limited way, it is also true that foundations simply could not impose their education vision, or implement programs and policies without the help of both state and local actors. Whites found the organizational repertoires of schooling in an industrial-training context to be nonthreatening, and were willing to support school organizations when based in agricultural work and domestic service.[12] However, black teachers used school-based programs to do far more than promote industrial education. Their work in developing agricultural clubs, commencements, county fairs, and other events helped teachers to extend schooling into the homes of every community member. These school-based organizations, shaped by the organizational repertoires of industrial education, were instrumental in expanding schooling, and in implementing and sustaining administrative reforms at the local level. These organizations were also central to local fundraising efforts for school improvement and created a common culture within and beyond local communities, which broadened frames of support for the pursuit of greater equality through education.[13]

While centralization in North Carolina created the possibility that differences between white and black schools would be reduced over the longer term, it was also detrimental to black participation at the local level.[14] State officials recognized the possibility that greater centralization might have an effect on community initiative. One report cautioned that with a "standard school" there was a strong probability that communities might get a feeling of self-satisfaction that would limit community initiative and organized effort.[15] Nathan Newbold acknowledged this explicitly following the 1932 Brookings report, when he recognized that centralization might actually give him fewer opportunities to work through Jeanes teachers in local communities. He understood that greater centralization might limit their power in North Carolina and advised them to "do the best we can with what we have, it will serve, I sincerely believe, to 'keep the light still burning' through these trying times, and when the next Legislature meets better provisions will be made for its continued usefulness."[16] He knew how important these teachers were to foundation work. He recognized, like the teachers, that centralization gave more power to the state but also limited the possibility of creating flexible programs that were tailored to a particular region. Of course, local control had also given the Jeanes teachers latitude to serve both the foundations and the community in rural areas.[17]

Schooling was central to community organizing in both states, and education was a flash point in the quest for civil rights. Black agency in Mississippi was more covert than in North Carolina, but it was definitely evident in the area of schooling, where local black teachers were successful at community organizing in the decades preceding national mobilization in the civil rights movement.[18] Indeed, the NAACP considered the teaching profession a good source for membership in the early part of the century.[19] Civil rights activist Aaron Henry recalled that in his Mississippi high school, one of his teachers convinced the entire senior class to join the youth council of the NAACP, and in his county, every black teacher was a member.[20] However, teachers' roles as community organizers evolved after World War II and moved the locus of organizing out of schools. While many teachers did join the NAACP like other black professionals in the 1930s, there were fewer on the rolls in Mississippi after *Brown v. Board of Education*. Winsom Hudson, another of Mississippi's civil rights activists, recalled in an interview that many teachers in that state had to choose not to be involved in the civil rights movement after 1954, when teaching applications required a series of questions about whether the applicant or a family member had ever been a member of the NAACP. Black applicants in Mississippi had to assert in a notarized form that they did not believe in the work of the organization.[21]

Southern whites had allowed black teachers to work on community organization through schooling not only because it was based in an industrial-education curriculum but also because many whites assumed that black citizens supported the idea of "separate but equal." Activist Aaron Henry also described a meeting in which Mississippi governors White and Barnett had called together members of the black community to get their support for a better model of separate but equal than what the state had been willing to consider for the first half of the century. The governors seemed surprised to learn that most blacks in Mississippi had never supported that ideal.[22] Henry recalled that when black leaders were preparing for the "separate but equal" discussion, the Union County Jeanes teacher expressed concern in advance of the meeting that black organizers were going to "bite the hand" that was feeding them. The teacher expressed concern about integrated schools, because white parents would "come around there looking for me with a shotgun" if he tried to discipline their kids. Indeed, all of the teachers had cause to worry. The Mississippi Sovereignty Commission, organized by Mississippi's state government to oppose integration, had collected meticulous records that included the names and addresses of every Jeanes teacher appointed in Mississippi and had investigated membership in the NAACP. One investigative letter from the commission observed, "two Negro school teachers, Mr. and Mrs. Herbert Ammons, at Tunica, Mississippi, had been fired because they were active in NAACP agitation."[23] Rural black schools were central to community outreach and organization in the early decades of the twentieth century. However, as the civil rights movement gained momentum, it became more difficult for black teachers, especially in Mississippi, to use schooling to mobilize for civil rights. Teachers risked losing their jobs and most citizens did not want to put their schools at risk. Schools had been and would remain central to the community. However, national organizations like the NAACP promoted the cause of black equality and churches became relatively "safer" institutions for black mobilization.

Ultimately, foundations wanted to institutionalize reform as part of state and local governments so that the system in the South would be publicly supported and serve all citizens. However, success varied and the strength of these emergent state systems of schooling had implications for both governance and the quest for greater equality that might come through expanded schooling. Historians and policy analysts have debated the extent to which institutions like the federal government, especially the judicial branch, provided the impetus for desegregation and civil rights. Some argue that there were powerful constraints on the courts that ultimately limited their ability to promote social reform. Others hold a more dynamic view, arguing that courts had the ability to produce significant social reform effectively when there were positive incentives to produce compliance and costs for not doing so. In order for that to occur, however, there must also be in place institutional capacity to implement change.[24] Public-private relationships in the South had some effect on the capacity of states to address each of these constraints. The creation of more centralized schooling produced venues in which desegregation could be implemented, and the means by which incentives to comply and costs for not complying could be imposed. This was not necessarily foundations' intent in the early twentieth century, when reformers hoped to promote national ideals in local areas and racial equality was not one of them. However, a more developed and centralized school system would create a more likely environment for new conceptions of both education and race.

For strong segregationists across the South, the possibility that the existing school system could accommodate integrated schools was deeply problematic. In states like North Carolina, they worried that the education system, which had become more centralized over previous decades, would lead naturally to the integration of schools. When Senator Robert Byrd of Virginia participated in the writing of the Southern Manifesto, he was less troubled by an excess of segregationist sentiment in that state than he was worried that Virginians might ultimately accept racial change as inevitable.[25] North Carolina, with its more centralized school system, could make a false effort at compliance by integrating students in such small numbers as to be inconsequential, in order to maintain "managed white supremacy." Of course, efforts like this were bound to have a more dynamic effect than state officials might have anticipated, giving blacks a taste of what desegregation might provide for them and a sense that what had been thought unattainable really could be attained. The more developed centralized school systems had already provided expanded political opportunities and organizational strength for rural blacks and contributed to the longer political process of developing new policy.[26]

At the same time, as with any form of policy development that occurs through indirect governance and collaboration, public support was ultimately more fragile in those relationships in which the collaboration was promoted by private rather than public interests.[27] Foundation efforts to influence schooling in the South during Jim Crow support that argument. In North Carolina, state education leaders promoted a public system of schooling and campaigned throughout the state to gain citizen support from white and blacks alike. Nathan Newbold, the state agent for Negro education, served as a liaison between private foundation interests, black citizens, state and local politicians, and local whites. Local reform in that state was publicly supported and funded, which allowed it to continue evolving throughout the early twentieth century, even though some in the state were opposed. Mississippi had weak administrative systems and little centralization of state functions. The private foundation interests pushed for black education reform, but the goals were never adopted by most of the state's white actors. There were successes in particular communities, but it was difficult to affect the public system in a meaningful and sustained way because the public did not generally initiate or support reform. The massive federal intervention that was required to promote change may have led to a more centralized education system, but likely without the support of local communities. Local whites in that state abrogated responsibility for rural black schools, kept local black schools isolated, and worked with state officials to place limits on what those schools might accomplish. Indeed, it would take much greater investment from the federal government after *Brown v. Board of Education* in states like Mississippi, because funding was needed not just to promote desegregation but also to create a more centralized system that could limit the power of local politics. The lack of a centrally institutionalized school system in Mississippi not only affected the ability of the federal government to develop incentives for compliance it also had a profound impact on the participation of the community.

While state political leaders in Mississippi were typically against integration, the lack of any threat to a centralized state institution may have made it easier to overlook the violence and massive resistance in local communities. The highly decentralized and local nature of schooling in Mississippi made it possible for strict segregationists to have a more receptive climate for promoting resistance in their local arena, which often took violent forms.[28] Michael Klarman's argument about the implications of this resistance is somewhat counterintuitive and ironic, asserting that success in achieving increased civil rights can actually be attributed to the massive white resistance that occurred because of local control in states like Mississippi.[29] The terror of local rule and the contentious political situation created by elite whites in local communities made it more difficult for blacks to mobilize as a community but ultimately shocked the rest of the country to change public opinion against the system of white supremacy.[30]

Indeed, it would be easier for foundations and government agencies generally to promote social policies in a public system of education that provided opportunities to reach into and affect local communities by disseminating ideas and implementing programs that included local citizens. Political scientists have distinguished between power and institutional political authority to enact change.[31] The philanthropists recognized that they had funding but no political authority in the South. Whites, who were committed to Jim Crow and typically hostile to universal education, controlled political authority at the local level almost completely. However, it would be possible for foundations to establish greater authority through institutions and formal changes in educational policy related to education. Through the institution of schooling, foundations could try to change the locus of control from local communities to the state, and it would be easier to influence a state system of schooling than thousands of local districts. It would help to ensure that the public assumed full responsibility for the education of its citizens. Schools were a site for socializing individuals and for state formation. Foundations understood that schooling and political development were related, and promoted a range of education programs that could strengthen government capacity at the state and local level. They created stronger administrative systems. Their expansive organization and ability to consider a range of complex issues gave them considerable policymaking leverage among competing interest groups in the South.[32] This did not give them greater authority but did provide more power than what already redounded to them through their largesse. They were able to establish consensus for their education program and build extensive and powerful networks to implement it. However, they could not completely control what happened in local schools or the decisions that individual states made about how to provide oversight to the emerging system of public schooling.

The modern foundations were self-conscious state builders and policy entrepreneurs who aimed to promote national ideals through a public system of education, efforts they believed to be critical in the South. Black education reform was an important component of this national agenda. However, the results were uneven. The best possible strategy for the foundations was to work with state and local officials, as well as local black educators. This research illustrates that, without the participation of all three, it was virtually impossible for foundation programs to be effective. North Carolina politicians and reformers collaborated with foundations to generate organizational capacity, creating a context in which foundations wielded considerable power in policy and political development. Their extensive efforts to create a more centralized and standard system of public education brought isolated and rural black schools into the public system. Schooling served as an important site for expanding governance capacity at the state and local level. Education reform incorporated efforts from the "bottom up," including elements of black agency, and challenged sectional politics. Mississippi politicians had almost the opposite experience.

This research has also illustrated that schooling provided opportunities to reorganize local communities and affect black agency in the process. Foundations could not impose their education vision, particularly in local black communities, and the collaboration that developed between foundation agents and local citizens had the potential to expand schooling and open political opportunity structures in rural areas. On this point, there were some similarities between the two states. The Jeanes teachers in both of these states worked to organize their communities to promote expanded educational opportunity in rural areas. All of these teachers saw community organization as central to their job descriptions. Foundation programs provided a vehicle to organize local communities in both states. However, teachers were more successful integrating the community with state and local governance structures in North Carolina. Rural black communities in Mississippi remained isolated, and a weak state administrative structure kept them relatively disconnected from governance. However, foundation programs provided opportunities for rural blacks in Mississippi to expose the extreme inequality of Jim Crow in the state and to work outside of the local political structure through foundation teacher networks and direct correspondence with foundation agents. These programs made clear that change would likely never happen without outside interference. That knowledge made people like Gladys Noel Bates work with the NAACP to challenge the racial structure of the state and promote the grassroots organizing that was vital to the quest for civil rights.

With more centralized schooling also came an increased role for both the federal government and the states, and the relative power of private interests in state and local schooling decreased. The early twentieth-century foundations were clear that private interests should not be in charge of a public system of schooling and anticipated that their administrative role would decrease over time. In the twenty-first century, philanthropists also exercise considerable power by virtue of the largesse that they provide, especially in the realm of education. Contemporary foundations have different concerns about political development. The themes of global competitiveness and the maintenance of American power continues to motivate many philanthropists and education reformers. The beginning of the twenty-first century, like the early twentieth century, has seen substantial sums of money contributed to shaping the future of schooling, and education systems have a great deal to gain by harnessing those resources. Further, much of the contemporary discourse among education reformers and foundation officials continue to focus on issues of opportunity and equity in schooling. Foundations have the power to promote extensive collaboration among reformers, teacher unions, business organizations, and state and local policymakers to generate support for reform. Yet, these efforts can also lead to protests from local groups who believe that private interests have exerted too much power and are stifling dissent. A significant part of this tension centers on the possibility that national ideals backed by private interests working in cooperation with federal agencies, will help to redefine schooling and diminish the power of state and local governance systems.

Schooling will remain an important site for redefining the relationship between local communities and states, between states and the federal government, and between local citizens and the federal government. Indeed, public discourse in both K–12 and higher education may lead to new efforts to redefine the relationship between education and the national state, which might lead to greater federal intervention and the potential for extensive foundation influence. However, the story of southern education development indicates that foundations will not be effective at imposing a new vision of education onto existing systems without the support of states, citizens, and private stakeholders. Both foundation officials and education reformers have much to gain by creating programs that are transparent and inclusive of state interests, elite political actors, and local communities. Reformers at every level of governance might learn from the public-private collaborations that developed in the South in the early twentieth century.

NOTES

INTRODUCTION

1. The original name was the Higgs Industrial Institute, and it became the Martin County Training School when it was turned over to the state as a public institution.

2. "Higgs Industrial Institute Will Receive $3,000 If It Can Raise $1,000," *The Enterprise* 11, no. 35 (June 17, 1910).

3. "Higgs Industrial Institute," *The Enterprise* 11, no. 34 (June 10, 1910).

4. Report of the Parmele Industrial School, Folder Reports and Outlines—Misc., 1913, Box 1, Division of Negro Education, Department of Public Instruction, State Archives of North Carolina, Raleigh; hereinafter referred to as SANC.

5. Report from *The Crisis* 7–8 (May 1914): 12.

6. Report of State Agent of Negro Rural Schools of North Carolina, December 30, 1914: 5, Folder 1042, Box 115, Series 1.1, Rockefeller Archive Center, Papers of the General Education Board, Rockefeller Archive Center, Pocantico Hills, NY; hereinafter referred to as RAC-GEB.

7. Parmar argues that foundations sought hegemonic control at the beginning of the century in order to promote their own power. See Inderjeet Parmar, *Foundations of the American Century: The Ford, Carnegie, and Rockefeller Foundations in the Rise of American Power* (New York: Columbia University Press, 2012), 32.

8. James Anderson, *The Education of Blacks in the South, 1860–1935* (Chapel Hill: The University of North Carolina Press, 1988); W. E. B. Du Bois, "Negro Education" and "Gifts and Education," in *W. E. B. Du Bois: A Reader*, ed. David Levering Lewis (New York: Henry Holt and Company, 1995); Du Bois, *Black Reconstruction in America, 1860–1880* (New York: Atheneum, 1992; orig. c. 1935); Ann Short Chirhart, *Torches of Light: Georgia Teachers and the Coming of the Modern South* (Athens: University of Georgia Press, 2005); Adam Fairclough, *Teaching Equality: Black Schools in the Age of Jim Crow* (Athens: University of Georgia Press, 2002); V. P. Franklin, *Black Self-Determination: A Cultural History of the Faith of the Fathers* (Westport, CT: L. Hill, 1984); Michael Fultz, "African American Teachers in the South,

1890–1940: Powerlessness and the Ironies of Expectations and Protest," *History of Education Quarterly* 35 (Winter 1995): 401–22; Mary Hoffschwelle, *The Rosenwald Schools in the American South* (Gainesville: University Press of Florida, 2006); Eric Anderson and Alfred Moss, *Dangerous Donations* (Columbia: University of South Carolina Press, 1999); James Leloudis, *Schooling the New South: Pedagogy, Self, and Society in North Carolina 1880–1920* (Chapel Hill: University of North Carolina Press, 1996); Vanessa Siddle-Walker, *Their Highest Potential: An African American School Community in the Segregated South* (Chapel Hill: University of North Carolina Press, 1996).

9. Percy H. Easom, "Mississippi's Negro Schools," *The Mississippi Educational Advance*, February 1937, Folder 872, Box 97, Series 1.1, RAC-GEB.

10. There is a history of philanthropic efforts to enhance the education of free blacks prior to the Civil War, mostly in Quaker communities. They were joined by other denominational organizations in this work, though none with as great an influence as the Quakers. For a brief history of philanthropic giving to black education, see Ullin W. Leavell, "Trends of Philanthropy in Negro Education: A Survey," *Journal of Negro Education* 2, no. 1 (January 1933): 38–52.

11. Ronald Butchart, *Schooling the Freed People: Teaching, Learning and the Struggle for Black Freedom, 1861–1876* (Chapel Hill: University of North Carolina Press, 2010), xiv. Butchart's research revises an accepted narrative that assumed that Reconstruction schooling was run primarily by denominational agencies and white missionary teachers. His work adds considerable nuance to our understanding of Reconstruction education efforts and the role of education in addressing the needs of the South.

12. Anderson, *Education of Blacks in the South;* Butchart, *Northern Schools, Southern Blacks and Reconstruction: Freedmen's Education, 1862–1875* (Westport, CT: Greenwood Press, 1980); Butchart, *Schooling the Freed People;* Du Bois, *Black Reconstruction in America;* Jacqueline Jones, *Soldiers of Light and Love: Northern Teachers and Georgia Blacks, 1865–1873* (Athens: University of Georgia Press, 1992); Robert Morris, *Reading, 'Riting and Reconstruction: The Education of Freedmen in the South, 1861–1870* (Chicago: University of Chicago Press, 1981).

13. Carl Kaestle, *Pillars of the Republic: Common Schools and American Society, 1780–1860* (New York: Hill and Wang, 1983), 192–212.

14. North Carolina called for systematic public education by the 1830s and established a state school fund for that purpose, though it was poorly administered and then bankrupted by the Civil War. Other states, including Georgia, Alabama, Mississippi, Louisiana, Arkansas, Texas, Tennessee, and Virginia passed school laws in the 1830s and 1840s, but the laws were ill-administered, viewed as vehicles to educate the poor, and did not gain popular traction. Bruce W. Eelman, "'An Educated and Intelligent People Cannot be Enslaved': The Struggle for Common Schools in Antebellum Spartanburg, South Carolina," *History of Education Quarterly* 44, no. 2 (Summer 2004): 251.

15. Hillary Moss, *Schooling Citizens: The Struggle for African American Education in Antebellum America* (Chicago: University of Chicago Press, 2009), 94–101.

16. Du Bois, *Black Reconstruction in America*, 638.

17. Ibid., 641.

18. Eric Foner, *Reconstruction: America's Unfinished Revolution, 1863–1877* (New York: Harper and Row, 1988), 144. By 1869, nearly three thousand schools, serving more than 150,000 students, reported to the bureau, though these figures did not include evening and

private schools operated by missionary schools and blacks themselves. The Peabody Fund was opposed to integrated schools in the South. Ibid., 367.

19. David Tyack, Thomas James, and Aaron Benavot, *Law and the Shaping of Public Education, 1785–1954* (Madison: University of Wisconsin Press, 1991), 14.

20. Nancy Beadie, *Education and the Creation of Capital in the Early American Republic* (Cambridge: Cambridge University Press, 2010), 325; Ira Katznelson and Margaret Weir, *Schooling for All: Class, Race, and the Decline of the Democratic Ideal* (New York: Basic Books, 1985); Tracy Steffes, *School, Society, and State* (Chicago: University of Chicago Press, 2012), 7.

21. *Report of the Commission on Country Life* (New York: Sturgis and Walton Company, 1917); Wayne Fuller, *RFD: The Changing Face of Rural America* (1964; repr., Bloomington: Indiana University Press, 1966). Good roads associations also flourished during this time period, especially in the South. See, *Southern Good Roads* (Lexington, NC: Southern Good Roads Publishing Company).

22. David B. Danbom, *Born in the Country: A History of Rural America,* 2nd ed. (Baltimore: Johns Hopkins University Press, 2006), 161–84.

23. Carl C. Plehn, "The Nature and Causes of the Tax Reform Movement in the United States," *The Economic Journal* 20, no. 77 (March 1910): 4–5; Edwin R. A. Seligman, "The Separation of State and Local Revenues," *State and Local Taxation: National Conference under the Auspices of the National Tax Association: Addresses and Proceedings*, vol. 1 (November 12–15, 1907), 485–88.

24. For a general discussion of the extractive policies of the Confederacy, see Richard Bensel, *Yankee Leviathan: The Origins of Central State Authority in America, 1859–1877* (Cambridge: Cambridge University Press, 1990). For a discussion of this issue in Mississippi, see Charles Hillman Brough, "State Taxation in Mississippi," in *Studies in State Taxation, with Particular Reference to the Southern States,* ed. J. H. Hollander (Baltimore: Johns Hopkins Press, 1900), 191–93. See also George Ernest Barnett, "Taxation in North Carolina," in *Studies in State Taxation, with Particular Reference to the Southern States,* ed. J. H. Hollander (Baltimore: Johns Hopkins Press, 1900). At the end of the nineteenth century, Georgia had one of the most prohibitive provisions for local taxes, for which each levy required the endorsement of grand juries and approval from two-thirds of registered voters. Charles D. McIver, "Problems in North Carolina," *Annals of the American Academy of Political and Social Science* 22 (September 1903): 302.

25. Robert A. Margo, *Race and Schooling in the South, 1880–1950: An Economic History* (Chicago: University of Chicago Press, 1994), 36. For a discussion of legislative reform in this regard, see Tyack, James, and Benavot, *Law and the Shaping of Public Education*, 133–53.

26. For an example, see *State Centralization in North Carolina* (Washington, DC: The Brookings Institution, 1932).

27. For general information about southern schooling, see Carl Kaestle, *Pillars of the Republic*, 192–217; William J. Reese, *America's Public Schools: From the Common School to "No Child Left Behind"* (Baltimore: The Johns Hopkins University Press, 2005), 75–78; Leloudis, *Schooling the New South.*

28. "Report of the Commissioner of Education," in *Reports of the Department of the Interior for Fiscal Year ended June 30, 1911, vol. 2* (Washington, DC: Government Printing Office, 1912), xxxiii, table 20.

29. Tyack, James, and Benavot, *Law and the Shaping of Public Education*, 75.

30. "Report of the Commissioner of Education." See also the *Digest of State Laws Relating to Public Education in Force, January 1, 1915*, Department of the Interior Bureau of Education Bulletin, 1915, no. 47 (Washington, DC, 1916), 628; and Louis Harlan, *Separate and Unequal* (New York: Atheneum, 1958).

31. Harlan, *Separate and Unequal*, 10–11. For a discussion of inequalities beginning with Reconstruction between black and white schools in five urban areas in the South, see Howard N. Rabinowitz, "Half a Loaf: The Shift from White to Black Teachers in the Negro Schools of the Urban South, 1865–1890," *Journal of Southern History* 40, no. 4 (November 1974): 565–94.

32. "General Aspects of Lynching in Recent Decades," Folder 977, Box 97, Series 3.8, Papers of the Laura Spelman Rockefeller Memorial Collection, Rockefeller Archive Center, Pocantico Hills, New York.

33. Oral history interview with Mrs. Minnie Ripley, Southern Mississippi History Digital Collection, Center for Oral History and Cultural Heritage, University of Southern Mississippi, Hattiesburg.

34. Notes from Reports of Mississippi Jeanes Teachers at Conference of Louisiana and Mississippi Jeanes Teachers, March 20, 1919, Folder 2125, Box 222, Series 1.2, RAC-GEB.

35. Reports from the GEB provide interesting data. In 1910, Georgia's per capita expenditures for all enrolled pupils was $10.70 according to the US Department of Education, while the GEB notes that the per capita expenditure in that same year for teaching was $1.76 for blacks and $9.58 for whites. Using the same sources to develop similar data for other states, Louisiana was $19.65 for all enrolled pupils, with $1.31 spent on teaching for blacks and $13.73 for whites; Mississippi was $10.20 per capita for enrolled students, with $2.26 and $10.60; North Carolina was $7.16, with $2.02 and $5.27; and South Carolina was $6.93, with $1.44 on teachers for blacks and $10.00 for whites. See "Report of the Commissioner of Education," June 30, 1911, and "Negro Public Education in the South," Southern Education Foundation Archives, Robert Woodruff Library, Atlanta University Center, Atlanta; hereinafter referred to as SEF-AUC. Within states, South Carolina illustrates the extent to which local politics both continued disparities within regions and prevented remedies in subsequent decades. As late as 1935, the county of Abbeville, South Carolina reported spending $4.58 on blacks ($73.56 on whites); Chesterfield County reported spending $7.52 on blacks ($45.90 on whites); Clarendon County reported $4.15 on blacks ($20.32 on whites); and Greenville $11.24 on blacks ($40.21 on whites). Reports from the Education Time Capsule, 1935, S152043, South Carolina State Department of Education, State Department of Archives and History.

36. Report of Bura Hilbun to the General Education Board, November 1917, Folder 876, Box 98, Series 1.1, RAC-GEB.

37. For a history of philanthropy and the American foundation, see David C. Hammack and Helmut K. Anheier, *A Versatile American Institution: The Changing Ideals and Realities of Philanthropic Foundations* (Washington, DC: Brookings Institution Press, 2013). Other scholars have similarly characterized foundation work as distinctive, referring to it as a period of "state centered philanthropic activism." See Mark Henderson, "Steering the State: Government, Nonprofits, and the Making of Labor Knowledge in the New Era," in *Politics and*

Partnerships: The Role of Voluntary Associations in America's Political Past and Present, ed. Elisabeth S. Clemens and Doug Guthrie (Chicago: University of Chicago Press, 2010). See also the discussion of Daniel Coit Gilman in Olivier Zunz, *Philanthropy in America: A History* (Princeton, NJ: Princeton University Press, 2012), 10.

38. Hammack and Anheier, *A Versatile American Institution*, 43–47.

39. The GEB charter was clear that the goal of the foundation was "the promotion of education within the United States of America, without distinction of race, sex or creed," making clear that the fund could be used to promote national education ideals. However, the next line made clear the organization's focus: "That the immediate intention of the Board is to devote itself to studying and aiding to promote the educational needs of the people of our southern states." *The General Education Board: An Account of its Activities, 1902–1914* (New York: General Education Board Publication, 1915), 216. An early history of the GEB can be found in Raymond B. Fosdick, Henry Pringle, and Katherine Douglas Pringle, *Adventure in Giving: The Story of the General Education Board, a Foundation Established by John D. Rockefeller* (New York: Harper and Row, 1962). For information about the Anna T. Jeanes Foundation, see "Certificate of Incorporation of Negro Rural School Fund," Folder 1924, Box 202, Series 1.2, RAC-GEB. For the Rosenwald Fund, see Hoffschwelle, *The Rosenwald Schools of the American South*, 9–48, 69; and, Peter M. Ascoli, *Julius Rosenwald: The Man Who Built Sears, Roebuck and Advanced the Cause of Black Education in the American South* (Bloomington: Indiana University Press, 2006), 135–53.

40. "The Conference and Community Organization," Folder 149, Box 6, Papers of the Southern Education Board, University of North Carolina Special Collections, Chapel Hill.

41. Edgar Gardner Murphy, *Problems of the Present South* (New York: Macmillan Company, 1904), 160.

42. *The General Education Board: An Account of its Activities*, 11.

43. Minutes from a meeting of the General Education Board, January 24, 1911, Folder 3651, Box 353, Series 1.2, RAC-GEB.

44. Robert C. Ogden, "The Conference for Education in the South," *Annals of the American Academy of Political and Social Science* 22 (September 1903): 272.

45. Murphy, *Problems of the Present South*, 245–46.

46. *Proceedings of the Fourth Conference for Education in the South Held at Winston-Salem, North Carolina, April 18, 19, 20, 1901* (Harrisburg, PA: Mount Pleasant Press, 1901), 11.

47. For a discussion of similar efforts in the present, see Frederick M. Hess, ed. *With the Best of Intentions: How Philanthropy Is Reshaping K–12 Education* (Cambridge, MA: Harvard University Press, 2005). Hess notes the importance of creating parallel systems and organizational capacity as an effective means to promote sustained reform. For a discussion of how southern parochialism helped to promote change through incremental reforms through local institution building, see Ann-Marie Szymanski, "Beyond Parochialism: Southern Progressivism, Prohibition, and State-Building," *Journal of Southern History* 69, no. 1 (February 2003): 107–37. For a discussion particular to schooling, see Joan Malczewski, "Weak State, Stronger Schools: Northern Philanthropy and Organizational Change in the Jim Crow South," *Journal of Southern History* 75, no. 4 (November 2009): 963–1000.

48. Bensel provides a detailed discussion of the ways in which reform impacted the struc-

tural capacity of national Confederacy and Union administrative systems during the Civil War, which have provided a useful framework for thinking about the ways that bureaucratic reforms can affect governance. See Bensel, *Yankee Leviathan*, 110.

49. Barry D. Karl and Stanley N. Katz, "Foundations and Ruling Class Elites," *Daedalus* 116, no. 1 (Winter 1987): 1–40; Karl and Katz, "American Private Philanthropic Foundations 1890–1930," *Minerva* 19, no. 2 (June 1981): 236–70. See also Ellen Condliffe Lagemann, *Private Power for the Public Good: A History of the Carnegie Foundation for the Advancement of Teaching* (Middletown, CT: Wesleyan University Press, 1983).

50. Samuel Hays, "The Politics of Reform in Municipal Government in the Progressive Era," *The Pacific Northwest Quarterly* 55, no. 4 (October 1964): 168–69.

51. Ibid., 157–69.

52. John Ettling, *The Germ of Laziness: Rockefeller Philanthropy and Public Health in the New South* (Cambridge, MA: Harvard University Press, 1981), 2.

53. Ibid., 118–21. One report claimed that public health demanded "not only effective federal, state and municipal health agencies, but . . . an effective county health service. Interest is focused as never before in conserving our natural resources; in bettering the farm and the farm home; in making the country school an effective educational agency; in redirecting the energies of the country church; in organizing country life for greater efficiency." Report of the County Health Service, July 8, 1912, Folder 149, Box 14, Rockefeller Foundation Archives, Rockefeller Archive Center, Pocantico Hills, NY; hereinafter referred to as RAC-RFA.

54. Steffes, *School, Society, and State*, 11. See also Natalie Ring, *The Problem South: Region, Empire, and the New Liberal State, 1880–1930* (Athens: University of Georgia Press, 2012), 19–20.

55. Steffes, *School, Society, and State*, 11.

56. Bensel, *Yankee Leviathan*, 236, 414–17. Bensel discusses the ways in which the structural capacity of government developed during the war, but in the aftermath the political economy was thoroughly devastated and disorganized. Class relations had been completely disrupted, southern representation was absent in national political institutions, the southern banking system was destroyed, and a massive redistribution of wealth out of the South into northern industrial markets and westward expansion occurred.

57. Ring, *The Problem South*, 18.

58. Ibid., 80.

59. Ibid., 52. Bensel also points out that questions about national modernization and state expansion after Reconstruction became associated with concerns about the underdeveloped South. See Bensel, *Yankee Leviathan*.

60. "Report from the Bureau of Investigation and Information of the Southern Education Board," *Proceedings of the Conference for Education in the South, the Sixth Session* (New York: Issued by the Committee on Publication, 1903), 45.

61. Joseph Soss, Richard C. Fording, and Sanford F. Schram, *Disciplining the Poor: Neoliberal Paternalism and the Persistent Power of Race* (Chicago: University of Chicago Press, 2011), 3–4. Scholars have argued that, in general, it is important to recognize that the American welfare state is more robust than most people recognize when the private dimensions of social spending and tax benefits are taken into account. Steffes explicitly makes this argument about schooling in Steffes, *School, Society, and State*. See also Jacob Hacker, *The Divided Welfare*

State: The Battle over Public and Private Social Benefits in the United States (Cambridge: Cambridge University Press, 2002); Christopher Howard, *The Welfare State Nobody Knows: Debunking Myths about US Social Policy* (Princeton, NJ: Princeton University Press, 2007); Howard, *The Hidden Welfare State: Tax Expenditures and Social Policy in the United States* (Princeton, NJ: Princeton University Press, 1997).

62. Robert J. Norrell, *Reaping the Whirlwind: The Civil Rights Movement in Tuskegee* (Chapel Hill: University of North Carolina Press, 1985); Adolph Reed, "The Study of Black Politics and the Practice of Black Politics: Their Historical Relation and Evolution," in *Problems and Methods in the Study of Politics*, ed., Ian Shapiro, Rogers Smith, and Tarek Masoud (Cambridge: Cambridge University Press, 2004), 106–43.

63. Lieberman describes the role that New Deal welfare policies had in defining the meaning of race in American society. The administrative structure could have profound consequences for the construction of racial differences. While there are important differences, schooling may have provided a similar function prior to the New Deal. See Robert Lieberman, *Shifting the Color Line: Race and the American Welfare State* (Cambridge, MA: Harvard University Press, 1998), 13.

64. Steffes, *School, Society, and State*, 201.

65. Nelson Lichtenstein, *State of the Union: A Century of American Labor* (Princeton, NJ: Princeton University Press, 2003), 197–99.

66. Robert J. Norrell, *Up from History: The Life of Booker T. Washington* (Cambridge, MA: Harvard University Press, 2009), 424–25.

67. "Negro School Buildings in the Southern States, 1917–1947," Folder 10, Box 76, Papers of the Rosenwald Fund, Franklin Library, Fisk University, Nashville, TN; hereinafter referred to as RFA-Fisk; "Rural Schools Aided by Fund," Folder 7, Box 53, Julius Rosenwald Papers, University of Chicago.

68. Rabinowitz, "Half a Loaf," 594.

69. Brian Balogh, *A Government Out of Sight: The Mystery of National Authority in Nineteenth-Century America* (Cambridge: Cambridge University Press, 2009); Eldon J. Eisenach, *The Lost Promise of Progressivism* (Lawrence: University of Kansas Press, 1994); Kimberly S. Johnson, *Governing the New American State* (Princeton, NJ: Princeton University Press, 2006); Ring, *The Problem South*.

70. Matthew Lassiter and Andrew Lewis, eds., *The Moderates' Dilemma: Massive Resistance to School Desegregation in Virginia* (Charlottesville: The University of Virginia Press, 1998). Notable exceptions include Prince Edward County, Virginia, which chose to close schools for a number of years rather than integrate and was conservative for the Upper South, and Tuskegee, Alabama, which was liberal for the Deep South.

71. Jack Goldstone, "Comparative Historical Analysis and Knowledge Accumulation in the Study of Revolutions," in *Comparative Historical Analysis in the Social Sciences*, ed. James Mahoney and Dietrich Rueschemeyer (Cambridge: Cambridge University Press, 2003), 41–90.

72. There is considerable evidence in the archives, and a notable example is in "Negro Public Education in the South: A Confidential Report for the Officers of the General Education Board," 1927: 7–7C, Folder 1, Box 33, SEF-AUC. The philanthropists noted whether lack of progress in black education was due to unfavorable public sentiment, a lack of money, or an unsympathetic superintendent. For more general information about the relationship between

sectional interests and policy development in the South, see Regina Werum, "Sectionalism and Racial Politics: Federal Vocational Policies and Programs in the Predesegregation South," *Social Science History* 21, no. 3 (Fall 1997); Richard Bensel, *Sectionalism and American Political Development, 1880–1980* (Madison: University of Wisconsin Press, 1987); Jill Quadagno and Debra Street, "Ideology and Public Policy: Antistatism in American Welfare State Transformation," *Journal of Policy History* 17, no. 1 (2005): 60.

73. Karen Orren and Stephen Skowronek, *The Search for American Political Development* (Cambridge: Cambridge University Press, 2004).

74. Elisabeth Clemens, "Lineages of the Rube Goldberg State: Building and Blurring Public Programs, 1900–1940," in *Rethinking Political Institutions: The Art of the State*, ed. Ian Shapiro, Stephen Skowronek, and Daniel Galvin (New York: NYU Press, 2006), 187–215. William Novak seeks to dispel the "myth" of a weak American state by pointing out that the United States exhibits "infrastructural power" that might not fit within definitions of classic state theory but nonetheless allows for "an extraordinary penetration of the state through civil society to the periphery." William Novak, "The Myth of the 'Weak' American State," *American Historical Review* (June 2008): 767. See also Pauline Vaillancourt Rosenau, ed., *Public-Private Policy Partnerships* (Cambridge, MA: MIT Press, 2000). For a comparative perspective, see Gosta Esping-Andersen, *The Three Worlds of Welfare Capitalism* (Princeton, NJ: Princeton University Press, 1990).

75. Brian Balogh has traced the power of the American federal government through governance that "spanned extensive territory and that delegated authority to distant agents." Brian Balogh, *A Government Out of Sight*, 6. An example can be found in federal efforts to manage the developing railroad system in the late nineteenth century. For scholarship on political development more broadly defined, see Skowronek, *Building a New American State*, chapter 5 and then subsequent contributions in American political development on this issue, including Scott James, "Prelude to Progressivism: Party Decay, Populism, and the Doctrine of 'Free and Unrestricted Competition' in American Antitrust Policy, 1890–1897," *Studies in American Political Development* 13 (Fall 1999): 288–336. For discussion of American political development and sectional and racial politics in the South, see Bensel, *Sectionalism and American Political Development*. Scholarship has focused on public-private partnerships beginning with the New Deal, but scholars have recently begun to consider partnerships earlier in American history. Foundation work in the South provides an early example of such collaboration as an important component of political development. See Peter B. Evans, Dietrich Rueschemeyer, and Theda Skocpol, eds., *Bringing the State Back In* (Cambridge: Cambridge University Press, 1985); Shapiro, Skowronek, and Galvin, eds., *Rethinking Political Institutions*; Rosenau, ed., *Public-Private Policy Partnerships*; Michael B. Katz, *The Price of Citizenship: Redefining the American Welfare State* (Philadelphia: University of Pennsylvania, 2001).

76. Balogh, *A Government Out of Sight*, 15–20. Suzanne Mettler provides another model, the "submerged state," in which the federal government creates programs that expand its reach through private initiatives. Suzanne Mettler, *The Submerged State: How Invisible Government Policies Undermine American Democracy* (Chicago: University of Chicago Press, 2011).

77. Parmar, *Foundations of the American Century*, 32.

78. Karl and Katz, "Foundations and Ruling Class Elites," 1–4. They point out that these

ideas may not be sufficient for considering foundation power because the United States lacked alternatives for coping with major welfare issues that emerged from rapid industrialization.

79. Karl and Katz, "American Private Philanthropic Foundations," 247–48.

80. Balogh, *A Government Out of Sight*, 17. Balogh discussed these efforts more extensively in chapter 9, where he describes the range of options regarding the relationship between state and society, Balogh, *A Government Out of Sight*, 352–78; Johnson, *Governing the New American State*, 19.

81. Tyack, James, and Benavot point out the government influenced national ideas about common schooling in two important ways: with grants to state common-school funds and by incorporating national ideas about education in the enabling acts that admitted new states into the union. Tyack, James, and Benavot, *Law and the Shaping of Public Education*, 20–22

82. In her exploration of marginalized groups in the Progressive Era, Clemens explicitly excludes rural blacks as being too marginal. Tracy Steffes includes rural black schooling in her analysis of schooling as a state-building project but as part of a broader study of school reform across the United States. Steffes acknowledges in her work that African Americans in segregated southern schools were usually left behind in the project of school building because resources were disproportionately provided to white schools first. Elisabeth Clemens, *The People's Lobby: Organizational Innovation and the Rise of Interest Group Politics in the United States, 1890–1925* (Chicago: University of Chicago Press, 1997), 92–93; Steffes, *School, Society, and State*.

83. Louis Galambos, "The Emerging Organizational Synthesis in Modern American History," *The Business History Review* 44 (Autumn 1970): 279–90; Samuel Hays, "The Social Analysis of American Political History, 1880–1920," *Political Science Quarterly* 80, no. 3 (September 1965): 373–94; and Robert Wiebe, *The Search for Order: 1877–1920* (New York: Hill and Wang, 1967). For a more recent analysis of organizational history in this context, see Balogh, "Reorganizing the Organizational Synthesis: Federal-Professional Relations in Modern America," *Studies in American Political Development* 5 (Spring 1991): 119–72.

84. Paul Pierson, *Politics in Time: History, Institutions, and Social Analysis* (Princeton, NJ: Princeton University Press, 2004), 137.

85. Lieberman, *Shifting the Color Line*, 29.

86. Shapiro, Skowronek, and Galvin, eds., *Rethinking Political Institutions*.

87. Scholars including Orren, Skowronek, and Lieberman have debated the relative power of ideas and institutions in political development. For an interesting discussion of this scholarship, see Rogers Smith, "Which Comes First, the Ideas or the Institutions?" in Shapiro, Skowronek, and Galvin, eds., *Rethinking Political Institutions*, 91–113.

88. Pierson, *Politics in Time*; Joseph Soss, Jacob Hacker, and Suzanne Mettler, *Remaking America: Democracy and Public Policy in an Age of Inequality* (New York: Russell Sage Foundation, 2010).

89. Foundations promoted education reform through an array of institutional configurations that operated within a policy-making void. The term "associated action" typically includes elite actors and does not adequately capture policy development at the level of individual states or localities. Interstitial collaboration expands the definition of associated action that is currently in the scholarship. Foundations often included marginalized black citizens in

policy development in a way that was unprecedented during Jim Crow and, in doing so, used their relationship to the black community to promote foundation programs. The foundations were effective at influencing policy making in areas that state and local political systems had simply ignored. For example, many southern states enacted laws in the early twentieth century to centralize and expand schooling through local consolidation and longer school terms, yet also failed to acknowledge that, for rural blacks, formal schoolhouses often did not exist, and school terms were based upon agricultural cycles because compulsory-school laws were not enforced. The formal systems and political will necessary to address these issues often did not exist.

90. Foundations were not a formal organizational structure like the judiciary and, indeed, had no official power to create or implement state and local policy, yet worked to fill gaps in both policy and the law. Interstitial law fills gaps that exist because Congress cannot be expected to cover everything and intentionally leaves gaps. Examples of intentional gaps include the Taft-Hartley Act and the Sherman Anti-Trust Act. One example of such legal gaps in the South, which foundations hoped to address, is taxation. State constitutions in the South often placed legislated caps on state and local taxes after Reconstruction. Some states lifted those caps in the early twentieth century by allowing special tax districts in which counties or school districts could collect tax revenues to extend school terms in local areas. However, many counties created the special tax districts but then purposely drew the district lines so that every black household was excluded. The foundations implemented programs that encouraged additional local taxation and minimum school terms in rural black communities. The scholarship on foundations and southern education typically indicts foundations for not using the power of their largesse to overturn the racial structure of the South, though foundations attempted to affect policy development in a context where the racial state created real social and legal constraints, some that were arguably unconstitutional (special tax districts that exclude black households would seem not be legal under *Plessy*). For more information about interstitial law, see Arthur D. Hellman, Laren Robel, and David R. Stras, *Federal Courts: Cases and Materials on Judicial Federalism and the Lawyering Process*, 2nd ed. (Massachusetts: LexisNexis, 2009), 419; Kevin Johnson, "Bridging the Gap: Some Thoughts about Interstitial Lawmaking and the Federal Securities Laws," *Washington and Lee Law Review* 48, no. 3 (June 1991): 879–936.

91. Julian E. Zelizer, "Introduction: New Directions in Policy History," *Journal of Policy History* 17, no. 1 (2005): 1–11.

92. Doug McAdam, *Political Process and the Development of Black Insurgency, 1930–1970* (Chicago: University of Chicago Press, 1999), 59.

93. For examples of collaborative relationships that developed and were central to political development and to the provision of social welfare, see Clemens, "Lineages of the Rube Goldberg State." In addition to the state-initiated collaboration that Clemens describes, another model is that of "leveraging," in which private entities use funding to compel state and local political systems to engage in reform. David Strong, Pamela Barnhouse Walters, Brian Driscoll, and Scott Rosenberg, "Leveraging the State: Private Money and the Development of Public Education for Blacks," *American Sociological Review* 65 (October 2000): 658–81.

94. Christine Woyshner, *The National PTA, Race, and Civic Engagement: 1897–1970* (Columbus: Ohio State University Press, 2009).

95. Harlan, *Separate and Unequal*, 253–54. In another more detailed discussion of the SEB's work, Harlan concludes that the board's efforts seemed to have "almost no effect on the Negro schools" because members' approach to the race issue in public education lacked moral firmness and was weakened by compromise. Harlan, "The Southern Education Board and the Race Issue in Public Education," *Journal of Southern History* 23, no. 2 (May 1957): 201–2.

96. Chance v. Lambeth, 186 F. 2d 879 (4th Cir. 1951). Chance's challenge, with the help of the NAACP, was an important precedent for the subsequent ruling in *Brown*. The district court upheld the railroad. The court of appeals reversed the decision, and the Supreme Court refused to hear the case.

CHAPTER 1

1. Curry also went by the name Jabez Lamar Monroe Curry.

2. "Progress of Anti-Slaveryism: Speech of Jabez Lafayette Monroe Curry, of Alabama, in the House of Representatives," December 10, 1859, *Congressional Globe, 36th Congress, 1st Session*, 39.

3. Jabez L. M. Curry, *Difficulties, Complications and Limitations Connected with the Education of the Negro*, The Trustees of the John F. Slater Fund, Occasional Papers, No. 5 (Baltimore: 1895), 33.

4. Curry was adamant in his support for the Blair Education Bill, which was debated in Congress throughout the 1880s and advocated the use of federal aid for education. He continued to call on the federal government to provide support to the South. In his speech to members of the Conference for Education in the South, Curry was clear: "When the government emancipated the negroes there was an imperative resulting of necessity to prepare them for citizenship and freedom, but the government has persistently and cruelly refused to give one cent to this indispensable work." Curry, "Education in the Southern States," *Proceedings of the First, Second, and Third Conferences for Christian Education in the South, Capon Springs, Virginia, 1898, 1899, 1900* (Washington, DC: Southern Education Board reprint), 26. For detailed discussion of Curry's views, though from the perspective of southern white reformers of the time period, see also Edwin Anderson Alderman and Armistead Churchill Gordon, *J. L. M. Curry, A Biography* (New York: Macmillan Company, 1911).

5. Curry wrote a paper for the Slater Fund in 1895 in which he asserted that the "poverty, wretchedness, hopelessness of the present life [of southern blacks] are sometimes in pitiable contrast to the freedom from care and anxiety, the cheerfulness and frolicsomeness, of antebellum days . . . every method and function of civilization have been secured and fostered by the Federal and State governments, ecclesiastical organizations, munificent individual benefactors, and yet the results have not been, on the whole, such as to inspire most sanguine expectations, or justify conclusions of rapid development or of racial equality." Curry, *Difficulties, Complications and Limitations*, 9–10.

6. Robert C. Ogden, "Annual Address of the President," in *Proceedings of the Fifth Conference for Education in the South* (Knoxville, TN: Gaut-Ogden Company by the Southern Education Board, 1902), 18.

7. *Proceedings of the Third Capon Springs Conference for Education in the South, 1900* (Washington, DC: Southern Education Board, 1900), 25.

8. The conference was originally billed as the Conference for Christian Education in the South, and organizers decided to change the name in order to appeal to a broader base of participants.

9. Edwin Alderman, "The Child and the State," *Proceedings of the Fifth Conference for Education in the South* (Knoxville, TN: Gaut-Ogden Company by the Southern Education Board, 1902), 55.

10. Curry, "Education in the Southern States," 30–31.

11. Ibid., 28.

12. *Proceedings of the Fifth Conference for Education in the South* (Knoxville, TN: Gaut-Ogden Company by the Southern Education Board, 1902), 7.

13. Steffes, *School, Society, and State,* 3.

14. Robert C. Ogden, "The Conference for Education in the South," *Annals of the American Academy of Political and Social Science,* 22 (September 1903), 275.

15. "A Survey of the Field by Rev. H. B. Frissell, Principal of the Hampton Institute," *Proceedings of the First Capon Springs Conference for Christian Education in the South, 1898* (Raleigh, NC: Capital Printing Co., 1898), 1. Frissell had helped to organize the conference at the suggestion of Reverend Edwin Abbot, who had been a devotee of the annual conferences at Lake Mohonk, New York, to discuss the "Negro Question" in the South. Abbott believed that the question would be more effectively discussed at a southern locale. For more information on the Mohonk Conferences, see Isabel C. Barrows, ed., *First Mohonk Conference on the Negro Question, held at Lake Mohonk, Ulster County, New York, June 4,5,6, 1890* (Boston: Geo H. Ellis, 1890). Edwin Abbott was also the brother of Reverend Lyman Abbot, author, social critic, and reformer, who had served as secretary of the Freedmen's Bureau and editor of the *Outlook,* a popular journal that promoted social reform and theology.

16. *Proceedings of the First Capon Springs Conference,* 10.

17. Hollis Frissell, "Memorial Auditorium to Memory of R. C. Ogden," *The New York Times,* November 7, 1915.

18. William Baldwin, "The Present Problem of Negro Education, Industrial Education," *Proceedings of the Second Capon Springs Conference for Christian Education in the South, 1899* (Capon Springs: The Conference, 1899), 70–75.

19. Calvin M. Woodward, "Manual Training in Education," reprinted in *Education in the United States, Volume 3–1810–1895,* ed. Sol Cohen (New York: Random House, 1974), 1866.

20. Francis W. Parker, "Notes of Talks on Teaching," reprinted in *Education in the United States,* 1856.

21. Carleton Gibson, "Industrial Education for the South," *Proceedings of the Fourth Conference for Education in the South: Athens Meeting, 1901* (Washington, DC: Southern Education Board, 1902), 92.

22. Charles Dabney to George S. Dickerman, January 18, 1899, Folder 1, Box 1, Series 1.1, Papers of the Southern Education Board, The Wilson Library, University of North Carolina, Chapel Hill; hereinafter referred to as UNC-SEB.

23. After providing initial gifts to Booker T. Washington for Tuskegee graduates, Anna Jeanes named Washington and Hollis Frissell, of the Hampton Institute, the trustees of the Negro Rural School Fund in her will. "The Last Will and Testament of Anna T. Jeanes," Folder Accounts of the Estate of Anna T. Jeanes, Swarthmore College Friends Library, Philadelphia.

With regard to the Rosenwald Fund, Booker T. Washington visited Rosenwald's home in 1914 in an effort to continue Rosenwald's funding for rural black schools, in particular his offer in 1912 for "Tuskegee off-shoots." For information about this incident and the fund's inception, see "Memo: Booker T. Washington Interview at the Palmer House, 4/23/14," Folder 12, Tuskegee Institute General (1912–1917), Box 53, Julius Rosenwald Papers, University of Chicago Special Collections Research Center, Chicago; hereinafter referred to as UC-JRF; and, Booker T. Washington to Wallace Buttrick, April 11, 1905, Folder 1924, Box 202, Series 1.2, RAC-GEB.

24. Ward McAfee, *Religion, Race and Reconstruction: The Public School in the Politics of the 1870s* (Albany: SUNY Press, 1998), 13.

25. Hollis Frissell to Morris K. Jesup, December 23, 1898, Folder 1, Box 1, Series 1.1, UNC-SEB.

26. Hollis Frissell to Henry E. Fries, January 2, 1899, Folder 1, Box 1, Series 1.1, UNC-SEB.

27. Hollis Frissell to Morris K. Jesup, December 23, 1898, Folder 1, Box 1, Series 1.1, UNC-SEB. Booker T. Washington had procured gifts from New York financier Morris Jesup and the Slater Fund for the agricultural extension wagon that had been developed at Tuskegee by George Washington Carver. The "Jesup Wagon" began its work in 1906 and reached more than two thousand rural blacks in its first summer of operation. Louis R. Harlan, *Booker T. Washington: The Wizard of Tuskegee, 1901–1915, Volume 2* (Oxford: Oxford University Press, 1986), 207.

28. Hollis Frissell to Henry Fries, January 2, 1899, Folder 1, Box 1, Series 1.1 UNC-SEB; Hollis Frissell to Morris K. Jesup, January 16, 1899, Folder 1, Box 1, Series 1.1, UNC-SEB.

29. Eugene Branson to Hollis Frissell, October 17, 1901, Folder 3, Box 1, Series 1.1, UNC-SEB.

30. *Proceedings of the Second Conference for Education in the South*, 8.

31. Dabney, "The Public School Problem in the South," in *Proceedings of the Fourth Conference for Education in the South*, 53.

32. George T. Winston, "Industrial Training in Relation to the Negro Problem," in *Proceedings of the Fourth Conference for Education in the South*, 105.

33. Murphy, *Problems of the Present South*, 80.

34. Ibid., 162.

35. Baldwin, "The Present Problem of Negro Education, Industrial Education," 74.

36. *Proceedings of the First Capon Springs Conference*, 1.

37. For more information about Curry's political views and the evolution of his education ideals, see Alderman and Gordon, *J. L. M. Curry, A Biography*.

38. Henry W. Grady, "The New South," in Edwin Du Bois Shurter, ed., *The Complete Orations and Speeches of Henry W. Grady* (New York: Hinds, Noble and Eldredge, 1910), 7.

39. Walter Hines Page, *The Rebuilding of Old Commonwealths: Being Essays Towards the Training of the Forgotten Man in the Southern States* (New York: Doubleday, Page & Company, 1902), 18–20.

40. Ibid., 18.

41. Murphy, *Problems of the Present South*, x.

42. Curry, *Education of the Negroes Since 1860* (Baltimore: The Trustees of the John F. Slater Fund, 1894), 26.

43. Remaining members included Wallace Buttrick, the first secretary and general officer of

the GEB, Edwin Alderman, Charles McIver, Albert Shaw, journalist and educator, and Hugh Henry Hanna, a businessman from Indianapolis and Trustee of the Tuskegee Institute.

44. *Proceedings of the Fourth Conference for Education in the South held at Winston-Salem*, 12.

45. Ogden, "The Conference for Education in the South," 276.

46. Ibid. William Baldwin, Albert Shaw, Walter Hines Page, and Hugh Hanna were added as members soon after the Board was established.

47. Wallace Buttrick to Frederick Gates, June 17, 1903, Folder 7414, Box 720, Series 1.5, RAC-RFA.

48. "A Fundamental Need of the Rural South is Community Organization," attachment III in A. P. Bourland to Wallace Buttrick, December 9, 1913, Folder 7415, Box 720, Series 1.5, RAC-RFA. Bourland noted in the letter that this had been published in a Kentucky newspaper.

49. *Proceedings of the Fifth Conference for Education in the South*, 14.

50. For information about Jeanes' Quaker roots, see "Born a Friend and Always a Friend, She Studied Buddha Faithfully. A Giver of Vast Sums," *Public Ledger–Philadelphia*, September 26, 1907, Folder PG7 Jeanes, Anna T., 1822–1907, (Philadelphia: Swarthmore College Friends Library). For information about her relationship to Booker T. Washington and the establishment of the fund, see James H. Dillard, *Fourteen Years of the Jeanes Fund 1909–1923*, reprint from *South Atlantic Quarterly* 22, no. 3 (July 1923), Folder PG7 Jeanes, Anna T., 1822–1907 (Philadelphia: Swarthmore College Friends Library); "Miss Jeanes Gives 5 Millions Away," *The Philadelphia Evening Bulletin*, September 30, 1907, Folder PG7 Jeanes, Anna T. 1822–1907 (Philadelphia: Swarthmore College Friends Library).

51. Peter M. Ascoli, *Julius Rosenwald: The Man Who Built Sears, Roebuck and Advanced the Cause of Black Education in the American South* (Bloomington: Indiana University Press, 2006).

52. Daniel Rodgers, "In Search of Progressivism" *Reviews in American History*, 10 (December 1982), 113–82; James J. Connolly, *The Triumph of Ethnic Progressivism: Urban Political Culture in Boston, 1900–1925* (Cambridge, MA: Harvard University Press, 1998). A discussion of the relationship between philanthropic concerns and progressive reforms can be found in Lagemann, in *Private Power for the Public Good*, 3; and, Judith Sealander, *Private Wealth and Public Life: Foundation Philanthropy and the Reshaping of American Social Policy from the Progressive Era to the New Deal* (Baltimore: Johns Hopkins University Press, 1997).

53. *Proceedings of the Fourth Conference for Education in the South*, 11.

54. Francis G. Peabody," Address—Knowledge and Service," *Proceedings of the Conference for Education in the South, the Sixth Session* (New York: The Committee on Publication, 1903), 128.

55. Allen J. Going, "The South and the Blair Education Bill," *The Mississippi Valley Historical Review* 44, no. 2 (September 1957), 269.

56. Daniel W. Crofts, "The Black Response to the Blair Education Bill," *Journal of Southern History* 37, no. 1 (February 1971): 43.

57. Going, "The South and the Blair Education Bill," 280.

58. Ibid., 290.

59. Dickerman, *Proceedings of the Fourth Conference for Education in the South*, 23.

60. Jill Quadagno, "Promoting Civil Rights through the Welfare State: How Medicare Integrated Southern Hospitals," *Social Problems* 47 (February 2000), 69.

61. *Proceedings of the Third Capon Springs Conference*, 26.

62. *Proceedings of the Fifth Conference for Education in the South*, 85–86.

63. Samuel Hays, "The Politics of Reform in Municipal Government in the Progressive Era," *The Pacific Northwest Quarterly*, 55, no. 4 (October 1964), 157–69.

64. Parmar, *Foundations of the American Century*.

65. Ramon G. Vela, "The Washington–Du Bois Controversy and African American Protest: Ideological Conflict and its Consequences." *Studies in American Political Development*, 16 (Spring 2002): 88–109.

66. Joan Malczewski, "Weak State, Stronger Schools: Northern Philanthropy and Organizational Change in the Jim Crow South," *Journal of Southern History*, 75, no. 4 (November 2009): 963–1000.

67. *The General Education Board: An Account of its Activities*, 5.

68. Balogh, *A Government out of Sight*.

69. Curry, *Education of the Negroes Since 1860*, 27.

70. *Proceedings of the Fourth Conference for Education in the South*, 85.

71. Skowronek, *Building a New American State*, chapter 5. See also James, "Prelude to Progressivism," which illustrates the stronger ties that developed between representatives from the South and the West, political alignments that were bound to affect the willingness of northeastern reformers and politicians to promote sweeping change across the South. See also William Bernhard and Brian Sala, "The Remaking of an American Senate: The 17th Amendment and Ideological Responsiveness," *Journal of Politics* 68, no. 2 (May 2006): 345, in which senators were shown to have had "little systematic incentive to shift their public ideologies in pursuit of reelection" but the "modern tendency for moderating ideological shifts prior to a reelection bid arose quickly in the wake of the direct election Amendment." This is a discussion that is continued by Wendy Schiller in "Building Careers and Courting Constituents: US Senate Representation 1889–1924," *Studies in American Political Development* 20 (Fall 2006): 185–97. This not only further weakened the power of partisanship in the South but also provided additional incentive to limit the black vote.

72. Szymanski, "Beyond Parochialism: Southern Progressivism, Prohibition, and State-Building," *Journal of Southern History* 69, no. 1 (February 2003): 107–37.

73. Liberty Hyde Bailey, *Report of the Country Life Commission* (Washington, DC: Government Printing Office, 1909), 22.

74. The commission was chaired by Professor Liberty Hyde Bailey of the New York College of Agriculture at Ithaca and included Iowan Henry Wallace, Gifford Pinchot of the United States Forest Service, President Kenyon Butterfield of the Massachusetts Agricultural College, and E. W. Allen as executive secretary. Charles Barret of Georgia and William Beard of California were added later.

75. Joan Malczewski, "Philanthropy and Progressive Era State Building through Agricultural Extension Work in the Jim Crow South." *History of Education Quarterly* 53, no. 4 (November 2013): 369–400; Sealander, *Private Wealth and Public Life*.

76. W. E. B. Du Bois to Liberty Hyde Bailey, November 23, 1908, Cornell University Manuscript Collections at http://rmc.library.cornell.edu/bailey/commission/commission_3.html#.

77. Bailey, *Report of the Country Life Commission*, 6–7.

78. Ibid., 19.

79. Ibid., 49.

80. Ibid., 54.

81. Monica Prasad, *The Land of Too Much: American Abundance and the Paradox of Poverty* (Cambridge, MA: Harvard University Press, 2012), 23.

82. Lagemann, *Private Power for the Public Good*, 1.

83. Ibid., 59.

84. Charles Postel, *The Populist Vision* (Oxford: Oxford University Press, 2007) 282–83. Historians have debated the extent to which populism included or excluded black interests. See also Charles Sydnor, "Democrats, Demagogues, and Negroes," *The South Atlantic Quarterly* XLIX (October 1950), 507–13.

85. Prasad, *The Land of Too Much*, 10; Postel, *The Populist Vision*, 282.

86. Ring, *The Problem South*, 120–74.

87. Scholars argue that contemporary social programs are part of a long history of efforts to regulate and reform such populations through policies designed to get cooperation and contributions and make communities more manageable. Soss, Fording, and Schram, *Disciplining the Poor*, 3.

88. Malczewski, "Philanthropy and Progressive Era State Building," 369–400

89. Du Bois, "Negro Education," 261–69.

90. Wickliffe Rose to Dr. Samuel Green, May 6, 1911, Folder 19, Box 1, Series 1.2, UNC-SEB, 1–2.

91. Malczewski, "Weak State, Stronger Schools," 963–1000.

92. Steffes, *Schools, Society, and State*, 88–89.

93. Ibid., 105.

94. Minutes of a Meeting of the General Education Board, January 24, 1911, Folder 3651, Box 353, Series 1.1, RAC-GEB, 1.

95. Ibid., 3–6.

96. Ibid., 8.

97. Ibid.

98. Hollis Frissell to Jabez L. M. Curry, September 30, 1902, Folder 4, Box 1, Series 1.1, UNC-SEB.

99. Hammack and Anheier point out that an assessment of foundations must focus on their interactions with those who share their objectives, and with those who are indifferent to them or oppose them. While it is interesting in this context to attempt to tease out the personal proclivities of individual reformers, far more can be learned from the way in which institutions developed over time, in ways that reflected the varied beliefs of interest groups. Hammack and Anheier, *A Versatile American Institution*, 10–13.

100. Circular letter from Charles W. Dabney, March 8, 1902, Folder 4, Box 1, Series 1.1, UNC-SEB.

101. "The Conference and Community Organization," Folder 149, Box 6, Series 2.2, UNC-SEB.

102. "The Work of the Southern Education Board," Folder 105, Box 4, Series 2.1, UNC-SEB.

103. *The General Education Board: An Account of its Activities*, 183.

104. "A Rural Organization Service," March 3, 1913, Folder 149, Box 14, Series 908, RAC-RFA, 1.

105. "For Southern Education: Fifteenth Conference to Be Held in Nashville," *New York Evening Post*, March 16, 1912.

106. *Negro Public Education: A Study of the Private and Higher Schools for the Colored People in the United States,* US Bureau of Education, "Bulletins, 1917, Nos. 38 and 39" (Washington, DC: Government Printing Office, 1917), 161. The report refers in this section to the GEB, Slater Fund, Jeanes Fund, Phelps-Stokes Fund, and the Rosenwald Fund.

107. Ibid., 162.

108. "Report of Professor Bailey of Mississippi for March, 1909," Folder 829, Box 93, Series 1.1, RAC-GEB, 2–3.

109. Ibid.

110. Philanthropic Funds and Negro Education, November 1, 1927, Folder 1070, Box 119, Series 1, RAC-GEB.

111. "New Developments," November 7, 1931, Folder 10, Box 57, Series 3.1, UC-JRF.

112. Minutes of the General Education Board, January 24, 1911, Folder 3651, Box 353, Series 1.2, RAC-GEB.

113. James Yadkin Joyner to Wallace Buttrick, April 25, 1912, Folder 1912, Box 1, Division of Negro Education, SANC. Many states actively sought GEB authorization before making such an appointment, though each state's willingness to collaborate with the foundations could have some effect on the appointment process. For example, when the state superintendent in Mississippi appointed two agents in 1928, including one assistant, he did so without prior approval, much to the consternation of the GEB. However, the appointments had to be justified in order to prevent the GEB from withdrawing funding. See Leo Favrot to Frank P. Bachman, June 20, 1928, Folder 872, Box 97, Series 1.1, RAC-GEB and Willard Bond to Wallace Buttrick, August 29, 1923, Folder 832, Roll 74, Series 1.1, The University of Mississippi (1906–1956), The General Education Board Archives, Mississippi Department of Archives and History, Jackson, Mississippi.

114. Abraham Flexner to Joseph Neely Powers, July 1, 1914, Folder 868, Box 97, Series 1.1, RAC-GEB; Abraham Flexner to James Y. Joyner, July 1, 1914, Folder 1914 J–L, Box 1, Division of Negro Education, SANC.

115. Skowronek, *Building a New American State*, 47–85; For more information about the extent to which local government in the South was determined by party affiliation throughout the nineteenth century, see Lawrence Powell, "Centralization and its Discontents in Reconstruction Louisiana," *Studies in American Political Development* 20 (Fall 2006): 105–31.

116. Minutes of the General Education Board, January 24, 1911, Folder 3651, Box 353, Series 1.2, RAC-GEB.

117. Lieberman describes three aspects of the administrative structure important for successfully delivering race-based social policy in the New Deal, which have similar characteristics to foundation efforts in promoting universal education. The first is the level of government involved, whether federal, state, or local. The second is the political permeability, defined as the position that the policy occupies in the government and the extent to which it is open to political influence. The third is the policy environment, which includes the array of institutions that produce the policy. See Lieberman, *Shifting the Color Line*, 17–18.

118. Pierson, *Politics in Time*.

119. Jeanes Fund Report of President, 1914, Folder 2125, Box 222, Series 1.2, RAC-GEB.

120. Wallace Buttrick to John D. Rockefeller, Jr., February 5, 1914, Folder 1937, Box 203, Series 1.2, RAC-GEB.

121. For information about the appointment of the state agents, see "Summary of New Legislation," March 26, 1921, Folder 1071, Box 118, Series 1, RAC-GEB. North Carolina created a division of Negro education within the state budget in 1921, one of the earlier states, but not the only one, to institutionalize the office of the state agent through legislation. In 1920, the South Carolina State Board of Education approved state aid for "several of the stronger colored high schools" based on the work of the state agent there and would consider a "full time . . . competent stenographer and office assistant." South Carolina Program of Work, 1920–21, Folder 1201, Box 121, Series 1.1, RAC-GEB.

122. "Negro Public Education in the South, 1927," 7-B, Folder 1, Box 33, Series 5, SEF-AUC.

123. Lieberman, *Shifting the Color Line*, 16.

124. "The Administration of Negro Public Education in State Departments of Education," October 6, 1927, Folder 3295, Box 315, Series 1.2, RAC-GEB, 1.

125. Ibid.

126. "Minutes of the Meeting of the Rosenwald Schoolhouse Building Agents, January 15–16, 1923," Folder 12, Box 187, RFA-Fisk, 2–3.

127. Ibid., 4.

128. Samuel L. Smith to W. B. Harrell, June 14, 1929, Folder 2, Box 128, RFA-Fisk.

129. "The Julius Rosenwald Fund Annual Report, 1924–1925," Folder 1, Box 81, RFA-Fisk, 7.

130. Steffes, *School, Society, and State.*

131. Jackson Davis to Wycliffe Rose, September 2, 1910, Folder Wycliffe Rose, Box 6, The Papers and Photographs of Jackson Davis, Alderman Memorial Library, University of Virginia, Charlottesville.

132. By 1935, for 390 Jeanes teachers in the South, the Jeanes Fund provided $105,230 (33 percent) of the total budget of $316,262, with the remaining $211,032 (67 percent) provided by public funds. North Carolina and Virginia provided the highest percentage of public funding (80 percent), while Alabama and Arkansas provided the lowest percentage (50 percent). "Jeanes Fund 1935–36," attachment found in Arthur Wright to Trevor Arnett, October 7, 1935, Folder 1931, Box 203, Series 1.2, RAC-GEB.

133. Circular Letter to Extension and Supervising Teachers and Organizers, April 7, 1910, Folder 2125, Box 222, Series 1.2, RAC-GEB.

134. This reflected 26 percent of the total in 1918, 44 percent of the total in 1930, and 49 percent by 1935. "Survey of Jeanes Teacher Areas in 14 States," March 1, 1933, Folder 17, Box 19, Series 3, SEF-AUC; "Rural Supervising Industrial Teachers, 1919–20," Folder 2122, Box 221, Series 1.2, RAC-GEB; "Survey of Jeanes Teacher Areas in 14 States," March 1, 1933, Folder 17, Box 19, Series 3, SEF-AUC; "Teachers and County Supervisors of Negro Schools," 1927–1930, Folder 2125, Box 222, Series 1.2, RAC-GEB; Arthur D. Wright to Trevor Arnett, October 7, 1935, Folder 1931, Box 203, Series 1.2, RAC-GEB.

135. Minutes from a meeting of the General Education Board, January 24, 1911, Folder 3651, Box 353, Series 1.2, RAC-GEB.

136. Minutes of the Executive Committee of the Negro Rural School Fund, circa 1909, Folder 3, Box 19, Series 3, SEF-AUC.

137. W. C. Bell to Trevor Arnett, June 15, 1929, Folder 4, Box 188, RFA-Fisk.

138. *Proceedings of the Second Conference for Education in the South 1899* (Capon Springs: The Conference, 1899), 8.

139. *Negro Public Education: A Study of the Private and Higher Schools for the Colored People in the United States,* US Bureau of Education, Bulletins, 1917, nos. 38 and 39 (Washington, DC: Government Printing Office, 1917), 177. The Phelps-Stokes Fund actually provided staff to the US Department of the Interior, the federal agency in charge of education, for whom a primary task would be data collection until 1917 when the fund decided not to continue the arrangement.

140. *Negro Public Education,* 177.

141. "A Review of Educational Legislation, 1935–1936," *Biennial Survey of Education in the United States: 1934–1936, Bulletin, 1937, no. 2* (Washington, DC: Government Printing Office, 1937), 4.

142. Wickliffe Rose to Dr. Samuel Green, May 6, 1911, Folder 19, Box 1, Series 1.2, UNC-SEB.

143. Notes Made at the Conference of State Agents for Negro Rural Schools, November 26–28, 1921, Record Group 193, Series 1.2, Box 208, Folder 2000, RAC-GEB.

144. Supplement to Negro Public Education in the South, 1927, 3, Folder 3297, Box 315, Series 1.2, RAC-GEB.

145. This strategy could be particularly effective given the politically contentious issues involved. One study on United States race policy argues that the "very limitations of the American state—its fragmentation and dispersion, its multiplicity, its lack of many of the characteristic tools of administrative control—might, in fact, under certain circumstances, be sources of strength that produce unexpectedly innovative, decisive, and effective policies." Robert Lieberman, "Weak State, Strong Policy: Paradoxes of Race Policy in the United States, Great Britain, and France," *Studies in American Political Development* 16 (Fall 2002): 161.

146. "Report of the Commissioner of Education," in *Reports of the Department of the Interior for Fiscal Year ended June 30, 1911, Volume II, Table 20* (Washington, DC: Government Printing Office, 1912), xxxiii. These disparities are also well documented in the literature. For a discussion of comparisons beginning with Reconstruction, see W. E. B. Du Bois, *Black Reconstruction*, chapter 15. Anderson, *The Education of Blacks in the South.*

147. "Report from the Bureau of Investigation and Information of the Southern Education Board," *Proceedings of the Conference for Education in the South, the Sixth Session* (New York: Issued by the Committee on Publication, 1903), 43.

148. Ibid.

149. *Biennial Survey of Education 1916–1918,* US Department of the Interior, Bureau of Education, Bulletin, 1919, no. 88 (Washington, DC: Government Printing Office, 1921), 442.

150. Ibid., 443.

151. Ibid., 509

152. Massachusetts, Connecticut, Delaware, Rhode Island, South Carolina, Utah, Wisconsin, and Missouri all enacted or amended state aid legislation during this time period. *Biennial Survey of Education 1916–1918,* US Department of the Interior, Bureau of Education, Bulletin, 1919, no. 88 (Washington, DC: Government Printing Office, 1921), 509–10.

153. Ibid., 776.

154. Robert Margo, *Race and Schooling in the South, 1880–1950: An Economic History* (Chicago: University of Chicago Press, 1990); J. Douglas Smith, *Managing White Supremacy: Race, Politics and Citizenship in Jim Crow Virginia* (Chapel Hill: University of North Carolina Press, 1990), 132–38; David S. Cecelski, *Along Freedom Road: Hyde County, North Carolina and the Fate of Black Schools in the South* (Chapel Hill: University of North Carolina Press, 1994).

155. Samuel L. Smith to William C. Strahan, March 29, 1930, Box 8013, Series 2342, Mississippi Department of Archives and History, Papers of the Department of Education, Division of Negro Education, Jackson; hereinafter referred to as MDAH.

156. For an interesting discussion of the relationship between taxes and the welfare state, see Prasad, *The Land of Too Much*, 148–71.

157. Edgar Garner Murphy to Wallace Buttrick, November 14, 1907, Folder 7414, Box 720, Series 1.5, RAC-RFA.

158. George S. Dickerman, "Agent's Report: The South Compared with the North in Educational Requirements," in *Proceedings of the Fourth Conference for Education in the South: Athens Meeting, 1901* (Washington, DC: Southern Education Board, 1901), 20.

159. Minutes of the General Education Board, January 24, 1911, Folder 3651, Box 353, Series 1.2, RAC-GEB. The Rosenwald Fund was clear that matching funds were central to achieving its goals. Between 1917 and 1936, 5,357 buildings were constructed in 883 southern counties, located in fifteen southern states for a total cost of $28,408,520. Of this amount, 15 percent came from the fund, 17 percent from black donations, 4 percent from white contributions, and 64 percent from state and county tax funds. The largest single number of buildings was in North Carolina with 813 schools. See "Negro School Buildings in the Southern States, 1917–1947," Folder 10, Box 76, Series 2.5, RFA-Fisk.

160. Abraham Flexner to Julius Rosenwald, June 20, 1919, Folder 6, Box 53, UC-JRF.

161. Abraham Flexner to Julius Rosenwald, November 28, 1925, Folder 2, Box 15, UC-JRF.

162. "Jeanes Fund for Extension School Terms; Slater Fund for County Training Schools," June 24, 1919, Folder 6, Box 53, Series 2.5, UC-JRF.

163. Summary of Reports of Mr. George D. Godard, State Agent for Negro Rural Schools of Georgia, January 1, 1916–November 30, 1916, Folder 4, Box 34, Series 5, SEF-AUC.

164. Between 1915 and 1927, the fund provided $529,436 to North Carolina, with $569,261 contributed by blacks, $68,615 by whites, and $2,226,738 from local tax dollars. Philanthropic Funds and Negro Education, November 1, 1927, Folder 1070, Box 119, Series 1, RAC-GEB.

165. *Digest of State Laws Relating to Public Education in Force January 1, 1915*, Department of the Interior Bureau of Education Bulletin, 1915, no. 47 (Washington, DC: Government Printing Office, 1916), 628, 903.

166. Ibid. 535, 628. For specific county data, see Negro Rural School Fund List of Counties, 1910–1911, Folder 2125, Box 222, Series 1.2, RAC-GEB. This report detailed counties across the South with terms of only three months, others with terms of eight months, and two counties (Jefferson, Louisiana, and Henrico, Virginia) at nine months.

167. David Tyack, Thomas James, and Aaron Benavot, *Law and the Shaping of Public Education, 1785–1954* (Madison: University of Wisconsin Press), 142.

168. Percy Easom to Mag Hanna, February 27, 1929, Box 8012, Series 2342, MDAH.

169. "To Julius Rosenwald Fund, Nashville, Tennessee: Application for Aid in Extension of Negro School Term," Box 8013, Series 2342, MDAH.

170. Restatement of a leaflet, "Plan for distribution of aid from the Julius Rosenwald Fund for building rural schoolhouses in the South," July 1920, Folder 7, Box 53, Series 2.5, UC-JRF.

171. For more information, see Ambrose Caliver, "Some Problems in the Education and Placement of Negro Teachers," *Journal of Negro Education* 4, no. 1 (January 1935): 99–112; Felton Clark, "General Administration and Control," *Journal of Negro Education* 1, no. 2 (July 1932), 137–62.

172. The Georgia system granted local superintendents and trustees, elected by white men in county school districts, an extraordinary amount of authority determining who could teach in their schools, with officials often favoring religious beliefs, morality, family connections, and regional ties over education and experience. Chirhart, *Torches of Light*, chapter 3.

173. *Negro Public Education: A Study of the Private and Higher Schools for the Colored People in the United States,* US Bureau of Education, Bulletins, 1917, nos. 38 and 39 (Washington, DC: Government Printing Office, 1917), 34.

174. Ibid.

175. Negro Public Education in the South, 1927, Folder 1, Box 33, Series 5, SEF-AUC, 18.

176. Reports of Jeanes Teachers, 1919, Record Group 375, Folder 2125, Box 222, Series 1.2, RAC-GEB.

177. Report on Conferences with State Superintendents of Education and State Agents of Schools for Negroes, January 3, 1928, Folder 2002, Box 208, Series 1.2, RAC-GEB.

178. Report on Conferences with State Superintendents of Education and State Agents of Schools for Negroes, January 3, 1928, Folder 2002, Box 208, Series 1.2, RAC-GEB.

179. William Allen to Frank Bachman, April 23, 1927, Folder 1075, Box 118, Series 1.1, RAC-GEB.

180. Minutes of the General Education Board, January 24, 1911, Folder 3651, Box 353, Series 1.2, RAC-GEB, 8.

181. Nathan Newbold to County Superintendents, January 22, 1914, Folder 1042, Box 115, Series 1.1, RAC-GEB.

182. "Important Word About County Training Schools," Folder D, Box 4, Division of Negro Education, SANC.

183. Desmond King and Robert C. Lieberman, "Ironies of State Building: A Comparative Perspective on the American State," *World Politics* 61 (July 2009): 571.

184. Percey Easom to W. W. Benson, September 30, 1929, Folder 1/7/30–5/30, Box 7985, Series 2342, MDAH.

185. Percy Easom to Edgar S. Bowlus, May 17, 1930, Folder 1/7/30–5/30, Box 7985, Series 2342, MDAH.

186. Jill Quadagno, "Promoting Civil Rights through the Welfare State," *Social Problems* 47 (February 2000): 68–89.

187. Abraham Flexner to Samuel Smith, December 11, 1914, Folder 869, Box 97, Series 1.1, RAC-GEB.

188. "Negro Public Education in the South, 1927," Folder 1, Box 33, Series 5, SEF-AUC, 12.

189. Nathan Newbold to Eugene Clyde Brooks, January 6, 1923, Folder B, Box 6, Division of Negro Education, SANC.

190. Facts and Figures on Negro Education in North Carolina, Folder Negro Education in NC, Data Sheets, Statistics, Surveys, 1898–1950, Box 4, Division of Negro Education, SANC. Many more teachers attended these training courses than would have been required as a result of minimum certification requirements. In 1923–24 the requirements were relatively new and teachers with provisional certificates were not at risk at that point of losing their positions; in fact, it was clear that most were needed regardless of certification.

191. Notes Made from Reports of Jeanes Teachers in March, 1919, Folder 2125, Box 222, Series 1.2, RAC-GEB.

192. Tracy Steffes provides a compelling discussion of the strengths of centralization, as well as the important role of decentralization to state building. See Tracy L. Steffes, *School, Society, and State: A New Education to Govern Modern America, 1890–1940* (Chicago: University of Chicago Press, 2012), 200–1.

193. "Conference of Trustees and Guests of the Julius Rosenwald Fund, April 29, 1928," File Rosenwald Fund, 1927–1929, Box 8, Division of Negro Education, SANC.

194. Ibid.

195. Karen Orren and Stephen Skowronek, *The Search for American Political Development* (Cambridge: Cambridge University Press, 2004), 125. The authors distinguish authority from power in a way that makes clear the difficulty of instituting change in the South. According to their definition, authority is "designated in advance, . . . works through institutions, [and] works through mandates that are enforceable . . . not simply coercive, but rather implies protection for those who carry out its dictates and sanctions against those who do not."

196. See Brian Balogh, "Reorganizing the Organizational Synthesis: Federal-Professional Relations in Modern America," *Studies in American Political Development*, 5 (Spring 1991): 146.

CHAPTER 2

1. J. R. Faison to Nathan Newbold, June 11, 1913, Folder 1913: Reports—Jeanes Teachers, Box 1, Division of Negro Education, SANC.

2. Conference of State Agents for Negro Rural Schools, Report of B. C. Caldwell as agent for the Jeanes and Slater Funds, November 26–28, 1921, Folder 1988, Box 208, Series 1.2, RAC-GEB.

3. J. R. Faison to Nathan Newbold, June 11, 1913, Folder 1913: Reports—Jeanes Teachers, Box 1, General Correspondence of the Director: 1907–1915, SANC, 3.

4. Ibid.

5. Ibid.

6. Ambrose Caliver, "The Role of the Teacher in the Reorganization and Redirection of Negro Education," *Journal of Negro Education* 5, no. 3 (July 1936): 516. For an interesting discussion of the expectations of black teachers in rural communities, see Michael Fultz, "African American Teachers in the South, 1890–1940: Powerlessness and the Ironies of Expectations and Protest," *History of Education Quarterly* 35, no. 4 (Winter 1995): 401–22. Fultz notes that these teachers were clearly at the top of their race educationally, and typically had even more

experience than many of the white teachers to whom they were compared, but for which they rarely received credit.

7. Thomas Jesse Jones, *Negro Education: A Study of the Private and Higher Schools for Colored People in the United States,* vol. 2 (Washington, DC: Government Printing Office, 1917), 447.

8. Robert Norrell, *The House I Live In* (Oxford: Oxford University Press, 2005), 43–73; Norrell, *Up from History: The Life of Booker T. Washington* (Cambridge, MA: Harvard University Press, 2009), 115–209.

9. James C. Scott, *Domination and the Arts of Resistance: Hidden Transcripts* (New Haven, CT: Yale University Press, 1990).

10. Description at Charles W. Chesnutt Library Archives and Special Collections, Fayetteville State University http://library.uncfsu.edu/archives/about-special-collections/finding-aid -for-anne-chesnutt-waddell/anne-chesnutt

11. "The Educational Equipment and Needs of North Carolina," January 27, 1904, Folder 104, Box 4, Series 2.1, UNC-SEB.

12. For a discussion of organizational repertoires and interest groups, see Elisabeth Clemens, *The People's Lobby: Organizational Innovation and the Rise of Interest Group Politics in the United States, 1890–1925* (Chicago: University of Chicago Press, 1997), 92–93. The use of these school models was central to their participation in reform. Connie L. Lester, in *Up from the Mudsills of Hell: The Farmers' Alliance, Populism, and Progressive Agriculture in Tennessee, 1870–1915* (Athens: University of Georgia Press, 2006), describes a similar role in the organization of the Grange in Tennessee.

13. W. E. B. Du Bois, *Black Reconstruction in America, 1860–1880* (New York: Atheneum, 1992; orig. c. 1935).

14. Butchart, *Schooling the Freed People.*

15. Black education leaders had supported the Blair Education Bill in the 1880s and support for federal intervention in schooling remained pervasive. In 1932, the *Chicago Defender* called for a federally appointed secretary of education with broader powers, and in 1933 an article in the *Chicago Defender* explicitly stated that only federal involvement would overcome the states' rights arguments for segregated education. See "A Secretary of Education," January 9, 1932, *Chicago Defender*, 14, and "Federal Control of Education," December 23, 1933, *Chicago Defender*, 14.

16. Jill Quadagno, "Promoting Civil Rights through the Welfare State: How Medicare Integrated Southern Hospitals," *Social Problems* 47 (February 2000), 69.

17. Robyn Muncy has illustrated in her work that female reformers in the Progressive Era lost control over their own reform initiatives when the institutions that they helped to create were moved into the public sphere. Robyn Muncy, *Creating a Female Dominion in American Reform: 1890–1935* (New York: Oxford University Press, 1991), 163.

18. Theda Skocpol, *Diminished Democracy: From Membership to Management in American Civil Life* (Norman: University of Oklahoma Press, 2003); Jennifer Hoschschild and Nathan Scovronick, *The American Dream and the Public Schools* (Oxford: Oxford University Press, 2003), 28–36. Quadagno, "Promoting Civil Rights," 69.

19. The establishment of the Tuskegee Institute provides an interesting example of how change is difficult to stop once set in motion. Norrell points out that southern white conservatives in Tuskegee came to realize that their grandfathers who had agreed to Tuskegee had "sown the winds of racial change." Robert Norell, *Reaping the Whirlwind: The Civil Rights Movement in Tuskegee* (Chapel Hill: University of North Carolina Press, 1985), 18.

20. Jackson Davis to Wycliffe Rose, September 2, 1910, Folder Wycliffe Rose, Box 6, The Papers and Photographs of Jackson Davis, Alderman Memorial Library, University of Virginia, Charlottesville.

21. Circular Letter to Extension and Supervising Teachers and Organizers, April 7, 1910, Folder 2125, Box 222, Series 1.2, RAC-GEB.

22. The Continuation and Extension of Jeanes Work, 1, Folder 19, Box 27, Series 5, SEF-AUC.

23. Ibid.

24. John R. Ellis to James H. Dillard, March 21, 1916, Folder 871, Box 97, Series 1.1, RAC-GEB.

25. "Some Problems Which Should Claim the Attention of Part-Time Supervisors; The Jeanes Teacher and Her Work," Folder Jeanes Misc. 1910, 1911, 1933, 1934, 1952, n.d., Box 5, Division of Negro Education, SANC.

26. Ibid.

27. Ibid.

28. "Itinerary Report Trips to Morgan and Taliaferro Counties, H. A. Whiting, 1935," Folder Helen Whiting Itinerary 1935–36, Box 2, Series Negro Education Division Director Subfiles, Papers of the Division of Negro Education, Georgia State Archives, Morrow, p. 10. Capital letters in the original.

29. By 1935, for 390 Jeanes Teachers in the South, the Jeanes Fund provided $105,230 (33 percent) of the total budget of $316,262, with the remaining $211,032 (67 percent) provided by public funds. North Carolina and Virginia provided the highest percentage of public funding (80 percent), while Alabama and Arkansas provided the lowest percentage (50 percent). Jeanes Fund 1935–36, attachment found in Arthur Wright to Trevor Arnett, October 7, 1935, Folder 1931, Box 203, Series 1.2, RAC-GEB.

30. "Jeanes Teachers," prepared by James Dillard, May 10, 1927, Folder 2125, Box 222, Series 1.2, RAC-GEB.

31. Bura Hilbun to Frank Bachman, April 22, 1925, Folder 872, Box 97, Series 1.1, RAC-GEB.

32. "Itinerary Record for Harris and Coweta Counties, November 19–22, 193, H. A. Whiting, Helping Teacher," Folder Helen Whiting Itinerary 1935–36, Box 2, Series Negro Education Division Director Subfiles, Papers of the Division of Negro Education, Georgia State Archives, Morrow.

33. Chirhart, *Torches of Light*.

34. Report of N. C. Newbold, State Agent Negro Rural Schools for the Month of February, 1915, Folder 1042, Box 115, Series 1, RAC-GEB.

35. "Monthly Progress Letter, April, 1916," Folder 1043, Box 115, Series 1.1, RAC-GEB.

36. Lautrec C. Brogden to Superintendent W. M. Hinton, September 9, 1914, Folder 1914 G-H, Box 1, Division of Negro Education, SANC.

37. Ibid.

38. Elisabeth Clemens, *The People's Lobby: Organizational Innovation and the Rise of Interest Group Politics in the United States, 1890–1925* (Chicago: University of Chicago Press, 1997), 92–93; Connie L. Lester, in *Up from the Mudsills of Hell: The Farmers' Alliance, Populism, and Progressive Agriculture in Tennessee, 1870–1915* (Athens: University of Georgia Press, 2006); Gunner Myrdal, *An American Dilemma: The Negro Problem and American Democracy* (New York: Harper and Bros., 1944); Theda Skocpol and Jennifer Lynn Oser, "Organization Despite Adversity: The Origins and Development of African American Fraternal Associations," *Social Science History* 28, no. 3 (Fall 2004): 367–437; Bayliss J. Camp and Orit Kent, "'What a Mighty Power We Can Be': Individual and Collective Identity in African American and White Fraternal Initiation Rituals," *Social Science History* 28, no. 3 (Fall 2004): 439–83.

39. "Notes Made at the Conference of State Agents for Negro Rural Schools," November 26–28, 1921, Folder 2000, Box 208, Series 1.2, RAC-GEB.

40. Ibid., 2.

41. Alabama Consolidated Report of Jeanes Teachers for the month ending October 31, 1923, Folder 2122, Box 221, Series 1.2, RAC-GEB.

42. Jackson Davis to Wallace Buttrick, July 13, 1916, Folder 2121, Box 221, Series 1.2, RAC-GEB.

43. Norrell, *The House I Live in*, 43–73.

44. "Jeanes Agent's Final or Term Report," Tunica, Mississippi, Box 7988, Series 2342, MDAH.

45. "Report of Jeanes Supervisors of Georgia, March 1935," Folder Jeanes Supervisors Final Reports 1934–35, Box 1, Series Department of Education Negro Education Division/Director Subfiles, Georgia State Archives, Morrow.

46. Sarah J. Anderson to Mrs. Millsap, April 19, 1935, Folder Jeanes Supervisors Final Reports 1934–35, Box 1, Series Department of Education Negro Education Division/Director Subfiles, Georgia State Archives, Morrow.

47. "Georgia Supervisor's Final Report, Elbert County," April 15, 1935, Folder Jeanes Supervisors Final Reports 1934–35, Box 1, Series Department of Education Negro Education Division/Director Subfiles, Georgia State Archives, Morrow.

48. The federal government generated biennial reports that provided detailed data at the state and local level about school systems in the South. Many states did not provide data that indicated the existence of an administrative structure for schooling. It was not until the 1930s that reports included the number of school board members, superintendents, and principals in particular states. Beyond that, it was not until 1940 that counties specifically recognized the number of black principals in their black schools registered with the state. Some states indicated in the 1934–36 report that the number of black teachers also included supervisors and principals, explicitly acknowledging that the teachers played a much broader role in school administration. See "Report of the Commissioner of Education, Biennial Survey of Education 1934–1936," US Department of the Interior, Bulletin, 1940, no. 16 (Washington, DC: Government Printing Office, 1940), 48; "Report of the Commissioner of Education, Biennial Survey of Education 1939–1940," US Department of the Interior, Bulletin, 1944, no. 16: (Washington, DC: Government Printing Office, 1944), 37.

49. "Some Problems Which Should Claim the Attention of Part-Time Supervisors: The

Jeanes Teacher and Her Work," File Jeanes Misc., 1910, 1911, 1933, 1934, 1952, n.d., Box 5, State Supervisor of Elementary Education 1910, 1911, 1933–56, Division of Negro Education, SANC.

50. "Monthly Progress Letter, April 1916," Folder 1043, Box 115, Series 1.1, RAC-GEB.

51. Ibid.

52. "Some Problems Which Should Claim the Attention of Part-Time Supervisors: The Jeanes Teacher and Her Work," File Jeanes Misc., 1910, 1911, 1933, 1934, 1952, n.d., Box 5, Division of Negro Education, SANC.

53. "Application for Jeanes Fund Aid," Treutlen County, Georgia, 1932, Folder 2, Box 23, SEF-AUC.

54. "State of Mississippi Department of Education, Jeanes Fund Contract," September 24, 1928, Box 7988, Series 2342, MDAH.

55. "Application for Jeanes Fund Aid," Yazoo, Mississippi, 1932, Folder 3, Box 23, Series 4 SEF-AUC.

56. "Application for Jeanes Fund Aid," Lincoln, Mississippi, 1932, Folder 3, Box 23, Series 4, SEF-AUC.

57. "Application for Jeanes Fund Aid," Georgia, 1932, Folder 2, Box 23, Series 4, SEF-AUC.

58. "Application for Jeanes Fund Aid," Jasper, South Carolina, 1932, Folder 5, Box 23, Series 4, SEF-AUC.

59. "Application for Jeanes Fund Aid," King George, Virginia, September 1, 1932, Folder 6, Box 23, SEF-AUC.

60. "Application for Jeanes Fund Aid," Knox and Jefferson, Tennessee, October 1, 1932, Folder 5, Box 23, SEF-AUC.

61. "Application for Jeanes Fund Aid," Anson County, North Carolina, August 19, 1932, Folder 5, Box 23, Series 4, SEF-AUC.

62. "Southern Education Foundation: Special Report of Jeanes Teacher for School Year 1939–40," Westmoreland, Virginia, Folder 7, Box 145, SEF-AUC.

63. "Southern Education Foundation: Special Report of Jeanes Teacher for School Year 1939–40," Caroline, Virginia, Folder 5, Box 145, SEF-AUC.

64. Circular letter from Mary E. Foster, January, 1918, Folder 1200, Box 131, Series 1.1, RAC-GEB.

65. Arthur D. Wright to Division Superintendents and School Trustees, June 28, 1919, Folder 8, Box 2, Papers of the State Board of Education, The Library of Virginia, Richmond.

66. W. C. Bell to Trevor Arnett, June 15, 1929, Folder 4, Box 188, RFA-Fisk.

67. "The Jeanes Teachers, April 1937," Folder 1206, Box 31, Series 1.1, RAC-GEB, 10.

68. "Conference of State Agents of Rural Schools for Negroes Held at Gulfport, Mississippi," January 7–8, 1925, Folder 2000, Box 208, Series 1, RAC-GEB, 17.

69. Ibid., 18.

70. "Application for Jeanes Fund Aid," Lincoln, Mississippi, August 25, 1932, Folder 5, Box 23, Series 4, SEF-AUC.

71. "Georgia Jeanes Supervisor's Final Report, Telfair County," Folder Jeanes Supervisors Final Reports, Box 1, Series Department of Education Negro Education Division Director Subfiles, Georgia State Archives, Morrow.

72. "School Report and Guide for Scoring," Folder 12, Box 336, RFA-Fisk.

73. J. Herbert Brannon to Jeanes Teachers and Principals of Training Schools, February 26, 1918, Folder 1200, Box 131, Series 1.1, RAC-GEB.

74. "Summary of Reports from the Jeanes Industrial Workers Scholastic Year 1914–1915," Folder 586, Box 67, Series 1.1, RAC-GEB.

75. Jeanes Agent's Final or Term Report from Oda Kirkland, 1928, Box 7988, Series 2342, MDAH.

76. "Opportunity for Cooperative Aid," in a Report of the General Agent of the GEB to the Trustees of the Peabody Education Fund, Folder 7410, Box 720, Series 1.5, RAC-GEB, 2.

77. Specifically, the act provided for an annual appropriation of $10,000 to each state and an additional increasing grant that would reach a maximum of $4,100,000 at the end of eight years, to be divided among the states according to their rural population. Herbert Kliebard has provided a comprehensive history of the development of vocational-education policies in the United States. Herbert M. Kliebard, *Schooled to Work: Vocationalism and the American Curriculum, 1876–1946* (New York: Teachers College Press, 1999). For more information about the history of vocational education, especially in the South, see Leon E. Cook, "The Federal Government and Vocational Education in the South," in *Secondary Education in the South*, ed. W. Carson Ryan, John Minor Gwynn, and Arnold Kimsey King (New York: Ayer Co. Pub, 1946); Chas. H. Thompson, "The Federal Program of Vocational Education in Negro Schools of Less than College Grade," *Journal of Negro Education* 7, no. 3 (July 1938): 202–18; Judith Sealander, *Private Wealth and Public Life: Foundation Philanthropy and the Reshaping of American Social Policy from the Progressive Era to the New Deal* (Baltimore: John Hopkins University Press, 1997).

78. Scholars have considered the relative importance of southern politics, agrarian interests, and agrarian politicians on political development. Ira Katznelson considers the central importance of legislative bodies to liberal democracy, highlighting the extent to which the South's commitments to a hierarchical racial order affected the whole range of New Deal policies. Monica Prasad acknowledges the strength of agrarian politicians in promoting state policies, while Charles Postel acknowledges the strength of agrarian interests in creating a populist vision while increasingly marginalizing the role of black farmers in policy. The federal role in promoting agrarian policies like extension work and vocational education, especially in cooperation with foundations, provides an interesting illustration of the overlap between these three perspectives on political development in the late nineteenth and early twentieth centuries. Ira Katznelson, *Fear Itself: the New Deal and the Origins of our Time* (New York: W. W. Norton & Co., 2013); Charles Postel, *The Populist Vision* (Oxford: Oxford University Press, 2007); Monica Prasad, *The Land of Too Much* (Cambridge, MA: Harvard University Press, 2012).

79. "General Education Board Relations with the Department of Agriculture," 1914, Folder 128, Box 15, Series 1.1, RAC-GEB, 15.

80. "Table V, Statement of Appropriations for Negroes," Folder 2009, Box 209, Series 1.2, RAC-GEB. For more information about the relationship between the GEB and USDA extension programs, see Joan Malczewski, "Agricultural Extension Work and the Organization of Rural Communities in the Jim Crow South," *History of Education Quarterly* (November 2013): 369–400. The North Carolina state agent used both Smith-Lever and GEB funding to pay a summer salary to Jeanes teachers to engage in extension work. See Nathan Newbold to Eugene Clyde Brooks, November 19, 1919, Folder 2122, Box 221, Series 1.2, RAC-GEB.

81. James Dillard to Wallace Buttrick, January 25, 1916, Folder 2121, Box 221, Series 1.2, RAC-GEB.

82. Nathan Newbold to E. C. Brooks, November 19, 1919, Folder 2122, Box 221, Series 1.2, RAC-GEB.

83. "Summarized Statement of Homemakers Club Work for the Summer of 1918 in the State of North Carolina," Folder 1048, Box 116, Series 1.1, RAC-GEB.

84. Ibid., 3.

85. Ibid.

86. "Reports from the Field on the Jeanes Industrial Work in Georgia, January 1, 1917," Folder 598, Box 68, Series 1.1, RAC-GEB.

87. "The Jeanes Teachers," April 1937, Folder 1206, Box 131, Series 1.1, RAC-GEB.

88. "Notes Made from Reports of Mississippi Jeanes Teachers at Conference of Louisiana and Mississippi Jeanes Teachers, March 20, 1919, Folder 2125, Box 222, Series 1.2, RAC-GEB.

89. Theda Skocpol and Jennifer Lynn Oser, "Organization Despite Adversity: The Origins and Development of African American Fraternal Associations," *Social Science History* 28, no. 3 (Fall 2004): 370.

90. Application for Jeanes Fund Aid," Dale, Alabama, October 10, 1933, Folder 7, Box 23, SEF-AUC.

91. "Application for Jeanes Fund Aid," Elmore, Alabama, September 1, 1933, Folder 7, Box 23, SEF-AUC.

92. "Southern Education Foundation: Special Report of Jeanes Teacher for School Year 1939–40," Rappahannock, County, Virginia, Folder 7, Box 145, SEF-AUC.

93. "Southern Education Foundation: Special Report of Jeanes Teacher for School Year 1939–40," Surry County, Virginia, Folder 7, Box 145, SEF-AUC.

94. Virginia Randolph to James Dillard, December 14, 1915, Folder 7, Box 27, SEF-AUC.

95. "Conference of State Agents of Rural Schools for Negroes, June 4–5, 1929," Folder 2000, Box 208, Series 1.2, RAC-GEB.

96. Nathan Newbold to Home-Makers' Club Agents, May 29, 1918, Folder 1044, Box 115, Series 1.1, RAC-GEB.

97. "Some Problems Which Should Claim the Attention of Part-Time Supervisors; The Jeanes Teacher and Her Work," Folder Jeanes Misc. 1910, 1911, 1933, 1934, 1952, n.d., Box 5, Division of Negro Education, SANC.

98. *Seventh Annual Report of the North Carolina Sanatorium for the Treatment of Tuberculosis, Under Control of the State Board of Health* (Raleigh, NC: Edwards and Broughton Printing Company, 1923). See also correspondence between Charles Coon, a more progressive superintendent in North Carolina, who complained bitterly about the lack of adequate funding to combat tuberculosis in the black community. Coon complained to state agent Nathan Newbold about the state's unequal approach to public health, and pointed out how unfair it was to use state funding to create sanitariums for whites with TB but only public health campaigns for blacks, that sought to have them "sleep with their windows open." Charles Coon to Nathan Newbold, October 16, 1917. Folder C, Box 3, Division of Negro Education, SANC.

99. *Seventh Annual Report of the North Carolina Sanatorium.*

100. Ibid.

101. This supports Valinda Littlefield's argument that the Jeanes teachers "often acted covertly and lived out the dictum 'we are not what we seem.'" Valinda Littlefield, "'To do the next needed thing': Jeanes Teachers in the Southern United States, 1908–1934," in *Telling Women's Lives: Narrative Inquiries in the History of Women's Education*, ed. Kathleen Weiler and Sue Middleton (Maidenhead, UK: Open University Press, 1999), 9. The popularity of these school-based organizations highlights the central role of schooling as a site for civic engagement. Robert Putnam argues that black citizens have been less civically engaged historically, due to slavery and the resulting problems of social capital, while Theda Skocpol and Jennifer Lynn Oser try to recapture the history of African American fraternal associations that were popular between the time of slavery and the late twentieth century. Robert Putnam, *Bowling Alone: The Collapse and Revival of American Community* (New York: Simon and Shuster, 2001); Skocpol and Oser, "Organization Despite Adversity: The Origins and Development of African American Fraternal Associations," *Social Science History* 28, no. 3 (Fall 2004): 367–437. See also Gunner Myrdal, *An American Dilemma: The Negro Problem and American Democracy* (New York: Harper and Brothers, 1944); Bayliss J. Camp and Orit Kent, "'What a Mighty Power We can Be': Individual and Collective Identity in African American and White Fraternal Initiation Rituals," *Social Science History* 28, no. 3 (Fall 2004): 439–83.

102. Georgia Jeanes Teacher Final Report from Jasper County, 1935, Jeanes Supervisors' Final Reports, Box 1, Director's Subject Files, 1928–1966, Papers of the Division of Education/Negro Education, Georgia State Archives, Atlanta.

103. "Summary of Reports of Mr. James L. Sibley, State Agent for Negro Rural Schools of Alabama, January 1, 1916–November 30, 1916," Folder 3, Box 34, Series 5, SEF-AUC, Ala 2.

104. For another example, see Christine Woyshner, *The National PTA, Race, and Civic Engagement: 1897–1970* (Columbus: Ohio State University Press, 2009).

105. Some Results of the Work of the State Agent in Mississippi, January 1938, Folder 873, Box 97, Series 1.1, RAC-GEB, 10.

106. Arthur Wright to W. G. Rennolds, July 24, 1919, Folder 9, Box 2, William G. Rennolds Papers, 1906–1947, Library of Virginia, Richmond, VA.

107. By M. H. Griffith, undated recollections from work begun as the Rosenwald agent in 1921, Folder 10, Box 76, Series 2.5, RFA-Fisk, 3.

108. Ibid.

109. "Summary of Reports of Mr. N. C. Newbold, State Agent for Negro Rural Schools of North Carolina, January 1, 1916 to December 31, 1916," Folder 4, Box 24, SEF-AUC, NC2.

110. "Supplement to 'Negro Public Education in the South,'" 1927, Folder 3297, Box 315, Series 1.2, RAC-GEB, 10.

111. Report of Miss Mary Sanifer, Folder 10, Box 76, RFA-Fisk.

112. Newbold to Home-Makers' Club Agents, May 29, 1918, Folder 1044, Box 115, Series 1.1, RAC-GEB.

113. Joan Malczewski, "The Schools Lost Their Isolation," *Journal of Policy History* 23, no. 3 (June 2011): 323–56.

114. Hollis Frissell to Henry E. Fries, January 3, 1899, Folder 1, Box 1, Series 1.1, Papers of the Southern Education Board, UNC-Chapel Hill.

115. Karl E. Weick, "Educational Organizations as Loosely Coupled Systems," *Adminis-*

trative Science Quarterly 26, no. 1 (March 1976): 1–19. In addition, with regard to progressive reforms in general, the dynamic nature of organizational change required that experts often compromise ideals or act upon competing ideals in order to create an effective organizational structure. See Robert Wiebe, *The Search for Order: 1877–1920* (New York: Hill and Wang, 1967), and Brian Balogh, "Reorganizing the Organizational Synthesis: Federal-Professional Relations in Modern America," *Studies in American Political Development* 5 (Spring 1991): 119–72.

116. Abraham Flexner to James Y. Joyner, July 1, 1914, Folder 1914 J–L, Box 1, Division of Negro Education, SANC.

117. "Conference of State Agents for negro Rural Schools Held at Hampton Institute, Hampton, Virginia," May 6–9, 1923, Folder 2000, Box 208, Series 1.2, RAC-GEB.

118. "Notes Made From Reports of Georgia Jeanes Teachers at Conference," March 28, 1919, Folder 2125, Box 222, Series 1.2, RAC-GEB.

119. Reports on Visits to County Training Schools in Georgia, January 8–January 11, 1924, Folder 596, Box 67, Series 1.1, RAC-GEB.

120. "Course of Study: Smithfield Training School, Johnston County," March 22, 1915, Folder 1046, Box 116, Series 1.1, RAC-GEB.

121. "Course of Study: Stonewall Training School, Pamlico County," March 24, 1915, Folder 1046, Box 116, Series 1.1, RAC-GEB.

122. "Conference of State Agents of Rural Schools for Negroes Held at Gulfport, Mississippi," January 7-8, 1925, Folder 2000, Box 208, Series 1, RAC-GEB, 4.

123. "Report of the Statesboro Summer School," June 9–July 4, 1919, Folder 599, Box 68, Series 1.1, RAC-GEB.

124. Ibid.

125. "Report of the Monroe County Summer School," June 9–July 4, 1919, Folder 599, Box 68, Series 1.1, RAC-GEB.

126. "Report of the Morehouse Summer School," June 9–July 4, 1919, Folder 599, Box 68, Series 1.1, RAC-GEB.

127. "Statement Covering the General Activities of the State Agents of Negro Schools in Georgia," attachment in Robert Cousins to Leo Favrot, January 17, 1928, Folder 589, Box 67, Series 1.1; "Itinerary Report Trips to Morgan and Taliaferro Counties by H. A. Whiting, 1935," Folder Helen Whiting Itinerary, 1935–36, Box 2, Series Negro Education Division Director Subfiles, Georgia State Archives, Atlanta, 5.

128. "Conference of State Agents for Negro Rural Schools Held at Hampton Institute, Hampton, Virginia," May 6–9, 1923, Folder 2000, Box 208, Series 1.2, RAC-GEB.

129. Samuel L. Smith to Percy H. Easom, March 17, 1930, Box 8013, Series 2342, MDAH.

130. A Suggestive Outline for Jeanes Supervising Teachers by Annie W. Holland, 1925, Folder 2125, Box 222, Series 12, RAC-GEB.

131. Joan Malczewski, "Weak State, Stronger Schools: Northern Philanthropy and Organizational Change in the Jim Crow South," *Journal of Southern History* 75, no. 4 (November 2009): 963–1000.

132. "Application for Jeanes Fund Aid," Sylvania, Georgia, 1932, Folder 2, Box 23, Series 4, SEF-AUC.

133. "Georgia Jeanes Supervisor's Final Report," May 24, 1935, Jeanes Supervisors' Final Reports, Box 1, Director's Subject Files, 1928–1966, Papers of the Division of Education Negro Education, Georgia State Archives Atlanta.

134. "The Jeanes Teachers, April 1937," Folder 1206, Box 31, Series 1.1, RAC-GEB, 2.

135. Ibid., 5.

136. Olivier Zunz, *American Philanthropy: A History* (Princeton, NJ: Princeton University Press, 2012), 23; Inderjeet Parmar, *Foundations of the American Century: The Ford, Carnegie, and Rockefeller Foundations in the Rise of American Power* (New York: Columbia University Press, 2012).

137. "Application for Jeanes Fund Aid," South Carolina, 1932, Folder 5, Box 23, Series 4, SEF-AUC. This is just one of many examples found in funding applications for Jeanes teachers across the South.

138. Scholarship has shown that strong political institutions are essential to the relationship between civil society and democracy, and that localism did much to promote and sustain discrimination and inequality in education. Theda Skocpol, *Diminished Democracy: From Membership to Management in American Civil Life* (Norman: University of Oklahoma Press, 2003); Jennifer Hoschschild and Nathan Scovronick, *The American Dream and the Public Schools* (Oxford: Oxford University Press, 2003), 28–36.

139. Jill Quadagno, "Promoting Civil Rights through the Welfare State: How Medicare Integrated Southern Hospitals," *Social Problems* 47, no. 1 (February 2000): 71.

140. Doug McAdam, *Political Process and the Development of Black Insurgency, 1930–1970* (Chicago: University of Chicago Press, 1982). This transfer of the educational infrastructure more fully to the public sphere ultimately affected the path dependency of racial incorporation that Lieberman describes. See Robert Lieberman, "Ideas, Institutions, and Political Order: Explaining Political Change," *American Political Science Review* 96, no. 4 (2002): 697–712.

141. Christine Woyshner, *The National PTA, Race, and Civic Engagement: 1897–1970* (Columbus: The Ohio State University Press, 2009).

142. Clemens, *The People's Lobby*, 92–93; Connie L. Lester, *Up from the Mudsills of Hell: The Farmers' Alliance, Populism, and Progressive Agriculture in Tennessee, 1870–1915* (Athens: University of Georgia Press, 2006). For more information about interest groups and policy reform, see Gunner Myrdal, *An American Dilemma: The Negro Problem and American Democracy* (New York: Harper & Bros., 1944); Theda Skocpol and Jennifer Lynn Oser, "Organization Despite Adversity: The Origins and Development of African American Fraternal Associations," *Social Science History* 28, no. 3 (Fall 2004): 367–437; Bayliss J. Camp and Orit Kent, "'What a Mighty Power We Can Be': Individual and Collective Identity in African American and White Fraternal Initiation Rituals," *Social Science History* 28, no. 3 (Fall 2004): 439–83.

143. Some notes regarding a meeting of state agents at Hampton, circa 1924, Folder 1998, Box 208, Series 1.2, RAC-GEB.

144. Robin D. G. Kelley, *Race Rebels: Culture, Politics, and the Black Working Class* (New York: Free Press, 1994); James Scott, *Weapons of the Weak: Everyday Forms of Peasant Resistance* (New Haven, CT: Yale University Press, 1985); Doug McAdam, *Political Process and the Development of Black Insurgency, 1930–1970* (Chicago: University of Chicago Press, 1982).

CHAPTER 3

1. Only Missouri and Oklahoma did not have a state agent by this date but were not considered to be a part of the region in which the foundations focused their efforts. It was in 1919 that Florida and Texas appointed their first agent. Samuel L. Smith, *Builders of Goodwill* (Nashville, TN: Tennessee Book Company, 1950), 175.

2. "Negro Public Education in the South: A Confidential Report for the Officers of the General Education Board, 1927," 7, Folder 1, Box 33, Series 5, SEF-AUC. The rankings were based upon a composite of each state's standing in literacy, teacher salaries, number of pupils per teacher, the length of the school term, the proportion of counties having high-school facilities and Jeanes teachers, and the percent of student population enrolled.

3. Ibid., 8.

4. "Education in Mississippi," Folder 101, Box 2, Series 2.1, UNC-SEB; "The Educational Equipment and Needs of North Carolina," Folder 104, Box 2, Series 2.1, UNC-SEB.

5. Tracy Steffes, *School, Society, and State: A New Education to Govern Modern America, 1890–1940* (Chicago: University of Chicago Press, 2012).

6. Financial support for the commission was provided by the Laura Spelman Rockefeller Memorial Fund, the Carnegie Corporation, the Phelps-Stokes Fund, and a number of church boards. The commission's board included trustees from northern foundations, and "two or more leading men" from each of the thirteen southern states. The commission also "secured the cooperation of the Governors of the states and the judges and leaders of all sections of the country, also of the Press." "Appeal of the Commission on Interracial Cooperation, Richmond, Virginia," January 24, 1922, Folder 974, Box 96, Series 3.08, Papers of the Laura Spelman Rockefeller Memorial Fund, Rockefeller Archive Center, Sleepy Hollow, NY; hereinafter referred to as RAC-LSRM. The general office also maintained a press service that reached "regularly all of the daily papers in the South, more than a hundred leading religious papers, and all the colored papers of the county . . . more than fifty releases were sent out during the year to one or all of these lists." "Progress in Race Relations: A Survey of the Work of the Commission on Interracial Co-operation for the Year 1923–24," Folder 978, Box 97, Series 3.08, RAC-LSRM, 14.

7. Ibid., 14–16.

8. "A General Survey of the Work of the Commission on Interracial Cooperation for 1922–23," Folder 975, Box 96, Series 3.08, RAC-LSRM.

9. Aiken provides a fascinating discussion of the relationship between geography and agricultural growth of the cotton industry. Gavin Wright relates the plantation economy to the development of New South sensibilities in the early twentieth century. Charles S. Aiken, *The Cotton Plantation South Since the Civil War* (Baltimore: Johns Hopkins University Press, 1998); Gavin Wright, *Old South, New South: Revolutions in the Southern Economy Since the Civil War* (Baton Rouge: Louisiana State University Press, 1997).

10. Aiken, *The Cotton Plantation South*, 5–7.

11. Aiken, *The Cotton Plantation South*; Wright, *Old South, New South*.

12. "Additional Facts to the Quarterly Report of July 1st, 1913," Folder 105, Box 4, Series 2.1, UNC-SEB. Most of Brogden's reports to his foundation benefactors focus on the creation of new tax districts.

13. These themes were evident in almost every state report that was submitted beginning in 1902 and the two subsequent decades. Joyner focused on the expansion of local tax districts and wrote extensively about the need for public funding. See "Some Reasons for Local Taxation," Folder Speeches, Resolutions, Sketches, Box Miscellaneous Papers 1900–1919, Papers of James Adkins Joyner 1873; 1902–1919, SANC. Joyner reported that more than one hundred had been created in the first decade of the twentieth century. See "Educational Expansion in North Carolina," Folder 104, Box 2, UNC-SEB. Newbold quickly took over this work for rural black communities. A comprehensive report issued in 1939 includes consolidation efforts beginning in 1914 as one of the criteria for evaluating the expansion of black education. See "Education of Negroes in North Carolina, 1914–1925–1939," State Department of Public Instruction in Raleigh, North Carolina, Folder 1045, Box 115, Series 1.1, RAC-GEB.

14. For more information about the 1898 elections, the Democratic Party, and the white supremacy campaign in North Carolina, see Eric Anderson, *Race and Politics in North Carolina, 1872–1901: The Black Second* (Baton Rouge: Louisiana State University Press, 1981); Helen G. Edmonds, *The Negro and Fusion Politics in North Carolina, 1894–1901* (Chapel Hill: University of North Carolina Press, 1951).

15. "A Keynote on the Amendment Campaign: Address Accepting the Democratic Nomination for Governor, April 11, 1900," in Robert Diggs, Wimberly Connor, and Clarence Poe, eds., *The Life and Speeches of Charles Brantley Aycock* (New York: 1912), 217.

16. Ibid., 219.

17. Aycock referred to his desire to build a state system of universal education throughout his speeches. See, for example, "How the South May Regain Its Prestige: An Address before the Southern Education Association, 1903," in Diggs, Connor, and Poe, *The Life and Speeches of Charles Brantley Aycock*, 279–86.

18. Ibid., 236.

19. Ibid., 235.

20. Charles Brantley Aycock, "Demand for Peace between the Races," in Diggs, Connor, and Poe, *The Life and Speeches of Charles Brantley Aycock*, 278.

21. Helen Edmonds, *The Negro and Fusion Politics in North Carolina, 1894–1901* (Chapel Hill: University of North Carolina Press, 1951), 205. Jonathan Pritchett provides an interesting analysis of tax policy in the state at the beginning of the twentieth century that makes clear that the relationship between the poll tax and schooling following disfranchisement weakens the argument that local whites redistributed significant sums received from the state. He points out that the loss of the black vote both limited the amount of taxes paid for schooling by the state's blacks and prevented them from voting for local tax levies in their communities. He argues that county and state tax revenues were more equitably distributed than scholars have recognized. See Pritchett, "North Carolina's Public Schools: Growth and Local Taxation," *Social Science History* 9, no. 3 (Summer 1985), 279.

22. "The New South," an address delivered at the Banquet of the New England Society, December 21, 1886 in *The Complete Orations and Speeches of Henry W. Grady*, ed., Edwin Du Bois Shurter (New York: Hinds, Noble, and Eldredge, 1910), 7.

23. The state's uniqueness was pointed out by V. O. Key in his early work on the politics of the South. It had the fewest number of slaves in the seven principle slave states, the smallest

number of slave owners, was initially opposed to secession, and bounced back more easily after the war. See V. O. Key, *Southern Politics in State and Nation* (New York: Vintage Books, 1949).

24. D. Gordon Bennet and Jeffrey C. Patton, *A Geography of the Carolinas* (Boone, NC: Parkway, 2007), 86.

25. Ibid., 171.

26. Bennett and Patton, *A Geography of the Carolinas*, 87; Phillip Wood, *Southern Capitalism: The Political Economy of North Carolina: 1880–1980* (Durham, NC: Duke University Press, 1986), 34.

27. Bennet and Patton, *A Geography of the Carolinas*, 88.

28. Ibid.

29. Key, *Southern Politics*.

30. Bennet and Patton, *A Geography of the Carolinas*, 90. Ready also points out that an almost "panic-like building of railroads" took place after 1870 with the help of private investors toward the goal of connecting all of North Carolina to both the rest of the South and the nation. Milton Ready, *The Tar Heel State: A History of North Carolina* (Columbia: University of South Carolina Press, 2005), 273.

31. For an interesting discussion of the relationship between roads and modernism, see Howard Lawrence Preston, *Dirt Roads to Dixie: Accessibility and Modernization in the South, 1885–1935* (Knoxville: University of Tennessee Press, 1991), 28–29, 103. The book provides a detailed analysis of the Good Roads Associations formed in the South during this time period, noting that North Carolina formed two such associations in 1901, the Northwestern Good Roads Association and the Appalachian Good Roads Association. More notable is the Good Roads Train, sponsored by the US Department of Agriculture and the Southern Railway Company, that traveled between Asheville and Raleigh in 1901 to demonstrate how the macadamized roadway could be constructed. It also sponsored a range of "good roads functions" that took place at train stops in urban areas that drew citizens from the surrounding counties. In 1909 reformers promoted an automobile race from New York to Atlanta, while the *Atlanta Journal* and the *New York Herald* sponsored the event and offered a cash prize to the county on the route with the best roads.

32. For 1915 alone, the periodical noted a successful bond campaign in the amount of $200,000 for sand-clay roads and three highways in Yadkin County, another $100,000 in Rutherford County; $150,000 in Gaston County for roads and $4,000 for a bridge. Yadkin also provided $60,000 to support a highway that would extend across the State. *Southern Good Roads* (January 1915): 27, 30–31, and *Southern Good Roads* (May 1915): 20. Another article noted that the road building outlook in the state "is better than ever before . . . there will not only be more miles built in 1915 than in 1914," and the money would be spent more wisely. *Southern Good Roads* (February 1915): 8.

33. National Highway Association, Good Roads Association Records, 1902–1917, Folder Article 1921, Box 1, SANC. See also *Southern Good Roads* (May 1915): 17. Further, while the "macadamizing process" of making roads with crushed rock was widespread in the North, it was atypical in the South in the early twentieth century, except in North Carolina, where cities like Charlotte and Asheville experimented successfully with the funding of these new roads and their use spread throughout the state. Robert E. Ireland, *Entering the Auto Age: The*

Early Automobile in North Carolina, 1900–1930 (Raleigh: State Archives of North Carolina, 1990).

34. Tammy Leigh Ingram, "Dixie Highway: Private Enterprise and State Building in the South, 1900–1930," (PhD diss., Yale University, 2009).

35. James M. Beeby, *Revolt of the Tar Heels: The North Carolina Populist Movement, 1890–1901* (Jackson: University Press of Mississippi, 2012), 14.

36. Helen G. Edmonds, *The Negro and Fusion Politics in North Carolina, 1894–1901* (Chapel Hill: University of North Carolina Press, 1951).

37. *Public School Law of North Carolina* (Winston, NC: M. I. and J. C. Stewart, Public Printers, 1895).

38. Ready, *The Tar Heel State,* 71, 279. V. O. Key noted the distinctiveness of the state in his early work on southern politics, and subsequent scholars have expounded on these themes. Gavin Wright provided an economic perspective on these differences, while Charles Aiken discusses a geographic one. See Key, *Southern Politics in State and Nation,* Aiken, *The Cotton Plantation South;* Wright, *Old South, New South.*

39. C. Vann Woodward, *Origins of the New South* (1951; repr., Baton Rouge: Louisiana State University Press, 2000).

40. Diggs, Connor, and Poe, *The Life and Speeches of Charles Brantley Aycock,* 219.

41. Ibid., 283.

42. Gregory P. Downs, "University Men, Social Science, and White Supremacy in North Carolina," *Journal of Southern History* 75, no. 2 (May 2009): 268.

43. James Leloudis provides the educational biographies of the three men who were close friends at the university and became political allies at the center of efforts to promote greater educational opportunity in the state after 1880. According to Leloudis, they sought to create a degree-granting institution for the training of teachers, which would lead to graded schools and better teacher training in the state. Edwin Alderman became the president of the University of North Carolina at Chapel Hill, Charles McIver became president of the North Carolina Normal and Industrial School for Women, and Joyner became the state superintendent for public instruction. James Leloudis, *Schooling the New South: Pedagogy, Self, and Society in North Carolina, 1880–1920* (Chapel Hill: University of North Carolina Press, 1996), 37–72.

44. Downs, "University Men, Social Science, and White Supremacy," 268.

45. Ibid., 296.

46. William E. King, "Charles McIver Fights for the Tarheel Negro's Right to an Education," *The North Carolina Historical Review* 41, no. 3 (July 1964): 365.

47. Leloudis, *Schooling the New South.*

48. North Carolina participants included McIver; George Winston, president of the North Carolina College of Agriculture and Mechanic Arts; Reverend Edward Rondthaler of Raleigh, appointed vice president of the 1901 conference; Reverend A. B. Hunter of Raleigh, appointed secretary and treasurer; Walter Hines Page (originally from North Carolina but residing in New York), appointed vice president of the 1901 conference; Charles Meserve, Raleigh; Francis Venable, president of UNC Chapel Hill. See *Proceedings of the Fourth Conference for Education in the South Held at Winston-Salem, North Carolina, April 18, 19, 20, 1901 (Harrisburg, NC: The Committee, 1901).*

49. "The Work in North Carolina," Report given by Charles D. McIver, District Director of the Southern Education Board, at the Fourth Conference, *Proceedings of the Fourth Conference for Education in the South*, 20.

50. *Proceedings of the Fourth Conference for Education in the South* and *Proceedings of the Fifth Conference for Education in the South, April 24, 25, 25 at Athens, Georgia* (Washington, DC: Southern Education Board, 1902).

51. Charles McIver, "The Child and the State," an address in *Proceedings of the Fifth Conference for Education in the South* (Knoxville: Gaut-Ogden Company by the Southern Education Board, 1902), 55.

52. Gregory Downs reached a similar conclusion. He argues that North Carolina education reformers viewed their white supremacy as different from the "reactionary" type that existed across the South and argued that education could serve reproductive and evolutionary purposes. He points out that in efforts to replace older more heroic accounts of white supremacy with more nuanced narratives of its leaders' tactics, scholars have lost track of the insight that the movement was "deeply modern and even liberal." See Downs, "University Men, Social Science, and White Supremacy," 279, 288, 269.

53. Ibid., 275–76.

54. Ibid., 297, 302.

55. "The Educational Equipment and Needs of North Carolina," 27, January 27, 1904, Folder 104, Box 2, Series 2.1, UNC-SEB.

56. William Link, *The Paradox of Southern Progressivism, 1880–1930* (Chapel Hill: University of North Carolina Press, 1992). Link argues that a significant goal of the progressive reform movement in the South required the creation of the bureaucracy necessary to oversee reform and the provision of social services and contends that progressivism in the North and the South differed because of the preexistence of bureaucracy in the North.

57. "Governor Aycock's Address," Speech by Governor Charles B. Aycock at the Fourth Conference for Education in the South, *Proceedings of the Fourth Conference for Education in the South*, 6.

58. *Proceedings of the Fourth Conference for Education in the South*, 11.

59. "Education and the Voluntary Tax," Speech by Governor Charles B. Aycock at the Fifth Conference for Education in the South, *Proceedings of the Fifth Conference for Education in the South*, 51–53.

60. George Ernest Barnett, "Taxation in North Carolina," in *Studies in State Taxation, with Particular Reference to the Southern States,* ed. J. H. Hollander (Baltimore: Johns Hopkins Press, 1900), 78–79. In 1900, the state rate, inclusive of the school tax, was forty-three cents on the hundred dollars, but only twenty-three and two-thirds cents were available for county purposes. The general assembly could increase the rate charged per hundred dollars of land, but most were reluctant to do so. Corporations in the state were included in the general property tax. An important problem was the undervaluation of land and the ability of corporations to escape taxation on large portions of their property.

61. Ibid., 102.

62. Ibid., 103.

63. "Education and the Voluntary Tax," Speech by Governor Charles B. Aycock at the Fifth Conference, *Proceedings of the Fifth Conference for Education in the South*, 51–53.

64. Notes on Negro Education, April 28, 1901, Folder Miscellaneous Correspondence, 1902–1959, Box Materials relating to life and to speeches, Papers of Charles Brantley Aycock, SANC.

65. "Two Open Fields for Investment in the South," Report by Charles D. McIver at the Fourth Conference for Education in the South, *Proceedings of the Fourth Conference for Education in the South*, 29–30.

66. King, "Charles McIver Fights," 362.

67. The state courts had already decided in 1886 that the Dortch Bill, giving white taxes to white schools and black taxes to black schools, was unconstitutional. King, "Charles McIver Fights," 367.

68. "The Work in North Carolina," Report given by Charles D. McIver, District Director of the Southern Education Board, at the Fifth Conference, *Proceedings of the Fifth Conference for Education in the South*, 21. *Biennial Report of the Superintendent of Public Instruction of North Carolina for the Scholastic Years 1900–1901 and 1901–1902* (Raleigh: Edwards & Broughton, State Printers, 1902), LIII-LIV. A detailed discussion of the campaign can also be found in James Leloudis, *Schooling the New South: Pedagogy, Self, and Society in North Carolina, 1880–1920* (Chapel Hill: University of North Carolina Press, 1996), 151-155.

69. Edgar Wallace Knight, *Public School Education in North Carolina* (New York: Negro Universities Press, 1969), 331–34

70. "The Work in North Carolina," Report given by Charles D. McIver, District Director of the Southern Education Board, at the Fifth Conference, *Proceedings of the Fifth Conference for Education in the South*, 22.

71. Charles D. McIver, "Problems in North Carolina," *Annals of the American Academy of Political and Social Science* 22 (September 1903): 296.

72. "The Work in North Carolina," 23.

73. McIver, "Problems in North Carolina," 302.

74. James Joyner to the GEB, January 30, 1918, Folder 1066, Box 118, Series 1.1, RAC-GEB. The North Carolina constitution required a minimum of four months at this point in time.

75. Press Release for the Report of the State Educational Commission on the Condition of Public Education in North Carolina, November, 1920, Folder 1072, Box 118, Series 1, RAC-GEB; "Summary of New Legislation," March 26, 1921, Folder 1071, Box 118, Series 1, Box 118, RAC-GEB.

76. Elisabeth Clemens, "Lineages of the Rube Goldberg State: Building and Blurring Public Programs, 1900–1940," in *Rethinking Political Institutions: The Art of the State*, ed. Ian Shapiro, Stephen Skowronek, and Daniel Galvin (New York: New York University Press, 2006), 187–215.

77. "Education in Mississippi," 25, Folder 101, Box 4, Series 2.1, UNC-SEB.

78. "Report of Thomas P. Bailey, Dean of Dept. of Education, Professor of Psychology and Secondary Education, University of Mississippi, to the General Education Board," October 12, 1908, Folder 829, Roll 74, Series 1.1, *The General Education Board Archives at The*

University of Mississippi (1902–1956), University of Mississippi, Jackson; hereinafter referred to as GEB-MDAH.

79. John C. Fant to Wallace Buttrick, June 10, 1919, Folder 828, Box 93, Series 1.1, RAC-GEB.

80. Wallace Buttrick to John C. Fant, June 19, 1919, Folder 828, Box 93, Series 1.1, RAC-GEB.

81. "General Education Board Relations with the Department of Agriculture," Folder 148, Box 15, Series 1.1, RAC-GEB, 20.

82. For more information about congressional discussions following the strikes, see Joan Malczewski, "Agricultural Extension Work and the Organization of Rural Communities in the Jim Crow South," *History of Education Quarterly* 53, no. 4 (November 2013): 369–400.

83. Robert B. Fulton, "Educational Progress in Mississippi," *Annals of the American Academy of Political and Social Science* 22 (September 1903): 62.

84. There are some exceptions, including the participation of Delta planters on levee boards that worked across states and with federal officials. The Delta planters were more willing to participate with the federal government or with organizations and private funders outside the state, if it redounded benefits to the Delta.

85. William F. Holmes, *The White Chief: James Kimble Vardaman* (Baton Rouge: Louisiana State University Press, 1970), 15. Holmes describes the intense relationship that Vardaman had to B. F. Ward, a confederate soldier and "unrepentant rebel" who mentored Vardaman throughout the late nineteenth century. Scholarship on Mississippi history also describes a culture wed to tradition and a sense of "place." See Dale Krane and Stephen D. Shaffer, *Mississippi Government and Politics: Modernizers versus Traditionalists* (Lincoln: University of Nebraska Press, 1992), 5–23.

86. Mary Duval, *History of Mississippi and Civil Government* (Louisville: Courier-Journal, 1892), 263.

87. "Geography of Mississippi," Mapsofworld.com, http://www.mapsofworld.com/usa/states/mississippi/geography.html.

88. For more information about the politics of flood control on the Mississippi River, see Georges Pabis, "Delaying the Deluge: The Engineering Debate over Flood Control on the Lower Mississippi River, 1846–1861," *Journal of Southern History* 64, no. 3 (August 1998): 421–54; Matthew Reonas, "Delta Planters and the Eudora Floodway: The Politics of Persistence in 1930s Louisiana," *Louisiana History: The Journal of the Louisiana Historical Association* 50, no. 2 (Spring 2009): 159–87; Mary G. McBride and Ann M. McLaurin, "The Origin of the Mississippi River Commission, *Louisiana History: The Journal of the Louisiana Historical Association* 36, no. 4 (Autumn 1995), 395; Robert W. Harrison, "Flood Control in the Yazoo-Mississippi Delta," *Southern Economic Journal* 17, no. 2 (October 1950): 148–58.

89. James Cobb, *The Most Southern Place on Earth: The Mississippi Delta and the Roots of Regional Identity* (New York: Oxford University Press, 1992), 95.

90. Ibid., 96.

91. James C. Geisen, "The Truth about the Boll Weevil": The Nature of Planter Power in the Mississippi Delta," *Environmental History* 14, no. 4 (October 2009): 683–704.

92. James E. Fickle, "'Comfortable and Happy'? Louisiana and Mississippi Lumber Workers, 1900–1950," *Louisiana History: The Journal of the Louisiana Historical Association* 40, no. 4 (Autumn 1999): 412.

93. "Report of Professor Bailey of Mississippi for March, 1909," Folder 829, Box 93, Series 1.1, RAC-GEB, 3.

94. Fickle, "'Comfortable and Happy,'" 411.

95. Dale Krane and Stephen D. Shaffer, *Mississippi Government and Politics* (Lincoln: University of Nebraska Press, 1992), 51–54.

96. Duval, *History of Mississippi*, 233

97. "Biennial Report and Recommendations of the State Superintendent of Public Education to the Legislature of Mississippi for the Scholastic Years 1906–1907 (Memphis, TN: General Books, reprint of state document, 1912).

98. Charles Hillman Brough, "State Taxation in Mississippi," in *Studies in State Taxation, with Particular Reference to the Southern States,* ed. J. H. Hollander (Baltimore: Johns Hopkins Press, 1900), 182. The privilege tax provided an opportunity for the majority landowners to transfer the tax burden to artisans and tradesmen, an effort that contributed at least as much revenue as the poll tax did by the end of the nineteenth century. This practice, common in many southern states, was quite extensive in Mississippi, which imposed the privilege tax on 119 occupations in 1898. One reason for the extensive use of this tax in Mississippi is that, in addition to property taxes, landowners in the two levee districts around the Mississippi River were required to pay ad valorem taxes for cotton production, which increases their burden relative to the rest of the state. The state also added personalty to the property tax much earlier than many other states, which included items such as pianos, weapons, watches, clocks, cattle, interest on loans, and capital.

99. In 1897, the amount appropriated for common schools was $923,500, while the poll tax receipts for the same year amounted to $250,257. Ibid., 205.

100. Poll tax policies in Mississippi reflect the strictness of white supremacy there. The tax existed before the territory became part of the union, when every white man paid his own tax and then a tax on every male slave. At that time, the system was another form of property tax on enslaved blacks. However, the state also used it as a means to encourage slavery by discriminating in the rates charged for "free males of color" and white males, making it substantially more expensive to be a free black male residing in Mississippi. Ibid., 212–13.

101. Fulton, "Educational Progress in Mississippi," 63.

102. Ibid., 193. Following Reconstruction, all but 250,000 acres was redeemed.

103. "Report of Professor Bailey of Mississippi for April, 1909," Folder 829, Box 93, Series 1.1, RAC-GEB, 5.

104. Ibid.

105. Ibid.

106. R. H. Watkins to Willard Bond, October 11, 1928, Folder 817, Box 92, Series 1.1, RAC-GEB.

107. Alan Ware, *The American Direct Primary: Party Institutionalization and Transformation in the North* (Cambridge: Cambridge University Press, 2002), 19.

108. Cal M. Logue and Howard Dorgan, *The Oratory of Southern Demagogues* (Baton Rouge: Louisiana State University Press, 1981), 6.

109. "The Deadly Parallel" and "Judge Vardaman by his record in the United States Senate," advertisements by the Vardaman Central Campaign Committee that appeared in *The Issue*, published by the Allied Printing Trades Council in 1922.

110. Ibid.

111. James D. Vardaman, "A Southern Senator's Views on the Race Situation in the South," from *Readings in Social Problems*, ed. Albert Benedict Wolf (Boston: Athenaeum Press, 1916), 705.

112. Ibid., 709. Vardaman tried to employ scientific language to support his views, claiming that, "The pureblooded negro reaches mental maturity soon after he passes the period of puberty. The cranial sutures become ossified by the time he reaches 20 years of age, and it is not uncommon to find one who reads fluently at 15 years of age not to know a letter in the book at the age of 25 or 30."

113. Ibid., 711.

114. Edwin Alderman, "The Work in Louisiana and Mississippi," *Proceedings of the Fifth Conference for Education in the South*, 33.

115. For more information about state law with regard to school funding, see Margo, *Race and Schooling in the South;* Tyack, James, and Benavot, *Law and the Shaping of Public Education*, 133–53.

116. *Biennial Report of the State Superintendent of Public Education: Mississippi State Department of Education, to the Legislature of Mississippi, for Scholastic Years 1891–92 and 1892–93* (Jackson, MS: Clarion-Ledger Publishing Company 1894), 3.

117. Ibid., 236.

118. There is a discussion of Vardaman's views in Holmes, *The White Chief*, 54–56 and 77–78. For a history of school-equalization funding policies in Mississippi, see Charles C. Bolton, "Mississippi's School Equalization Program, 1945–1954: 'A Last Gasp to Try to Maintain a Segregated Educational System,'" *Journal of Southern History* 61, no. 4 (November 2000): 781–814.

119. Holmes, *The White Chief*, 132–33 and chapters 5 and 10. Holmes explores the actual policies of Vardaman's tenure as governor and then as senator, illustrating that he voted consistently with progressive reforms except with regard to race. However, even as governor, while he promoted lynching through race baiting demagoguery, he also personally intervened to stop a lynching in Batesville, Mississippi, though it doesn't quite make sense to laud him for his actions given that his words may have prompted such events to begin with.

120. "Reject Rockefeller Aid: Amendment Accepted in Senate—Ashurst Denounces Carnegie Also," *New York Times*, May 6, 1914, 4.

121. "Repeal Passes Senate, 50–35: 37 Democrats and 13 Republicans Vote for Tolls Bill—11 Democrats Against it . . . Vardaman and West Exchange Recriminations over Carnegie Endowment's Activities," *New York Times*, June 12, 1914.

122. Holmes, *The White Chief*, 171.

123. "Report of Thomas P. Bailey, Dean of Dept. of Education, Professor of Psychology and Secondary Education, University of Mississippi, to the General Education Board," January, 1909, Folder 829, Roll 74, Series 1.1, GEB-MDAH, 3.

124. "Report of Professor Bailey of Mississippi for March, 1909," Folder 829, Box 93, Series 1.1, RAC-GEB, 3.

125. Andrew A. Kincannon to Wallace Buttrick, April 20, 1909, Folder 826, Box 93, Series 1.1, RAC-GEB.

126. Ibid.

127. "Reports of Supervisors of Rural Elementary Schools, March–June, 1911—Mississippi: Mr. W. H. Smith," Folder 120, Box 5, Series 2.1, SEB-UNC.

128. Ibid.

129. Harlan, *Separate and Unequal*; Anderson, *The Education of Blacks in the South*, Anderson and Moss, *Dangerous Donations*; Fairclough, *Teaching Equality*; and Hoffschwelle, *The Rosenwald Schools of the American South*.

130. Jill Quadagno, "Promoting Civil Rights through the Welfare State: How Medicare Integrated Southern Hospitals," *Social Problems* 47 (February 2000): 69, 71.

CHAPTER 4

1. *State Centralization in North Carolina* (Washington, DC: The Brookings Institution, 1932). The report focused on public schools, public roads, and local government and finance. It also included a long chapter on the state administrative reorganization.

2. The state had originally agreed to a budget of $5,000 for the study but then cut the funding to only $1,000, after which James Joyner requested the GEB to provide another $5,000 and the GEB complied. The request argued that the study would form a basis for advanced legislation in 1921 and continued progress on the reform agenda. James Joyner to the GEB, January 30, 1918, Folder 1066, Box 118, Series 1.1, RAC-GEB.

3. Joan Malczewski, "The Schools Lost their Isolation," *Journal of Policy History* 23, no. 3 (June 2011): 323–56.

4. "The Educational Equipment and Needs of North Carolina," 25, January, 1904, Folder 104, Box 2, Series 2.1, UNC-SEB.

5. Edwin Alderman graduated from the University of North Carolina, was the first president of the University of Virginia, and also served as president of the University of North Carolina and then Tulane. Charles McIver also graduated from the University of North Carolina and was the founder and first president of the University of North Carolina at Greensboro.

6. Edwin Alderman, "The Child and the State," an address in *Proceedings of the Fifth Conference for Education in the South* (Knoxville, TN: Gaut-Ogden Company by the Southern Education Board, 1902), 59.

7. James Joyner's Trinity School Commencement Speech, 7, undated, Folder Joyner, James Y. Papers, Speeches, Resolutions, Sketches, Box 1, Series PC171.5, Papers of James Yadkin Joyner, SANC.

8. Gregory P. Downs, "University Men, Social Science, and White Supremacy in North Carolina," *Journal of Southern History* 75, no. 2 (May 2009).

9. James Joyner's Trinity School Commencement Speech, 7.

10. "Some Reasons for Local Taxation," Folder Speeches, Resolutions, Sketches, Box Miscellaneous Papers 1900–1919, Papers of James Yadkin Joyner, SANC.

11. "The Work in North Carolina," Report given by Charles D. McIver, District Director of the Southern Education Board, at the Fifth Conference, *Proceedings of the Fifth Conference for Education in the South*; James Leloudis, *Schooling the New South: Pedagogy, Self, and Society in North Carolina, 1880–1920* (Chapel Hill: University of North Carolina Press, 1996), 153.

12. *Public School Laws of North Carolina* found in *Public Laws and Resolutions of the State of North Carolina Passed by the General Assembly at its Session of 1901* (Raleigh: Presses of Edwards & Broughton, 1901), 50.

13. Ibid., 57.

14. Ibid., 63.

15. Minutes of the General Education Board, January 24, 1911, Folder 3651, Box 353, Series 1.2, RAC-GEB.

16. James Yadkin Joyner to Wallace Buttrick, April 25, 1912, Folder 1912, Box 1, Papers of James Yadkin Joyner, SANC.

17. Informational and explanatory letter about industrial work in public schools of the state, J. Y. Joyner, 1913. Folder 1913 Reports and Outlines, Misc., Box 1, Papers of James Yadkin Joyner, SANC.

18. Nathan Newbold to Wallace Buttrick, February 27, 1914. Folder 1038, Box 115, Series 1.1, RAC-GEB.

19. Arthur Wright to the General Education Board, December 20, 1932, Folder 2124, Box 222, Series 1.2, RAC-GEB.

20. "Report of State Agent of Negro Rural Schools for North Carolina," 3. December 30, 1914, Folder 1042, Box 115, Series 1.1, RAC-GEB.

21. Ibid.

22. Informational and explanatory letter about industrial work in public schools of the state, James Y. Joyner, Folder 1913, Box 1, Reports and Outlines, Misc., Papers of James Yadkin Joyner, SANC.

23. Reports of Nathan C. Newbold, Box 115, Folder 1042, Series 1.1, RAC-GEB.

24. "The Educational Equipment and Needs of North Carolina," 27.

25. Circular letter from James Yadkin Joyner, E. E. Sams, and Nathan Newbold, November 28, 1913, Folder 1913 A–G, Box 1, Division of Negro Education, SANC.

26. J. Douglas Smith, *Managing White Supremacy*.

27. Program: Rural School Day, June 12, 1914, Folder 1914 Reports, Outlines, Misc., Box 1, Division of Negro Education, SANC.

28. Charlotte Hawkins Brown to Nathan Newbold, June 10, 1914, Box 1, Folder 1914B, Division of Negro Education, SANC.

29. Nathan Newbold to Mary Battle, March 15, 1915, Folder 1915 Reports, Outlines, Misc., Box 1, Division of Negro Education, SANC.

30. Mary Battle to Nathan Newbold, July 13, 1916, Folder B, Box 2, Division of Negro Education, SANC.

31. Joseph Debnam to Nathan Newbold, June 18, 1916, Folder B, Box 2, Division of Negro Education, SANC.

32. Nathan Newbold to Joseph Debnam, June 19, 1916, Folder B, Box 2, Division of Negro Education, SANC.

33. Mary Battle to Nathan Newbold, July 14, 1916, Folder B, Box 2, Division of Negro Education, SANC.

34. Nathan Newbold to Thomas Jesse Jones, January 18, 1917, Folder J–K, Box 3, Division of Negro Education, SANC.

35. "Minutes First North Carolina Conference for Negro Education," 2, December 12, 1913, Folder 1042, Box 115, Series 1.1, RAC-GEB.

36. Ibid.

37. A. C. Monahan to Nathan Newbold, October 20, 1913, Folder 1913 H–P, Box 1, Division of Negro Education, SANC.

38. "Report of N. C. Newbold, for the Month of January, 1914," 4–5, Folder 1042, Box 115, Series 1.1, RAC-GEB.

39. Ibid., 5.

40. Ibid., 4.

41. James E. McCulloch, *The Human Way: Address on Race Problems at the Southern Sociological Congress, Atlanta, 1913* (Nashville, TN: Southern Sociological Congress, 1913), 22.

42. Ibid., 7–12.

43. "Report of N. C. Newbold, for the Month of December, 1914," Folder 1042, Box 115, Series 1.1, RAC-GEB.

44. Nathan Newbold to William M. Hinton, September 9, 1914, Folder 1914 G–H, Box 1, Division of Negro Education, SANC.

45. Ms. Williams to Nathan Newbold, September 7, 1916, Folder W, Box 3, Division of Negro Education, SANC.

46. Nathan Newbold to Williams, September 11, 1916, Folder W, Box 3, Division of Negro Education, SANC.

47. Nathan Newbold to Eugene C. Brooks, November 9, 1919, Folder B, Box 4, Division of Negro Education, SANC.

48. "Unfolding of a Philosophy," File Some Facts about the Education of Negroes by G. H. Ferguson, Box 1, Division of Negro Education, SANC.

49. "Supplement to 'Negro Public Education in the South,'" 1, 1927, Folder 3297, Box 315, Series 1.2, RAC-GEB.

50. Nathan Newbold to James Dillard, August 17, 1915, Folder 1914D, Box 1, General Correspondence of Director: 1907–1915, Division of Negro Education, SANC.

51. Ibid.

52. Nathan Newbold to Abraham Flexner, May 17, 1919, Folder E–G, Box 4, Division of Negro Education, SANC.

53. Summary of Reports of N. C. Newbold, July 1, 1915–June 20, 1916, Folder 1043, Box 115, Series 1.1, RAC-GEB.

54. Report of N. C. Newbold, for the month of July, 1915, Folder 1043, Box 115, Series 1.1, RAC-GEB.

55. Nathan Newbold to Abraham Flexner, May 17, 1919, Folder E–G, Box 4, Division of Negro Education, SANC.

56. "Summary of Reports of N.C. Newbold," July 1, 1915–June 30, 1916, Folder 1043, Box 115, Series, 1.1, RAC-GEB.

57. Nathan Newbold to Abraham Flexner, May 17, 1919, Folder E–G, Box 4, Division of Negro Education, SANC.

58. This refers to "borrowing organizational capacity." Elisabeth Clemens, "Lineages of the Rube Goldberg State: Building and Blurring Public Programs, 1900–1940," in *Rethinking*

Political Institutions, ed. Ian Shapiro, Stephen Skowronek, and Daniel Galvin, 187–215 (New York: New York University Press, 2006).

59. Rural Schools aided by Fund, Folder 7, Box 53, Series 2.5, UC-JRF.

60. Nathan Newbold to Clinton Calloway, January 3, 1923, Folder C, Box 6, Division of Negro Education, SANC.

61. Arch T. Allen to Frank Bachman, April 23, 1927, Folder 1075, Box 118, Series 1.1, RAC-GEB.

62. Louis Ray, *Charles H. Thompson: Policy Entrepreneur of the Civil Rights Movement, 1932–1954* (Lanham, Maryland: Rowman & Littlefield Pub Group, 2012), 53–54.

63. Report of W. F. Credle, Supervisor Rosenwald Fund," March, 1929, Folder Rosenwald Fund W. F. Credle Reports, Box 8, Division of Negro Education, SANC.

64. Ibid.

65. "Report of George E. Davis, Supervisor of Rosenwald Buildings for North Carolina, State Department of Education," September 1924, Folder Rosenwald Fund George E. Davis Reports, Box 8, Division of Negro Education, SANC.

66. "Exhibit B" from "Report of W. F. Credle, Supervisor of Rosenwald Fund," May, 1924, Folder Rosenwald Fund, W. F. Credle Reports, Box 8, Division of Negro Education, SANC.

67. Nathan Newbold to Abraham Flexner, September 22, 1917, Folder 1039, Box 115, Series 1.1, RAC-GEB.

68. Nathan Newbold to Abraham Flexner, April 22, 1921, Folder 1074, Box 118, Series 1.1, RAC-GEB.

69. Nathan Newbold to Wallace Buttrick, May 22, 1922, Folder 1039, Box 115, Series 1.1, RAC-GEB.

70. Wallace Buttrick to Nathan Newbold, May 26, 1923, Folder 1039, Box 115, Series 1.1, RAC-GEB.

71. Wallace Buttrick to Nathan Newbold, April 9, 1923, Folder 1039, Box 115, Series 1.1, RAC-GEB.

72. Nathan Newbold to Arch T. Allen, June 27, 1923, Folder Correspondence, Box 7, Division of Negro Education, SANC.

73. "The Unfolding of a Philosophy," 3, File Some Facts about the Education of Negroes by G. H. Ferguson, Box 1, Division of Negro Education, SANC.

74. For a description of the role of institutionalization in sustaining organizations, see Walter W. Powell and Paul J. DiMaggio, *The New Institutionalism in Organizational Analysis* (Chicago: University of Chicago Press, 1991): 1–9.

75. Ann Short Chirhart, *Torches of Light: Georgia Teachers and the Coming of the Modern South* (Athens: University of Georgia Press, 2005); Adam Fairclough, *Teaching Equality: Black Schools in the Age of Jim Crow* (Athens: University of Georgia Press, 2002); Michael Fultz, "African American Teachers in the South, 1890–1940: Powerlessness and the Ironies of Expectations and Protest," *History of Education Quarterly* 35, no. 4 (Winter 1995): 401–22; Vanessa Siddle-Walker, *Their Highest Potential: An African American School Community in the Segregated South* (Chapel Hill: University of North Carolina Press, 1996); James Leloudis, *Schooling the New South* (Chapel Hill: University of North Carolina Press, 1996).

76. Joan Malczewski, "The Schools Lost Their Isolation," *Journal of Policy History* 23, no. 3 (June 2011): 323–56.

77. Summary of Reports, August 1921–June 30, 1922, G. H. Ferguson, Assistant Director Negro Education. Folder F, Box 5, Division of Negro Education, SANC.

78. 1932 numbers represented somewhat of a decrease from the total, given the nation's economy. By 1925, North Carolina had placed Jeanes teachers in forty-one of its one hundred counties. James Dillard to the General Education Board, February 1, 1926, Folder 2122, Box 221, Series 1, RAC-GEB.

79. "The Unfolding of a Philosophy," File Some Facts about the Education of Negroes by G. H. Ferguson, Box 1, Division of Negro Education, SANC.

80. J. R. Faison to Nathan Newbold, June 11, 1913, Folder 1913 Reports—Jeanes Teachers, Box 1, Division of Negro Education, SANC.

81. Ibid.

82. Oscar B. Martin to Nathan Newbold, January 12, 1914, Folder 1914M, Box 1, Division of Negro Education, SANC.

83. Oscar B. Martin to Nathan Newbold, December 3, 1913, Box 1, Folder 1913 H–D, SANC.

84. Extract from Report of N. C. Newbold since beginning of his work June, 1913, Folder 1048, Box 116, Series 1.1, RAC-GEB.

85. Oscar B. Martin to Nathan Newbold, January 12, 1914, Folder 1914M, Box 1, Division of Negro Education, SANC.

86. Oscar B. Martin to Nathan Newbold, January 5, 1914, Folder 1914M, Box 1, General Correspondence of the Director 1907–1915, Division of Negro Education, SANC.

87. Circular letter to county supervisors, March 24, 1914, Box 1, Folder 1913 H–D, SANC.

88. Circular letter from Nathan Newbold to County Superintendents, June 26, 1918, Folder 115, Box 1044, Series 1.1, RAC-GEB.

89. "Monthly Progress Letter for December, 1913," Folder 1042, Box 115, Series 1.1, RAC-GEB.

90. "Summary of Reports of Home-Makers Club Agents North Carolina, 1915," Folder 1048, Box 116, Series 1.1, RAC-GEB.

91. Progress Letter, March 6, 1924, Box 90, Folder Division of Negro Education 1923, Division of Negro Education, SANC.

92. "Report of Nathan C. Newbold, Month of October, 1918, 1–2, Folder 1044, Box 115, Series 1.1, RAC-GEB.

93. "Report of N. C. Newbold, Month of October, 1918, 3, Folder 1044, Box 115, Series 1.1, RAC-GEB.

94. Summary of Reports of Nathan C. Newbold, July 1, 1916–June 30, 1916, Folder 1043, Box 115, Series 1.1, RAC-GEB.

95. "Report N. C. Newbold, May, 1914," 3, Folder 1042, Box 115, Series 1.1, RAC-GEB.

96. "Report N. C. Newbold, January, 1915," 3, Folder 1042, Box 115, Series 1.1, RAC-GEB.

97. Elisabeth Clemens, *The People's Lobby: Organizational Innovation and the Rise of Interest Group Politics in the United States, 1890–1925* (Chicago: University of Chicago Press, 1997), 92.

98. Progress Letter, June 5, 1924, Folder 1924, Box 92, Division of Negro Education, SANC.

99. "Summary of Reports of Home-Makers Club Agents North Carolina, 1915," Folder 1048, Box 116, Series 1.1, RAC-GEB.

100. "Monthly Progress Letter, December, 1915," January 10, 1916, Folder 1043, Box 115, Series 1.1, RAC-GEB.

101. "Summary of Reports of Home-Makers Club Agents North Carolina, 1916," Folder 1048, Box 116, Series 1.1, RAC-GEB.

102. "Report of N. C. Newbold, State Supervisor Rural Schools for Negroes for North Carolina, for the Month of February, 1914," Folder 1042, Box 115, Series 1.1, RAC-GEB.

103. Nathan Newbold to Home-Makers Club Agents, May 29, 1918, Folder 1044, Box 115, Series 1.1, RAC-GEB.

104. "Application for Jeanes Fund Aid," Alamance County, August 16, 1932, Folder 5, Box 23, Series 4, SEF-AUC; "Application for Jeanes Fund Aid," Catawba County, August 31, 1932, Folder 5, Box 23, Series 4, SEF-AUC.

105. "Application for Jeanes Fund Aid," Anson County, August 31, 1932, Folder 5, Box 23, Series 4, SEF-AUC.

106. "Application for Jeanes Fund Aid," Bladen County, August 31, 1932, Folder 5, Box 23, Series 4, SEF-AUC.

107. Wallace Buttrick to Nathan Newbold, August 24, 1926, Folder 1075, Box 118, Series 1.1, RAC-GEB. The same letter points out that the GEB also provided an additional $433,432 for private-school enterprises in the state, mostly colleges and universities. Both James Anderson, in *Education of Blacks in the South*, and Eric Anderson and Alfred Moss, in *Dangerous Donations*, point out that overall the amount provided by the GEB for black education was relatively small. For example, as Anderson and Moss illustrate, the general appropriations of the GEB between 1902 and 1918 were $24,693,368, and the amount provided in total for black education was only $2,462,079. See James Anderson, *The Education of Blacks in the South, 1860–1935* (Chapel Hill: The University of North Carolina Press, 1988); Eric Anderson and Alfred Moss, *Dangerous Donations: Northern Philanthropy and Southern Black Education, 1902–1930* (Columbia: University of Missouri Press, 1999), 220.

108. Clinton Calloway to Nathan Newbold, July 7, 1916. Folder Rosenwald Fund, Box 2, Division of Negro Education, SANC.

109. Ibid.

110. Between 1915 and 1927, the fund provided $529,436 to North Carolina, with $569,261 contributed by blacks, $68,615 contributed by whites, and $2,226,737.85 from local tax dollars. See Philanthropic Funds and Negro Education, November 1, 1927, Folder 1070, Box 119, Series 1.1, RAC-GEB.

111. The Julius Rosenwald Fund Schoolhouse Construction Summary for 1923–1924, Folder Reports, Outlines, Misc., Box 7, Division of Negro Education, SANC.

112. List of Counties in North Carolina Asking for Aid from the Rosenwald Fund in the Erection of Rural Public School Houses for Negroes, October 1916, Folder Rosenwald Fund, Box 2, Division of Negro Education, SANC.

113. Progress Letter, June 5, 1924, Folder 1924, Box 92, Division of Negro Education, SANC.

114. *State Centralization in North Carolina* (Washington, DC: The Brookings Institution, 1932), 10.

115. D. J. Whitener, "Education for the People," *The North Carolina Historical Review* 36, no. 2 (April, 1959), 190.

116. Ibid. Whitener points out on pages 190 and 194 that the state equalization fund was $250,000 in 1913 and $3,209,290 by 1927.

117. Superintendent McLeod to Nathan Newbold, February 5, 1916, Folder Ma–Mc, Box 2, Division of Negro Education, SANC.

118. *State Centralization in North Carolina* (Washington, DC: The Brookings Institution, 1932), 15–59.

119. Initially local taxpayers limited increased taxes when the North Carolina Supreme Court ruled in favor of taxpayer S. Barksdale in 1885 in Sampson County after the county attempted to levy special taxes in order to meet state mandates to maintain a four-month school term. The case was a reflection of public sentiment, and the court overturned that ruling in the Granville case in 1907. *State Centralization in North Carolina* (Washington, DC: The Brookings Institution, 1932).

120. Fletcher Harper Swift, "State Taxes as Sources of Public School Revenue," *Bulletin of the National Tax Association* 14, no. 3 (December 1928), 76.

121. Harvey Walker, "The Poll Tax in the United States," *Bulletin of the National Tax Association* 9, no. 3 (December 1923), 71. Walker also points out that the poll tax existed in states across the nation, though many recognized the futility of collecting it from men who owned no property, which made it both expensive to administer and an unreliable source of income. For example, the tax commissioner in South Dakota said that he believed the poll tax to be the "most difficult to enforce of any laws we have on our statute books . . . the assessor in many cases fails to list the persons liable for the tax, and in my cases the tax authorities, either township, board, or county commissioners, who are delegated the power to make levies, fail in their duty, either from neglect or from the fact that they do not favor such taxes." Ibid., 69.

122. Plan for Erection of Rural Schoolhouses, July 7, 1916, Folder Rosenwald Fund, Box 2, Division of Negro Education, SANC.

123. Nathan Newbold to County Superintendents, January 22, 1914, Box 115, Folder 1042, Box 115, Series 1.1, RAC-GEB.

124. Arch T. Allen to Frank Bachman, April 23, 1927, Folder 1075, Box 118, Series 1.1, RAC-GEB.

125. Notes from a meeting of the GEB, January 24, 1911, Folder 3651, Box 353, Series 1.2, RAC-GEB, 7.

126. Annual Report of Jeanes Teachers in North Carolina, Folder 1044, Box 115, Series 1.1, RAC-GEB.

127. Nathan Newbold to Wallace Rogers, July 24, 1920, Folder R, Box 4, Division of Negro Education, SANC.

128. "Length of Term in Rosenwald Schools," May 5, 1923, Folder Rosenwald Fund, 1921–25, Box 8, Division of Negro Education, SANC.

129. William F. Credle to Samuel L. Smith, August 6, 1923, File Rosenwald Fund 1921–1925, Box 8, Division of Negro Education, SANC.

130. The teacher-training issue was overstated by many white reformers. The teachers were often well trained by private schools. Further, philanthropists and white southerners alike often defined "trained" not in terms of academic credentials and extensive teaching experience but rather as those teachers who were willing and able to promote industrial training, and some

counties did not want trained teachers because it would materially improve education. Yet, a successful campaign for universal education would dramatically increase the number of children enrolled, for longer periods of time, increasing the need for teachers. Ambrose Caliver, "Some Problems in the Education and Placement of Negro Teachers," *Journal of Negro Education* 4, no. 1 (January 1935): 99–112; Felton Clark, "General Administration and Control," *Journal of Negro Education* 1, no. 2 (July 1932): 137–62; Chirhart, *Torches of Light.*

131. Nathan Newbold to George E. Davis, September 17, 1920. Box 5, Folder D, Division of Negro Education, SANC.

132. Nathan Newbold to Arch T. Allen, June 26, 1923, Box 7, Folder Correspondence of the Director, Division of Negro Education, SANC.

133. Nathan Newbold to Eugene C. Brooks, January 6, 1923, Folder B, Box 6, Division of Negro Education, SANC.

134. "The Unfolding of a Philosophy," 5, File Some Facts about the Education of Negroes by G. H. Ferguson, Box 1, Division of Negro Education, SANC.

135. Ibid., 6.

136. "Some Problems Which Should Claim the Attention of Part-Time Supervisors: The Jeanes Teacher and Her Work," File Jeanes Misc., 1910, 1911, 1933, 1934, 1952, n.d., Box 5, State Supervisor of Elementary Education 1910, 1911, 1933–56, Division of Negro Education, SANC.

137. "State Wide Conference on Negro Education, Shaw University—Raleigh, NC," November 27, 1931, File State Conferences on Negro Education, Shaw University, Box 8, Division of Negro Education, SANC.

138. Ibid.

139. Report of Reading Circle Work of Colored Teachers, North Carolina 1923–1924, Folder 1924, Box 92, Division of Negro Education, SANC.

140. Sallie Joyner-Martin to Nathan Newbold, December 8, 1919, Folder M, Box 4, Division of Negro Education, SANC.

141. Annual Report of Annie W. Holland, Supervisor of Elementary Schools, North Carolina, September 1923–24, Folder 1924, Box 92, Division of Negro Education, SANC.

142. "A Suggestive Outline for Jeanes Supervising Teachers by Annie W. Holland, 1925," Folder 2125, Box 222, Series 1.2, RAC-GEB.

143. Ibid.

144. Conference of State Agents of Rural Schools for Negroes, June 5 and 6, 1930, Folder 5, Box 188, RFA-Fisk, 26.

145. "Effects of the Rosenwald Work in North Carolina," Folder Rosenwald Fund n.d., Box 8, Division of Negro Education, SANC.

146. "Report of G. E. Davis, Supervisor of Rosenwald Buildings for North Carolina, State Department of Education, for September, 1924," File Rosenwald Fund, G. E. Davis Reports, Box 8, Division of Negro Education, SANC.

147. Economic, Social and Political Situation Since 1900, Excerpt from Newbold's thesis, June 1922, Box 115, Folder 1039, Box 115, Series 1.1, RAC-GEB.

148. Nathan Newbold to William Credle, April 29, 1922, Folder C, Box 5, Division of Negro Education, SANC.

149. Paul Vernon Betters, *State Centralization in North Carolina* (Washington, DC: The Brookings Institution, 1932).

150. J. R. Collie Appellant v. Commissioners of Franklin County (supreme court of North Carolina, August term, 1907), 145 N.C., 170. See also Betters, *State Centralization in North Carolina*, 21–29.

151. Betters, *State Centralization in North Carolina*, 27–28.

152. Ibid., n. 48. For a full discussion, see the McLean Law, chapter 10, *Public Laws of 1931*. For a discussion of the development of public school legislation in North Carolina History, see S. H. Thompson, "The Legislative Development of Public School Support in North Carolina," (PhD diss., University of North Carolina, 1936).

153. Betters, *State Centralization in North Carolina*, 49.

154. Ibid., 147.

155. Jill Quadagno, "Promoting Civil Rights through the Welfare State: How Medicare Integrated Southern Hospitals," *Social Problems* 47 (February 2000): 69, 71. Robyn Muncy points out that after women galvanized reformers to promote legislation that would address social policy, women's leadership on social issues was passed to the state. See Robyn Muncy, *Creating a Female Dominion in American Reform: 1890–1935* (New York: Oxford University Press, 1991).

156. "Jeanes Teachers, North Carolina, 1933–34," File Jeanes, Misc. 1910, 1911, 1933, 1934, 1952, n.d., Box 5, Division of Negro Education, SANC.

157. Ibid.

CHAPTER 5

1. *Institute for Government Research of the Brookings Institution, Report on a Survey of the Organization and Administration of State and County Government in Mississippi* (Washington, DC: The Brookings Institution, 1932), 445–51.

2. "Negro Public Education in the South: A Confidential Report for the Officers of the General Education Board, 1927," Folder 1, Box 33, Series 5, SEF-AUC, 8.

3. S. B. Henson to William Strahan, September 3, 1929, Folder General Correspondence August 7, 1928–November 6, 1929, Box 7986, MDAH.

4. "Report of Professor Bailey of Mississippi for March, 1909," Folder 829, Box 93, Series 1.1, RAC-GEB, 5.

5. Ibid., 6.

6. "Duck Hill School," *Fisk University Rosenwald Fund Card File Database,* www .rosenwald.fisk.edu.

7. Henryetta Fullilove to Julius Rosenwald, January 12, 1929, Folder S. L. Smith General Correspondence, Box 8013, MDAH.

8. Jackson Davis to Wallace Buttrick, November 8, 1919, Folder 872, Box 97, Series 1.1, RAC-GEB.

9. Arthur Wright to the General Education Board, December 20, 1932, Folder 2124, Box 222, Series 1.2, RAC-GEB; "Negro School Buildings in the Southern States, 1917–1947," Folder 19, Box 76, RFA-Fisk.

10. "Mississippi Statement of Activities of the State Supervisor of Rural Schools during month of January, 1914," Folder 125, Box 5, UNC-SEB.

11. Specifically, a county could expend as much as one teacher's salary on transportation to support consolidated schools, and two teachers' salaries if four schools were consolidated and the second allowed a tax-levy in the consolidated district to maintain the school term and for incidental expenses, such as transportation. "Recent Progress in Rural Education, especially in 1911 and 1912, by J. C. Fant," 1, Folder 830, Box 93, Series 1.1, RAC-GEB.

12. For information about the teacher's relationship to the GEB, see, for example, Susie Powell to Wickliffe Rose, July 20, 1911, Folder 20, Box 1, UNC-SEB. For information about her efforts in rural schools, see "School Improvement Prizes, 1911–12," Folder 21, Box 1, UNC-SEB.

13. Abraham Flexner to Joseph Neely Powers, July 1, 1914, Folder 868, Box 97, Series 1.1, RAC-GEB.

14. Samuel L. Smith, *Builders of Goodwill* (Nashville, TN: Tennessee Book Company, 1950), 28.

15. Ibid., 31.

16. Leo Favrot to Frank P. Bachman, June 20, 1928, Folder 872, Box 97, Series 1.1, RAC-GEB.

17. Jackson Davis to Frank Bachman, July 29, 1928, Folder 872, Box 97, Series 1.1, RAC-GEB.

18. Willard Bond to Wallace Buttrick, August 29, 1923, Folder 832, Roll 74, Series 1.1, The University of Mississippi (1906–1956), GEB-MDAH.

19. Interview with Superintendent J. S. Vandiver and Leo Favrot, August 21, 1935, Series 1, Subseries 1, Folder 873, Box 97, RAC-GEB.

20. Ibid.

21. Bura Hilbun and William Strahan to Frank Bachman, 2, April 22, 1925, Folder 872, Box 97, Series 1.1, RAC-GEB.

22. Percy Easom to James Dillard, January 28, 1929, Folder General Correspondence November 14, 1929–December 21, 1929, Box 7986, Series 2342, MDAH.

23. "Field Work," Report of Bura Hilbun for November, 1917, Folder 876, Box 98, Series 1.1, RAC-GEB.

24. Jackson Davis to Wallace Buttrick, August 14, 1920, Folder 872, Box 97, Series 1.1, RAC-GEB.

25. Bura Hilbun to Willard Bond, August 31, 1920, Folder 877, Box 98, Series 1.1, RAC-GEB.

26. John C. Fant to Abraham Flexner, October 26, 1917, Folder 827, Box 93, Series 1.1, RAC-GEB.

27. Ibid.

28. Bura Hilbun to Willard F. Bond, June 2, 1921, Folder 877, Box 98, Series 1.1, RAC-GEB.

29. Percy Easom to John D. Henderson, Folder General Correspondence Rosenwald Pending Matters, 1929–30, Box 7987, Series 2343, Papers of the Julius Rosenwald Fund, MDAH.

30. "Poor School System Cause of Migration," *Chicago Defender*, October 2, 1920.

31. "Secretary of Labor to Seek Better Schools: Poor Educational Facilities is Prime Cause for Labor Leaving South," *Chicago Defender*, January 17, 1925.

32. Percy Easom to Jessie Littleton, January 31, 1929, Folder General Correspondence Rosenwald Pending Matters 1928–29, Box 7987, Series 2343, MDAH

33. Wallace Buttrick to Joseph Neely Powers, September 19, 1919, Folder 828, Box 93, Series 1.1, RAC-GEB.

34. The authorities of the state university and the administrators of the public school system had reached an understanding in 1892 and 1893 that the two organizations would be recognized as parts of one system. Robert B. Fulton, "Educational Progress in Mississippi," *Annals of the American Academy of Political and Social Science* 22 (September 1903): 63.

35. "Report of Professor Bailey of Mississippi for April, 1909," 1, Folder 829, Box 93, Series 1.1, RAC-GEB.

36. "High School Progress in Mississippi since 1908," July 1912, Folder 830, Box 93, Series 1.1, RAC-GEB. The university had provided for the position of high school inspector in 1904 to support high-school development, but the position was dropped after one year from the university budget and left vacant for three years.

37. John C. Fant to Dr. E. C. Sage, February 5, 1917, Folder 827, Box 93, Series 1.1, RAC-GEB. Fant also served as dean of the School of Education at the University of Mississippi and then president of the Mississippi College for Women, where a library is named for him today. He also received his doctorate in pedagogy at New York University, where he wrote a thesis titled, "A Survey of Secondary Education in Mississippi." See *Annual Catalogue New York University* (New York: The University, 1914).

38. "Report of Professor Bailey of Mississippi for April, 1909," 4, Folder 829, Box 93, Series 1.1, RAC-GEB.

39. Wallace Buttrick to J. N. Powers, September 19, 1919, Folder 828, Box 93, Series 1.1, RAC-GEB.

40. John C. Fant, "Recent Progress in Rural Education, especially in 1911 and 1912," 6, Folder 830, Box 93, RAC-GEB.

41. John C. Fant to Chancellor Andrew A. Kincannon, March 4, 1914, Folder 827, Box 92, Series 1.1, RAC-GEB.

42. John C. Fant to E. C. Sage, April 4, 1914, Folder 827, Box 93, Series 1.1, RAC-GEB.

43. John C. Fant to Chancellor Andrew A. Kincannon, March 4, 1914, Folder 827, Box 92, Series 1.1, RAC-GEB.

44. John C. Fant to E. C. Sage, November 10, 1913, Folder 826, Box 93, Series 1.1, RAC-GEB.

45. "High School Progress in Mississippi since 1908," July 1912, Folder 830, Box 93, Series 1.1, RAC-GEB.

46. Robert Fulton to Wallace Buttrick, June 20, 1908, Folder 822, Roll 73, Series 1.1, The University of Mississippi (1906–1956), GEB-MDAH.

47. Roswell Rogers to Wallace Buttrick, December 11, 1921, Folder 823, Roll 73, Series 1.1, The University of Mississippi (1906–1956), GEB-MDAH.

48. In 1930, the AAUP made an initial list of "Censured Institutions," a list that would become formal practice in 1938. The initial list included three Mississippi institutions—the University of Mississippi, the Mississippi Agricultural and Mechanical College, and the Mississippi State College for Women—the result of Bilbo summarily dismissing a number of faculty and university employees as part of his quest to dispense political favors throughout the state. See Jonathan Knight, "The AAUP's Censure List," *Academe* 89, no. 1 (January–February 2003): 44–49, and "Censured Administrations, 1930–2002," *Academe* 89, no. 1 (January–February 2003): 50–59.

49. Fant's request provided detail about school terms, including that a third of the counties went only four to five months with white teachers receiving less than $160 annually and black teachers far less. He noted that twenty-six counties made no school levy, running schools solely with state allocations of the common school fund. John C. Fant to Wallace Buttrick, June 10, 1919, Folder 828, Box 93, Series 1.1, RAC-GEB.

50. The foundation pointed out that they were happy to fund the professorial position and the state agents but did not want to participate so overtly in swaying public opinion and voter action. This is different from their response to James Joyner in North Carolina. In fact, in their letter to Fant, the GEB made the dubious claim that it "never thought it wise to make appropriations of this character, designed, of course, to influence public sentiment." It is possible that the political context was difficult enough that their long-term efforts with regard to building collaborative relationships would be thwarted by bad press, which they had already experienced previously with the resignation and imprisonment of their state agent for Negro education, John Ellis. Regardless, Fant was writing the memos and doing the work that Newbold was doing as state agent, and there are few such memos from the Mississippi state agents Wallace Buttrick to John C. Fant, June 19, 1919, Folder 828, Box 93, Series 1.1, RAC-GEB.

51. "Report of Professor Bailey of Mississippi for April, 1909," Folder 829, Box 93, Series 1.1, RAC-GEB, 2–3.

52. John C. Fant to Wallace Buttrick, March 8, 1911, Folder 826, Roll 74, Series 1.1, The University of Mississippi (1906–1956), GEB-MDAH.

53. Mag Hanna to Percy Easom, January 15, 1929, Box 7986, Series 2342, MDAH and Percy Easom to Mag Hanna, January 19, 1929, Box 7986, Series 2342, MDAH.

54. Mag Hanna to Percy Easom, January 22, 1929, Box 7986, Series 2342, MDAH.

55. Percy H. Easom to W. H. Joyner, August 23, 1928, Box 7986, Series 2342, MDAH.

56. William Strahan to Samuel Smith, September 28, 1928, Folder S. L. Smith General Correspondence, Box 8013, Series 2342, MDAH.

57. Percy Easom to May E. Irvine, August 29, 1929, Folder General Correspondence August 7, 1928–November 6, 1929, Box 7986, Series 2342, MDAH.

58. Walter Strahan to Ermine Pitts, February 20, 1930, Folder General Correspondence January 29, 1929–April 5,1 1930, Box 7986, Series 2342, MDAH.

59. Ibid.

60. John C. Fant to W. W. Brierley, August 22, 1914, Folder 827, Box 93, RAC-GEB, 2.

61. W. H. Smith to Abraham Flexner, January 14, 1915, Folder 869, Box 97, Series 1.1, RAC-GEB and Abraham Flexner to W. H. Smith, June 10, 1915, Folder 869, Box 97, Series 1.1, RAC-GEB.

62. John C. Fant to Wallace Buttrick, March 8, 1911, Folder 827, Roll 74, Series 1.1, GEB-MDAH.

63. Abraham Flexner to John Fant, August 6, 1917, Folder 827, Box 93, Series 1.1, RAC-GEB.

64. "Report of J. C. Fant, Professor of Secondary Education in Mississippi—1918," Folder 832, Roll 74, Series 1.1, GEB-MDAH.

65. "Recent Progress in Rural Education, especially in 1911 and 1912, by J. C. Fant," 3, Folder 830, Box 93, Series 1.1, RAC-GEB.

66. S. J. Ingram to Percy Easom, February 3, 1930, Box 7986, Series 2342, MDAH.

67. Percy Easom to S. J. Ingram, February 5, 1930, Box 7986, Series 2342, MDAH.

68. Percy Easom to W. B. Jackson, May 28, 1929, Folder Correspondence August 7, 1928–November 6, 1929, Box 7986, Series 2342, MDAH.

69. Samuel Smith to Percy Easom, February 12, 1930, Box 8013, Series 2342, MDAH.

70. Percy H. Easom to Samuel L. Smith, February 18, 1930, Box 8013, Series 2342, MDAH.

71. "Research Problems," 4, circa 1932, Folder 5, Box 188, RFA-Fisk.

72. David Strong, Pamela Barnhouse Walters, Brian Driscoll, and Scott Rosenberg, "Leveraging the State: Private Money and the Development of Public Education for Blacks," *American Sociological Review* 65 (October 2000): 658–81.

73. The appointment of Leo Favrot in Arkansas provides an interesting illustration. He had been appointed as the state agent in Louisiana, with payment provided by the GEB. However, the newly elected governor of Louisiana wrote to the GEB in 1912 requesting that Favrot's salary be redirected to a new state agent whom the governor had just appointed. The GEB withdrew all aid for secondary education in Louisiana, and transferred Favrot to Arkansas to be its first state agent in 1913. See S. L. Smith, *Builders of Goodwill: The Story of the State Agents of Negro Education in the South, 1910–1950* (Nashville, TN: Tennessee Book Company, 1950), 17.

74. Bura Hilbun to Willard Bond, January 5, 1920, Folder 877, Box 98, Series 1.1, RAC-GEB.

75. Percy H. Easom to James H. Dillard, January 28, 1929, Folder Correspondence August 7, 1928–November 6, 1929, Box 7986, Series 2342, MDAH.

76. J. S. B. King to Percy Easom, December 7, 1929, Folder Correspondence August 7, 1928–November 6, 1929, Box 7986, Series 2342, MDAH.

77. J. C. McGehee to Percy Easom, March 30, 1930, Folder School Term Extension Approved Applications 1929–30, Box 8013, Series 2342, MDAH.

78. "Education in Mississippi," Miss. 18, Folder 101, Box 4, UNC-SEB.

79. Fletcher Harper Swift, "State Taxes as Sources of Public School Revenue," *Bulletin of the National Tax Association* 14, no. 3 (December 1928): 70.

80. Institute for Government Research of the Brookings Institution, *Report on a Survey of the Organization and Administration of State and County Government in Mississippi* (Washington, DC: The Brookings Institution, 1932), 16–21.

81. This is an interesting outcome, given that the work of the Brookings Institution was initiated by the Mississippi State Board of Development, a nonprofit agency supported by private institutions that sought a remedy to ongoing state indebtedness in twenty-three of twenty-nine years preceding 1930. While it might have been politically wise to respond to the report, given constituent dissatisfaction with government, most legislators were "hesitant to abandon the patronage inherent in a sprawling administrative organization whose personnel management is weak." Robert Highsaw and Charles Fortenberry, *The Government and Administration of Mississippi* (New York: Thomas Cromwell Company, 1954), 99.

82. Ibid., 30.

83. "Rural Schools aided by Fund," from Report J.R. Fund: Review of Two Decades, by E.R. Embree (1936), Folder 7, Box 53, Series 2.5, UC-JRF; "Negro School Buildings in the Southern States, 1917–1947," Folder 10, Box 76, RFA-Fisk.

84. "Negro School Buildings in the Southern States, 1917–1947," Folder 10, Box 76, RFA-Fisk.

85. A. M. Strange to Percy Easom, Folder General Correspondence Pending Matters 1928–29, Box 7987, Series 2342, MDAH.

86. Frank Roberson, "Recent Fiscal Legislation in Mississippi, *Bulletin of the National Tax Association* 3, no. 8 (May 1918): 188. The commission ultimately filed a written report that led to a set of tax bills including a new inheritance tax and an act authorizing the reassessment of land whenever counties desired but at least biennially.

87. *Institute for Government Research of the Brookings Institution, Report on a Survey of the Organization and Administration of State and County Government in Mississippi* (Washington, DC: The Brookings Institution, 1932), 16.

88. Alfred W. Garner, "A Note on the Mississippi Sales Tax," *Southern Economic Journal* 1, no. 2 (January 1934): 24.

89. "Mississippi School Expenditures, 1937–38," Folder 973, Box 97, Series 1.1, RAC-GEB.

90. Percy Easom to Judge J. Morgan Stevens, January 3, 1930, Folder General Correspondence January 28, 1929–June 2, 1930, Box 7986, Series 2342, MDAH.

91. Percy Easom to Monroe Johnson, March 25, 1930, Folder General Correspondence January 7, 1930–May, 1930, Box 7986, Series 2342, Negro Education Division Records, Papers of the Department of Education, MDAH. The actual application indicated that the principal earned fifty dollars per month; one teacher earned just thirty-eight dollars, while the other two teachers earned only thirty-five dollars per month. "For School to which no Term Extension Aid has been given, To Julius Rosenwald Fund, Nashville, Tennessee," Folder General Correspondence Rosenwald Pending Matters, 1928–29, Box 8013, Series 2342, Records of the Julius Rosenwald Fund, MDAH.

92. May Irvine to Percy Easom, March 19, 1930, Folder School Term Extensions—Pending Correspondence 1929–30, Box 7986, Series 2342, MDAH.

93. May Irvine to Percy Easom, as a postscript to a letter sent from Easom to Irvine, January 23, 1931, Folder General Correspondence Rosenwald Pending Matters, 1928–29, Box 8013, Series 2342, Records of the Julius Rosenwald Fund, MDAH

94. William C. Strahan to G. L. Orr, March 27, 1930, Box 8013, Series 2342, MDAH.

95. Percy Easom to Samuel L. Smith, May 6, 1930, Folder General Correspondence Rosenwald Pending Matters, 1928–29, Box 8013, Series 2342, Records of the Julius Rosenwald Fund, MDAH. Easom noted that the Sunflower County superintendent had dropped a forty-dollar teacher, "on account of reduced enrollment," making the application for school-term extension viable. The superintendent followed up with a note that was even more revealing, explaining that the teacher had been fired, but "should this not be satisfactory, however, perhaps we could strain a point and keep this teacher on at fifty dollars." R. M. Yarbrough to Percy Easom, April 29, 1930, Folder General Correspondence Rosenwald Pending Matters, 1928–29, Box 8013, Series 2342, Records of the Julius Rosenwald Fund, MDAH

96. Percy Easom to Samuel Smith, April 25, 1930, General Correspondence Rosenwald Pending Matters, 1928–29, Box 8013, Series 2342, Records of the Julius Rosenwald Fund, MDAH

97. Samuel L. Smith to Percy Easom, April 5, 1930, Folder School Term Extensions—Pending Correspondence 1929–30, Box 7986, Series 2342, MDAH.

98. Percy H. Easom to Samuel L. Smith, February 25, 1930, Box 8013, Series 2342, MDAH.

99. Percy Easom to R. M. Yarbrough, May 28, 1930, Folder School Term Extension Approved Applications 1929–30, Box 8013, Series 2342, MDAH.

100. "Jeanes Fund, 1927–28," Folder 2123, Box 222, Series 1.2, RAC-GEB. The states in which counties provided more than 50 percent of the cost included Alabama, Florida, Louisiana, North Carolina, Tennessee, and Virginia. The states in which counties provided less than 50 percent were Arkansas, Georgia, Kentucky, Mississippi, South Carolina, and Texas.

101. Samuel Smith to Percy Easom, March 6, 1930, Folder School Term Extension Approved Applications 1929–30, Box 8013, Series 2342, MDAH.

102. Ibid.

103. Samuel Smith to Percy Easom, March 17, 1930, Box 8013, Series 2342, MDAH.

104. Samuel Smith to Alfred Stern, June 13, 1930, Folder 6, Box 128, RFA-Fisk.

105. Walter Strahan and Willard F. Bond, *Mississippi Negro Rural and Elementary Schools: County Normal Manual and Teacher's Guide, 1932–33,* Bulletin no. 2, MDAH.

106. Ivy to Willard Bond, May 2, 1922, Folder 832, Roll 74, GEB-MDAH.

107. Percy Easom to Edgar Bowlus, May 17, 1930, Folder General Correspondence January 7, 1930–May, 1930, Box 7986, Series 2342, MDAH.

108. Percy Easom to W. W. Benson, September 30, 1929, Folder General Correspondence January 7, 1930–May, 1930, Box 7986, Series 2342, MDAH.

109. William C. Strahan to Jackson Davis and Leo Favrot, September 13, 1929, Box 7986, Series 2342, MDAH.

110. Leo Favrot to William C. Strahan, September 17, 1929, Folder General Correspondence November 14, 1929, Box 7986, Series 2342, MDAH.

111. State Department of Education to County Superintendents, February 10, 1917, Folder 871, Box 97, Series 1.1, RAC-GEB.

112. Circular letter to County Superintendents from the State Department of Education in Mississippi, February 10, 1917, Folder 871, Box 97, Series 1.1, RAC-GEB.

113. C. H. Curd to Percy Easom, April 16, 1930, Folder General Correspondence March 26–May 24, 1930, Box 7986, Series 2342, MDAH.

114. W. E. Granberry to Percy Easom, Folder Summer School Financial File Correspondence 1929–30, Box 7986, Series 2342, MDAH.

115. Mag Hanna to Percy H. Easom, February 21, 1929, Box 8012, Series 2342, MDAH.

116. Percy H. Easom to Mag Hanna, February 27, 1929, Box 8012, Series 2342, MDAH.

117. "Grenada County," an inadequately titled monthly report from Bura Hilbun to Willard Bond, March 1918, Folder 876, Box 98, Series 1.1, RAC-GEB.

118. This supports Quadagno's argument that it was helpful, over time, to oppressed local majorities to move social programs into the public sphere in order to get decision making out of the hands of oppressive local majorities, though detrimental to local black agency in the short term. See Jill Quadagno, "Promoting Civil Rights through the Welfare State: How Medicare Integrated Southern Hospitals," *Social Problems* 47 (February 2000): 69, 71.

119. Percy Easom to Richard Tate, January 21, 1929, Box 7986, Series 2342, MDAH.

120. Richard Tate to Percy Easom, February 11, 1929, Box 7986, Series 2342, MDAH.

121. William Strahan to Blanch Hall, February 9, 1929, Folder General Correspondence November 14, 1929–December 21, 1929, Box 7986, Series 2342, MDAH.

122. M. A. B. Buckingham to Percy Easom, June 18, 1930, Box 7986, Series 2342, MDAH, and Percy Easom to Prof. M. A. Buckingham, June 21, 1930, Box 7986, Series 2342, MDAH.

123. Walter Strahan to J. A. Riddell, February 1, 1929, Folder Financial Records 1928–29, Box 7988, Series 2342, MDAH.

124. C. M. Johnson to Percy Easom, March 10, 1930, Folder School Term Extensions— Pending Correspondence 1929–30, Box 7986, Series 2342, MDAH.

125. Percy Easom to C. M. Johnson, March 12, 1939, Folder School Term Extensions— Pending Correspondence 1929–30, Box 7986, Series 2342, MDAH.

126. J. C. McGehee to Percy H. Easom, April 14, 1930, Folder General Correspondence Rosenwald Pending Matters, 1928–29, Box 8013, Series 2342, Records of the Julius Rosenwald Fund, MDAH.

127. Percy Easom to George Lee Orr, August 27, 1928, Folder General Correspondence August 7, 1928–November 6, 1929, Box 7986, Series 2342, MDAH.

128. M. M. Leak to Percy Easom, February 27, 1929, Folder General Correspondence August 7, 1938–November 6, 1929, Box 7986, Series 2342, MDAH.

129. Percy Easom to R. H. Watts, April 1, 1929, Folder General Correspondence Rosenwald Pending Matters, 1928–29, Box 7987, Series 2343, Records of the Julius Rosenwald Fund, MDAH.

130. Percy Easom to Noah Expose, April 1, 1929, Folder General Correspondence Rosenwald Pending Matters, 1928–29, Box 7987, Series 2343, Records of the Julius Rosenwald Fund, MDAH.

131. J. H. Dean to F. J. Hubbard, April 25, 1929, Folder General Correspondence Rosenwald Pending Matters, 1928–29, Box 7987, Series 2343, Records of the Julius Rosenwald Fund, MDAH.

132. Percy Easom to H. R. Watts, April 19, 1929, Folder General Correspondence Rosenwald Pending Matters, 1928–29, Box 7987, Series 2343, Records of the Julius Rosenwald Fund, MDAH.

133. Ibid.

134. Percy Easom to L. B. Spinks, November 26, 1928, Folder General Correspondence Rosenwald Pending Matters, 1928–29, Box 7987, Series 2340, Records of the Julius Rosenwald Fund, MDAH.

135. "Recent Progress in Rural Education, especially in 1911 and 1912, by J. C. Fant," 3, Folder 830, Box 93, Series 1.1, RAC-GEB.

136. Percy Easom to John Henderson, November 5, 1929, Folder General Correspondence Rosenwald Pending Matters, 1930, Box 7987, Series 2343, Records of the Julius Rosenwald Fund, MDAH.

137. R. S. Lee to William Strahan, April 15, 1930, Folder General Correspondence Rosenwald Pending Matters, 1930, Box 7987, Series 2343, Records of the Julius Rosenwald Fund, MDAH.

138. Henriette Jackson to William Strahan, November 22, 1929, Folder General Correspondence August 7, 1928–November 6, 1929, Box 7986, Series 2342, MDAH.

139. William Strahan to Henriette Jackson, December 2, 1929, Folder General Correspondence August 7, 1928–November 6, 1929, Box 7986, Series 2342, MDAH.

140. Percy Easom to Samuel Smith, October 9, 1929, Folder General Correspondence Rosenwald Pending Matters, 1929–30, Box 7987, Series 2343, Records of the Julius Rosenwald Fund, MDAH.

141. Leo Favrot, "Negro Education in the South," *The Bulletin* 9, no. 7 (June–July 1929): 5–9.

142. "Prominent Educators to Address Teachers at National Meeting," *The Bulletin* 9, no. 7 (June–July 1929): 10.

143. John Sullivan to William Strahan, May 19, 1930, Folder General Correspondence January 28, 1929–June 2, 1930, Box 7986, Series 2342, MDAH.

144. For example, see "Application for Jeanes Fund Aid," to employ Avenue Thompson, August 12, 1932, Folder 3, Box 23, Series 4, and "Application for Jeanes Fund Aid," to employ Hattie Williams, August 15, 1932, Folder 3, Box 23, Series 4, SEF-AUC.

145. "Application for Jeanes Fund Aid," to employ Beulah Alexander, August 25, 1932, Folder 3, Box 23, Series 4, SEF-AUC.

146. "Application for Jeanes Fund Aid," to employ Cresie Franklin, August 18, 1932, Folder 3, Box 23, Series 4, SEF-AUC.

147. "Application for Jeanes Fund Aid," to employ Laura Little, August 12, 1932, Folder 3, Box 23, Series 4, SEF-AUC; "Application for Jeanes Fund Aid," to employ Oda Kirkland, August 18, 1932, Folder 3, Box 23, Series 4, SEF-AUC; "Application for Jeanes Fund Aid," to employ Ella Key, August 12, 1932, Folder 3, Box 23, Series 4, SEF-AUC.

148. "Application for Jeanes Fund Aid," to employ Louise Webb, August 18, 1932, Folder 3, Box 23, Series 4, SEF-AUC.

149. "Application for Jeanes Fund Aid," to employ Lina Brookens, August 12, 1932, Folder 3, Box 23, Series 4, SEF-AUC.

150. "State of Mississippi Department of Education, Jackson, Jeanes Fund Contract," October 23, 1928, for Leake County, Box 7988, Series 2342, MDAH.

151. "State of Mississippi Department of Education, Jackson, Jeanes Fund Contract," October 29, 1928, for Leflore County, Box 7988, Series 2342, MDAH.

152. "State of Mississippi Department of Education, Jackson, Jeanes Fund Contract," October 23, 1928, for Monroe County, Box 7988, Series 2342, MDAH.

153. "Application for Jeanes Fund Aid," to employ Bessie Little, August 18, 1932, Folder 3, Box 23, Series 4, SEF-AUC.

154. "Application for Jeanes Fund Aid," to employ Nannie Gillis, August 27, 1932, Folder 3, Box 23, Series 4, SEF-AUC.

155. "Application for Jeanes Fund Aid," to employ Alice McLemore, August 30, 1932, Folder 3, Box 23, Series 4, SEF-AUC.

156. "Application for Jeanes Fund Aid," to employ Miriam Howard, October 1, 1932, Folder 3, Box 23, Series 4, SEF-AUC.

157. "An Interview with Mrs. Ann Britton, November 19, 1977," interviewed by Daisy M. Greene, Mississippi Department of Archives and History and the Washington County Library System Oral History Project: Greenville and Vicinity, MDAH.

158. "Notes from Reports of Mississippi Jeanes Teachers at Conference of Louisiana and Mississippi Jeanes Teachers," March 20, 1919, Folder 2125, Box 222, Series 1.2, RAC-GEB.

159. Frances Mathis to Percy Easom, April 8, 1930, Box 8011, Series 2342, MDAH.

160. "State of Mississippi Department of Education, Jackson, Jeanes Fund Contract, October 23, 1928, for Pike County, Box 7988, Series 2342, MDAH

161. H. Hopkins to Percy Easom, February 6, 1930, Folder General Correspondence January 7, 1930–May, 1930, Box 7986, Series 2342, MDAH.

162. Percy Easom to H. Hopkins, February 10, 1930, Folder General Correspondence January 7, 1930–May, 1930, Box 7986, Series 2342, MDAH.

163. Marie Ellison to Julius Rosenwald, January 14, 1920, Folder S. L. Smith General Correspondence, Box 8013, Series 2342, MDAH.

164. Samuel Smith to Marie Ellison, February 7, 1929, Folder S. L. Smith General Correspondence, Box 8013, Series 2342, MDAH.

165. Percy H. Easom to Wm. H. Harrison, January 6, 1930, Box 8013, Series 2342, MDAH.

166. Samuel L. Smith to Wm. H. Harrison, January 4, 1930, Box 8013, Series 2342, MDAH.

167. S. S. Gaston to Julius Rosenwald, January 12, 1930, Folder General Correspondence Rosenwald Pending Matters, 1929–30, Box 7987, Series 2343, Records of the Julius Rosenwald Fund, MDAH.

168. Samuel Smith to S. S. Gaston, February 21, 1930, Folder General Correspondence Rosenwald Pending Matters, 1929–30, Box 7987, Series 2343, Records of the Julius Rosenwald Fund, MDAH.

169. "Annual Summary of the Jeanes Work, 1928–29," Box 7988, Series 2342, MDAH.

170. "Jeanes Agent's Final or Term Report," Adams County, circa 1928, Box 7988, Series 2342, MDAH.

171. "Jeanes Agent's Final or Term Report," Amite County, circa 1928, Box 7988, Series 2342, MDAH.

172. "Jeanes Agent's Final or Term Report," Bolivar County, circa 1928, Box 7988, Series 2342, MDAH.

173. "Jeanes Agent's Final or Term Report," Kemper County, circa 1928, Box 7988, Series 2342, MDAH.

174. "Jeanes Agent's Final or Term Report," Lamar County, circa 1928, Box 7988, Series 2342, MDAH.

175. Joan Malczewski, "Agricultural Extension Work and the Organization of Rural Communities in the Jim Crow South," *History of Education Quarterly* 53, no. 4 (November 2013): 369–400.

176. "Summarized Statement of Homemakers Club Work for the Summer of 1917 in the State of Mississippi," Folder 881, Box 98, Series 1.1, RAC-GEB.

177. "Jeanes Agent's Final or Term Report," Leake County, circa 1928, Box 7988, Series 2342, MDAH.

178. "Jeanes Agent's Final or Term Report," Leflore County, circa 1928, Box 7988, Series 2342, MDAH.

179. "Jeanes Agent's Final or Term Report," Walthall County, circa 1928, Box 7988, Series 2342, MDAH.

180. "Jeanes Agent's Final or Term Report," Warren County, circa 1928, Box 7988, Series 2342, MDAH.

181. "Jeanes Agent's Final or Term Report," Winston County, circa 1928, Box 7988, Series 2342, MDAH.

182. C. J. Murphy to Percy Easom, April 1, 1930, Folder School Term Extensions—Pending Correspondence 1929–30, Box 7986, Series 2342, MDAH.

183. Percy Easom to C. J. Murphy, April 5, 1930, Folder School Term Extensions—Pending Correspondence 1929–30, Box 7986, Series 2342, MDAH.

184. Kenneth T. Andrews, *Freedom Is a Constant Struggle: The Mississippi Civil Rights Movement and Its Legacy* (Chicago: University of Chicago Press, 2004), 71.

185. Elisabeth Clemens, "Lineages of the Rube Goldberg State: Building and Blurring Public Programs, 1900–1940," in *Rethinking Political Institutions: The Art of the State,* ed. Ian Shapiro, Stephen Skowronek, and Daniel Galvin (New York: New York University Press, 2006), 187–215.

186. For example, in 1932, the Chicago Defender called for a federally appointed secretary of education with broader powers, and an article in 1933 in the *Chicago Defender* explicitly stated that only federal involvement would overcome the states' rights arguments for segregated education. See "A Secretary of Education," January 9, 1932, *Chicago Defender* and "Federal Control of Education," December 23, 1933, *Chicago Defender*.

187. Percy H. Easom, "Mississippi's Negro Schools," *The Mississippi Educational Advance*, February, 1937, folder 872, Box 97, Series 1.1, RAC-GEB.

188. Florence O. Alexander and Mary G. Whiteside, "Negro Higher and Professional Education in Mississippi," *Journal of Negro Education* 17, no. 3 (Summer 1948): 314–15.

189. "Negro School Buildings in the Southern States, 1917–1947," Folder 19, Box 76, RFA-Fisk.

CHAPTER 6

1. Interview with Gladys Noel Bates, the University of Southern Mississippi Center for Oral History and Cultural Heritage, December 23, 1996.

2. Ibid., 11.

3. Jason Sokol describes variation in white attitudes about race in the South after World War II. His periodization acknowledges that the war and the New Deal were the kind of unprecedented events that could shift beliefs in profound ways. His assessment is accurate, though there was also variation in white attitudes about race in the early part of the century, but within more rigid parameters. See Jason Sokol, *There Goes My Everything: White Southerners in the Age of Civil Rights, 1945–1975* (New York: Vintage Books, 2006), 11.

4. "Report of Professor Bailey of Mississippi for March, 1909," Folder 829, Box 93, Series 1.1, RAC-GEB.

5. *State Centralization in North Carolina* (Washington, DC: The Brookings Institution, 1932).

6. Scholarship has shown that strong political institutions are essential to the relationship between civil society and democracy, and that localism did much to promote and sustain dis-

crimination and inequality in education. Theda Skocpol, *Diminished Democracy: From Membership to Management in American Civil Life* (Norman: University of Oklahoma Press, 2003); Jennifer Hoschschild and Nathan Scovronick, *The American Dream and the Public Schools* (Oxford: Oxford University Press, 2003), 28–36.

7. Robert Lieberman describes the administrative structure necessary to promote successfully race-based social policy and is a useful framework for considering North Carolina's progress in developing publicly funded education for both white and black citizens. See Robert Lieberman, *Shifting the Color Line, Race and the American Welfare State* (Cambridge, MA: Harvard University Press, 1998), 17–18.

8. *Institute for Government Research of the Brookings Institution, Report on a Survey of the Organization and Administration of State and County Government in Mississippi* (Washington, DC: The Brookings Institution, 1932), 451.

9. Natalie Ring, *The Problem South: Region, Empire, and the New Liberal State, 1880–1930* (Athens: University of Georgia Press, 2012), 52.

10. J. Douglas Smith, *Managing White Supremacy: Race, Politics and Citizenship in Jim Crow Virginia* (Chapel Hill: University of North Carolina Press, 2002).

11. Glenda Gilmore, *Gender and Jim Crow: Women and the Politics of White Supremacy in North Carolina, 1896–1920* (Chapel Hill: University of North Carolina Press, 1996).

12. For a discussion of organizational repertoires and interest groups, see Elisabeth Clemens, *The People's Lobby: Organizational Innovation and the Rise of Interest Group Politics in the United States, 1890–1925* (Chicago: University of Chicago Press, 1997), 92–93. Connie L. Lester, in *Up from the Mudsills of Hell: The Farmers' Alliance, Populism, and Progressive Agriculture in Tennessee, 1870–1915* (Athens: University of Georgia Press, 2006), describes a similar role in the organization of the Grange in Tennessee. While there is a body of literature that provides evidence of black participation in interest groups, such as fraternal organizations, there is less evidence of the relationship between participation in interest groups and educational policy reform. See Gunner Myrdal, *An American Dilemma: The Negro Problem and American Democracy* (New York: Harper & Bros., 1944); Theda Skocpol and Jennifer Lynn Oser, "Organization Despite Adversity: The Origins and Development of African American Fraternal Associations," *Social Science History* 28, no. 3 (Fall 2004): 367–437; Bayliss J. Camp and Orit Kent, "'What a Mighty Power We Can Be': Individual and Collective Identity in African American and White Fraternal Initiation Rituals," *Social Science History* 28, no. 3 (Fall 2004): 439–83.

13. See David Snow, Steven Worden, E. Burke Rochford Jr., and Robert D. Benford, "Frame Alignment Processes, Micromobilization, and Movement Participation," *American Sociological Review* 51 (August 1986): 464–81. Doug McAdam, *Political Process and the Development of Black Insurgency*, 1930–1970 (Chicago: University of Chicago Press, 1982). The transfer of the educational infrastructure more fully to the public sphere ultimately affected the path dependency of racial incorporation. See Robert Lieberman, "Ideas, Institutions, and Political Order: Explaining Political Change," *American Political Science Review* 96, no. 4 (2002): 697–712.

14. Jill Quadagno, "Promoting Civil Rights through the Welfare State: How Medicare Integrated Southern Hospitals," *Social Problems* 47 (February 2000): 69, 71

15. "Standardization of Rural Elementary Schools: Meaning and Nature of standardization," Folder 105, Box 4, Series 2.1, UNC-SEB.

16. "Jeanes Teachers, North Carolina, 1933–34," File Jeanes, Misc. 1910, 1911, 1933, 1934, 1952, n.d., Box 5, Division of Negro Education, SANC.

17. Robyn Muncy, *Creating a Female Dominion in American Reform: 1890–1935* (New York: Oxford University Press, 1991).

18. Deanna Gillespie, "'First Class' Citizenship Education in the South," *Journal of Southern History* 80, no. 1 (February 2014): 109–42. Gillespie discusses the role of citizenship education programs in the Delta during the 1950s in promoting collective action, an important precursor to grassroots organizing for the civil rights movement in the Delta. This work argues that the relationship between schools and grassroots organizing began much earlier in the century, even if CEP adult programs were a more overt example.

19. Adam Fairclough, *Race and Democracy: The Civil Rights Struggle in Louisiana, 1915–1972* (Athens: University of Georgia Press, 1995), 12.

20. An Oral History with Aaron Henry, The University of Southern Mississippi Center for Oral History and Culture, May 1, 1972, 7–8.

21. An Oral History with Ms. Winson Hudson, The University of Southern Mississippi Center for Oral History and Cultural Heritage, August 31, 1995, 11.

22. An Oral History with Aaron Henry, the University of Southern Mississippi Center for Oral History and Culture, May 1, 1972, 44.

23. Zack VanLandingham to Director, State Soverignty [sic] Commission, November 7, 1958, SCR ID# 2-9-0-3-1-1, Sovereignty Commission Online, MDAH.

24. Gerald N. Rosenberg, *The Hollow Hope: Can Courts Bring About Social Change?* 2nd ed. (Chicago: University of Chicago Press, 2008), 33

25. Anthony Badger, "The South Confronts the Court: The Southern Manifesto of 1956," *Journal of Policy History* 20, no. 1 (2008): 128.

26. McAdam describes a political process model, in which you must look at the entire span of years during which conditions facilitative of insurgency are developing, in McAdam, *Political Process and the Development of Black Insurgency,* 65.

27. Paul Pierson, *Politics in Time*; Joseph Soss, Jacob Hacker and Suzanne Mettler, *Remaking America: Democracy and Public Policy in an Age of Inequality* (New York: Russell Sage Foundation, 2010).

28. George Lewis, "Virginia's Northern Strategy: Southern Segregationists and the Route to National Conservatism," *Journal of Southern History* 72, no. 1 (February 2006): 123.

29. Michael J. Klarman, *From Jim Crow to Civil Rights: The Supreme Court and the Struggle for Racial Equality* (Oxford: Oxford University Press, 2004).

30. McAdam makes a case for the need to recognize the extent to which periods of elite contention are necessary for the popular resistance of social movements and points out that it was nationalization of the local conflict that accounted for the singular importance of the Montgomery bus boycott. McAdam, *Political Process and the Development of Black Insurgency*, xxviii.

31. Karen Orren and Stephen Skowronek, *The Search for American Political Development* (Cambridge: Cambridge University Press, 2004), 125. The authors distinguish authority from

power in a way that makes clear the difficulty of instituting change in the South. According to their definition, authority is "designated in advance, . . . works through institutions, [and] works through mandates that are enforceable . . . not simply coercive, but rather implies protection for those who carry out its dictates and sanctions against those who do not."

32. See Brian Balogh, "Reorganizing the Organizational Synthesis: Federal-Professional Relations in Modern America," *Studies in American Political Development* 5 (Spring 1991): 146. Balogh describes the increased power of professional experts in the early decades of the century, describing the compromises that existed between experts and the decentralized political structure to gain political support for reforms.

Abbott, Edwin, 274n15

Abbott, Lyman, 274n15

African Americans. *See* blacks

agency: administrative reorganization and, 191–93; definition of, 113; foundation programs and, 29–30; local control *vs.* centralization, trade-off of, 249–50; in Mississippi school reform, 224–25, 255–56; schooling and, 260; of southern blacks, 4, 13, 16–17, 29, 79, 113, 249, 317n118; of teachers, 113

Agriculture, US Department of: agricultural extension services, 45–47, 97–99, 134, 138; Bureau of Plant Industry, 174; Newbold, collaboration with, 174

Aiken, Charles S., 294n9

Alabama: budget system in, 60; Jeanes teachers in, 100–101, 103, 280n132, 286n29; rural black education, GEB ranking regarding, 114; state agent funded by the GEB in, 55; teachers and teacher training, lack of, 68

Alderman, Edwin: background and career of, 297n43, 303n5; Bureau of Information and Investigation, director of, 38; Conference for Education in the South, speech at, 27; as North Carolina reformer, 125, 153; SEB, member of, 276n43

Alexander, Florence, 110

Allen, A. T., 168

Allen, E. W., 277n74

Anderson, Bula, 70

Anderson, Eric, 308n107

Anderson, James, 308n107

Anheier, Helmut K., 278n99

Arizona, 62

Arkansas, 55, 114, 280n132, 286n29, 315n73

Armstrong, Samuel Chapman, 31

associated action, 271n89

Association of State Superintendents of the Southern States, 51

Atlantic Coast Line Railroad, 25

Aycock, Charles Brantley: educated workforce, recognition of need for, 16; education, vision of universal but unequal, 14, 120–21, 124–32, 153, 179, 295n17; foundations and reformers, links to, 121, 124–28, 131–32, 154, 191; tax reform, support for, 128–29, 180; white supremacy, campaign for, 119–20, 124, 127, 130, 146

Bailey, Liberty Hyde, 277n74

Bailey, Thomas P.: administrative impediments to reform, reports highlighting, 208; difficulties faced by foundations in